Das Lehrwerk **Challenge Bundesausgabe** entspricht den Lehrplänen für die Jahrgangsstufen 11 bis 13 des Beruflichen Gymnasiums. Alle zu erreichenden Kompetenzen und Prüfungsformate werden intensiv trainiert.

1. Mit jedem Topic Schritt für Schritt sicher zum Abitur

- Einstiegsdoppelseite **Topic**: Vorbereitung auf das jeweilige Thema
- 5 Doppelseiten mit **aktuellen, authentischen Texten** – begleitet von **englisch-deutschen Wortangaben** für einen schnelleren Zugang zum Text und **differenzierten Aufgaben**, die ausgewogen alle Kompetenzbereiche trainieren und auf die in der Abiturprüfung vorgesehenen Prüfungsformate vorbereiten
- Fokusseite **Spot on language:** Wortschatzübungen und Vertiefung der wichtigsten **Grammatikkenntnisse**
- Fokusseite **Hotspot:** Handlungsorientierte Themenbearbeitung **mit vielen Projekt- und Internetaufgaben**
- Doppelseite **Exam practice:** **Testaufgabe im Abiturformat**
- **Video lounge**: Authentische BBC-Videos zum Training des Hör-/Sehverstehens
- Berufsbezug durch **Reading for your exam:** mit je drei Texten zu den Bereichen Technik, Wirtschaft & Verwaltung sowie Soziales & Gesundheit plus Aufgaben

2. „Your challenge" bietet umfangreiches Material zur individuellen Förderung

- **Self-assessment:** Kategorien zur Selbsteinschätzung
- **Assessment tests:** Thematisch verknüpfte Aufgaben zur Selbsteinschätzung und zur Lernwegdokumentation
- **Helping hand:** Differenzierungsangebot zu komplexen Aufgabenstellungen
- **Grading grid:** Bewertungsbogen für Englisch
- **Skills files:** Alle Kompetenzen prägnant und mit vielen *Phrases* (Redewendungen)
- **Grammar files:** Kompaktgrammatik zum Wiederholen und Nachschlagen
- **Dictionary:** Alphabetisches Vokabelverzeichnis

3. Training und Prüfungsvorbereitung

- **Challenge-Code:** Über den Challenge-Code können Sie sich das *Talking vocabulary* (vertonte Wortlisten) als MP3-Dateien zum Anhören der korrekten Aussprache kostenlos unter www.klett.de herunterladen.
- **3-in-1-Workbook:** Für die Jahrgangsstufen 11 bis 13 bieten wir Ihnen ein Workbook zzgl. Prüfungsvorbereitung und Audio-CD:
  - Grammatikintensivtraining im Arbeitsheft zum Hineinschreiben
  - Hörverstehensübungen mit beiliegender Audio-CD
  - intensive Prüfungsvorbereitung mit Hinweisen zum Abitur und Wiederholung der wichtigsten *Skills* mit Prüfungsaufgaben auf Abiturniveau im *EXAM TRAINING*
- **Vocabulary Notebook:** Das Vokabellernheft für die Jahrgangsstufen 11 bis 13 ist der thematische Aufbauwortschatz, der gebündelt nur die wichtigen Vokabeln aus den Texten sowie zusätzlichen Wortschatz mit vielen Aufgaben zum Hineinschreiben trainiert.

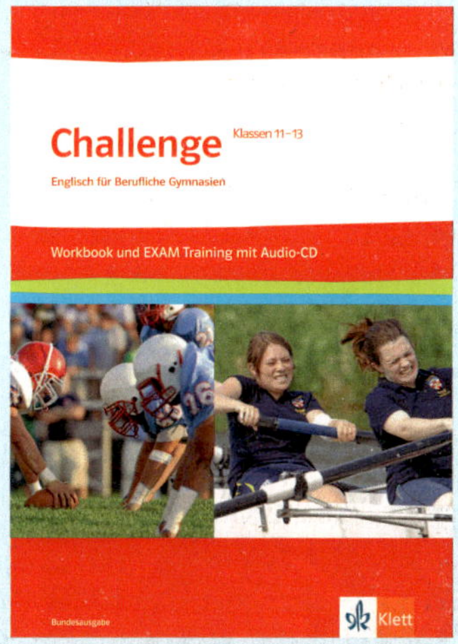

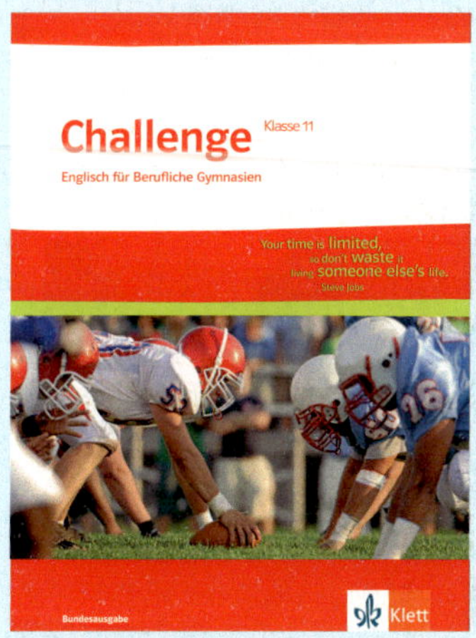

Symbole und Abkürzungen

p9v2et	Challenge-Code mit *Talking vocabulary*: vertonte Wortlisten als MP3-Download
A 1.1	Audio: Für den Lehrer auf den Audio-CDs im Lehrerhandbuch. Für die Schüler teilweise auf der Audio-CD im Workbook.
[1] **to improve** – (sich) verbessern	Lernvokabular ist in den Topics schwarz hervorgehoben
	Partneraufgabe
	Gruppenaufgabe
→	Verweise auf die *Skills* und *Grammar files* im Anhang
	Aufgaben zur selbstständigen Recherche im Internet
p. 84	Aufgaben mit Differenzierungsangeboten im Anhang (*Helping hand*)

Topic 1
The English language in use

x8w9uk

163 nations use English to communicate with other UN member states

medium for 80% of the information stored in the world's computers

more than half of the world's technical and scientific periodicals are in English

most widely learned second language in the world

official language in 52 countries

some 380 million native speakers

dominant language in electronic communication

Globish
skills modernity future
global hybrid language
lingua tomorrow
immigrants change globalisation worldwide
Mandarin technology international Hinglish Pidgin
negotiations second Shakespeare working
non-native vehicular music
business politics barrier
Internet franca
Asian

influence on cinema, music, broadcasting, science, and the Internet

language with the greatest number of native speakers: Mandarin Chinese

working knowledge is a basic skill in many fields and occupations

of all the world's languages (over 2,700) English is the richest in vocabulary

more than 700 million people speak English as a foreign language

people who count English as their mother tongue make up less than 10% of the world's population, but possess over 30% of the world's economic power

most widely spoken and written language worldwide

Getting started

1 a) What aspects of the English language are included in the cluster? What do you know about these aspects? Re-arrange them in a word web adding further details. → Word webs, p. 251

b) Present your word web to your partner.

2 Study the information on the yellow slips of paper and complete your word web about the English language. Then give a three-minute talk to the class about English as a global language. → Presentation, p. 264

3 A class survey about languages → Questionnaires and surveys, p. 262
Draw up a class survey about the languages which
- you speak,
- you would like to be able to speak (stating your reasons, too),
- are spoken in your homes.

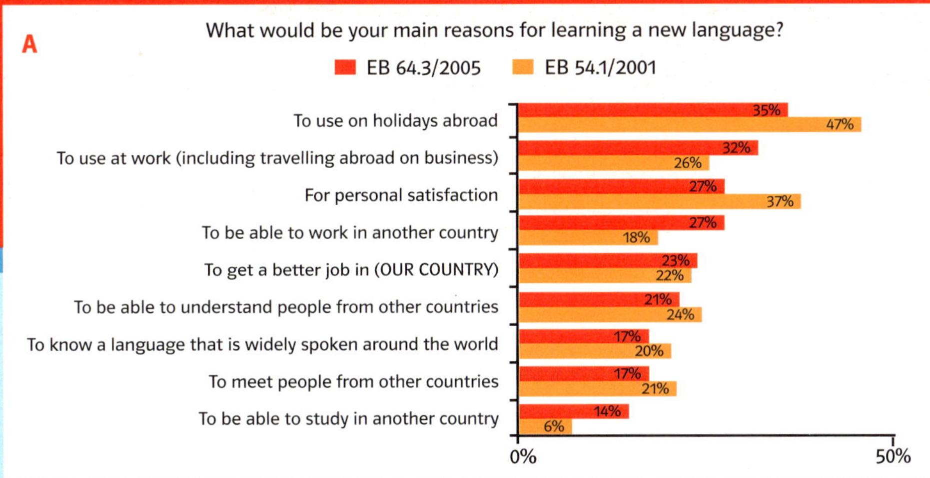

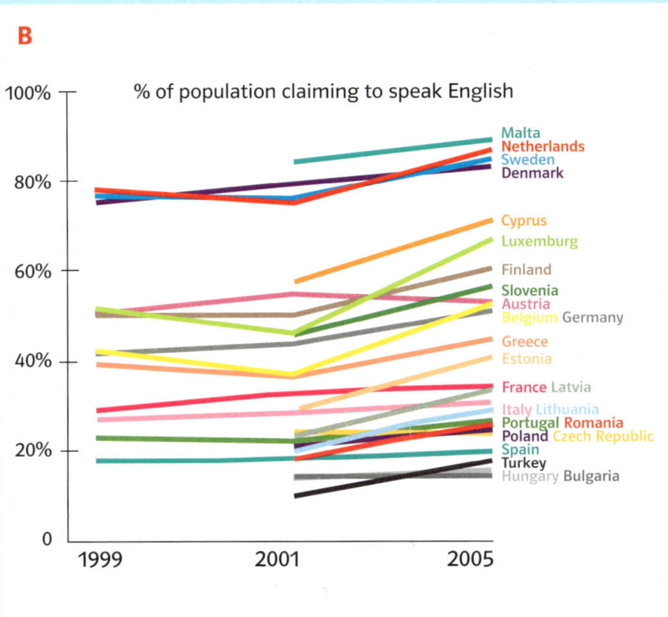

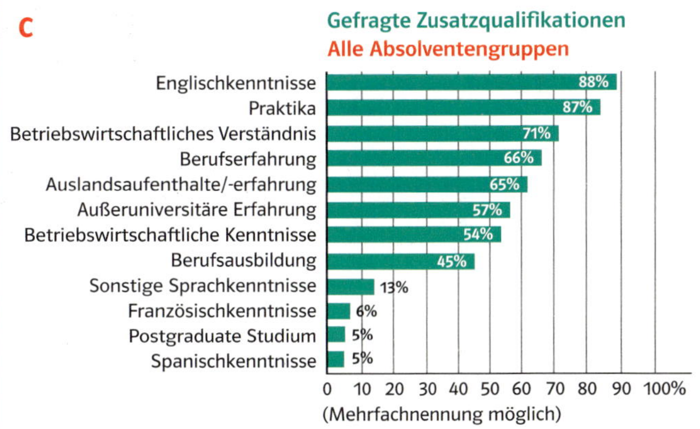

Wer keine Englischkenntnisse und Praktika vorweisen kann, wird es schwer haben, einen attraktiven Arbeitgeber zu finden. Die internationale Geschäftssprache zu beherrschen und praktische Erfahrungen mitzubringen, gehört mittlerweile zum Pflichtprogramm: Jeweils an die 90 Prozent der Unternehmen erwarten dies von ihren Bewerbern. Nur Unternehmen mit Bedarf an Juristen nennen betriebswirtschaftliches Verständnis als zweitwichtigste Kompetenz nach Englischkenntnissen. Auslandsaufenthalte und außeruniversitäre Erfahrungen sind weitere wichtige Pluspunkte beim Berufseinstieg.

Source (A and B): European Union, Eurobarometer

Source (C): Job Trends Deutschland 2011, Staufenbiel Institut

4 **The Eurobarometer (EB) is a series of surveys by the European Commission which are carried out in all European member states.** → Describing diagrams, p. 243

a) Study and summarise diagrams A and B. What do the two Eurobarometer surveys say about the importance of the English language?

b) Choose one diagram and analyse it in detail.

5 **Additional qualifications and skills** → Mediation, p. 245
German companies were asked to name the additional qualifications and skills university graduates need to get a job on the German labour market. Summarise the findings in diagram C in English.

6 **Research project** → Hotspot 1, p. 21

Word bank

highest number of speakers • % of those who took part in the survey say … • international language of business • … % of the population claim to speak English • a good knowledge of English • to be fluent in English • to have work experience • to spend a year abroad • work placement • key qualifications

A English as a lingua franca

1 Before you read → Brainstorming, p. 253

a) Why do people all over the world learn English? Make a list of reasons.

b) This advert by the British council in Hungary tries to motivate people to learn English. Analyse the ad and say if it works. Give reasons.

A 2.1

European Commission

LANGUAGES

Search GO

English as a lingua franca

Throughout history, whenever and wherever different groups have come into contact, there has been a constant need for a common language enabling communities with different mother tongues to communicate. What is new is the scale of international communication today. The past few decades have witnessed unparalleled increases, emphasising the need for one or more vehicular languages that can overcome language barriers. That this role is mainly played by English at the moment can scarcely be disputed. It is against this backdrop that labels such as "World English", "International English", "English as a Lingua Franca", "Global English", or "Globish" have been coined.

Learn English. The most popular language in the universe.

English is the working language or one of the working languages of all international organisations. Besides the United Kingdom, Ireland, the United States, Canada, Australia, and New Zealand, most countries belonging to the former British Empire have adopted it as their – at times sole – official language and new countries are promoting its use (e.g. Rwanda designated English as the official language of education in 2008 and English is gaining ground on French as the chief foreign language even in former French colonies like Algeria, Tunisia and Morocco). It is also the main language of international business and is chosen ever more frequently as the corporate language in multinational corporations and in academic, technological and scientific contexts or in sports events. Its prestige is unchallenged in the media and the entertainment industry worldwide: the number of music bands singing in English instead of their mother tongue clearly shows the appeal of English, as does the number of people drawn to it as the language of their idols.

Thus English has become a symbol of modernity and speaking it means sharing and being part of a global culture through which local barriers can be overcome. Starting mainly from the 1960s and 1970s, through popular music, English has become in many countries a symbol of freedom and rebellion and in serious crises it still proves a powerful weapon against censorship. As the

3 **scale** – Ausmaß
4 **vehicular language** – Verkehrssprache
6 **scarcely** – kaum
23 **corporate language** – offizielle Sprache in einem Unternehmen
25 **prestige** – Prestige, Ansehen

main language of new communication channels, such as blogs and social networks, it has often allowed the opponents of totalitarian regimes to make their voices heard worldwide in spite of the harsh censorship put in place by such governments to crush and silence them. The events which followed the Iranian presidential elections in 2009 very clearly showed the importance of a vehicular language to break isolation and circulate information. The official media did not cover the protests and manifestations which spontaneously broke out in the days immediately after the official results were announced, but news of the riots and casualties could reach the outside world thanks to these new tools, and universal use of English meant that the news spread rapidly and afar. Even those who fight its supremacy recognise it as a powerful medium to make themselves heard. A few years ago during a march in support of Hindi against English organised in India, demonstrators carried banners in English to reach a wider public. Another interesting example is the protest of fundamentalist Muslims after satirical cartoons making fun of Muhammad were published in Denmark: they protested against the Western world, but did so using slogans in English, even though it is the language of "the Great Satan" and is perceived as the very symbol of Western predominance.

However, whilst the phenomenon is widely acknowledged, it is far from being unanimously welcomed given the perceived risk of serious dangers not only for the survival of other languages, and as a consequence of other cultures, but also for English itself. On the one hand, the more English develops, the more fears are voiced that it propagates a new form of imperialism. According to this view, together with their language, English speaking countries (notably the US) impose their cultures and values, as well as their economic and political supremacy, the final outcome being global uniformity and homogenisation. Therefore, positive and clear action is called for to counter this trend and promote cultural diversity by protecting smaller languages and cultures endangered by the advance of English. On the other hand, the global reach of English is claimed to have a negative impact on English itself, as standards fall and mistakes and local idiosyncrasies increase, leaving native speakers feeling dispossessed of their own language. (711 words)

34 **harsh censorship** – strenge Zensur
40 **supremacy** – Vormachtstellung
46 **predominance** – Dominanz, Vorherrschaft
47 **unanimously** – einhellig
56 **idiosyncracy** – Eigenart
57 **dispossessed** – enteignet, enterbt

2 Comprehension

a) In your own words summarise the reasons for English as a lingua franca that are mentioned in the text.

b) Outline the criticism against English as a lingua franca according to the text.

3 Working with words

a) Read the text again and collect all the technical terms that have to do with English as a lingua franca.

b) Cluster or categorise your technical terms in a logical way (e.g. word web).

4 Having a discussion → Discussions, p. 246

a) Prepare a panel discussion about the pros and cons of English as a lingua franca. Before you start, decide on roles that should be included in your discussion.

b) Collect arguments to prepare for the roles.

c) Make notes of the best arguments for both sides that come up in your discussion.

5 Research projects → Hotspots 2 and 3, p. 21

B The language of tomorrow?

1 Before you read → Brainstorming, p. 253

a) Look at the photo and the headline of the article. What do you think the text is about?

b) Work with a partner and agree on five questions that you expect the text to answer.

THE INDEPENDENT

British schools import China's teachers for lessons in "language of tomorrow"

All the country's 250 specialist language schools have been told by a government adviser that they should put Mandarin on the curriculum as "the language of tomorrow". Sir Cyril Taylor, chairman of the Specialist Schools and Academies Trust, said it should be seen as the key language for future generations to learn – replacing European languages. The trust, which represents 90 per cent of England's 2,950 state secondary schools, has clinched a deal with the Chinese government, which will send 200 teachers a year over to the UK to teach Mandarin in schools. Pupil exchanges are also being arranged, Sir Cyril revealed at a meeting of the Commons Select Committee on Education yesterday. He told MPs: "I want all language colleges to be teaching Mandarin. It is a strategic world language. The difficulty in the past has been getting Chinese teachers. However, exchanges between our schools and Chinese schools will help to change that. We learn from them and they learn from us."

Around 4,000 pupils in the UK are studying GCSE Chinese. However, most of them are of Chinese origin and Sir Cyril wants to extend its take-up. Richard Cairns, headmaster of Brighton College – the independent school which became the first school in the country to make the language compulsory for all pupils and introduced it to youngsters from the age of three – said he believed it would replace German in the "pecking order" of languages. Sir Cyril added: "The state of modern language teaching in this country means we need to do a lot more to promote it. I'd like to see all language colleges having Mandarin on the curriculum as soon as possible and I'd like to extend it to a number of other schools as well." In his government inquiry into language teaching, Lord Dearing successfully argued that ministers should drop the requirement for all schools to teach a European language from the ages of 11 and 14. Instead,

2 **government adviser** – Regierungsberater(in)
4 **curriculum** – Lehrplan
11 **to clinch a deal** – eine Vereinbarung treffen
21 **to make the language compulsory** – eine Sprache verpflichtend machen
23 **pecking order** – Hackordnung

they should be allowed to include Mandarin, Arabic and Urdu on the list of languages that could be taught.
Answering questions from MPs, Sir Cyril also called for schools to use a lottery to determine admissions if they were oversubscribed. He said he would like to see all specialist schools and academies introduce "fair banding" – taking an equal number of pupils from each of several different ability bands. "If a school is oversubscribed, random allocation could be used," he added. Brighton became the first authority in the country to plan the introduction of ballots earlier this year – but the proposal prompted an outcry from parents who believed their children could be denied a place even if they lived near the school.
Sir Cyril argued, though, that it was fair and was already being practised successfully by the Haberdashers' Aske's Academy in Lewisham, south London. He also said that many of the country's brightest pupils were being denied the chance to succeed at A-level – because they had to switch school at 16. "Half of our secondary schools are for 11 to 16-year-olds," he said. "Only 20 per cent of the very able children get three A grades at A-level if they move school at 16." He said schools should work in partnership in their neighbourhoods to ensure post-16 courses for all pupils locally. (561 words)

32 **admission** – Aufnahme (an einer Schule)
33 **fair banding** – Zuordnungsprinzip von Schülern zu Schulen durch ein Testsystem in verschiedenen Kompetenzbereichen
35 **over-subscribed** – *hier:* mehr Anmeldungen als freie Plätze
35 **random allocation** – Zuweisung nach dem Zufallsprinzip
36 **ballot** – Abstimmung
42 **to switch school** – die Schule wechseln

2 Comprehension

a) Which of your five questions from task 1 b) can be answered now?

b) Ask your partner questions about specific information in the text. Your partner has to answer the question and also indicate the line where the correct answer can be found. **Example:**
How many GCSE students are studying Chinese at the moment?
4,000 GCSE students in the UK are studying Chinese at the moment.
This can be found in line 18 of the text.

3 Mediation → Mediation, p. 245

Prepare a German summary of the text for your school magazine in which you focus on the decision to introduce the Chinese language Mandarin.

4 Analysis → Text analysis, p. 228

Analyse the use of quotes and reported speech in the text and explain its effect on the reader.

5 Text production: A letter to the headmaster → Writing a personal letter, p. 233

As a German living in the UK, you are a parent of a 12-year-old boy attending a specialist language school in an English town. As a result of the *Specialist Schools and Academies Trust* strategy, the school has decided to replace German with Mandarin. Write a letter to the headmaster in which you either criticise or welcome this decision.

6 Making a poster → Presentation, p. 264

Design a poster for an advertising campaign for the *Specialist Schools and Academies Trust* strategy to put Mandarin on the curriculum of the country's specialist language schools. Present your posters to the class and decide which one you like best.

C Language and immigration

1 Before you read
What difficulties might immigrants face if they cannot speak the language of the country they move to? Make a list with a partner and report back to the class.

theguardian

News | Sport | Comment | Culture | Business | Money | Life&Style | Travel | Environment

Comment is free > Canada   Search [ ] GO

Canada to raise language bar

Requiring new immigrants to speak English or French to a higher level will improve their economic prospects say ministers but others fear the policy will target favoured nationalities.

The Canadian government's plan to raise language fluency requirements for prospective skilled immigrants has some experts concerned that it may tilt migration patterns toward the English-speaking world.

Canada's immigration minister Jason Kenney said earlier this year that some immigration applicants will soon have to demonstrate high levels of English or French fluency to gain entry to Canada. The proposed new requirements would apply to the largest class of immigrants, the federal skilled worker category, which accounts for nearly 100,000 of the roughly 250,000 immigrants who come to Canada every year. The decision is aimed at improving economic outcomes for immigrants in the country, which have been steadily declining over the last 30 years. Today a new immigrant earns only about 60% of the wages of a similarly educated Canadian-born citizen, compared with nearly 90% three decades ago. Meanwhile a flood of research has shown that language ability is one of the best predictors of rapid integration and economic success.

But Naomi Alboim, a public policy professor at Ontario's Queen's University and a former provincial deputy minister of citizenship, expects the policy will also have other consequences. The most striking will be a significant shift in source countries, she said. Alboim anticipates a decline in the number of migrants from China, for example, and a rise in the number from English-speaking countries.

Such a shift would make Canada's immigrant intake more similar to Australia's. The Australian government raised immigrant language requirements

0 **to raise the bar** – *(idiom)* die Messlatte höher legen
2 **prospect** – Aussicht, Perspektive
2 **policy** – Strategie, Richtlinie
3 **to target sb.** – sich jdn zur Zielgruppe nehmen
3 **favoured** – bevorzugt
4 **fluency** – Flüssigkeit
4 **requirement** – Anforderung
5 **prospective** – zukünftig
5 **to tilt** – neigen
6 **pattern** – Muster
9 **to gain entry** – eingelassen werden
9 **proposed** – geplant
10 **to apply to sb.** – für jdn gelten
13 **to account for** – ausmachen
14 **roughly** – ungefähr
17 **to aim at** – zielen auf
18 **outcome** – Ergebnis
21 **to decline** – abnehmen
23 **decade** – Jahrzehnt
23 **meanwhile** – mittlerweile
24 **predictor (for)** – Anzeichen (für)
28 **striking** – auffallend
28 **shift** – Verschiebung, Verlagerung
29 **to anticipate** – erwarten
32 **intake** – Aufnahme

over the last decade and its immigrants have fared better economically than those in Canada. But Australia also receives proportionally larger numbers from English-speaking countries such as the UK, Ireland and New Zealand, who tend to integrate more quickly.

"A focus on language does make eminent sense. But I think we have to be careful about how high we are setting the bar and whether that is going to exclude a whole group of people who can contribute to a very significant degree with a little bit of assistance," Alboim said.

"We don't need to restrict our entire federal skilled worker intake to only those who have a high level of language, because that can develop over time." […]

While anyone can, in theory, learn a language, English or French fluency is more common in some parts of the world and Canada may be taking a step, intentional or not, towards targeting source countries.

Debbie Douglas, executive director of the Ontario Council of Agencies Serving Immigrants, fears that the new policy will screen out people from the global south. "We can't discriminate against folks who don't sound like us. That might mean more propping up of language teaching [for new immigrants] but that's a very small price to pay for helping people contribute to building our country," Douglas said. […]

Kenney has said it is hard to predict what impact the new language requirements might have on source countries, as they tend to ebb and flow for a variety of reasons, including global economic conditions as well as selection criteria. His goal is to create a more flexible language grid that will contribute to improving the economic fortunes of those who are selected. […]

While an emphasis on language might produce better economic outcomes for immigrants in the short term, it could also have other effects. Canada may struggle to find enough people with sufficient levels of fluency to maintain its very high immigration levels, for example. A sudden shift in the attainability of immigration may have an impact on Canada's ties to a country such as China and studies have shown that trade ties increase through immigration. […]

(628 words)

34 **to fare well** – *(ugs.)* gut fahren
38 **eminent** – hervorragend
40 **to contribute** – beitragen
42 **entire** – ganz
48 **to screen out** – aus-sortieren
49 **to discriminate against sb.** – jdn diskriminieren
50 **to prop up** – (finanziell) stützen
53 **impact** – Auswirkung
56 **grid** – Netz
57 **fortune** – Schicksal
58 **emphasis** – Betonung, Schwerpunkt
60 **to struggle** – sich schwer tun
60 **sufficient** – ausreichend
60 **to maintain** – aufrechter-halten
61 **attainability** – Erreich-barkeit
62 **tie** – Bindung

2 Comprehension: Table completion
Read the text. In a table, collect all the pieces of information the text gives you on the following:

a) reasons why the Canadian government plans to raise the 'language bar",

b) positive effects of this plan,

c) negative effects of this plan.

3 Analysis → Describing cartoons, p. 242
Describe and analyse the cartoon and relate it to the text.

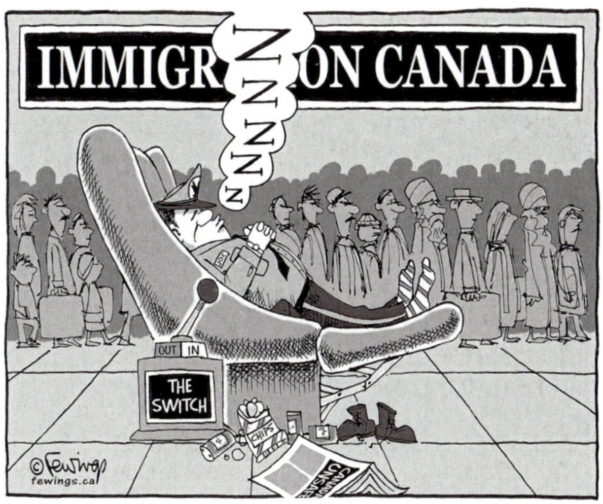

D Whose English is it anyway?

1 Before you listen
"I find children's manipulation of language very exciting. They mix two words up in the bat of an eyelid," she said. "It's incorrect to mix it up but who says it's incorrect? English is a mongrel language anyway."

a) Looking at this quote and the headline *Schoolchildren now speak "The Queen's Hinglish"*, guess what the listening text is about.

b) What is your opinion about the statement: "It's incorrect to mix it up but who says it's incorrect?"

A 2.4 p. 200 **2 Listening comprehension: Schoolchildren now speak "The Queen's Hinglish"**
→ Listening, p. 221
Copy and complete the following table.

Definition of Queen's Hinglish	Development of Queen's Hinglish	Future of Hinglish

A 2.6 **3 Listening comprehension: Whose English is it anyway?**
→ Listening, p. 221, Mediation, p. 245
Listen to the recording. Make notes and summarise them in a German text concentrating on what David Crystal and Bill Bryson say about the aspect of power.

p. 201 **4 Analysis** → Describing cartoons, p. 242
Describe and analyse the cartoon.

E Shakespearian English

1 Shakespeare: Famous quotes and themes

a) The following quotes by Shakespeare are world famous. Match them with the sentences in the right column to express what they mean.

1.	Give every man thy ear, but few thy voice.	A	There is something wrong here.
2.	To be, or not to be: that is the question.	B	Making a fuss about something which is not important.
3.	All the world's a stage, And all the men and women merely players.	C	This is the plain truth.
4.	This is the short and the long of it.	D	Some things look more valuable than they really are.
5.	All that glitters is not gold.	E	Life is just a play.
6.	All's well that ends well.	F	Anything is OK as long as it turns out well in the end.
7.	Much ado about nothing.	G	Listening is often wiser than talking.
8.	Something is rotten in the state of Denmark.	H	Is an unhappy life better than death?

to make a fuss about sth. – viel Aufhebens um etw. machen
to glitter – glitzern
plain truth – reine Wahrheit
ado – Getue, Aufwand

b) In his plays, Shakespeare repeatedly focussed on the following themes. What do they mean in your own words?

The corrupting power of too much ambition • The impossibility of certainty • Fate versus free will, the inevitability of fate • The possibility of justice in the world • Self-interest versus love • The nature of evil • Love as a cause for suffering, love as a cause of death

c) Which of these themes do you consider important today?

Apart from his dramas, William Shakespeare also wrote many sonnets. Sonnet 116 is one of his most famous.

Sonnet 116

Let me not to the marriage of true minds
Admit impediments. Love is not love
Which alters when it alteration finds,
Or bends with the remover to remove:
O no! it is an ever-fixed mark
That looks on tempests and is never shaken;
It is the star to every wandering bark,
Whose worth's unknown, although his height be taken.
Love's not Time's fool, though rosy lips and cheeks
Within his bending sickle's compass come:
Love alters not with his brief hours and weeks,
But bears it out even to the edge of doom.
If this be error and upon me proved,
I never writ, nor no man ever loved.

2 Vocabulary → Working with a dictionary, p. 255
Look up the following words appearing in the sonnet in an English-English dictionary and explain their meaning to a partner.

impediment (l. 2) • to alter (l. 3) • mark (l. 5) • tempest (l. 6) • to wander (l. 7) • bark (l. 7) • sickle (l. 10) • compass (l. 10)

3 Comprehension
A sonnet can be divided into four parts. Find the parts in the sonnet on page 17 and write down what each one is about.

4 Analysis

a) Instead of directly stating what love is, the speaker uses a number of metaphors to define love. List and explain them.

b) Analyse the structure of the sonnet and explain how this supports its main theme.

5 Shakespeare goes interactive
In *Macbeth*, Shakespeare tells a story of prophecy, ambition, murder and fate. Macbeth is prophesied to one day become King of Scotland. In order to speed things up, he and his wife kill King Duncan, but in the end they have to pay for their crime.

theguardian

News | Sport | Comment | Culture | Business | Money | Life&Style | Travel | Environment

Comment is free > Literature   Search GO

Schools test 'interactive graphic novel' version of Macbeth

Classical Comics is set to launch a multimedia version of the play for children and teenagers, featuring the voices of Juliet Stevenson and Derek Jacobi

Classical Comics' Interactive Macbeth

The latest attempt to get an audience of multimedia-savvy schoolchildren and teens engaged with Shakespeare is an interactive graphic novel version of the play, complete with voiceovers by Derek Jacobi and Juliet Stevenson.

Classical Comics has done well with a series of graphic novels of famous titles (including Jane Eyre, A Christmas Carol and Frankenstein) which it launched two years ago, but the publisher decided that the next step in its quest to make classic stories accessible would be to bring the text alive. Its new version of Macbeth, which it will preview to schools this week before launching in June, takes the artwork of comicbook artist Jon Haward from its original graphic novel and animates it, adding audio from Jacobi and Stevenson.

"That which hath made them drunk hath made me bold: what hath quenched them hath given me fire," proclaims Stevenson as Lady Macbeth, descending a stone staircase framed by gargoyles as two dogs growl over a piece of meat. And later, "I have

4 **multimedia-savvy** – bewandert in Multi-Media
6 **voiceovers** – Synchronstimmen
9 **quest** – Plan, Unterfangen
14 **bold** – mutig, entschlossen
14 **to quench** – Durst löschen
16 **gargoyles** – Wasserspeier

Generations of students have found it difficult to access the original text of what is considered to be one of the world's greatest works of literature. However, there have been modern versions that try to get Shakespeare across to today's audience.

a) If you were asked to make a 400 year old drama more interesting for students, how would you do it? Think about the media you would use, the language, costumes, etc.

b) Go online and watch a demo version of the interactive graphic novel of Macbeth, which was created by *Classical Comics*, a UK publisher. What do you think about it?

6 Comprehension

a) Read the text and outline the reasons for deciding to publish the interactive graphic novel version of Macbeth.

b) In your own words, briefly describe the features of the interactive graphic novel version of Macbeth.

7 Comment

"Publishing Shakespeare dramas as interactive graphic novels helps to get younger readers interested in the work of Shakespeare." Comment.

8 Project → Hotspot 4, p. 21

done the deed," gasps Jacobi as the Thane of Cawdor, gripping two bloody daggers. "Didst thou not hear a noise?"

"It's been in the planning for a while," said Classical Comics managing director Clive Bryant of the Macbeth project. "We thought of it at the beginning of last year and it's taken this long to get it together. Having Derek Jacobi and Juliet Stevenson involved was incredible – we were recording it in a small studio in north London, which had a large contact list, which was how we managed to secure them. It just adds that extra dimension to it: hearing Macbeth with Derek Jacobi in the classroom – you can't get much better than that."

He visualises teachers using the interactive graphic novel (which comes in three versions: the original Shakespearean text, a contemporary rendering, and a quick, reduced version for younger viewers) on the whiteboard for a whole class. Alternatively groups of students might discuss the novel around a computer. Readers can choose to view one panel at a time or sit back and watch in "movie mode", with context notes provided explaining the Shakespearean language.

Jacobi called the concept "truly inspirational, creating, as it does so magnificently, an accessible and fascinating mix of visual and audible drama ... The stage and the page brought vividly to life". "The artwork of Jon Haward is both dramatically compelling and beautifully illustrative," he added. "His pictures illuminate the words to perfection and bring these great works leaping to mind and eye. This format is immediate, vital, energetic and engaging."

If the venture proves popular with schools, Classical Comics is planning a whole range of other interactive graphic novels, including Romeo and Juliet, Julius Caesar and A Midsummer Night's Dream, Bryant said. (497 words)

27 **rendering** – *hier:* Ausgabe, Version
30 **panel** – Blende
35 **compelling** – fesselnd
36 **to leap** – springen

Working with words

These strategies work for all topics. The more words you know for one aspect / idea, the more flexible you become. Looking up words in a thesaurus will certainly help.

a) Synonyms and short definitions

For the following words that have to do with the English language in use, find at least two words or a short definition with the same or a similar meaning, e.g. global: wordwide, all over the world, all-encompassing.

immigrant • lingua franca • negotiations • globalisation • hybrid language • international • skills • technology • texting • abbreviations • multicultural

b) Language functions

For the following verbs, collect as many words with the same language function as possible, e.g. outline: to show, to illustrate, to sketch, to draft.

say • refer to • show • explain • agree • argue • believe • convince • detail • report

c) Odd one out

Find the word which does not belong in the list. Give reasons for your choice.

1. Pidgin • Globish • Hinglish
2. texter • sender • writer
3. communicate • chat • socialise
4. abbreviation • text message • email
5. global • international • multinational
6. language barrier • misunderstanding • unknown words
7. working language • mother tongue • native language
8. communication channel • blog • post

d) Find the words to fill the gaps. Pay attention to the correct forms of the verbs.

misunderstand • combine • discourage • well • abstract • decrease • advantage • polite • difficult • temporary

Some speakers find it very difficult to express **1** ideas in a foreign language.
Misunderstandings **2** learners of a foreign language.
Even when speaking a lingua franca it is very important to remain **3**.
If you learn an international language **4**, you can easily communicate with a variety of people.
In international meetings it is essential not to be **5**.
Therefore, speaking more than one foreign language can be an **6**.
The influence of the English language on other languages is not just **7**.
Many students of English find Shakespeare's dramas **8** to understand.
Children often **9** words from two languages and unknowingly create hybrid expressions.
The percentage of websites in English has **10**.

1 Research project: The influence of English → Presentation, p. 264
Do some research and prepare a talk about the influence of English on German computer/technology language. Make sure to give examples to illustrate what you want to say. Include your own opinion about this trend.

2 Research project: Anglicisms → Internet research, p. 260
Do some research about anglicisms (a word that is borrowed from English to be used in another language, i.e. *Wir müssen das Wording überdenken.*) or the blending of two languages for special effects in advertising, like in the example. Prepare a talk in which you outline how these adverts work. Give further examples and also state your opinion about them.

3 Research project: Lingua francas → Internet research, p. 260

a) Go online and do some research about the following lingua francas and pidgins: Volapük, Esperanto and Interlingua. Present your findings to the class.

b) Go online and do some research on the history of Pidgin English. Include video examples (e.g. Pidgin English spoken on the Solomon Islands, Hawaian Pidgin, Nigerian Pidgin, etc.) in your presentation for the class.

4 Project: Shakespeare's plays → Projects and group work, p. 261
Work in groups. Each group chooses one of Shakespeare's plays, collects all relevant information and then prepares a poster about it. Present your poster to the class.

A 2.9

8 **rise** – increase
10 **to coin** – to invent
11 **paralyzed** – unable to move
13 **to plunge ahead** – to carry on without worries
14 **heedless** – without concern for
16 **latter** – *here:* last
20 **maven** – expert
21 **to riff on sth.** – to say sth. which is based on sth. else
35 **drill** – exercise

THE CHRISTIAN SCIENCE MONITOR

Search GO

World | USA | Commentary | Business | Environment | Innovation | Science |

'Globish' and the open-sourcing of English

This form of 'English lite' is out from under the control of native speakers; does that matter?

Do you speak Globish – "global English"? Can you stand it when others do? Globish is a much simplified form of English used, especially in business, where neither party is a native speaker of English. Globish is how a Venezuelan talks to a Chinese, or a Turk to an Algerian. Unlike "Spanglish," for instance, it's not a meld of English and something else. And unlike Basic English or Esperanto, Globish arose naturally.

Its rise would seem to illustrate the saying that Britain and the United States are two countries separated by a common language. Jean-Paul Nerrière, the former IBM executive credited with coining the term "Globish," noticed that at his company's international conferences, Americans and Britons would tend to be paralyzed by the endless minor differences between their two brands of English. Meanwhile, people from other parts of the world would plunge ahead into conversation with one another, heedless of their bad grammar and limited vocabulary.

I'm not sure I buy this. Somehow the idea of an American at a conference hesitating to chat up a British contact for fear the latter would say something like "different to" seems unlikely. On the other hand, anyone who has ever traveled outside his or her linguistic comfort zone has probably found how helpful just a few words in a common language can be.

British language maven Robert McCrum has called Globish "the worldwide dialect of the third millennium." A blogger riffing on Mr. McCrum compared Globish to "open source" software – available for anyone to adapt to his own uses. He added, "I think that if Globish were to be defined by the International community as a whole, this would greatly help to abstract the language from the western, English-speaking culture." But language and culture are so closely linked that culture-free language would be like tasteless food or colorless paint. That idea of ownership, however, is important.

"*Anglophones* no longer own English," the Toronto Star quoted Mr. Nerrière as saying last year. "It's now owned by people in Singapore, Ulan Bator, Montevideo, Beijing, and elsewhere." *Anglophone* isn't used very much in American English, but it's common in French and in officially bilingual Canada. Dictionaries tend to define *Anglophone* as simply one who speaks English – never mind whether as native tongue or something else.

I first learned *Anglophone* at summer school at the University of Aix-Marseille in France. For phonetics drills, we were segregated by mother tongue. The idea was that native English speakers face different issues in learning to make the sounds of

French than do, say, native speakers of German. So I tend to think of *Anglophone* as meaning specifically one who makes the sounds of English.

This, I suspect, is how Nerrière understands it, too. His book, "Don't Speak English, Parlez Globish," was a bestseller in France. His codification of Globish has a vocabulary of just 1,500 words – only a fraction of the 615,000 or so of the Oxford English Dictionary.

Globish, Iman Kurdi wrote in the Arab News, "is based on short sentences, simple grammar, repetition and the avoidance of complex syntax. It is rather ugly, clumsy and certainly painful to the ears of native English speakers. But," he continued, "it is also democratic and accessible ... It is something to get you by."

Globish isn't pretty. But it works. (575 words)

40 **parlez** *(French)* – speak
40 **codification** – *here:* list
41 **fraction** – very small part

1 Comprehension

a) Summarise the facts about Globish mentioned in the text in your own words.

b) Explain why Globish is called a culture-free language.

2 Analysis

→ Describing diagrams, p. 243
Describe and analyse the diagram "Which two languages, apart from your mother tongue, do you think children should learn?"

3 Comment

Taking into consideration the text and the diagram, comment on whether children should learn one or two foreign languages or rather Globish.

Which two languages, apart from your mother tongue, do you think children should learn?

	English	French	German	Spanish
EU25	**77%**	**33%**	**28%**	**19%**
BE	88%	50%	7%	9%
CZ	89%	9%	66%	4%
DK	94%	13%	62%	13%
DE	89%	45%	3%	16%
EL	96%	34%	50%	3%
ES	85%	44%	14%	4%
FR	91%	2%	24%	45%
IE	3%	64%	42%	35%
IT	84%	34%	17%	17%
CY	98%	49%	19%	2%
LU	59%	83%	43%	2%
HU	85%	4%	73%	3%
NL	90%	22%	40%	21%
AT	84%	29%	2%	10%
PL	90%	7%	69%	1%
PT	90%	60%	8%	7%
SI	96%	6%	69%	3%
SK	87%	7%	75%	3%
SE	99%	17%	35%	31%
UK	5%	71%	34%	39%
BG	87%	13%	49%	5%
HR	82%	5%	69%	2%
RO	64%	34%	17%	7%
TR	72%	12%	52%	1%

= **First language**

= **Second language**

Source: European Union, Eurobarometer

Topic 2
The United States – then and now

c63e6w

A

"The American Dream is ownership … a house, a car, a vacation home and, even better, your own business."
Mario Batali, famous chef

B

"The American Dream is something that every immigrant brought to this country, as my parents did, and that is the ability to go as far as you can in life, limited only by your own dreams and willingness to work hard. And above all, the American Dream for these folks meant that your children will have the opportunity to do better than you will."
General Colin Powell, former Secretary of State

C

Getting started

1 Think – pair – share

a) Look at the pictures and compile a list of five aspects you consider typically American.

b) Compare your list with that of a partner and agree on five aspects between you.

c) Share your results with another pair and agree on five aspects again. Was it easy to agree? Which of the ideas do you consider stereotypes rather than fact?

E

folks *(coll.)* – Leute
attainable – erreichbar
to impel – antreiben
to achieve sth. – etw. erreichen

"The American Dream is equal protection under the law and equal opportunity. The American Dream does not promise equal results, but it does promise equal opportunity."
The Rev. Jesse Jackson, civil rights activist and political leader

D

"The American Dream, whether attainable or not, is to have freedom, freedom in all things. To go as far as ambition impels us, in work, in play, and religion and even in love."
Maya Angelou, author and civil rights activist

F

"The American Dream is about fulfilling your potential to the max. It's not a chase for material goods; it's about learning what inspires you in life and creating a plan to turn it into your life's work. The way to achieve the dream is to follow the plan and pay attention to the details, because it's those details that make or break you."
Tyra Banks, supermodel and host of 'America's Next Top Model'

2 **From the quotations, filter out the basic idea of the American Dream. Where do these famous Americans agree and where do they disagree? Arrange your answers in a word web.**

3 **In the Declaration of Independence, America's founding fathers declared that God had given us all the right to "Life, Liberty and the Pursuit of Happiness". Discuss in class what these rights mean to you.** → Discussions, p. 246

Word bank

proud • Stars and Stripes • front lawn • rodeo • conservative • religious • extreme views • preacher • protest • demonstration • funeral • coffin • casualty of war • vanity • plastic surgery • appearance • superficial

A The history of the United States

12,000 BC The people we now call Native Americans came from Siberia to Alaska. Recent discoveries suggest, however, that the first humans to arrive in America came from Southeast Asia by boat long before that.

1492 AD Christopher Columbus wanted to sail to India by a new route around the globe. He reached some islands in the Caribbean instead and thought he was in India. That is why he called the natives "Indians". Soon after 1492, the European powers, especially Spain, started to explore and colonize America.

1607 The first permanent English settlement in America was founded: Jamestown in Virginia.

1620 The ship "The Mayflower" brought 102 people (many of them Puritans – the Pilgrims) from England to America. They came for religious reasons. To this day, Americans celebrate the Pilgrims' first harvest as "Thanksgiving" every November.

1675 – 1676 There had always been conflicts between European settlers and Indians, but most of the time there was peace during the early years. King Philip's War in 1675 – 76 (Philip was an Indian chief) was the first serious war and started two centuries of bloody warfare between whites and Native Americans.

1775 – 1783 On July 4, 1776, the American Colonies declared independence from Britain because they were unhappy about the way the mother country treated them. With the help of the French, the American revolutionary army, led by George Washington, won the War of Independence against Britain. Then delegates from the former 13 colonies signed the Constitution of the United States. Washington later became the first president of the US.

1791 The Bill of Rights was added to the Constitution because references to human and civil rights were missing.

1803 After having bought large parts of North America from the French (the Louisiana Purchase), President Jefferson sent the famous explorers Lewis and Clark out West to see what he had bought. As more and more settlers came, the Native Americans were pushed further and further West.

1861 – 1865 The North and the South of the US drifted apart: the South was a slave-holding, agricultural society, the North was more industrialized. Because of these differences, the southern states wanted to be separate, and a terrible Civil War followed (1861 – 65). The victory of the North saved the unity of the United States and freed the slaves in the South.

1869	After the Civil War, the Industrial Revolution spread across the US. The railroad, which was extremely important for linking the different regions of the huge country, was part of it. In 1869 it was finally possible to travel non-stop from East to West by train.
1914–1918	The US Army entered World War I in 1917 and helped to end the war. By that time the US had become one of the leading industrial countries in the world.
1929–1938	The US, together with the rest of the world, entered a period of economic depression. A radical shift in economic policy (President Franklin D. Roosevelt's so-called "New Deal") helped to overcome the crisis.
1939–1945	When Japan attacked the US at Pearl Harbor (Hawaii) in 1941, the US entered World War II to fight against Japan, Germany and Italy. After the war, the US decided to help reconstruct Europe again (with the Marshall Plan) because it needed the western allies against the Soviet Union.
1946–1993	The US and the Soviet Union were rival superpowers until the Soviet Union collapsed in 1993. Several times their "Cold War" almost turned into a nuclear war.
1950s and 60s	Rosa Parks and Martin Luther King Jr., among others, protested against the unjust treatment of African Americans. Eventually, protests grew so strong that the policy of segregation came to an end. This, however, didn't mean the end of race problems in the US.
1964–1973	The US fought on the side of South Vietnam against Communist North Vietnam, which was supported by the Soviet Union. In 1975, two years after the US had withdrawn from a war it could not win, North Vietnam invaded South Vietnam and the war was over.
2001	With the terrorist attacks on the World Trade Center in NYC and on the Pentagon in Washington on September 11, Americans realized how vulnerable they were. Fighting terrorism with military means turned out to be very problematic, especially the American invasion of Iraq in 2003. Many of America's allies were against this war.
2009	Barack Obama was elected the first black president of the US.

(756 words)

1 Look at the pictures. Which events in the timeline do they represent?

2 Presentation: A market place → Presentation, p. 264
The class chooses at least six topics from the timeline that are worth considering in more detail (e.g. Native Americans, Bill of Rights, Civil War, 9/11, etc.) and then splits up into groups. Each group works on one of the topics and prepares an informative poster. Display the posters in a market place.

B The American Dream

1 Before you read
What do you associate with the American Dream? Discuss your ideas with your partner.

7 **reliable** – zuverlässig
12 **requisite** – unerlässlich
13 **mobster** – Mitglied der Mafia
13 **to dishonor** – entehren
29 **self-evident** – selbstverständlich
29 **to endow** *(formal)* – ausstatten
30 **inalienable** – unveräußerlich
36 **betrayal** – Verrat, Treuebruch
36 **to hit home** – ankommen (Botschaft)

The American Dream

The Founding Fathers sign the Declaration of Independence, 1776

I'm going to start out today by going back just over a month ago. It's Sunday night, April 16 – the sixth episode of the sixth season of "The Sopranos" is on. Vito Spatafore – the most reliable and loyal captain in the New Jersey crime family run by Tony Soprano – is on the run. The story is out – Vito has a wife, two kids, the requisite mistress, but he's been seen in a gay bar, dressed like the biker in the Village People. The other mobsters want him dead; he's dishonored them all.

Heading north, Vito's been on the road for hours. His cellphone rings; he throws it out the window. He has no idea where he is. His car breaks down. He makes it into the next town, finds an inn, puts his gun under his pillow.

The next day he wakes up in a little New Hampshire village, where gay people walk the streets without fear. In a diner, looks pass between Vito and the counterman. A male couple comes in, sits down, and begins speaking a language Vito has never before heard in the light of day, only in the dark. He's confused: What does it mean to be in a place where, for the first time in your life, you might feel at home in your own skin? Could that even be right?

He goes into an antique shop. He picks up a vase, and the gay owner compliments him on his taste: "That's the most expensive item in the store." But then Vito sees something else, probably the cheapest thing in the store: an old New Hampshire license plate. "Live Free or Die" reads the slogan across the top. [...]

Vito stares. "Live Free or Die" – it's as if the metal can talk. It's just a license plate; for him it might as well be the Declaration of Independence, ringing its bell. "We hold these truths to be self-evident, that all men are created equal, that they are endowed by their Creator with certain inalienable Rights, that among these are Life, Liberty, and the pursuit of Happiness," Jefferson wrote – and suddenly, as it has for so many for so long, through that license plate the Declaration is speaking to Vito as if it were addressed to him. "Live free or die" – what if all this, the shock in his face says, was meant for him as much as anyone?

It's one of those signal moments when the whole weight of the national story, its promises and its betrayals, hits home – leaving the citizen at once part of a community and completely alone. It doesn't matter that, well, yes, of course, on the fourth of July,

1776, when the Declaration of Independence was presented, everyone understood that all men meant men, not women; whites, not blacks; Christians, not Jews or Hindi or heathen; decent people, not Sodomites. The idea that "all men are created equal" was not a "self-evident truth", Sen. John Pettit said on the floor of the Senate in 1853: it was "a self-evident lie". It was in the midst of the debates over the Kansas-Nebraska Act; Pettit was arguing for voiding the Missouri Compromise of 1820 and opening the territories to slavery. It was a debate: "The great declaration cost our forefathers too dear," Sen. Benjamin Franklin Wade of Ohio replied to Pettit, "to be so lightly thrown away by their children." [...] "Life, liberty, and the pursuit of happiness" – it's what the rest of the world understands by America when America isn't forcing the rest of the world to understand America as something else. "We are caught in a world of limits where there's no such thing as the self-made man," said a graduate student in France last week; Claire de la Vigne was speaking to a New York Times reporter about the French university system, where doors are made to be closed, not opened. "We are never taught the idea of the American Dream, where everything is possible," she said. It's what Americans understand by America, when the facts of everyday American life somehow recede, and an idea of America takes their place. [...]

There's a way in which you can see every American story as a version of the Declaration of Independence: every story an attempt to make it true, or prove it a lie. In 1941, Henry Luce called the 20th century "the American century"; he meant this was the century when America became a colossus from which the rest of the world would have to step back, trembling with awe. But if that American century was truly American, you can almost see Lincoln reminding us – or, if not Lincoln, the doorkeeper at Independence Hall – that the story of the American century is the story of all sorts of previously excluded, marginalized, scorned, despised, ignored or enslaved people – laborers, women, African-Americans, Asian Americans, Jews, Latinos, gay men and women – entering into full citizenship and full participation in national life. If not full citizenship, a more complete citizenship than even Lincoln or the doorkeeper could in fact have imagined – as, again and again, decade after decade, those echoing words of the Declaration of Independence sounded as if for the first time. (888 words)

by Greil Marcus, delivered as a commencement address at the University of California at Berkeley, 2006

43 **to void** – ungültig machen, auflösen
53 **to recede** – sich entfernen
57 **colossus** – Koloss
58 **to tremble with awe** – vor Ehrfurcht erschauern
60 **marginalized** – an den Rand gedrängt
61 **scorned** – verachtet
61 **despised** – verschmäht

2 Comprehension
What are the main ideas of the Declaration of Independence? How does Vito Spatafore's story compare to the promises made in the Declaration of Independence?

3 Mediation
What meaning does the fulfillment of the Declaration's promise have for those who have previously suffered injustice? Answer in complete German sentences.

4 Vocabulary → Taking notes, p. 254
Make a list of words in this text that you can use to define the American Dream and use them to write a short definition.

5 Comment
"We are caught in a world of limits where there's no such thing as the self-made man." (l. 48). Do you agree with the French student?

6 Research project → Hotspot 1, p. 37

C The American political system

The voters

direct vote

indirect vote (via state electors)

Legislative
- Senate
- House of Representatives

The legislative branch (also known as Congress)
Congress has two chambers, the Senate and the House of Representatives.

- Senate:
  100 Senators, elected for a 6-year term, one third are elected every two years.
- House of Representatives:
  435 members, elected every two years. States with a high population have more representatives than states with a low population.

The House and Senate can reject each other's bills. Congress decides on the federal budget (how federal money is spent).

The Capitol, Washington D.C., the seat of Congress

The President suggests legislation and can veto laws passed by Congress.

Congress can pass laws over the President's veto by a two-thirds majority. Congress ratifies treaties and declares war.

The Court can declare laws unconstitutional.

The Senate must confirm the President's judicial appointments.

The President appoints federal judges.

The Court can declare presidential acts unconstitutional.

Executive
- President
- Cabinet

The executive branch
The President is elected every four years and can hold office for two full terms only. The President is Head of State and Commander-in-Chief of the armed forces. The President appoints a Cabinet and the Cabinet is approved by the Senate. Cabinet members need not be members of Congress.

The US President's office, the Oval Office

Judicial
- Supreme Court
- Federal Courts

The judicial branch
The Supreme Court has nine judges. They are appointed for life. The Supreme Court is responsible for seeing that the Constitution is upheld and that laws that are made are allowed under the Constitution.
There are eleven US Courts of Appeals and 90 US District Courts.

The seal of the US Supreme Court

The electoral process

US citizens over the age of 18 who are registered to vote can do so, but voters must register themselves as there is no automatic registration. At a general election all registered voters vote for the candidate of their choice and the candidate who gets the most votes is the winner (winner-takes-all system).

How the President is elected

The presidential elections are the most important elections of the US. They are held every four years and there are six basic stages.

Stage 1: Who can run for president?

US-born citizens over the age of 35 who had lived in the US for at least 14 years can decide to run for the post of president. Usually there are a number of applicants from the main parties as well as independent candidates.

Stage 2: Primaries

These are state-wide (not nation-wide) elections held between January and June of the election year in which voters choose delegates who will go to the party's national convention to finally select the party's presidential candidate. At the primaries the ordinary party members indicate by selecting their delegates who they would prefer as their party's presidential candidate.

Stage 3: National conventions

Republican and Democratic conventions are held in July or August and at the end of these 4-day meetings with speeches, political declarations and colourful shows, the party's official candidate for presidency is chosen by the delegates and officially announced. Then the candidates start an intensified campaigning tour through all US states.

Stage 4: General election

Election day is the Tuesday following the first Monday in November. Voters cast their vote for their favourite presidential candidate. In fact, the voters are selecting the members of the electoral college, who will finally vote for a certain candidate.

Stage 5: The Electoral College

The number of electors a state has depends on the number of members it has in Congress (e.g. 47 for a big and densely populated state like California, three for the District of Columbia). On the Monday following the second Wednesday in December each elector casts one vote for a presidential candidate. The candidate who wins the majority of electoral votes becomes president (at least 270 out of 538).

Stage 6: Inauguration

The results of the Electoral College vote is declared on January 6 and the newly elected president and vice president are sworn in on January 20 following the November election.

National convention of the Republican Party

12 **applicant** – Bewerber(in)
13 **primary** – *hier:* Vorwahl
16 **convention** – *hier:* Parteitag
18 **delegate** – Vertreter(in), Repräsentant(in)
30 **Electoral College** – Wahlmännergremium
33 **District of Columbia** – Regierungssitz (Washington)
37 **inauguration** – Amtseinsetzung, (feierliche) Ernennung

1 **If you are a party member in the US and want to become president, you have to carry out two successful campaigns. Explain and illustrate the differences in these campaigns.**

2 **Research project** → Hotspot 2, p. 37

D Racial (in)equality

1 Before you read
Make assumptions about the content of the article based on the headline. Share your ideas with a partner.

5 **to ring out** – schallen
10 **eerie** – gespenstisch
13 **irreversibly** – unumkehrbar
19 **uncanny** – unheimlich
19 **premonition** – Vorahnung
21 **to reverberate** – nachhallen
25 **to ascend** – aufsteigen
32 **to detoxify** – entgiften
36 **to expel** – ausschließen

theguardian

40 years after King's death, Jackson hails first steps into promised land

Jesse Jackson has no difficulty remembering his last conversation with Martin Luther King. The leader of the civil rights movement and his young apprentice were preparing to go to dinner with a local pastor. The shot rang out a second later. "Next thing I heard," says Jackson, "someone was saying 'Get low! Get low!' The police were coming towards us with guns drawn. I remember crawling to the steps. There was blood everywhere, and a photographer scooped up a cup of it. It was eerie."

Those few moments, 40 years ago tomorrow, are carved not only into Jackson's memory but into the collective narrative of America. They certainly changed his life, driving an already keen activist, then 26, deeply and irreversibly into the pursuit of racial justice. "It put on us a burden not to stop, to say we must not allow one bullet to kill a whole movement," he says now. But in a wider sense they changed everyone else's reality too. They were what he calls "a defining moment in American history".

Jackson was on stage with King in the Mason Temple in Memphis the night before he was assassinated, when King made his famous "mountaintop" speech. King talked with almost uncanny premonition about the "threats out there" and what might happen to him at the hands of "some of our sick white brothers".

"It doesn't matter with me now," King concluded in words that will forever reverberate, "because I've been to the mountaintop … And I've looked over. And I've seen the promised land."

Forty years on, Jesse Jackson is still weighing up how far up the mountain African Americans have ascended. As someone who has stood at the front of that march for four decades, Jackson believes that there remains some way to go. Politically, he says, African Americans have come a long way. In 1965 there were about 300 black elected politicians in America; now there are some 10,000.

He sees a substantial step forward too in other areas of public life, notably entertainment and athletics. "Take the Super Bowl between the [New York] Giants and the [New England] Patriots. Millions of people watched the game and race never came up. It was the red team versus the blue team. That has detoxified racial relations."

But there are several headline figures that tell a very different story. A quarter of African Americans live in poverty, compared with 8% of whites; seven out of 10 black boys drop out before finishing high school; in several states such as New Jersey black children are 60 times more likely to be expelled from school than whites; there are more black men in jail than in college; and the most shocking statistic: on average black men die more than six years earlier than their white equivalents.

"People of colour have higher infant mortality rates, shorter life expectancy, greater unemployment, less education. We pay more for less. That is our characteristic 40 years later." Jackson has an explanation for this piercing disparity between the advancement of black people in many areas of public life coupled with stagnation or even deterioration in their overall standards of living. He points out that the legal underpinning of Jim Crow segregation in the South was negated in a series of landmark legal actions starting in 1954. Then the civil rights movement led by King began the process that would remove cultural impediments to black progress. But the issue with which he had only begun to grapple at the time of his death – economic inequalities experienced by black as well as white working-class communities – remains a festering sore. "Yes, blacks have been elected to political office, but the economic problems that King had started to turn to are still there. The result is you get black mayors presiding over the worst inner-cities in America, where jobs are leaving, investment is leaving, guns and drugs are coming; where there are first-class jails and second-class schools."

(675 words)

39 **infant mortality** – Säuglingssterblichkeit
41 **piercing** – stechend
41 **disparity** – Ungleichheit
42 **deterioration** – Verschlechterung
43 **to underpin** – untermauern
44 **to negate** – zunichtemachen
46 **impediment** – Hindernis
46 **to grapple with sth.** – sich auseinandersetzen mit
48 **to fester** – eitern
48 **sore** – Wunde

2 Comprehension: True or false?

Read the statements below and decide whether they are true or false. Quote or paraphrase words from the text which confirm or disprove the ideas in the statements.

a) Martin Luther King was assassinated while giving a speech.

b) Jesse Jackson was inspired to devote himself to the fight for racial equality after Martin Luther King was killed.

c) Shortly before his death, King predicted that his life was in danger.

d) In Jackson's opinion, sport in America is still heavily affected by debates about race.

e) According to Jackson, the increasing number of black people in American politics shows that economic inequality between black and white Americans is decreasing.

3 Mediation

What evidence does the text give to suggest that black people suffer from a lower quality of life than white people in America? Find six reasons. Answer in complete German sentences.

4 Listening comprehension: Comparing two speeches → Listening, p. 221

Go online and find the texts and the audio files for King's "I have a dream" speech and Malcolm X's "Message to the grass roots" speech. Compare the styles, the references and the aims of the two speeches and how they were delivered.

5 Text production

"Forty years on, Jesse Jackson is still weighing up how far up the mountain African Americans have ascended." (ll. 24 – 25)
Describe the development of African Americans' status in US society.

6 Presentation → Presentation, p. 264

Find out in which areas of public life African Americans were segregated before the civil rights movement. Write down the most important cue-words on a transparency and use this to present your findings in class.

7 Research project → Hotspot 3, p. 37

Word bank

Talking about civil rights
to stage a sit-in • to boycott • to strike • act of non-violence / civil disobedience • to demand / claim / gain your rights • to give / grant / deny sb. his / her rights • to violate sb.'s right

E America's responsibility

Manhattan and the Statue of Liberty on September 11, 2001

1 Before you read

a) Describe the photo taken on September 11, 2001.

b) In your opinion, is this photo historic/memorable/impressive/thought-provoking/symbolic? Why (not)?

c) Work in pairs. Discuss what happened on September 11, 2001 and how the international public and US government responded to this event.

d) From today's perspective, what long-term effects has 9/11 had in political, economic or psychological terms? Consider the different viewpoints, e. g. that of the Americans, of the Europeans, of Muslim fundamentalists, etc.

e) Suggest suitable captions for the photo from each subjective viewpoint.

4 **authoritarian** – autoritär
5 **regime change** – Regimewechsel
10 **to intervene** – einschreiten
14 **to spark** – entzünden
17 **deep-seated** – tiefsitzend

US soldiers cover a statue of Saddam Hussein before tearing it down

America's role in the world: four options

Option 1:
Lead the world to democracy

American values of democracy and freedom are the standard by which all other nations should be measured. Therefore, authoritarian states must become democratic ones through regime change. Relationships with tyrannical regimes should be avoided and the military may be used to keep international troublemakers in check.

- Supporting arguments:
  - Aggressive tyrants and oppressive regimes will be stopped only when the United States intervenes.
  - Democracies are much less likely to start wars. Thus, the world will be more peaceful by spreading democratic values.
- Concerns:
  - Pressuring other governments will spark criticism that the United States is trying to control the world.
  - Many societies reject the US definition of democracy and human rights.
  - Deep-seated forces of history and culture need to be accepted.

Option 2:
Protect US global interests

We must focus on our main interests, i.e. our own security, our trade relationships, our access to crucial raw materials, and stopping the spread of nuclear weapons. We must be prepared to intervene around the globe if our vital interests are at stake.

- Supporting arguments: …
- Concerns: …

An American soldier checks a young Iraqi boy during a patrol

Option 3:
Build a more cooperative world

Today's world is interdependent and we cannot stand alone. We must take the initiative to bring the nations of the world together. We have no choice but to play a leadership role in strengthening the UN's role. We must be willing to give up a part of our sovereignty to the UN and to support its initiatives.

- Supporting arguments: …
- Concerns: …

Option 4:
Protect the US homeland

The US has spent billions of dollars on its allies and the developing countries but its recent military involvements overseas have only made it new enemies.
It is time for the US to bring its troops overseas home and to face the challenges at home, e.g. a sagging economy, decaying schools, a shaky health care system and the protection against terrorism.

- Supporting arguments: …
- Concerns: …

(343 words)

Fighter jets fly over Mount Rushmore

2 Comprehension
Read the four policy options and describe the pictures. Discuss to what extent they illustrate the four policy options.

3 Having a discussion → Discussions, p. 246

a) Prepare a panel discussion about America's four policy options. Before you start, decide on roles which should be included in your discussion.

b) Collect supporting arguments and concerns about these four options to prepare for the roles.

c) Make notes of the best arguments for each role that come up in your discussion.

4 Comment → Writing a comment, p. 229
"After years of waging war against terrorism unsuccessfully, how should the western world respond to the danger of further terrorist acts?" Write a newspaper article in which you give your own opinion on the above question.

Phrasal verbs

a) Read the texts and replace the words in bold type with an appropriate phrasal verb from the box.

> break out • call off • draw in • give up • go off • go on • rule against • send in • set off • sign up • step in

The struggle for equality

1954	The Supreme Court **overturns (1)** the law of segregation in public schools. It is now unconstitutional to have separate facilities, as they are inherently unequal.
1955	NAACP member Rosa Parks refuses to **surrender (2)** her seat to a white passenger at the front of a bus. Her arrest **starts (3)** a bus boycott in Montgomery, Alabama, that **lasts (4)** for over a year. The young Baptist minister, Martin Luther King, Jr., leads the boycott and receives national attention for his efforts.
1956	Busses are desegregated in Montgomery, and the boycott is **canceled (5)**.
1957	King's principles of non-violent resistance and civil disobedience **attract (6)** many followers. State and federal troops **intervene (7)** on behalf of the nine African American students who are denied entry to their new high school in Little Rock, Arkansas.
1962	James Meredith is the first black student to go to the University of Mississippi. The violence and riots following his enrollment cause president Kennedy to **dispatch (8)** 5,000 federal troops.
1963	About 200,000 people join the March on Washington. King delivers his famous "I have a dream" speech. Four teenage girls are killed when a bomb **explodes (9)** at the 6th Street Baptist Church in Birmingham, Alabama, a popular location for civil rights meetings. Riots **erupt (10)**.
1965	Black nationalist Malcolm X is shot to death. Activists begin a March to Montgomery in support of voting rights. On this "Bloody Sunday", 50 marchers are hospitalized after police use tear gas, whips, and clubs against them. The Voting Rights Act is passed five months later, making it easier for blacks to **register (11)** to vote.
1968	Martin Luther King is assassinated in Memphis, Tennessee.

b) Translate the phrasal verbs into German.

c) Choose four of the phrasal verbs above and make a sentence with each one.

d) Work with a partner. Choose a text in your book and list all the phrasal verbs you can find. Then try and find synonyms for them and translate them into German. Use a monolingual dictionary to help you. → Working with a dictionary, p. 255

1 Research project: The American Dream → Internet research, p. 260
Research people who have realised the American Dream – e.g. people with a relatively poor background who went from "rags to riches". Then prepare a presentation in class.

2 Research project: 2012 election in the US → Internet research, p. 260
With the help of the map and the Internet, find the names of the 15 most important states for the Electoral College and say which party won them. Comment on the geographical distribution of Republican and Democratic states.

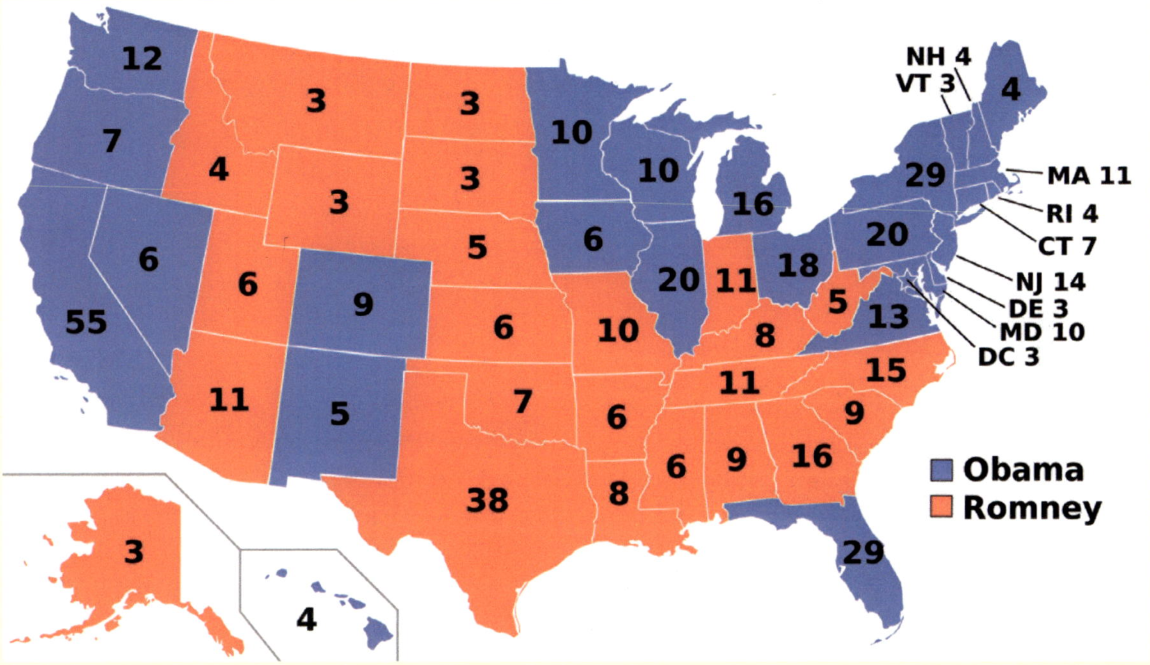

3 Research project: Writing a biography → Internet research, p. 260
Go online and find out about the life of one of the following people:

Malcolm X • Rosa Parks • Jesse Jackson • Martin Luther King

Produce a short biography, creating your own summary of the major events in their life and their contributions to the fight for racial equality. You can choose between the following ways to present your information: a poster, a handwritten text, or a timeline.

A 2.12

4 **to gentrify** – to modernize
8 **subprime mortgage crisis** – US real estate crisis
10 **to foreclose** – to confiscate
12 **to leave sth. in one's wake** – to leave sth. behind oneself
14 **unkempt** – not taken care of
16 **desolate** – abandoned
19 **to deter sb. from doing sth.** – to keep sb. from doing sth.
22 **gloomy** – depressing
23 **foreclosure** – ceditor reclaims property when borrower fails to make payments
25 **to emerge** – to appear
33 **rundown** – in bad condition
35 **commute** – journey to and from work
37 **mass transit** – public transport
41 **to gain momentum** – to increase influence

CNN

Search GO

Is America's suburban dream collapsing into a nightmare?

When Shaun Yandell proposed to his longtime girlfriend Gina Marasco on the doorstep of their new home in the sunny suburb of Elk Grove, California, four years ago, he never imagined things would get this bad. But they did, and it happened almost overnight.

Suburban neighborhoods are becoming refuges for those outpriced in gentrifying innercities. "It is going to be heartbreak," Yandell told CNN. "But we are hanging on."

Yandell's marriage isn't falling apart: his neighborhood is.

Devastated by the subprime mortgage crisis, hundreds of homes have been foreclosed and thousands of residents have been forced to move, leaving in their wake a not-so-pleasant path of empty houses, unkempt lawns, vacant strip malls, graffiti-sprayed desolate sidewalks and even increased crime.

In Elk Grove, some homeowners not only cut their own grass but also trim the yards of vacant homes on their streets, hoping to deter gangs and criminals from moving in. […]

For Yandell, his wife and many other residents trying to stick it out, the white picket fence of an American dream has faded into a seemingly hopeless suburban nightmare. "The forecast is gloomy," he told CNN.

While the foreclosure epidemic has left communities across the United States overrun with unoccupied houses and overgrown grass, underneath the chaos another trend is quietly emerging that, over the next several decades, could change the face of suburban American life as we know it.

This trend, according to Christopher Leinberger, an urban planning professor at the University of Michigan and visiting fellow at the Brookings Institution, stems not only from changing demographics but also from a major shift in the way an increasing number of Americans – especially younger generations – want to live and work.

"The American dream is absolutely changing," he told CNN.

This change can be witnessed in places like Atlanta, Georgia, Detroit, Michigan, and Dallas, Texas, said Leinberger, where once rundown downtowns are being revitalized by well-educated, young professionals who have no desire to live in a detached single family home typical of a suburbia where life is often centered around long commutes and cars. Instead, they are looking for what Leinberger calls "walkable urbanism" – both small communities and big cities characterized by efficient mass transit systems and high density developments enabling residents to walk virtually everywhere for everything – from home to work to restaurants to movie theaters.

The so-called New Urbanism movement emerged in the mid-90s and has been steadily gaining momentum, especially with rising energy costs, environmental concerns and health problems associated with what Leinberger calls "drivable suburbanism" –

a low-density built environment plan that emerged around the end of World War II and has been the dominant design in the US ever since.
But now, Leinberger told CNN, it appears the pendulum is beginning to swing back in favor of the type of walkable community that existed long before the advent of the once fashionable suburbs in the 1940s. He says it is being driven by generations molded by television shows like "Seinfeld" and "Friends," where city life is shown as being cool again – a thing to flock to, rather than flee. […]
Recent market research indicates that up to 40 percent of households surveyed in selected metropolitan areas want to live in walkable urban areas, said Leinberger. The desire is also substantiated by real estate prices for urban residential space, which are 40 to 200 percent higher than in traditional suburban neighborhoods – this price variation can be found both in cities and small communities equipped with walkable infrastructure, he said. The result is an oversupply of depreciating suburban housing and a pent-up demand for walkable urban space, which is unlikely to be met for a number of years.
It is estimated that as a result of the coming structural transformation in 2025 there will be a surplus of 22 million large-lot homes that will not be left vacant in a suburban wasteland but instead occupied by lower classes who have been driven out of their once affordable inner-city apartments and houses. […]
In Shaun Yandell's neighborhood, this has already started to happen. Houses once filled with single families are now rented out by low-income tenants. Yandell speculates that they're coming from nearby Sacramento, where the downtown is undergoing substantial gentrification, or perhaps from some other area where prices have gotten too high. He isn't really sure. But one thing Yandell is sure about is that he isn't going to leave his sunny suburban neighborhood unless he has to, and if that happens, he says he would only want to move to another one just like it.
"It's the American dream, you know," he said. "The American dream." (786 words)

47 **to mold** – to have a great influence on

49 **to flock to sth.** – to come in great numbers to sth.

52 **to substantiate sth.** – to confirm sth.

55 **to depreciate** – to lessen in value

55 **pent-up demand** – accumulated demand

64 **gentrification** – modernization

1 Comprehension

a) Outline the changes that have taken place in many of America's suburbs and give reasons for this development.

b) Explain the term "walkable urbanism" (l. 36) in your own words and state why many find it attractive.

2 Analysis

a) Describe the consequences of the demographic shift from suburban areas to city centres.

b) "Devastated by the subprime mortgage crisis, hundreds of homes have been foreclosed and thousands of residents have been forced to move, […]" (ll. 8–12) The global financial crisis has changed millions of lives around the world. Illustrate how people in America and beyond have been affected.

3 Comment: Choose one of the following tasks

a) For many people the city is the place to be. In your opinion, is it better to live in an urban area or a rural area? Discuss this, giving arguments for both.

b) People either love or hate the USA. Why does this country arouse such a range of mixed feelings – from admiration to rejection?

Topic 3

8qv4b9

The United Kingdom – then and now

“No motto please, we’re British.” David, London

“Mind your own business!” Brian Clacey

A

B

“Dipso, fatso, bingo, asbo, Tesco.” JCL

“We apologise for the inconvenience.” Matthew Bailey

C

“Smile, you’re on CCTV.” Les

“Britain – the birthplace of freedom.” Kat

In 2007, the Times asked its readers to come up with a national motto for Britain. Over 2,000 ideas were submitted – ranging from tongue-in-cheek suggestions to more serious ones. The newspaper then chose the best 10 and asked readers to vote for their favourite.

> Once mighty empire, slightly used.

J Harris

> Try writing history without us!

Simon Ludkin

D

E

tongue-in-cheek – ironisch
dipso *(coll.)* – jmd, der oft betrunken ist
fatso *(coll.)* – übergewichtige Person
asbo (Anti-Social Behaviour Order) – einstweilige Verfügung wegen antisozialen Verhaltens
Tesco – britische Supermarktkette
CCTV (closed circuit television) – Videoüberwachung

> Free, tolerant, fair-minded & true.

Benj

> Mathematically, we could still qualify.

Wobbly

Getting started

1 **Look at the photos A–E. Explain what they show.** → Describing pictures, p. 241

2 **Read the mottos. Choose one for each picture.**

3 **Share your ideas with a partner and give reasons for your choice.**

4 **In pairs, come up with your own motto for Britain and report back to the class.**

5 **With the same partner, find a similar motto for Germany. What are the differences and similarities between Germany and the UK?**

Word bank

Giving opinions
I think that … • In my opinion … • I believe that … • It seems to me … • I agree/disagree because … • What do you think? • What is your opinion on this?

A The British Empire and the Commonwealth

1 Before you read → Brainstorming, p. 253
What comes to your mind when you hear the word "empire"? Brainstorm your ideas with a partner and report back to the class.

3 **hence** – daher, deshalb
4 **foremost** – führend
7 **to encompass sth.** – etw. umfassen
10 **indigenous people** – Einheimische
11 **to aid** – helfen
17 **monopoly** – Monopol
19 **despotism** – Willkür
20 **urge** – Drang, Trieb
21 **to scramble for sth.** – um etw. kämpfen
22 **British Raj** [rɑ:dʒ] – British-Indien
25 **longing** – Sehnsucht
39 **suttee** – Witwenverbrennung (in Indien)

How big was the British Empire?

At its height in the nineteenth century the British Empire was the largest in world history, covering about a quarter of the world's land surface, hence the expression "The sun never sets on the British Empire". It was also the world's foremost global power. Ever since the first British colony was established in Jamestown (America) in 1607, the Empire kept changing as Britain gained and sometimes even lost new territories. At different times it encompassed large areas of North America, Australia, Africa and Asia.

How did such a small country come to rule so much territory?

Britain was a powerful and wealthy nation which defeated other European countries and conquered indigenous peoples thanks to its army and navy. In addition, rapid technological advances in the 19th century aided expansion. Inventions such as the telegraph, railroads and steamships meant that Britain had an advantage over local peoples who did not have access to such things.

What were the motives behind Britain's expansion?

The motives behind Britain's expansion were diverse. They included:
- **trade** – the desire to benefit British companies and secure trade routes, e.g. the British-owned East India Company had a monopoly on trade with Asia,
- **economics** – the desire to increase Britain's wealth; George Orwell once wrote that the Empire was "a despotism with theft as its final object",
- **politics** – the urge to prevent other European countries from becoming too powerful, as can be seen with the so-called 'scramble for Africa' at the end of the 19th century,
- **ambition** – Sir James Fitzjames Stephen (1829–1894) wrote that the Raj was "founded not on consent but on conquest",
- **religion** – the desire to spread Christianity,
- **adventure and curiosity** – the longing to explore and learn about new countries and peoples.

What legacy did the British Empire leave?

The British Empire has had a huge impact on the world. The formation of the Commonwealth has meant that most of the former colonies still have links with Britain. Many of them are parliamentary democracies with a legal system based on British law, a military, police and civil service system based on British models, and English is still the main or secondary language.

What changes did the Empire bring about?

The British Empire is often said to have been liberal. It was guided by the principle that colonial government was to be exercised for the good of the subject peoples, who would eventually be given the right to self-rule. Many empire builders thus tried to improve the welfare of the indigenous peoples, giving them better medical care, better legal, education and transport systems, and tried to eliminate practices that they considered barbaric, e.g. suttee, cannibalism and slavery (having, however, first profited from it a century before!). On the other hand, the British often arrogantly considered the indigenous peoples to be 'children' who needed to be 'educated'. Whilst those like the author Rudyard Kipling, who spent years in India, understood that "East is East, and West is West, and never the twain shall meet", others tried to turn the locals into Englishmen. So they not only endured the loss of their lands, but also their culture and met with discrimination and prejudice.

Why did the Empire decline?

The First and Second World Wars not only led to a decline in Britain's wealth and prestige but also lessened the political impact of the Empire. After the wars, the British were more interested in rebuilding their own country than in concentrating on far-away places. They were also beginning to realise that it was no longer feasible to run such a large empire. The dominions (Australia, New Zealand, Canada, the Irish Free State and South Africa) had already officially been given the power to rule themselves by the Statute of Westminster in 1931, even though in practice they had been doing so for some time. This set an example to which many other colonies now began to aspire. The British lost a prized colony, the 'Jewel in the Crown', in 1947, when India was partitioned. After this, colonies were either given self-governing dominion status or became independent. By the late 1960s most of British territories had become independent, although this did not always happen peacefully, especially in the case of Ireland. (718 words)

42 **twain** *(old)* – die Zwei
43 **to endure** – ertragen, aushalten
49 **feasible** – machbar
50 **dominion** *(old)* – Herrschaft, Machtgebiet
53 **to aspire** – anstreben
54 **to partition** – aufteilen

2 Comprehension
In your own words, answer the questions posed in each of the six subheadings in the text. Write between 2–3 sentences for each question.

3 Analysis → Describing cartoons, p. 242
On July 1, 1997 the UK handed Hong Kong – its last significant colony – back over to China. Describe the cartoon that was drawn at the time and explain the symbols used. What points is the cartoonist making about the British Empire?

4 Listening comprehension → Listening, p. 221
Listen to the opening of a lecture given in November 2007 by Don McKinnon, the former Secretary-General of the Commonwealth, entitled *The Modern Commonwealth: challenges in the 21st century*. Give short answers in English.

a) Which event led to the downfall of the "British Commonwealth" and when did it happen?

b) How many countries and people make up the Commonwealth?

c) Which two expressions did McKinnon use to describe the values and goals of the Commonwealth?

d) Name two countries in which Commonwealth representatives are active.

e) What positive outcome did an idea of the Commonwealth have for 30 of the world's poorest countries?

f) According to McKinnon, which two characteristics must the Commonwealth have?

5 Research project → Hotspot 1, p. 53

B Britishness

1 Before you read

What do you associate with being British? Together with a partner, make a list, then share your ideas with another pair.

0 **disunited** – entsolidarisiert, uneinig
1 **notion** – Idee
3 **decreasingly** – immer weniger
3 **to rally to sth.** – sich um etw. scharen
4 **division** – Trennung
5 **Marmite** – Hefe-Brot-aufstrich
6 **Coronation Street** – britische Soap
7 **strain** – Belastung, Anspannung
8 **referendum** – Bürger-entscheid
9 **to prompt** – veranlassen
9 **to shatter** – zerschlagen
10 **regardless of** – unabhängig von
15 **grip** – Griff
17 **nationhood** – nationale Identität
19 **arguably** – wohl
21 **to unfold** – sich entfalten
27 **crucial** – entscheidend, aus-schlaggebend
28 **undoubtedly** – zweifellos
28 **extent** – Ausmaß
33 **intriguingly** – verblüffen-derweise
33 **evidence** – *hier:* Befunde
33 **devolution** – Übertragung von parlamentarischer Gewalt

theguardian

News | Sport | Comment | Culture | Business | Money | Life&Style | Travel | Environment

Comment is free > UK > Search GO

Identity crisis: are we becoming a disunited kingdom?

Surveys suggest notions of Britishness are changing

So what makes us? We share the same islands, but we aren't all British. We call ourselves Scots, Irish, Welsh, English and often, but decreasingly, British. Every four years, we rally to the union flag for the Olympics, but when it comes to rugby and football, the divisions open up. There is much shared culture, whether in pop music, clothing, fish and chips, curries and Marmite, comedians and Coronation Street. […]

But now, for the first time in several centuries, that notion of Britishness is under intense strain. Alex Salmond, the first minister of Scotland, will soon lead the country into a referendum that could prompt Scotland to declare independence, a move that would shatter a 304-year-old political union. Regardless of the Scottish referendum, the UK has four separate governments and now the three devolved administrations, in Scotland, Wales and Northern Ireland, are winning greater economic and legal powers, cutting London's grip on the country. And in each part of the UK, notions of nationhood and Britishness are changing and, arguably, the links are weakening.

Because of this unfolding political situation, the Guardian invites readers to enter the debate about national identity and air your attitudes on Britishness. […] We will be asking if it is more and more becoming a "disunited kingdom"?

There is much to suggest this is the case. John Curtice, from the Scottish Centre for Social Research, […] said: "The crucial thing to realise is that in Scotland, British is now very definitely a secondary identity; that's undoubtedly true to a far greater extent than it is in Wales." In England there are plenty of people who, if asked whether they're British or English, will say 'what's the difference?'. Comparing all the latest social attitudes surveys gives us this contrast: if voters are forced to choose, 52% of English voters choose British first compared to 19% of Scots, and 30% of Welsh. […]

Intriguingly, the latest evidence from Wales suggests that devolution may be making the Welsh feel more British. That is one reading of a new study of 3,029 voters by the Economic and Social

Research Council, carried out in the runup to the 2011 referendum, which found overwhelming support for giving the Welsh Assembly greater powers.

Its results [...] find that 16% of Welsh voters now feel "British not Welsh", compared to 9% in 2007 and in 2003. Meanwhile, only 19% felt "Welsh not British", a fall from 24% in 2007, with 30% feeling equally Welsh and British.

Roger Scully, from Aberystwyth University and the study's co-author, is cautious about reading too much into the Welsh figures since different survey methods were used in 2011.

"The bigger picture is that basic identity in Wales has not changed much under devolution, or even if you go back and look at the evidence from 1979, since the first devolution referendums," he said. "People have very different views now about how Wales should be governed. But not because they have become, in some crude sense, more Welsh."

In Northern Ireland, identity can be far more complex; loyalty to a larger nation splits between those feeling British and Irish, mostly down religious or ethnic lines. The 2010 Northern Ireland Life and Times surveys [...] have shown that 37% see themselves as British, 26% Irish and 29% Northern Irish, with 3% choosing Ulster.

But asked the multiple-choice question, 58% of voters in Northern Ireland in 2007 saw themselves, to varying degrees, as both British and Irish. In 1998, 51% of those given a straight choice said they were British. It is 37% now.

In England last year, 52% described themselves as British and just 34% as English in a straight choice between the two. That is the widest margin since 1997.

Behind such figures emotions run deep. Yet, is national identity in the UK purely a personal badge to be worn with pride at sporting events – or could it fundamentally change the nature of the British (and Northern Irish) state? (670 words)

35 **runup** – Vorlauf
35 **overwhelming** – überwältigend
36 **assembly** – Versammlung
40 **cautious** – vorsichtig
45 **crude** – derb, grob
51 **varying** – wechselnd
54 **margin** – Spanne
55 **badge** – Ansteckschildchen

2 Comprehension

a) What information can you find in the text about the following numbers?

304 • 9% • 16% • 37% • 51% • 52%

b) Describe in your own words why the "notion of Britishness is under intense strain." (l. 7)

c) Outline where in the UK, according to the text, the number of people who feel British might be on the rise. Give reasons.

3 Vocabulary → Working with a dictionary, p. 255

a) Define the following terms. Compare your definitions with the ones in the dictionary.

1. independence • 2. political union • 3. government • 4. national identity • 5. attitude • 6. loyalty • 7. ethnic • 8. emotion • 9. pride

b) Find the corresponding adjectives for numbers 1., 3., 6., 8., and 9.
c) Find the corresponding verb for number 3.
d) Find the corresponding noun for number 7.

4 Presentation → Presentation, p. 264

Think of ideas that characterise Germany. How would you explain "Germanness" to a foreigner? Write down your main points on a transparency and use this to present your ideas to the class.

C The British political system

The House of Commons

The House of Lords

Number 10 Downing Street

16 **approximately** – ungefähr
17 **constituency** – Wahlkreis
19 **advisory** – beratend
20 **to delay** – verzögern
24 **to appoint** – ernennen
36 **assembly** – Versammlung; *hier:* Parlament
40 **predominantly** – vorwie-ge[illegible]

The constitution

The British constitution is not set down in a single document, it is made up of a whole range of laws and conventions instead.

The monarchy

The monarch is the official **Head of State**, the head of the executive and of the judiciary, the Commander-in-Chief of the armed forces and the 'supreme governor' of the **Church of England**. The monarch formally appoints the **Prime Minister** (PM). However, the monarch's duties are largely ceremonial.

Parliament

Parliament is made up of the **House of Commons**, and the **House of Lords**. The Prime Minister decides exactly when a **general election** is to be held within a five year term.

The House of Commons

The House of Commons is where new laws are passed and the main business of government is done. The House of Commons is elected in general elections and consists of approximately 650 **Members of Parliament** (MPs), one from each of the constituencies.

The House of Lords

The House of Lords acts in a mainly controlling and advisory capacity but it can delay bills for up to a year. The number of members is not fixed.

Government and opposition

The party which wins the most seats (though not necessarily the most votes) at a general election forms the Government. The leader of the party is appointed Prime Minister by the Sovereign. The Prime Minister's official residence is **Number 10 Downing Street**. The Prime Minister forms a cabinet by appointing ministers who are usually in charge of a government department. Most ministers are known as "Secretary of State" or "Minister" unless they have a special title, such as the **Chancellor of the Exchequer**, who is responsible for financial and monetary issues. Other important ministers are the **Home Secretary**, responsible for internal affairs and the **Foreign Secretary**, responsible for foreign affairs. The largest minority party in the House of Commons becomes the official opposition with its own leader and "shadow cabinet".

Traditionally Britain has been governed centrally from **Westminster** (London) with Scotland and Wales being represented there by Secretaries of State. Since June 1998 Northern Ireland has had its own assembly (the **New Northern Ireland Assembly**), and since 1999 Wales and Scotland have had their own assemblies with some limited powers.

The political parties

[illegible] the past 150 years a predominantly two party system has existed in Bri[illegible] After 1945 power was held either by the **Conservative Party** (Tories), a righ[illegible]tre party, or by the **Labour Party**, a left of centre party. In 2010 the 'To[illegible]med a coalition with the **Liberal Democrats** (LibDems), who make up the third biggest party in Britain. There is a Green Party in Britain but it is not represented in parliament, partly because the electoral system gives small parties almost no chance of winning any seats. There are two nationalist parties: **Plaid Cymru** (Welsh Nationals) and the **Scottish National Party** (SNP), which play an important role in Wales and Scotland respectively. In Northern Ireland the most important parties are the Ulster Unionist Party and Sinn Féin, the political wing of the IRA.

The electoral system

For electoral purposes Britain is divided into about 650 **constituencies**. Each constituency is represented by one MP in the House of Commons. The current system that is used at general elections in the UK is the **simple majority** or "first-past-the-post" (FPTP) system. Each **elector** has one vote. Electors vote for the candidate of their choice. The candidate who gets the most votes in a constituency wins the seat. The main advantages of FPTP is that it is simple to understand and produces strong single party governments rather than coalitions, and that it provides a close link between MPs and their constituencies. (613 words)

49 **respectively** – beziehungsweise

59 **to provide** – sorgen für

1 Comprehension: True or false?

Read the statements below and decide whether they are true or false. Quote or paraphrase words from the text which confirm or disprove the ideas in the statements.

a) The British constitution was written in one sitting.

b) The members of the House of Commons are elected in their constituencies.

c) The law-making body is the House of Lords.

d) The electorate decides who will become Prime Minister.

e) The Prime Minister and his ministers form the shadow cabinet.

f) The building of homes lies in the responsibility of the Home Secretary.

g) Coalitions have always been a common phenomenon in Britain.

h) The PM chooses a date for the next general election.

2 Analysis → Describing diagrams, p. 243
Describe and analyse the pie charts.

3 Project → Hotspot 2, p. 53

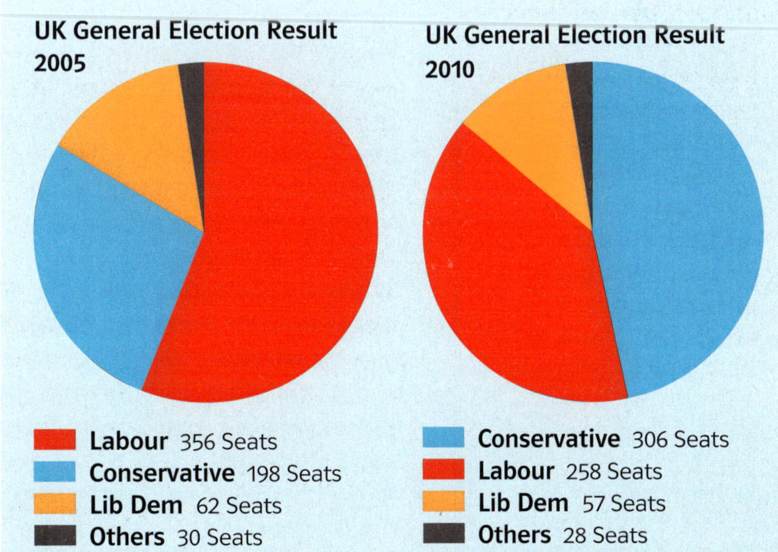

Source: The Huddersfield Daily Examiner

D The Royal Family

1 Before you read

Which members of the royal family can you name? What do you know about them? Discuss with a partner and report back to the class.

2 Comprehension

a) Outline why, according to the text, the royals need an "intense PR campaign" (l. 20) and describe what this campaign includes.

b) Summarise, in your own words, Jennie Bond's and Walter Bagehot's opinions on the new royals.

theguardian

News | Sport | Comment | Culture | Business | Money | Life&Style | Travel | Environment

Comment is free > Society Search GO

How the royals became cool

Princes William and Harry are seen as being down-to-earth regular guys. The Duchess of Cambridge is supposedly one of us. How did our stuffy and out-of-touch monarchy suddenly get its mojo back? The other day, Cheryl Cole had a lovely dream. "I married Prince Harry and was a real-life princess," she said. "It's true. And Charles was my father-in-law." The last bit sounds like every girl's nightmare, but that's not important now.

More important are the ramifications of this dream for the British constitution. Until very recently, pop stars didn't dream of marrying members of the royal family, still less blab about it. The royals were too tweedy and facially equine for such dreams to do anything but damage a pop chanteuse's fanbase. But all that has changed. How? […]

"Of course there's a policy," says former BBC royal correspondent Jennie Bond. "The young royals are making the monarchy enormously cool." […] Graham Smith, head of anti-monarchy pressure group Republic, agrees. "There is, after all, a good reason for the intense PR campaign being run by the palace: it knows the public are fast losing interest in the royals, and that as the Queen nears the end of her life any residual affection for her is unlikely

1 **down-to-earth** – bodenständig
2 **supposedly** – angeblich
2 **stuffy** – spießig *(ugs.)*
2 **out-of-touch** – abgehoben, lebensfremd
2 **mojo** – Glücksbringer
6 **ramification** – Auswirkung
10 **tweedy** – konservativ
11 **facially equine** – *hier:* pferdeähnlich aussehend
12 **chanteuse** – Barsängerin
23 **residual** – restlich
23 **affection** – Zuneigung
24 **heir** – Thronfolger
24 **to be better off without sth.** – ohne etw. besser dran sein
25 **state funding** – staatliche Förderung
26 **scrutiny** – Kontrolle, Prüfung
26 **to reverse** – umkehren
27 **alleged** – angeblich
27 **decline** – Rückgang

3 Analysis → Text analysis, p. 228

a) Explain the following terms from the text in your own words:
1. to blab about sth. (l. 9)
2. to trade groovy moves (l. 30)
3. to be off your head (l. 33)
4. pop (l. 34)
5. to be plastered (l. 49)

b) Analyse what effect the use of informal language in the text has on the reader.

c) Explain the following phrase: "I think the biggest enemy is apathy among young people." (l. 52)

03 **4 Comment**
"The British Monarchy has no place in modern society." Discuss.

5 Research project → Hotspot 3, p. 53

to transfer to her son and heir,". Smith argues that at least a quarter of Britons believe we'd be better off without the monarchy, more than half want an end to its state funding and two-thirds want the royal household opened up to more scrutiny. Maybe, just maybe, making the royals cool could reverse that alleged decline in interest.

It seems only five minutes ago that Prince Harry was a swastika-sporting throwback who called his Asian friend "paki". Three stories show how his image has changed. During his tour of the Caribbean, Harry traded groovy moves with Jamaican sprinter Usain Bolt, yielding the kind of picture spreads of which no previous British prince, with the possible exception of Henry, Prince of Wales, circa 1505, would have been capable. Then Harry emerged from a 4am lock-in at a bar called Bunga Bunga, dancing to his waiting car like any other twentysomething English yeoman off his head on too much pop. [...]

Harry's rehabilitation looks like part of a bigger campaign to make the royals seem normal, while paradoxically – and this would be a brilliant campaign if it could be pulled off – glamourising them and reinforcing their regal status. "It's a marvel to behold," says PR expert Mark Borkowski, "and it seems to be working. What you have now is an amazing PR turnaround in an infinitesimally small amount of time."

The branding of Kate, Duchess of Cambridge, is key to this turnaround. She is simultaneously our future queen, the world's hottest magazine cover girl and a woman feted as a cut-price royal who, while William was bravely defending the Falklands from wicked Sean Penn, modestly made her debut as a public speaker wearing her mother's hand-me-down dress in, there's no easy way to say this, Ipswich. [...]

But isn't there a tension for the monarchy in all this? Victorian thinker Walter Bagehot distinguished the dignified from the efficient parts of the constitution. By the former he meant the monarchy, which has a symbolic function; by the latter he meant parliament and government. If the royals seem ordinary, the dignified part of the constitution could be doomed. Where, after all, is the dignity in Harry spilling out of a lock-in evidently plastered?

Bond thinks otherwise. She argues that if the monarchy has a future, then members of the royal family must be like us but cooler. "Not long ago they seemed to be the most dysfunctional family on the planet. Now they're cool. It's brilliant. I think the biggest enemy is apathy among young people." [...]

(631 words)

28 **swastika** – Hakenkreuz
30 **to yield** – hervorbringen
32 **capable** – fähig
32 **to emerge** – herauskommen
32 **lock-in** – Privat-Party in einer Bar/einem Pub
33 **yeoman** – Freibauer
36 **to pull sth. off** – etw. zustande bringen *(ugs.)*
37 **to reinforce** – verstärken
37 **regal** – königlich
37 **marvel** – Wunderwerk
37 **to behold** – anschauen
38 **infinitesimally** – winzig
41 **to fete** – feiern
41 **cut-price** – Billig-
42 **wicked** – böse
43 **hand-me-down** – gebraucht
45 **tension** – Spannung
45 **to distinguish** – unterscheiden
46 **dignified** – würdevoll
48 **doomed** – verdammt
48 **to spill out of sth.** – *hier:* aus etw. herauskommen *(ugs.)*
49 **evidently** – offensichtlich
50 **otherwise** – anders
51 **dysfunctional** – gestört, zerrüttet
52 **apathy** – Gleichgültigkeit, Teilnahmslosigkeit

E Britain and Europe

1 Before you read
What advantages and disadvantages might EU membership have for a country? Share your ideas with a partner.

THE INDEPENDENT

What if Britain left the EU?

Eurosceptics want a vote on the ultimate question – and the PM does not seem entirely opposed. Ben Chu examines the consequences of saying bye bye to Brussels

Exports

The European Union is easily Britain's biggest single export market, with 53 per cent of our goods purchased by our fellow European nations in 2011. This sector of our economy, directly and indirectly, supports three million jobs, according to Sir Iain Begg, a professorial research fellow at the European Institute of the London School of Economics. Without export growth last year, we would have fallen back into recession much earlier. If we were to leave the EU, we would almost certainly still be allowed to sell goods into the single market. Norway, Iceland and Switzerland already do so through a free-trade agreement. The difference would be that the UK would not be able to set the rules that govern the European single market. It would, of course, have to implement those rules to keep selling into those markets though. The argument sometimes deployed by those who want out of the EU is that leaving would, somehow, encourage British manufacturers to concentrate on exporting to the likes of China, Brazil and India.

Imports

Britain also imports a great deal from other nations in the EU – more than it exports, in fact. In 2011, we exported £159bn of goods to the EU and imported goods worth £202bn – an annual trade deficit of £42bn. Some argue that this deficit gives us leverage to demand more opt-outs and budget rebates from our European partners. The argument is: "They need us more than we need them." The problem is that we import a lot of European goods, not because we are doing the Europeans a favour, but because our people want to buy things that cannot be produced at home – think of all those German cars and French luxury goods. If Britain were to leave the EU, the Government might decide to impose large tariffs on European imports, but this probably wouldn't prove very popular. The likelihood is we would still run a trade deficit with the EU, but, as with imports, we would have no say over the rules governing the single market. […]

Growth

Would foreign capital still want to invest in the UK if it were not part of the EU bloc? Some economists say overseas investors would be put off. The National Institute of Economic and Social Research, for example,

1 **eurosceptic** – Europagegner(in)
1 **entirely** – gänzlich
2 **to be opposed to sth.** – gegen etw. sein
5 **to purchase** – erwerben
8 **recession** – Konjunkturabschwung
9 **free-trade agreement** – Freihandelsabkommen
12 **to govern** – leiten, lenken
12 **European single market** – europäischer Binnenmarkt
13 **to implement** – umsetzen
16 **to deploy** – einsetzen
25 **trade deficit** – Handelsdefizit
25 **leverage** – Einfluss, Druckmittel
25 **opt-out** – Ausstiegsmöglichkeit
26 **rebate** – Nachlass, Ermäßigung
29 **to impose** – auferlegen
30 **tariff** – Zoll
30 **likelihood** – Wahrscheinlichkeit
34 **bloc** – Staatenblock
35 **overseas** – ausländisch

estimates that foreign direct investment would fall. And, mainly for this reason, it argues that our GDP would permanently be 2.25 per cent lower if we left the EU. However, Capital Economics argued last month that, because of the eurozone crisis, levels of foreign investment in the UK could actually go up if we left the EU, because we would seem like a safe haven.

Immigration

If Britain left the EU, the Government would not be required to permit the free movement of all citizens of the 27 nations of the union into Britain, nor their right to work here. About 165,000 EU citizens migrated to the UK in the year to September 2011, after 182,000 arrived in the 12 months to September 2010. Proponents of withdrawal argue that stopping such flows would improve quality of life because there would be less strain on public services and infrastructure. Opponents argue that immigrants are an economic benefit for Britain, filling holes in our labour market and boosting overall productivity. But the free movement of people is two-way. An estimated 748,010 Britons live or work in the European Union. Many have holiday homes in France and Spain. If we decided to restrict inflows of EU citizens to Britain, the European Union would be likely to respond in kind. [...]

Politics

Europe is more social democratic than the UK. Even countries with centre-right governments tend to tax more, spend more on welfare and are less laissez-faire when it comes to markets. Those on the left in Britain tend to be in favour of the UK's continued membership because they feel it will help to move the country in this direction. Those on the right tend to be opposed for similar reasons; they feel Europe is helping to undermine Britain's social and economic freedoms. Yet there are global politics to consider, too. The right wants to rely on Britain's "special relationship" with the US, but Washington prefers Britain to work in closer partnership with the EU. Rising Asian giants such as India and China also seem to regard Britain's membership of the EU as a good reason to build economic and diplomatic ties with us.

(772 words)

36 **GDP (Gross Domestic Product)** – Bruttoinlandsprodukt
39 **safe haven** – sicherer Ort
41 **to permit** – erlauben
44 **proponent** – Befürworter(in), Anhänger(in)
44 **withdrawal** – Ausstieg
45 **strain** – Belastung
45 **opponent** – Gegner(in)
46 **labour market** – Arbeitsmarkt
46 **to boost** – in die Höhe treiben
51 **to tax** – besteuern
52 **welfare** – Sozialwesen
52 **laissez-faire** – lax
55 **to undermine sth.** – etw. untergraben
56 **to rely on** – setzen auf, bauen auf
58 **to regard** – betrachten
58 **tie** – Beziehung, Bindung

2 Mediation → Mediation, p. 245

You are doing an internship at a local German newspaper. The editor would like to print an article based on the text above in the newspaper's international section. Summarise the text in German using the subheadings to help you.

46 **3 Listening comprehension: A British vision for Europe** → Listening, p. 221

Listen to the article and find out whether Angela Merkel's or David Cameron's points of views are reflected in the following statements:

a) We want to be less involved with Europe.

b) We are, for the most part, Eurosceptics.

c) Us European countries should work more closely together.

d) We did not choose to be in charge, but it is our responsibility.

e) If you expect us to support you financially, you have to listen to what we have to say.

f) We are in a dilemma: if we step back, you say we are not interested, and if we take the lead, you accuse us of pushing you around.

g) What we need is a "networked Europe".

h) 49% of our citizens want to leave the EU, anyway.

4 Project → Hotspot 4, p. 53

Transitions

The purpose of transitions is to connect. They lead into the next paragraph and the next point or make a connection back to the previous paragraph before introducing a new point. Transitional phrases or sentences come at the end of one paragraph or at the beginning of the next.

This may be a reason for … Another reason for this is … That's not the only reason for … Furthermore, … In addition, … In fact, …	Another example is … Let's take a look at another example. For example/instance … To demonstrate … To illustrate … In particular, …	On the other hand, … More importantly, … Even before … In order to … With this in mind … In comparison/contrast to …

a) Read the first part of the comment below and improve the flow of the text by adding transitions.

The pros and cons of moving to the United Kingdom

There are many reasons why people choose to move to the UK: 1 there might be more employment opportunities. While a person's native country may have a weak economy and a high unemployment rate, it is possible that the UK offers a great deal of job possibilities. 2 some countries may be politically unstable, making them unsafe for people to live. 3 the person or people may have fled the country to escape a civil war. 4 a large number of immigrants leave their home country and move to the UK for this reason.

5 not all people move countries for these reasons. 6 some people may simply move because of the lifestyle, or for personal reasons. For many people, moving to the UK offers them a fresh start. 7 these people can also face many problems. 8 they may not speak English or be able to adapt to British culture. Or, 9 they could find that their new home does not offer the opportunities they had hoped for or had been promised.

10 migrants may find themselves under pressure not only to support themselves in a new country, but also the friends and relatives they have left behind in their country, especially those from poorer parts of the world. […]

b) Find more arguments and continue writing the comment using transitions.

c) Look at a comment you have recently written and improve its style by adding transitions where possible.

1 Research project: The British Empire and the Commonwealth
→ Internet research, p. 260

a) In groups, create an illustrated timeline on the British Empire and/or the Commonwealth, including dates, pictures, short texts, and if possible quotations.

b) Go online and find out more about the Commonwealth Games. Look at the history of the Games, the most recent Games, and how they differ from the Olympics.

2 Project: 2010 elections in the UK → Projects and group work, p. 261
The general elections in the UK in 2010 caused a completely new situation in the political landscape in the UK. Find out about the results of this election and explain the new situation.

3 Research project: Monarchies in Europe → Internet research, p. 260
Use the Internet to find out which countries in Europe still have a monarch as head of state. Find out what role they play, how much political influence they still have, and what relationship they have with their people.

4 Project: Britain and Europe → Discussions, p. 246
Work in small groups. Read the fact file and then look at the cartoon. What point is the cartoonist making? Do you agree with him? Give reasons and report back to the class.

Britain and Europe
After twice being denied membership, Britain finally joined the Common Market in 1973. This was mainly for economic reasons such as to promote trade. During the Thatcher era (1980s), opposition to a "United States of Europe" was strong. Nevertheless, Britain did sign the Single European Act in 1987 and join the Exchange Rate Mechanism in October 1990. In 1994 the opening of the Eurotunnel lessened Britain's geographical isolation. When the Labour government came to power in 1997, Britain signed the Social Charter (guaranteeing social and economic human rights), which the Conservatives had refused to do, thus giving the country a more pro-European image. However, one of the biggest issues is the euro. Britain has stayed with its decision to keep its own currency unless the people choose to accept the euro in a referendum. Whatever the British feel about Europe, they cannot really leave. As Gordon Brown said, "The European Union is essential to the success of Britain and a Britain fully engaged in Europe is essential to the success of the European Union."
(177 words)

A 2.20

theguardian

News | Sport | Comment | Culture | Business | Money | Life&Style | Travel | Environment

Comment is free > Society > Search [ ] GO

Why India needs aid

Most of its population are still poor. The row over British aid shows how many people confuse rapid growth with wealth.

Underlying the debate raging over British aid to India is the myth that the subcontinent's strong, market-driven growth of the past two decades has pulled hundreds of millions out of poverty. The economy is taking off; its people no longer need much aid, it is said.

In reality, since 1991, during which time India has experienced the highest growth in recent history, there has been no significant reduction in poverty or hunger. Two in every five children remain malnourished. A third of adults have an abnormally low body-mass index. Half of women of childbearing age are anaemic, a proportion far higher than in sub-Saharan Africa. More than 500 million Indians have no electricity, and less than a third have toilets.

The neoliberal policies unleashed by the prime minister, Manmohan Singh, when he was finance minister in the early 90s, have widened class disparities obscenely. Numbers such as 8% growth, and the fact there are 153,000 dollar millionaires, mean little to most Indians.

The debate in the UK was fuelled by anger at India's decision to buy French Rafale jets rather than the Eurofighter Typhoon, prompting shrill accusations of "ingratitude". International develop-

0 **aid** – (financial) help
0 **row** – fight
1 **to underlie** – to be the cause or basis of
2 **myth** – common belief
6 **to take off** – to start
14 **to remain** – to stay
14 **malnourished** – starved
17 **childbearing age** – age from which women can have children
17 **anaemic** – not having enough blood
22 **to unleash** – to release
26 **disparity** – inequality
26 **obscenely** – *here:* greatly
30 **to fuel** – to inflame
33 **to prompt** – to start
33 **accusation** – a charge or claim that someone has done sth. illegal or wrong
34 **ingratitude** – ungrate-fulness

ment secretary Andrew Mitchell even admitted that the focus of aid to India included "seeking to sell the Typhoon" – in violation of the stated rationale of British overseas aid, to fight poverty and promote health and education.

So if India can spend billions on nuclear weapons, aircraft carriers and nuclear submarines, and on a moon mission, does it deserve aid? As was revealed this weekend, India has itself told Britain it doesn't want aid.

But this confuses the nature of aid – which is about poor people, not poor countries. Many Indians question the government's ballooning military expenditure, which has more than tripled since the 1998 nuclear blasts. Instead they want substantially improved public services, including food security, drinking water, health-care (India's public health spending proportionate to GDP is among the world's lowest), sanitation, and education at affordable prices. Great struggles are under way on these issues, which have the potential to reshape Indian politics.

Besides, aid is much less wasteful than commonly thought. A small part of the international development department's budget might go towards GPS devices on buses in Bhopal, with dubious benefits. But more than 60% has gone in recent years into education and healthcare. [...]

Britain would be morally and politically wrong to terminate aid to India, home to the largest number of the world's poor. Giving aid not only acknowledges the injustice of colonial exploitation, it also arises from an obligation to redress the gross structural imbalances that continue to mark the world despite recent power shifts between states.

Good aid programmes can make humane existence possible for millions who have been denied it. Rather than Mitchell's aim to "invest more in the private sector" and public-private partnerships – which charge user fees the poor cannot afford – Britain should target schemes with a social transformation potential. Programmes that resemble a sovereign wealth fund and seek financial returns are less beneficial than building up people's human potential.

(533 words)

38 **violation** – breach
38 **rationale** – philosophy
40 **to promote** – to support
45 **to reveal** – to make known
50 **ballooning** – increasing
51 **expenditure** – money spent
52 **blast** – explosion
57 **GDP (Gross Domestic Product)** – the total value of goods and services that is produced by a nation, measure of a nation's economic activity
58 **sanitation** – the provision of clean drinking water and adequate sewage disposal
59 **affordable** – not too expensive
62 **to reshape** – to reform
68 **benefit** – advantage
72 **to terminate** – to stop
75 **to acknowledge** – to recognize
75 **injustice** – unfairness
76 **exploitation** – misuse
77 **to redress** – to set right
77 **gross** – large
80 **shift** – change
90 **to resemble** – to be similar to
92 **beneficial** – useful

1 Comprehension

a) Outline the contrast between India's recent economic development and the actual standard of living for most of its population.

b) Describe why there is a debate whether India deserves financial aid or not.

c) Summarise what Indians criticise about the way their government is spending the country's money.

2 Analysis

Analyse whether the author of the text supports or opposes British aid to India. Quote examples from the text to support your answer.

3 Comment → Writing a comment, p. 229

Write a letter to the author of the text in which you discuss the pros and cons of foreign aid to poor places such as India or Africa, taking into account the aspects mentioned in the text.

Topic 4
World of work

r8tj62

Word bank

to have an interview • to be nervous / creative • CV • to design • to work overtime / outdoors • dangerous • to install • solar panel • green company • to be responsible for • to work in education / with children

Getting started

1 **Work on your own. Look at the photos and brainstorm words that describe what is shown in each of them.** → Describing pictures, p. 241

2 **Compare your list of words with a partner and agree on a final list of five words for each photo.**

3 **With the same partner, think of three questions you would like to ask each of the four young people shown in the photos.**

You're logical and enjoy learning. Your ideal job: one where you need to solve problems and that has a high salary, e.g. an IT specialist or a marketing manager.

You're active and practical. Your ideal job: one that needs a lot of energy, e.g. a police officer, an electrician, an athlete.

You're friendly and helpful. Your ideal job: something where you can assist people, e.g. a flight attendant, a nurse, a sales assistant.

You're communicative and creative. Your ideal job: something that involves interaction or artistic talent, e.g. a makeup artist, a journalist, an actor/actress.

You're smart and independent. Your ideal job: something with language and words, e.g. a writer, a language teacher.

You're creative and practical. Your ideal job: something that needs organisational skills or creative talent, e.g. a tourist guide, a secretary, a graphic designer.

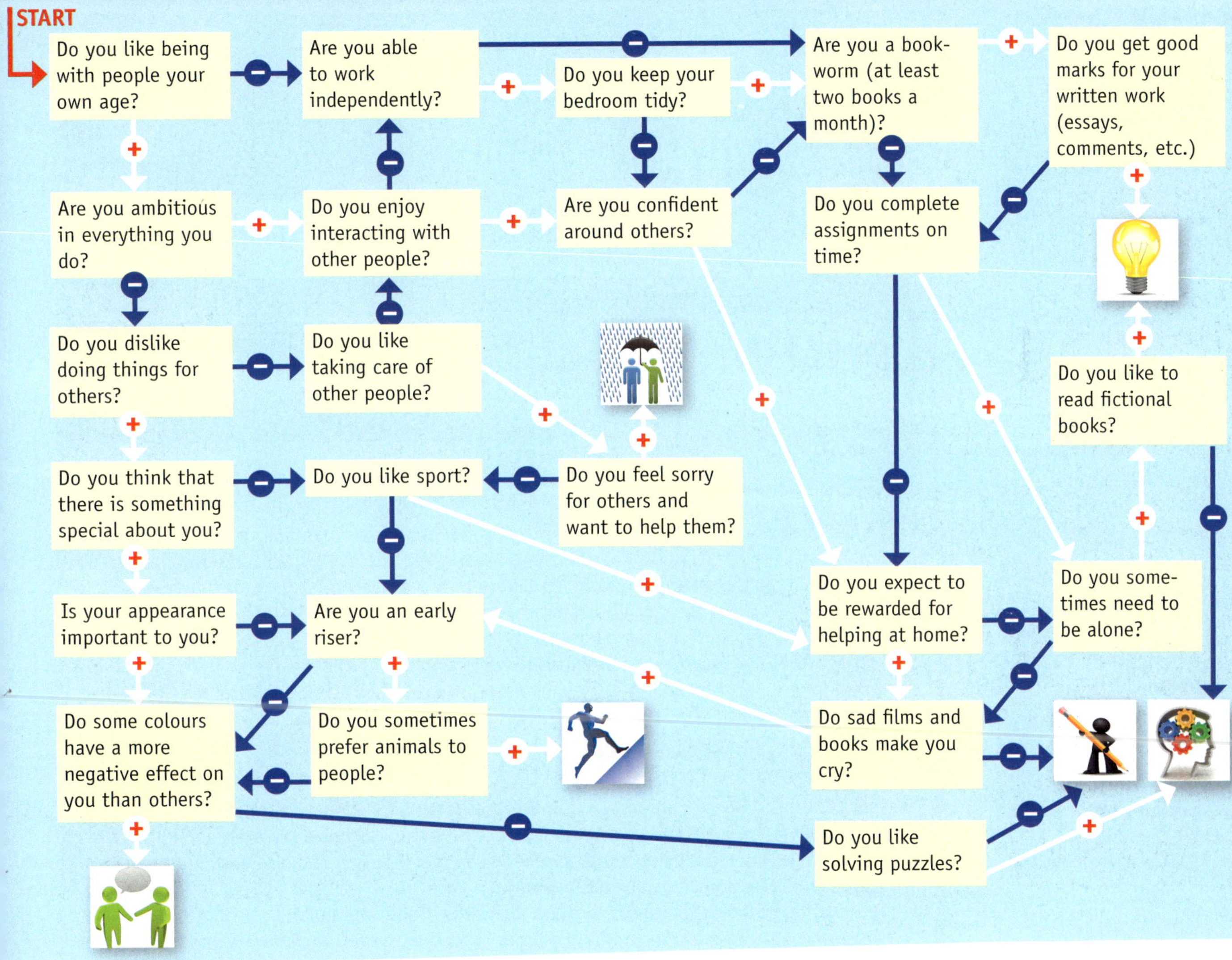

4 Do you already know what you're going to do when you leave school? If not, don't worry. Check out the chart, find out what kind of person you are and which direction you should take.

a) Work with a partner. Partner A asks the questions in the chart, partner B closes his/her book and answers the questions truthfully with "yes" or "no". When you get to one of the symbols, look at the list for a suitable job. Then swap roles.

b) What do you think about your results? Does this reflect your interest? Would you consider one of the jobs? Why (not)?

A Applying for a job

1 Before you read

a) Do you know which documents are generally included in a job application? Look at the box below and find the correct documents.

copy of driving license • curriculum vitae (CV)/résumé • pictures of your family • bank details • letter of application • school certificates • references • birth certificate • medical records

b) Compare your answers with a partner, then report back to the class.

eHOW

Search GO

family | food | health | home | money | style | more

How to make a job skills portfolio

A CBS News report stated there are 4.5 job seekers for every open position. With so many qualified individuals crowding the job market, the successful candidate needs more than a killer résumé. An old idea, generally reserved for artists, designers and architects, is making a comeback for anyone looking for a job. The job portfolio expands on the traditional résumé with hard-copy examples of past work, projects, recommendations, writing samples and other documented items. It is worth the time to write and compile this powerful tool to give life to résumés through concrete examples of past work.

Instructions: Things you'll need

Three-ring portfolio binder

Copies of sample work documents

1. Compile your documents in a three-ring portfolio. A zippered style looks professional and will keep everything neat and clean. Organize the portfolio into sections with a table of contents and dividers. You should be able to easily remove and replace the sections for job customization.

2. Write, gather and assemble the documents. Begin the portfolio with a clear objective statement and summary of your work experience. Include your past experience, areas of expertise and personal traits. Request copies of transcripts, certifications or other documents verifying education or certification training and include them in a separate section.

3. Prepare regular and scannable versions of your résumé. Many companies scan résumés into their applicant tracking systems. Your résumé may be rejected if it does not comply with their system.

4. Include work samples relevant to the position. Sample spreadsheets, P&L statements or annual reports showcase your work as an accountant. Training manuals or employee satisfaction surveys are relevant to a human resources position. Reports, projects, PowerPoint presentations, technical drawings, graphic design projects showcase your particular skills that set you apart from the others. Be sure work samples do not include confidential or proprietary information.

2 **to crowd** – überfüllen
3 **killer** *(coll.)* – *hier:* sehr gut
5 **to expand on** – aufbauen auf
5 **hard-copy** – in Papierform
6 **recommendation** – Empfehlung
6 **sample** – Beispiel
7 **to compile** – zusammenstellen
10 **binder** – Ordner
11 **zippered** – Reißverschluss-
13 **table of contents** – Inhaltsverzeichnis
13 **divider** – Trennblatt
14 **customization** – Anpassung
15 **to gather** – sammeln
15 **to assemble** – zusammenstellen
16 **objective** – Absicht
17 **expertise** – Fachkenntnis
17 **trait** – Charakterzug
17 **transcript** – Zeugnis
18 **to verify** – belegen
21 **applicant** – Bewerber(in)
21 **to track** – verfolgen
21 **to reject** – ablehnen
22 **to comply with** – übereinstimmen mit
23 **work sample** – Arbeitsprobe
23 **spreadsheet** – Tabelle
23 **P&L (profit & loss) statement** – Gewinn- und Verlustrechnung
24 **annual report** – Jahresbericht
24 **to showcase** – demonstrieren
24 **training manual** – Schulungshandbuch
25 **survey** – Umfrage
28 **confidential** – vertraulich
28 **proprietary** – geschützt

5. Share awards and recognitions. Include copies of award certificates, letters of recognition, reference letters, customer appreciation letters and emails. Remove any personal information such as email addresses, street addresses, and phone or fax numbers from outside correspondence. This can be provided in a second interview.

6. Select relevant material. While jobs require a variety of skills and experience, do not overload the portfolio. Help prospective employers focus on significant information. Too much can be confusing and appear disorganized.

7. Create an electronic version of the portfolio. Scan the documents and copy to a flash drive or CD to include in the portfolio. Plastic dividers for electronic media will give your portfolio an updated look. (517 words)

29 **recognition** – Anerkennung
29 **letter of recognition** – Empfehlungsschreiben
30 **appreciation** – Wertschätzung
37 **flash drive** – USB-Stick

2 Comprehension: Multiple choice

Read the text and choose the answer (1., 2., or 3.) which you think fits best according to the text.

a) According to the text, there are currently
1. more qualified applicants than available jobs.
2. more available jobs than qualified applicants.
3. as many qualified applicants as available jobs.

b) At the start of your portfolio, you should have
1. school certificates.
2. a reference from a former employer.
3. information about your previous jobs.

c) Your portfolio should not contain
1. personal details.
2. samples of your work.
3. examples of positive feedback from customers.

d) Having a hard-copy of your job skills portfolio is
1. unnecessary.
2. recommended.
3. obligatory.

04 ## 3 Mediation → Mediation, p. 245

A friend of yours would like to apply for a job at a company in the USA, and for her application she needs to make a *job skills portfolio*. Use the text above and create a list of tips. Write your answers in complete German sentences.

3 ## 4 Listening comprehension: A job interview → Listening, p. 221, Taking notes, p. 254

Barbara Meyer has applied for a summer job in a coffee shop.

a) Listen to the interview twice and find out the following information:

1. name of manager • 2. opening hours (weekdays) • 3. opening hours (Sundays) • 4. working hours • 5. possibility of working overtime • 6. duties (three items) • 7. necessary qualifications

b) What does the manager learn about Barbara Meyer? Write down the notes she might have made about: 1. Barbara's age; 2. nationality; 3. family; 4. her English skills; 5. experience; 6. place of residence. Then listen again and check your answers.

5 Projects → Hotspots 1 and 2, p. 69

B Work placements

1 Before you read → Brainstorming, p. 253

a) Have you ever done a work placement? If you could do a three-month work placement with any company, which one would you choose? Give reasons for your choice. Share your ideas with the class.

b) Would you be prepared to pay €2,000 for the work placement you have just chosen? Explain why or why not.

theguardian

News | Sport | Comment | Culture | Business | Money | Life&Style | Travel | Environment

Comment is free > Career   Search [ ] GO

Career-boosting internships for sale

The pressure to get experience on their CV leads students not only to work for free in internships, but to pay for the privilege … if they can afford it.

About a decade ago the word internships was barely used in a British context. Today, internships are both ubiquitous and highly contentious. There are campaigns denouncing the ethics of requiring young people already saddled with thousands of pounds of debt from their degree studies to do unpaid work, and debate over the morality of a system that allows those from well-to-do families to exploit their connections and secure opportunities that give them even greater advantage over those from humbler backgrounds.

Growing numbers of recent graduates are paying thousands of pounds to companies that specialise in securing placements overseas. And auctions held in aid of charity continue to offer internships to the highest bidder.

Work experience placements donated to four charities by the auction house Christie's over the last year have each raised up to £3,000, while, in November, the charity Pilotlight, which sends volunteers from the world of business into small charities to help them work more efficiently, attracted a top bid of £3,000 in an online auction for a week at GQ magazine.

Meanwhile firms offering to arrange internships abroad for a fee, usually in China or Australia, are growing in size and number. One, CRCC Asia, has increased the number of placements it offers in Beijing and Shanghai fivefold in three years.

This year, 3,600 students applied for its one or two month internships, easily filling the 1,300 places. Students, who are assessed for suitability, pay £1,495 for a month in Beijing and £100 more for Shanghai. As well as a fee for arranging the placement, the figure includes accommodation, a visa and other extras. But students must cover their flights and living costs while in China, separately.

The one-year-old company Standout Internships offers placements in Sydney, in everything from finance, banking and law to fashion and event planning. Jonathan Manning quit his City job to co-found the firm with a friend after seeing graduate friends struggle to get jobs because of a lack of work experience. Manning says, "The fact that students are doing an internship helps them in their applications for a paid job. You need the experience to get the job and if you have to pay for it then it is worth it."

3 **privilege** – Privileg
4 **to afford sth.** – sich etw. leisten können
7 **ubiquitous** – allgegenwärtig
8 **contentious** – umstritten
8 **to denounce** – verurteilen
10 **debt** – Schuld, Schulden
13 **well-to-do** – wohlhabend
13 **to exploit** – ausbeuten
14 **humble** – bescheiden
16 **overseas** – im Ausland
16 **in aid of** – zur Unterstützung von
16 **charity** – Wohltätigkeit, Wohltätigkeitsverein
17 **bidder** – Bietende(r)
18 **to donate** – spenden
19 **volunteer** – Freiwillige(r), Ehrenamtliche(r)
22 **fee** – Gebühr
26 **to assess** – beurteilen
26 **suitability** – Eignung
27 **accommodation** – Unterbringung
30 **to co-found** – mitgründen

Critics disagree. Already concerned that unpaid internships put poor students at a disadvantage, they say asking students to spend large sums for such opportunities harms social mobility even more.
Sophie Corcut applied for an internship through CRCC Asia after studying history and French at Bristol and finding herself unsure what career she wanted to pursue. While at university she had already done several unpaid placements, mostly arranged through personal contacts.
Using a combination of savings, paid work and a loan of £1,500 from her parents, she got together the £3,500 she needed to cover the trip, including flights, and spent two months in Beijing doing a marketing internship at a fair trade company. On her return she was quickly accepted on a graduate scheme at management consultants Accenture.
Corcut says she is sure the internship played a big role in her getting the job. "Coming back from China, you've got this one thing on your CV that makes you stand out," she says.
Martin Birchall, managing director of High Fliers Research (HRF), says it's no surprise graduates are so keen to find placements. "Employers have been looking for more than just the basic degree for some time, and the recession accelerated that process," he says. "In the past work experience was a 'nice to have'. Now it has, in effect, becoming a pre-requisite." (852 words)

39 **to pursue** – verfolgen
41 **loan** – Darlehen, Kredit
43 **graduate scheme** – Traineeprogramm für Hochschulabsolventen
49 **to accelerate** – beschleunigen
50 **pre-requisite** – Voraussetzung

204 **2 Comprehension: Table completion**

a) What are the pros and cons of the kind of internships described in the text? Make a table and list as many pros and cons as you can find.

Pros	Cons

b) Explain the following sentence in your own words: "[…] asking students to spend large sums [of money] for such opportunities harms social mobility […]" (l. 36).

3 Role play → Discussions, p. 246
Prepare a panel discussion with the title "Internships for sale: a fair trade?" with the following roles. You can use the pros and cons you have collected in task 2 to prepare your arguments.

a) A recent graduate who is looking for work experience to increase his career prospects. ("I'd rather not have to pay, but if it gets me the job …")

b) A parent of a recently graduated student who is not able to support their child financially. ("We simply can't afford it.")

c) A human resources manager from a major company. ("Nowadays, work experience is a pre-requisite.")

d) The manager of a company selling overseas work placements. ("You need the experience. If you have to pay for it, then it's worth it.")

e) Another role you believe is missing in this discussion.

24 **4 Listening comprehension: Work experience** → Listening, p. 221, Taking notes, p. 254
Listen to a British teenager talking about her work experience in a London store. Take notes about her work experience and make a grid. Use the following keywords:

employer / type and location of company • length of stay • feelings before starting work • first impressions • normal duties • additional duties • positive aspects of the job • negative aspects of the job • achievements

5 Projects → Hotspots 3 and 4, p. 69

C Teenage unemployment

1 Before you read → Brainstorming, p. 253
The following text is about Neets, i.e. teenagers who are *not in education, employment or training*. It provides us with facts and figures, reasons for the present situation and also names measures to fight this problem. Before you read, discuss the following questions in class:

a) What might be reasons for young people to become Neets?

b) Which measures might be taken to fight this problem?

BBC NEWS EDUCATION & FAMILY — Search GO

Home | UK | Africa | Asia-Pac | Europe | Latin America | Mid-East | South Asia

Rise in youths out of work and education in England

The proportion of 16-24-year-olds not in employment, education or training in England at the end of 2010 was up on previous years, official figures show.
A total of 938,000 – 15.6% of 16-24-year-olds – were in this category (Neet) in December 2010, the highest final-quarter figure since 2005. The government said the number was "still too high". Last week the youth unemployment rate hit a new peak. Critics called for more investment in education rather than cuts. (...) The increase comes amid concerns that young people have been hit particularly hard by the recession, as rising numbers of graduates battle for jobs and fill vacancies traditionally taken by school and college leavers.

'Back of the queue'

The proportion of 16-18-year-olds not in education, employment and training, however, has reached its lowest level, 162,000 (8.5%) since 2005. This follows a push in recent years to encourage more 16-year-olds to stay on in education. A government spokesperson said: "The number of young people who are Neet is still too high. It is young people who bear the brunt in any recession or downturn, which is why we are so focused on tackling the deficit and promoting growth." The Conservative-Liberal Democrat coalition says it plans to fund 75,000 extra adult apprenticeship places, as well as offering a new Work Programme to provide "personalised support and training to help unemployed young people into work".
A spokesman from youth charity The Prince's Trust said: "As thousands of unemployed graduates flood the jobs market, Britain's most disadvantaged young people are being pushed to the back of the queue. These young people may have come from households where no-one works, with no positive role models, or struggled at school, leaving with few qualifications. It is these vulnerable young people who need our support to help them into jobs," the spokesman said.
Last week, the youth unemployment rate reached 20.5%, its highest since comparable records began in 1992.
The government has axed the Education Maintenance Allowance study support grant for low-income students in England, and the Future Jobs Fund, which has been used to fund temporary employment for 18-24-year-olds in England, Scotland and Wales who have been out of work for more than six months.

6 **to hit a peak** – den höchsten Stand erreichen
9 **to battle** – kämpfen
9 **to fill vacancies** – freie Stellen besetzen
14 **to encourage** – ermutigen
16 **to bear the brunt** – die volle Last tragen
16 **to tackle** – angreifen
21 **youth charity** – Jugendhilfsorganisation
22 **disadvantaged** – benachteiligt
25 **vulnerable** – verletzlich
29 **to axe** – *hier:* abschaffen

Sally Hunt, general secretary of the University and College Union, said these moves, at a time when youth unemployment was at its highest in years, "could come back and haunt this country".
"Instead of erecting barriers to study, such as tripling the cost of tuition fees, the government should be following the example of other countries and be investing in education, not cutting the very services young people need," she said. Figures for Neet young people are published separately in Wales, Scotland and Northern Ireland.

(466 words)

34 **to haunt** – *hier:* später zu schaffen machen
36 **to erect barriers** – Barrieren errichten
36 **to triple** – verdreifachen
36 **tuition fees** – Studiengebühren

2 Comprehension: True or false?

Read the statements below and decide whether they are true or false. Quote or paraphrase words from the text which confirm or disprove the ideas in the statements.

a) The proportion of 16-18-year-olds not in education, employment and training, however, has reached its highest level in many years.

b) Only a fifth of all 16-24-year-olds in England were in education, employment and training at the end of 2010.

c) One reason for this increased youth unemployment is the recession of 2010.

d) Many disadvantaged young people in Britain simply do not want to be trained or work.

e) Critics of the government demanded that more money should be invested in education and training.

f) A high number of Neets come from households where no-one works, with no positive role models.

g) The Future Jobs Fund is a government programme to help young people in England, Scotland and Wales who have been unemployed for over half a year.

h) The government has already been criticised for increasing tuition fees making education more expensive.

3 Analysis → Understanding non-fictional texts, p. 222

Analyse the function of the quotations in the text. In order to get a better overview, first copy and fill in the table below:

quotation by	summary of quotation in your own words	function of this quotation

"Yes, I've been looking for a job but I haven't seen any yet."

4 Analysis → Describing cartoons, p. 242

Describe and analyse the cartoon.

5 Research project → Hotspot 5, p. 69

D Corporate culture

1 Before you read

a) Look at the photo. What can you see?

b) Find words that best describe the kind of working environment you think it represents.

c) Would you like working in a large office? Why (not)?

2 Comprehension → Understanding fictional texts, p. 224
In your own words, describe a day at the office for the employees in the text.

Joshua Ferris (American writer, born in 1974)

Then We Came to the End *is set during the downturn of the Internet boom at the end of the 1990s. The story takes place in an advertising company in Chicago and is a satire of American office environment.*

Then We Came to the End

WE WERE FRACTIOUS AND overpaid. Our mornings lacked promise. At least those of us who smoked had something to look forward to at ten-fifteen. Most of us liked most everyone, a few of us hated specific individuals, one or two people loved everyone and everything. Those who loved everyone were unanimously reviled. We loved free bagels in the morning. They happened all too infrequently. Our benefits were astonishing in comprehensiveness and quality of care. Sometimes we questioned whether they were worth it. We thought moving to India might be better, or going back to nursing school. Doing something with the handicapped or working with our hands. No one ever acted on these impulses, despite their daily, sometimes hourly contractions. Instead we met in conference rooms to discuss the issues of the day.

Ordinarily jobs came in and we completed them in a timely and professional manner. Sometimes fuckups did occur. Printing errors, transposed numbers. Our business was advertising and details were important. If the third number after the second hyphen in a client's toll-free number was a six instead of an eight, and if it went to print like that, and showed up in Time magazine, no one reading the ad could call now and order today. No matter they could go to the website, we still had to eat the price of the ad. Is this boring you yet? It bored us every day. Our boredom was ongoing, a collective boredom, and it would never die because we would never die.

1 **fractious** – mürrisch
3 **to lack sth.** – etw. vermissen lassen
11 **unanimously** – einstimmig
11 **to revile sb.** – jmdn schmähen
12 **infrequently** – selten, unregelmäßig
13 **astonishing** – erstaunlich
13 **comprehensiveness** – Umfang
15 **handicapped** – Behinderte(r)
16 **to act on** – auf etw. reagieren
16 **despite** – trotz
17 **contraction** – Zusammenziehen
19 **ordinarily** – für gewöhnlich, normalerweise
20 **transposed** – vertauscht
22 **hyphen** – Bindestrich
22 **toll-free** – kostenlos

205 △ **3 Analysis** → Text analysis, p. 228

a) Analyse the language the author uses to show how the employees in this company feel. First, collect positive and negative examples showing the employees' attitudes towards their job and workplace in a table. Then use this information to explain their feelings. Include the corresponding lines.

b) Explain the phrase "No matter they could go to the website, we still had to eat the price of the ad." (ll. 24–25)

c) Analyse the perspective from which the text is written and its effect on the reader. Give some examples from the text to support your answer.

05 △ **4 Comment** → Writing a comment, p. 229
Imagine you have been offered a job at the company in the text. Would you like to work there? Give reasons for and against.

We didn't know who was stealing things from other people's workstations. Always small items – postcards, framed photographs. We had our suspicions but no proof. We believed it was probably not for the loot so much as the excitement – the shoplifter's addictive kick, or maybe it was a pathological cry for help. Hank Neary, one of the agency's only black writers, asked, "Come on, now – who would want my travel toothbrush?"

In those days it wasn't rare for someone to push someone else down the hall really fast in a swivel chair. Games aside, we spent most of our time inside long silent pauses as we bent over our individual desks, working on some task at hand, lost to it – until Benny, bored, came and stood in the doorway. "What are you up to?" he'd ask. […]

It could have been any of us. "Working" was the usual reply. Then Benny would tap his topaz class ring on the doorway and drift away.

How we hated our coffee mugs! Our mouse pads, our desk clocks, our daily calendars, the contents of our desk drawers. Even the photos of our loved ones taped to our computer monitors for uplift and support turned into cloying reminders of time served. But when we got a new office, a bigger office, and we brought everything with us into the new office, how we loved everything all over again, and thought hard about where to place things, and looked with satisfaction at the end of the day at how well our old things looked in this new, improved, important space. There was no doubt in our minds just then that we had made all the right decisions, whereas most days we were men and women of two minds. Everywhere you looked, in the hallways and bathrooms, the coffee bar and cafeteria, the lobbies and the print stations, there we were with our two minds. There seemed to be only the one electric pencil sharpener in the whole damn place.

We had visceral, rich memories of dull, interminable hours. Then a day would pass in perfect harmony with our projects, our family members, and our co-workers, and we couldn't believe we were getting paid for this. (762 words)

29 **suspicion** – Verdacht
30 **loot** *(AE, coll.)* – Geld
31 **addictive** – süchtig machend
31 **pathological** – krankhaft
35 **swivel chair** – Drehstuhl
41 **mug** – Becher
43 **uplift** – Auftrieb
43 **cloying** – anwidernd
47 **satisfaction** – Zufriedenheit
48 **doubt** – Zweifel
49 **whereas** – während, wohingegen
54 **visceral** – tief sitzend
54 **dull** – langweilig
54 **interminable** – unendlich

E Job satisfaction

1 Before you read → Brainstorming, p. 253

a) Work on your own. Write a list of at least five things which you would need to be happy in your future job.

b) Write a short definition of "job satisfaction" and share it with the class.

1 **tangible** – materiell
2 **reward** – Belohnung
2 **generous** – großzügig
2 **benefit** – Leistung, Vorteil
3 **increasingly** – zunehmend
4 **intangible** – immateriell
7 **gorgeous** – sehr schön
9 **praise** – Lob
9 **supervisor** – Leiter(in), Kontrolleur(in)
9 **to go out of one's way** – keine Mühen scheuen
10 **to bother** – sich die Mühe machen
16 **sincere** – aufrichtig
17 **accomplishment** – Leistung
18 **to escalate** – sich zuspitzen
19 **to appreciate sth.** – etw. schätzen
23 **survey** – Umfrage
24 **honesty** – Aufrichtigkeit, Ehrlichkeit
28 **to nurture** – etw. fördern
32 **executive** – leitende(r)
33 **merely** – nur
35 **to determine** – bestimmen
37 **sympathetic** – mitfühlend
37 **crucial** – entscheidend, äußerst wichtig

THE CHRISTIAN SCIENCE MONITOR

Search GO

World | USA | Commentary | Business | Environment | Innovation | Science |

Seven things employees want most to be happy at work

Ask bosses what makes employees happy at work, and many are likely to think in terms of tangible rewards: a good salary, a pleasant office, generous benefits.
Those play a role in job satisfaction, of course. But increasingly, workplace specialists are discovering that for many workers, the "happiness factor" depends heavily on intangibles, such as respect, trust, and fairness. Here are seven intangibles workers want most, according to experts:

1

"If the office is gorgeous, the pay is good, and the work is interesting, of course that helps," says Michal Ann Strahilevitz, a marketing professor at Golden Gate University in San Francisco. "However, there is one huge factor that does not cost an employer money: praise. So many supervisors go out of their way to let employees know what they have done wrong, but don't bother to congratulate and praise them for success. Praise does not cost anything to give, but its benefits on employee morale are priceless."

2

"The most important factor in keeping employees happy is treating them with fairness and respect," says Pamela Skillings, a career coach in Jackson Heights, N.Y. "People want to be paid what they're worth, treated like adults, and rewarded for their good work." Those rewards can be simple and spontaneous. "A sincere thank you or short note often means a great deal when it is recognizing an accomplishment or specific effort," says Mrs Sarikas, Career Specialist, Northeastern University, Boston. She finds that job dissatisfaction escalates when employees are not treated with respect or feel that their work is not appreciated.

3

Going hand in hand with respect is trust. "You have to trust the people you work for, and enjoy the people you work with," says Julie Clarkson, assistant professor of business at Wartburg College in Waverly, Iowa. In a nationwide survey of 500 employees about what matters most in their relationship with a manager, 90 percent of workers rank honesty, fairness, and trust as their top three needs, says Terry Bacon, author of "What People Want."

4

What people also want is an opportunity to grow and learn on the job. "No matter how we make a living, each of us is nurtured by our own professional and personal growth," says Michael Neece, cofounder of Pongo.com, which provides résumé-writing services. "Employees want to understand how their efforts contribute to the business and want to feel that they are making a difference to their team, their department, and the company." "The presence of money is a condition of work, and its absence is a demotivator," says Alan Weiss, an executive coach in East Greenwich, R.I. "But if you give more money to an unhappy employee, you merely have a wealthier, unhappy employee."

5

Bosses also play key roles in determining a worker's happiness factor. More than half of employees responding to an annual job-satisfaction survey by Yahoo! HotJobs admit that they don't leave companies, they leave bosses. "Having a fair, sympathetic manager who makes employees feel valued is a crucial element to an employee's job satisfaction," says Tom Musbach, managing editor of Yahoo! HotJobs. By contrast, if bosses aren't honest with workers, don't listen to them, and don't care about them, employees either leave or become disengaged in their work, says Terri Levine, president of Comprehensive Coaching U in North Wales, Pennsylvania.

6

"You need to feel good about the people you work with and the people you work for," Sarikas says. "You don't have to be best friends and probably shouldn't be, but you need to be able to respect them for their knowledge and experience as well as for their ethics." Similarly, employees need to find an organization where the corporate culture fits their personality and work style. For some, that includes work-life balance.

7

"Most people find happiness at work when they feel connected to the core purpose of the organization," Clarkson says. "When we are able to find work that uses our capabilities and allows us to address important values in our life's purpose, it is the best way to find happiness at work."
Whatever an individual's personal recipe for happiness on the job, Jeff Garten, author of the forthcoming book "Career Contentment," urges people to take the long view. "Career contentment is different from job satisfaction," he says. "It is a deeper state of mind about one's direction, fulfillment, calling, engagement. Job satisfaction comes and goes with each job, but career contentment is a lifelong quest and mind-set." (944 words)

40 **disengaged** – gelöst
45 **ethics** – Werte
49 **core** – Kern
50 **capability** – Fähigkeit
52 **recipe** – Rezept
53 **to urge** – drängen
54 **calling** – Berufung
55 **quest** – Suche
56 **mind-set** – Einstellung

2 Comprehension: Multiple matching → Scanning, p. 221

a) Look at the headlines below and match them with the appropriate sections (1–7) of the text. There are three headlines that don't fit.

Compatible co-workers • Financial rewards • Appreciation • A good boss • Trust • Individual growth • Generous holidays • Respect • Social events • A sense of purpose

b) Summarise each of the 7 sections in one or two sentences. Use your own words.

c) Compare the definition of job satisfaction given in the text with your definition. What are the similarities and differences?

3 Comment → Writing a comment, p. 229

"A high salary is the most important factor for job satisfaction." Comment on this statement.

4 Partner interview: School satisfaction → Discussions, p. 246

Interview your partner about the things that are necessary for him or her to be satisfied at school. Ask them how satisfied they are in these areas. The words in the box should give you some ideas, but you should also include your own.

marks • teachers • classmates • timetable • tests • catering • location of school • facilities • …

5 Listening comprehension: Job satisfaction → Listening, p. 221

Listen to an interview with the director of Oxfam in Britain, Barbara Stocking, and find out the following:

- What did Barbara want to be as a child? Why?
- How did she get the job at Oxfam?
- What are Barbara's top interview tips?
- How does she describe her work-life balance?

Oxfam Deutschland

Oxfam International is a confederation of 13 organisations which work together with more than 3,000 partners in over 100 countries to find long-term solutions to poverty and injustice.

Formal and informal language

a) Choosing the right register

Decide for the following words and expressions if they are formal, informal or part of a professional register (a variety of a language that is used in a particular professional context). Find a formal term for informal expressions.

what makes us tick • incentives • rewards • household pattern • bestie • friend • mate • parents • pal • sista • bro • dad • old man • fam • relatives • mommy • big daddy • peer support • social networks • peer pressure • motivation chart • marriage patterns • family structures • sibling • guardians • push factors • to save sth. for a rainy day

b) Rewriting a text

You have been asked to write a short text for your school's partner college in England. They would like you to write about German teenagers, friendships and finding the right job. Put the notes into a formal English text. You can use a thesaurus (= a book of synonyms, often including related and contrasting words and antonyms) to help you. Online thesauruses are a fast way of finding the words and expressions you need.

Notes:

- the German teenagers I know are open and don't have any stereotypes, they just get along well with everybody no matter if boy or girl, German or foreigner
- they just ask one question: do I like this person, are they cool?
- when it comes to finding the right job after school: no typically male / female job; only concern: What am I good at? What will my mates do? Will I lose touch when I go somewhere else?
- many of them have a hard time finding the perfect job for themselves
- but then they help each other because they're going through the same things
- when choosing a job, money doesn't seem that important as long as the people are cool and the work is fun
- they don't like others nagging all the time and telling them what to do, they want to be independent and also share responsibility
- if someone is getting on their nerves, they might freak out and risk getting into trouble
- all in all the teenagers I know are open and honest …

Start like this:

I was asked to write a short text about German teenagers, friendships and finding the right job. Of course I cannot speak for all German teenagers; I can only speak from my own experience. Generally speaking, German teenagers are open-minded and do not have any particular prejudices. …

1 Project: A job skills portfolio → Presentation, p. 264
Prepare a job skills portfolio for yourself. You do not need to write out full sentences. However, be prepared to tell your classmates what you would like to include in your job profile when applying for a job.

2 Project: Interview do's and don'ts → Projects and group work, p. 261

a) Work in groups of four. Go online and find a video with expert advice about job interviews. While you are watching, make a list of the do's and don'ts mentioned in the clip. Type "job interview, do's and don'ts, video clip" into a search engine.

b) Discuss your results in your group and add your own ideas.

c) Split the group into two smaller groups. Group 1 should write a script for a good interview, and Group 2 for a bad interview.

d) Act out your interviews in front of the class and ask them to point out the do's and don'ts.

3 Project: "Duales Ausbildungssystem" (Mediation) → Presentation, p. 264
Imagine you work in a German company with business partners abroad. In the near future, your boss is going to be visited by some Chinese business partners. He asks you to prepare a short presentation on the *duales Ausbildungssystem* in Germany. You can use a search engine and these two German key words to find information. Sum up the most important ideas about the German dual vocational education system in English. Prepare a transparency with key words to use in your presentation.

4 Project: "Juniorenfirma" (Mediation) → Projects and group work, p. 261

a) Some schools in Germany have a so-called "Juniorenfirma". Find out which class at your school is in charge of it. Then prepare a list of questions in English to ask the students involved. Collect information that you can use to create a leaflet about the "company" in English. You can present your findings at the end of this short project.

b) If there is no such "Juniorenfirma" in your school, imagine you are asked to set one up. Which services and products could you offer in your school? List your services and products, invent a marketing slogan to go with each item and think up a name for your company.

5 Research project: Job descriptions and necessary skills → Internet research, p. 260

a) Go online and find the job description for a job that interests you. Make notes on the most important tasks and necessary skills and qualifications for this job.

b) Now go online again and find a report from an intern/trainee about their experiences in the job you have chosen. What positive and negative experiences did they have and how useful was it for their future careers?

c) Copy your results from a) and b) onto a transparency and present them to the class.

A 2.29

THE INDEPENDENT

Working at home grows in popularity

Billions of people have ditched the commute to the office in favour of working from home – and the number of home-based workers is set to rise dramatically. According to research […] by consumer think tank the Future Foundation, 8.6 per cent of the work force – 2.5 million people – work from home for one or more days a week.

It expects that number to rise by 200,000 a year for the next four years. By 2020, it reckons that 16 per cent of the working population will be at least partially based at home.

Employers increasingly allow well-paid, high-flying professionals, as well as traditional teleworkers, to work away from the office. The report, commissioned by Brother, the electronics and manufacturing company, also identifies a new type of worker, who is based at the office but e-mails clients from their BlackBerry on the train or makes work-related phone calls from home.

Describing them as "free workers", it says this group accounts for 46 per cent of the work force but will rise to 80 per cent by 2020.

"The question by then will be not who sometimes works at home but who doesn't," says report author William Nelson. "There are positive benefits

1 **to ditch** – to give up
4 **to be set** – to be about to
12 **to reckon** – to estimate
13 **partially** – partly
16 **high-flying** – successful
18 **to commission sth.** – to order sth.
26 **to account for** – to constitute

to skipping the daily commute and increasing productivity by working at home. Highly-skilled workers who are in demand may find their company would rather allow them to work flexibly, rather than lose them."

In a separate report, published recently by the Management Consultancies Association, a third of the 1,200 respondents claimed that remote working is now common in their organisation. However, despite the potential gains for the employer, 93 per cent said it was the employees who were choosing to work away from the office, rather than their employer encouraging them to do so.

It also found that the majority of companies were unwilling to fund the arrangements. Only 40 per cent said that their employer covered the costs of remote working.

The Flexible Working Regulations, which came into force in 2003, provide parents with children under six – or 18 if the child has a disability – with the right to request flexible working arrangements, which may include working from home.

The employment solicitor James Upton, from Hill Dickinson Solicitors, says: "This means an employer has to follow certain procedures to consider their request for flexible working. It doesn't mean they are automatically able to work from home. Neither does it mean that employees without children can't ask their boss to let them work from home."

If you're a valued employee with bags of experience, you're more likely to convince your employer that you can work from home effectively, than if you're fairly junior, only started last month and need constant supervision. [...]

(461 words)

33 **to skip sth.** – to leave out
36 **in demand** – desired
42 **remote working** – working from home
44 **gain** – benefit
50 **to fund** – to finance
57 **disability** – handicap
60 **solicitor** – lawyer
69 **valued** – appreciated
70 **you're more likely to ...** – there's a higher chance that you ...
74 **supervision** – *here:* guidance

1 Comprehension

a) In your own words, summarise what the article tells us about today's world of work.

b) Outline what the "Flexible Working Regulations" (l. 54) are and what they mean for employees as well as employers.

2 Analysis → Text analysis, p. 228

Analyse the language and structure used in the text and show whether the authors' opinions about teleworking become perceptible to the reader. Quote from the text to support your findings.

3 Comment

Comment on the benefits and inconveniences of teleworking for both employers and employees.

Topic 5
Science, technology and society

gq988z

A

“Men have become the tools of their tools.” Henry David Thoreau

“Civilization advances by extending the number of important operations which we can perform without thinking of them.” Alfred North Whitehead

“Everybody gets so much information all day long that they lose their common sense.” Gertrude Stein

B

“Any sufficiently advanced technology is indistinguishable from magic.” Arthur C. Clarke

Getting started

1 Look at the photos and think of different ways in which technology is part of our lives. What are the positive effects, what are the negative developments?

2 **a)** Choose one of the technologies in the pictures and imagine life without it. What would your life look like? Discuss with a partner.

b) Choose one of the technologies in the pictures and discuss some positive and negative effects of this technology with a different partner.

D

> Our technological powers increase, but the side effects and potential hazards also escalate.
> Alvin Toffler

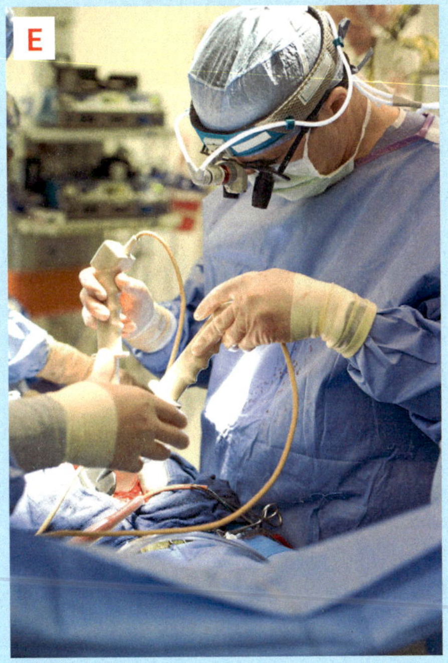

E

> Technology is the knack of so arranging the world that we don't have to experience it.
> Max Frisch

C

> It is only when they go wrong that machines remind you how powerful they are.
> Clive James

> The real problem is not whether machines think but whether men do.
> B.F. Skinner

3 Work in groups. In your group, agree on the most important machine in history. Collect arguments and convince your classmates of your choice.

4 Famous quotes

Choose two quotes that in your opinion best describe the role technology plays in our lives. Give reasons for your decision and share your arguments with your classmates.

5 Research project → Hotspot 1, p. 85

Word bank

minimally invasive surgery • robotic arm • wind power station • nuclear power plant • solar panels • to advance • to progress • to live without sth. • it's hard to imagine • not all that is possible is acceptable • to meet the demands • to develop solutions • to make life easier • a double-edged sword

A Genetics

1 Before you read

Do you agree with the following statements? Why (not)?

- Couples should be allowed to use genetic engineering to make sure that they have a healthy baby.
- Insurance companies should be allowed to use genetic testing before giving someone health or life insurance.
- Sports officials should be allowed to use genetic testing of young athletes before supporting and sponsoring careers.
- Scientists should be allowed to clone human embryos to grow organs for transplant operations.

The Telegraph

Search GO

Home | News | Sport | Finance | Comment | Culture | Travel | Lifestyle | Fashion

Stem cell research: a new age dawns in healthcare

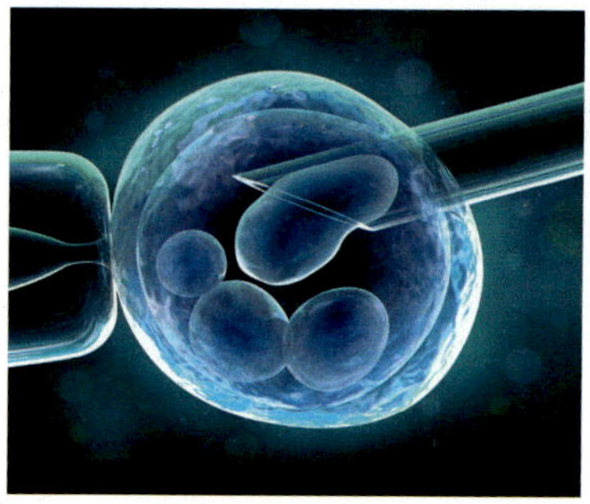

Scientists working in stem cell research believe that they are about to change medicine forever, writes Michael Day.

Professor Pete Coffey, of University College London, like many other stem cell scientists, has a spring in his step these days. His team is set to conduct the first test of an embryonic stem cell-based treatment on patients in the UK.

Approval from the Medicines and Healthcare products Regulatory Agency (MHRA) to test a therapy that he hopes will cure macular degeneration, the most common form of blindness among older people in the western world, is unlikely before 2012. However, Prof Coffey is confident that the regulator will give the go-ahead.

This is due in no small part to events in the US, where it was announced last week that doctors had begun the first trial in which patients with spinal cord injuries will receive tissue grown from human embryonic stem cells. The study by the Geron Corporation is primarily designed to test the safety of the procedure; larger trials will be needed to gauge its effectiveness. But the fact that the US Food and Drug Administration approved the trial is testimony to important advances in stem cell research. [...] The other important change is political. With George W. Bush out of the White House, the US, the world's powerhouse for biomedical research, is once more publicly funding medical research with embryonic stem cells left over from fertility treatments. The Geron scientists have grown oligodendrocyte precursor cells from their stem cells.

0 **stem cell** – Stammzelle
0 **to dawn** – beginnen
5 **a spring in his step** – federnder Schritt, er strahlt Zuversicht aus
5 **to conduct** – durchführen
7 **approval** – Zustimmung
7 **regulatory agency** – Prüfbehörde
8 **macular degeneration** – Makuladegeneration, Verlust von Sehkraft am „Gelben Fleck"
10 **to give the go-ahead** – grünes Licht geben
12 **spinal cord** – Rückenmark
13 **tissue** – Gewebe
14 **trial** – Versuch
15 **to gauge** – beurteilen, messen
15 **US Food and Drug Administration (FDA)** – amerikanische Regierungsinstitution, die für die Sicherheit von Nahrungsmitteln, Medizin etc. verantwortlich ist
16 **testimony** – *hier:* Beweis
16 **advance** – Fortschritt
19 **fertility treatment** – Fruchtbarkeitsbehandlung
20 **oligodendrocyte** – eine Form von Gehirnzellen
20 **precursor** – Vorläufer(in)

They hope that, once injected at the site of recent spinal injury, these will populate the area and help regenerate damaged tissue.

Prof Coffey's group is using stem cells to develop cells that support the retina, the photosensitive area at the back of the eye. In patients with macular degeneration, these cells start to disappear. He hopes that a patch containing the reared cells delivered behind the retina will restore patients' vision. "If we start testing, we should know quite quickly whether it works. The question is simple: can the patients see again?"

He believes treatments for conditions like macular degeneration, which are well-understood and don't require complex interactions between curative cells and host tissue, will be the first to appear. "Liver disease, heart conditions, perhaps diabetes, where the concept of getting insulin-producing cells into the body is quite simple, might be the first to be treated."

He predicts stem cell treatments for more complex and less well-characterised conditions, including brain diseases like Alzheimer's or Parkinson's, will take longer to appear. But ultimately he is in no doubt that stem cells "will change medicine for ever". This is a view shared by his UCL colleague Chris Mason, professor of regenerative medicine bioprocessing. "There are still many years of rigorous testing ahead and there will be setbacks and failures before we have safe and effective cell-based therapies," he says. "But this first in man [Geron] study marks the dawn of the 'Stem Cell Age'."

(502 words)

22 **to regenerate** – neu beleben
23 **retina** – Netzhaut
25 **patch** – Flicken, Pflaster
25 **reared** – herangezüchtet
26 **to restore** – wiederherstellen
30 **curative** – heilend

2 Comprehension: True or false? → Comprehension questions, p. 228

Read the statements below and decide whether they are true or false. Quote or paraphrase words from the text which confirm or disprove the ideas in the statements.

a) The tests for a stem cell-based cure for macular degeneration have been approved by the regulatory agency.

b) In the USA, a study has been started that will find out how well stem cell therapy works in healing spinal cord injuries.

c) Former US president George W. Bush was opposed to funding medical stem cell research.

d) Researchers hope to make blind patients see again by introducing photosensitive cells grown from stem cells into the patients' eyes.

e) Parkinson's and Alzheimer's will soon be curable as well.

3 Mediation → Mediation, p. 245

Summarise the current developments and possibilities of stem cell research and stem cell treatment as mentioned in the article in a German text.

4 Analysis → Text analysis, p. 228

Analyse the structure of the text and state if the author includes his personal opinion about stem cell research in this article. Quote examples from the text to support your answer.

5 Research project → Hotspot 2, p. 85

B Human spare parts

1 Before you read → Brainstorming, p. 253
Why do people have babies? Discuss reasons with a partner. To what extent can these reasons influence a person's relationship with his / her parents, and what effect might this have on their self-image and self-esteem?

2 Comprehension → Understanding fictional texts, p. 224

a) Make a list of the reasons the narrator gives for why people have babies.

b) Briefly outline the circumstances surrounding the narrator's own birth.

3 Analysis
Explain the sentence: "[…] we practically set a place for Death at the dinner table." (ll. 41 – 42)

Jodi Picoult
(American writer, born in 1967)

The following text is a passage from "My Sister's Keeper", a novel by Jodi Picoult.

- 1 **mystery** – Rätsel
- 2 **mechanics** *(pl)* – Ablauf
- 12 **to file for divorce** – die Scheidung einreichen
- 17 **flattering** – schmeichelhaft
- 20 **to hook up** – *hier:* zusammenfügen
- 21 **precious** – wertvoll
- 23 **more than I bargained for** – mehr als ich erwartet hatte

Anna

When I was little, the great mystery to me wasn't how babies were made, but why. The mechanics I understood – my older brother Jesse had filled me in – although at the time I was sure he'd heard half of it wrong. Other kids my age were busy looking up the words penis and vagina in the classroom dictionary when the teacher had her back turned, but I paid attention to different details. Like why some mothers only had one child, while other families seemed to multiply before your eyes. Or how the new girl in school, Sedona, told anyone who'd listen that she was named for the place where her parents were vacationing when they made her ("Good thing they weren't staying in Jersey City," my father used to say).

Now that I am thirteen, these distinctions are only more complicated: the eighth grader who dropped out of school because she got into trouble; a neighbor who got herself pregnant in the hopes it would keep her husband from filing for divorce. I'm telling you, if aliens landed on earth today and took a good hard look at why babies get born, they'd conclude that most people have children by accident, or because they drink too much on a certain night, or because birth control isn't one hundred percent, or for a thousand other reasons that really aren't very flattering.

On the other hand, I was born for a very specific purpose. I wasn't the result of a cheap bottle of wine or a full moon or the heat of the moment. I was born because a scientist managed to hook up my mother's eggs and my father's sperm to create a specific combination of precious genetic material. In fact, when Jesse told me how babies get made and I, the great disbeliever, decided to ask my parents the truth, I got more than I bargained for. They sat me down and told me all the usual stuff, of course – but they also explained that they chose little embryonic me, specifically, because I could save my sister Kate. "We loved you

4 Role play → Discussions, p. 246

a) Write down two or three sentences in which you describe the relationship between the characters in the text. Since the text isn't explicit about this, you have to use your imagination. Write about how:
- the narrator feels about her parents / her sister / herself,
- the parents feel about their daughter Kate / the narrator.

b) Now prepare a role play in which the family come together to discuss their feelings. Work in groups of four and assign a role to each person. Then, on your own, collect arguments to support your position. You can use your ideas from exercise a) to help you.

5 Comment
Is it ethically acceptable to artificially create a child in order to save another life? Discuss this question using the results from the previous task.

6 Project → Hotspot 3, p. 85

even more," my mother made sure to say, "because we knew what exactly we were getting."
It made me wonder, though, what would have happened if Kate had been healthy. Chances are, I'd still be floating up in Heaven or wherever, waiting to be attached to a body to spend some time on Earth. Certainly I would not be part of this family. See, unlike the rest of the free world, I didn't get here by accident. And if your parents have you for a reason, then that reason better exist. Because once it's gone, so are you. […]
My parents tried to make things normal, but that's a relative term. The truth is, I was never really a kid. To be honest, neither were Kate and Jesse. I guess maybe my brother had his moment in the sun for the four years he was alive before Kate got diagnosed, but ever since then, we've been too busy looking over our shoulders to run headlong into growing up. You know how most little kids think they're like cartoon characters – if an anvil drops on their heads they can peel themselves off the sidewalk and keep going?
Well, I never once believed that. How could I, when we practically set a place for Death at the dinner table?
Kate has acute promyelocytic leukemia. Actually, that's not quite true – right now she doesn't have it, but it's hibernating under her skin like a bear, until it decides to roar again. She was diagnosed when she was two; she's sixteen now. Molecular relapse and granulocyte and portacath – these words are part of my vocabulary, even though I'll never find them on any SAT. I'm an allogeneic donor – a perfect sibling match. When Kate needs leukocytes or stem cells or bone marrow to fool her body into thinking it's healthy, I'm the one who provides them. Nearly every time Kate's hospitalized, I wind up there too. (680 words)

38 **to run headlong into sth.** – überstürzt in etw. hineinrennen
39 **anvil** – Amboss
43 **promyelocytic leukemia** – Promyelozytenleukämie
44 **to hibernate** – überwintern, *hier:* vorübergehend inaktiv sein
46 **relapse** – Rückfall
46 **granulocyte** – eine Form weißer Blutkörper
46 **portacath** – transportabler Katheder, durch den ständig Medizin in den Körper geleitet werden kann
47 **SAT (scholastic aptitude test)** – Test vor der Zulassung zu einem College
47 **allogenic donor** – Spender, dessen Gene ähnlich, aber nicht identisch mit denen des Empfängers sind
48 **bone marrow** – Knochenmark

C Green clubbing

1 Before you read

a) Many people think that nightclubs are loud, create lots of rubbish and use large amounts of energy. But how can nightclubs be 'green'? Work with a partner and make a list of ideas.

b) Share your list with the class. Which ideas do you think would be easy/difficult to introduce? Discuss.

SPIEGEL ONLINE

Search GO

Home | Berlin | Politik | Sport | Kultur | Welt | Meinung

Erste Öko-Disco der Welt: Schwoofen für Strom

Hüpfen, schwingen, springen – jede Tanzbewegung im „Club Watt" erzeugt Strom. Das aktuell produzierte Energie-Level der Tänzer lässt sich von Leuchttafeln ablesen. Die erste Öko-Disco der Welt hat jetzt in Rotterdam eröffnet.

Rotterdam – Diesen Werbeslogan kann man wörtlich nehmen: „We want your energy" heißt es in der ersten Öko-Disco der Welt. Wer in dem Beton- und Glasbau an der West-Kruiskade im einst als Drogenquartier berüchtigten Chinesenviertel von Rotterdam tanzt, erzeugt Strom und hilft damit der Umwelt. In der Nacht zum Freitag wurde der Club von energiegeladenen Tänzern eröffnet. „Man fühlt sich dabei wie ein Kraftwerk", schwärmte eine Besucherin aus Deutschland. „Der erste nachhaltige Dance Club der Welt setzt einen Trend", hofft der Architekt Herman Kossmann. „Er beweist, dass Umweltschutz und Spaß bestens zusammenpassen." Früher war der Laden als „Nighttown" für aufregende Shows von Iggy Pop, Nirvana oder Amy Winehouse berühmt. Stars werden auch künftig kommen. Doch jetzt heißt die mit Millionengeldern niederländischer Privatinvestoren völlig neu gestaltete Disco „Club Watt" – und wer hier auftritt, legt damit auch ein grünes Bekenntnis ab.

Das Kernstück der Öko-Disco ist die flexible elektromechanische Tanzfläche. Der Boden unter den Füßen gibt um einige Millimeter nach. Die durch Schwingungen erzeugte Bewegungsenergie wird nach dem Dynamo-Prinzip in Elektrizität umgewandelt und in Akkus gespeichert. Fast ein Drittel des Stroms, den die DJ-Bühne verbraucht, sollen die Tänzer als „menschliche Energieerzeuger" liefern.

Tanzt, auf dass die Birnen erglühen

Leuchtdioden im Boden sowie Lampen an der Bühne zeigen an, wie stark die Stromerzeugung jeweils ist. Wer sich austobt, sorgt für eine individuelle Lichtshow. „Leute, tanzt auf dass die Birnen erglühen!", feuert DJ Ted Langenbach die Gäste an. Der 48-jährige Party-Guru der

Rotterdamer Szene gehört zu den Initiatoren des „Club Watt“. „Dieses Projekt hat mich gefesselt. Es gibt eben doch noch etwas Neues auf dem alten Tanzboden.“

Allerdings ist die Eigenstromerzeugung gemessen am Gesamtbedarf des Clubs, der 2000 Gäste aufnehmen kann, mit bis zu zehn Watt pro Tanzendem noch gering. Doch dabei soll es nicht bleiben. „Dies ist Club Watt in der Version 1.0“, sagt Martin Jordans vom Rotterdamer Architektenbüro Döll. „Wir arbeiten bereits an verbesserten Konzepten mit weit höherer Ausbeute.“

Dafür werden auch die künftigen Erfahrungen des Italieners Lucien Gambarota berücksichtigt, der als einer der „Väter“ der Nutzung „menschlicher Energie“ gilt. Gambarota richtete in Hongkong den „California Fitness“-Club ein, wo Sporttreibende immerhin so viel Strom erzeugen, dass damit die Beleuchtung, die Musik und Elektronik der Trainingsgeräte betrieben werden können.

Anfragen aus aller Welt

Im „Club Watt“ geht es nicht allein ums Stromsparen. Im „Club Watt“ ist alles verpönt, was Abfall erzeugt oder unnötig Ressourcen verbraucht. So werden die Toiletten mit Regenwasser gespült. Die eingesparte Wassermenge soll dem Jahresbedarf von 13.000 Menschen entsprechen. Und an den beiden Zero-Waste-Bars (etwa: Null-Müll-Theken) werden Getränke ausschließlich in wiederverwertbare Hartplastikgläser eingeschenkt. Wegwerfprodukte sind verpönt, darunter auch Flyer.

„Den meisten Leuten ist noch gar nicht bewusst, dass normale Discos mit allem drum und dran enorme Stromfresser und Umweltverschmutzer sind“, sagt der Miterfinder des „Club Watt“-Konzepts, Michel Smit. Mit seiner Firma SDC – die Abkürzung steht für Sustainable (nachhaltiger) Dance Club – hofft er auf Aufträge aus aller Welt. Wohl nicht zu unrecht.

Vor Anfragen - darunter auch aus Berlin und anderen deutschen Städten - können sich die „Watt Club“-Macher inzwischen kaum retten. (538 Wörter)

2 Vocabulary → Working with a dictionary, p. 255

Find the German equivalents of the following words in the above text.

illuminated panel • sustainable • environment protection • private investors • electromechanical • vibrations • kinetic energy • to transform • storage battery • bulbs • lighting • taboo • waste • annual consumption • exclusively • recyclable • disposable products • enquiries

3 Mediation → Mediation, p. 245

You are doing an internship at an international event management company in Dublin. Your boss has heard about *Club Watt* and asks you to find out more about it. Use the information in the text and summarise the main points for her in English.

4 Presentation → Presentation, p. 264

It is not only nightclubs which produce a lot of waste and use masses of energy, but any place where many people gather and spend time - for example, your school. How could you make your school greener? Work in small groups and think of some ideas to make your school more environmentally friendly. Present your ideas to the class, using a poster to display your main points.

D Smart homes

1 Before you read
Look at the picture and the headline of the article. What do you think the text is about? Which features would your own smart house have? Why?

1 **to grab** – sich etw. schnappen
2 **kettle** – Wasserkocher
3 **induction coil** – Induktionsspule
5 **to defrost** – auftauen
6 **surface** – Oberfläche
6 **to sense** – *hier:* registrieren
15 **thawing** – tauend
17 **far-fetched** – weit hergeholt
26 **sophisticated** – *hier:* hochentwickelt
27 **real-time** – Echtzeit
27 **monitoring** – Kontrolle, Überwachung
30 **slew** – Menge

BBC | Search [ ] GO

News | Sports | Travel | Weather | TV

Building smart homes of the future

1

You come home after a long, hard day at work. Having grabbed a frozen meal on the way home, you set it down on the coffee table and turn the kettle on. Seems normal, right? Only that your frozen meal has smart packaging and the coffee table has induction coils built in. So that as soon as you set the meal down – anywhere on the table – it starts to defrost the meal and keep it at that temperature. And because the kettle is also powered wirelessly, you can leave it anywhere in the house. The surface senses a kettle has been set down and starts to power it up. The surface is using magnetic fields to heat directly into the metal inside the product, and only the coil, meaning that you will not burn your hand if you put it next to your thawing meal or boiling kettle.

2

That may seem far-fetched, but according to Dave Barman of the US firm Fulton Innovations – which makes this cordless induction-heating technology – we could be only three years away from this being a reality if manufacturers want it to happen. "It's more efficient than gas and electric," he says. "When installed properly, there shouldn't be any cost difference between the traditional method and an induction zone."

3

The smart home of the future, featured in science fiction movies and cartoons like the Jetsons, is almost upon us. While we are not quite at the state of transporters and instant food makers a la Star Trek, our homes are getting smarter and more sophisticated. Real-time monitoring of every aspect of your house is here already, from plumbing to electrics, while companies like Google are trying to get the internet into your TV. But it takes a lot of power to make this happen, and a much more sophisticated approach to home construction, presenting opportunities for a whole slew of companies out there.

4

In the UK, for example, low-energy "green" buildings are extremely uncommon, according to John Alker, head of policy at the UK Green Building Council, an industry body formed by the biggest homebuilders in the country. But this is set to change. The new government has stuck to targets mandating that all new residential homes must be carbon neutral by 2016, with commercial and public buildings to follow three years later.

5

A UK firm, Green Structures, is developing a passive heat recovery system using heat pipes and a thermal accumulator that stores the night's cool or hot air for daytime release, saving both the cost of air-conditioning and winter heating. This technology can also provide savings to the public sector – albeit in macabre ways. Mr Alker says that one council recently announced it was going to warm its swimming pool using wasted heat – from the local crematorium.

6

Fulton Innovations is also trying to reuse wasted energy, by for example having the sensor on urinals powered by the energy of the flush, or a shower radio derive its charge from the shower itself. But this only goes so far. The shower cannot power the washing machine or the heating system, as it would take too much power out of the system. "If you try to push too much power from the plumbing, it goes back to the source," Mr Barman says. "We're not trying to get free energy." That, at least, is a long way off yet. (579 words)

34 **to mandate** – anordnen
34 **residential** – Wohn-
35 **carbon neutral** – CO2-neutral
37 **recovery** – Rückgewinnung
38 **pipe** – Rohr
38 **accumulator** – *hier:* Speicher
39 **release** – Freisetzung
40 **albeit** – obgleich, wenn auch
40 **macabre** – makaber, grausig
44 **urinal** – Pissoir, Urinal
44 **flush** – Spülung
44 **to derive sth. from** – etw. beziehen aus

2 Comprehension: Multiple matching → Scanning, p. 221

a) Read the text and choose from the headings A – H the one which fits each gap. There are two extra headings that you do not need to use.

A Green buildings • **B** Smart but limited • **C** Intelligence at a price • **D** Convenient cooking • **E** Recycling heat • **F** Fiction becoming reality • **G** Hidden dangers • **H** More efficiency, same costs

7 **b)** In your own words, summarise the features that smart homes of the future might have, and the opportunities they could offer.

3 Vocabulary → Working with a dictionary, p. 255

Find one synonym and one antonym for the words below. Use an English-English dictionary if necessary.

smart (l. 3) • properly (l. 22) • traditional (l. 23) • sophisticated (l. 26) • uncommon (l. 31)

4 Analysis → Describing cartoons, p. 242

Describe the cartoon, analyse it and relate it to the text.

5 Project → Hotspot 4, p. 85

"Sorry I'm late. My smart house overslept."

E The next fifty years

1 Before you read

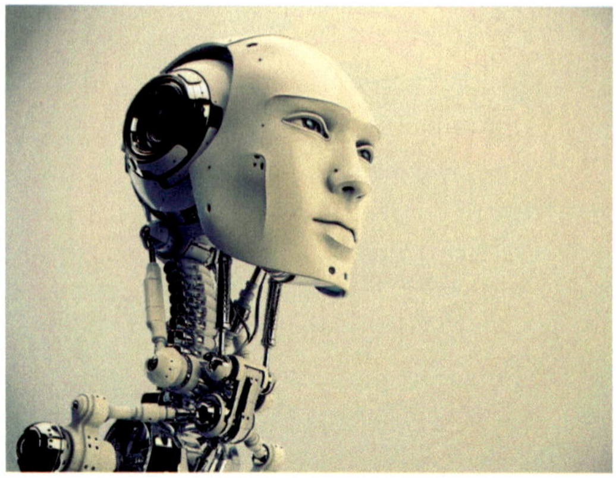

a) Look at the picture and brainstorm adjectives that express how you feel when looking at the cyborg. Agree on five words in your group.

b) Based on the discussion in your group, come up with ten sentences that all begin with "In fifty years' time there will be (won't be) …".

c) Share your adjectives and your sentences with your classmates. Which predictions do you find promising or useful, which ones do you rather find threatening? Explain why?

Promising predictions	Threatening predictions

Five trends that will transform science and technology

Nanotechnology

Nanotech is the hyped technology of the new millennium. It's unlikely to disappoint either, because it's disruptive. Nanotech will affect every industry from aerospace and construction to energy and medicine and will create products that we cannot possibly imagine now. However, public debate about it will be almost invisible until there is a major high-profile nanotechnology accident.

Biotechnology

We had Dolly the cloned sheep in 1996 and since then we've had cloned mice, cows, rabbits, horses and dogs. A human clone can't be far away, although it's unlikely that it will come from a US or Western laboratory. A clone will certainly grab the headlines, but a more threatening concept is perhaps the idea of genetically enhancing humans to strengthen or remove certain traits. There is also the alarming prospect of tests to judge personality or future actions based on genetic makeup and hereditary factors. In the future, everything from careers to relationships will involve genetic issues. Anyone for genetically engineered mosquitoes? How about one that glows in the dark so that you can see it coming? Or what about genetic enhancements and tests for unborn children?

Emotionally aware machines

Much has been written about artificial intelligence, but personally I think that AI in any meaningful sense is a long way off. Having said that, can you imagine the implications if an internet of the future did actually become aware of its own existence? Ohmygawd. As for the foreseeable future, a more immediate driver of change will be emotional intelligence – or emotionally aware machines. In the future we will see cars that link the emotional state of the driver with various safety controls and mood-sensitive features, computers that can tell whether we are

2 **nanotech (nanotechnology)** – Nanotechnologie
2 **hyped** – angesagt, hochgejubelt
3 **disruptive** – bahnbrechend
8 **clone** – Klon
12 **traits** – Charaktermerkmale
14 **hereditary** – Erb-
17 **enhancement** – Verbesserung
22 **foreseeable** – vorhersehbar

in a good mood and voice-recognition systems that can judge if we are king. How about therapeutic robots or radios and televisions that tune into happy programs when we're feeling sad? Or what about online retailers tailoring their home pages, product offerings and even product descriptions to the emotional state of individual customers?

Ethics

Science and, to a lesser extent, technology have always operated within a political context, but until recently they were more or less left alone. Not any more. Both will come under the microscope as society debates not whether something is possible but whether its consequences are desirable. Top of the list of gatekeepers will be government, with its own national and international agenda based on political philosophy, the economy and defense. Privacy will also become a key issue once people realize that computers are everywhere and almost no place on Earth is free from surveillance. No form of communication will be safe. Other people will know who you are, where you are, what you are doing and perhaps even what you are thinking. Privacy in a digital and connected age is dead. Gen Y knows this and doesn't care. Gen X and the Boomer Generation either don't realize or are horrified. In the future we will even debate questions such as whether it is wrong for an adult to love a machine or whether people should marry robots or have sex with them.

Robotics

Robotic soldiers anyone? They're coming, but should such machines feel pain or regret? And if (when) there's an accident, who should be held responsible? Would you trust a robot to administer a general anaesthetic and perform surgery on you? Or what about when someone makes a robot that your child loves more than you? The convergence of a handful of trends is about to transform the field of robotics. First, the cost of computing power (processing and storage) is dropping fast. Second, distributed computing, voice and visual-recognition technologies and wireless broadband connectivity are similarly becoming cheaper and more available. Personal robots will be cleaning floors, dispensing medicine and keeping an eye open for intruders, while industrial robots will operate dangerous machinery and handle hazardous materials. On a smaller scale, robots could carry our bags from the supermarket, work as guide dogs for the visually impaired, or replace care workers in hospitals or nursing homes. Whether a machine will ever fully replace human or animal contact is a big question, to which most people currently answer no. However, attitudes may shift over time. (719 words)

from: Richard Watson, Future files: A brief history of the next 50 years

28 **to tailor** – maßschneidern
35 **gatekeeper** – Türsteher, Kontrolleur
39 **surveillance** – Überwachung
48 **anaesthetic** – Narkosemittel
48 **to perform surgery** – operieren
50 **convergence** – Annäherung, allmähliche Übereinstimmung
52 **visual-recognition** – visuelle Erkennung, biometrische Erkennung
56 **hazardous** – gefährlich
56 **scale** – Ausmaß
57 **impaired** – eingeschränkt, behindert

2 Comprehension: Table completion

Complete your table "Promising predictions – Threatening predictions" with information from the text.

3 Analysis → Text analysis, p. 228

Analysing the language used in this extract, show how the author includes his personal opinion in his predictions about the future and what effect it has on the reader.

4 Listening comprehension: The next fifty years → Listening, p. 221

Listen to the recording and complete your table "Promising predictions – Threatening predictions".

5 Project → Hotspot 5, p. 85

Connectives

Connectives are conjunctions, adverbs or phrases that make the logical link between two clauses or two sentences explicit. Their functions are to indicate, for example, addition, contrast, reinforcement, explanation, the cause or result of something, etc.

a) Complete the statements.

1. Rationalisation and automation meant the introduction of many new machines, so …
2. The Industrial Revolution saw the invention of many machines. Above all, …
3. In the near future nanotechnology will become more important. Presumably …
4. Technology is becoming more complex. Consequently, …
5. Life without sophisticated technology would be less comfortable, but …

b) Odd one out

Find the odd one out, i.e. the word that does not have the same function as the others.

1. moreover – besides – otherwise – furthermore
2. to start with – then – next – so
3. above all – instead of – especially – indeed
4. all in all – moreover – finally – in summary
5. meanwhile – therefore – thus – consequently
6. but – however – still – likewise
7. for instance – for example – such as – except
8. yet – but – above all – however

c) Synonyms

Think of a connective with the same function as the word or phrase given in the left column. Then use the new connective to develop the idea of the prompt given in the right column. Be careful: some connectives are used to link two clauses in the same sentence (a), some connectives are used to begin a new sentence (b).

1. therefore	Hard and dirty work has become unpopular …

Examples:

a. Hard and dirty work has become unpopular, so we have invented a lot of machines.

b. Hard and dirty work has become unpopular. Consequently, we have invented a lot of machines.

2. but	Technology means more comfort …
3. furthermore	More machines meant fewer jobs …
4. as a result	Today's global problems demand intelligent solutions …
5. however	With the help of technology, possibilities seem to be endless …
6. because	Today's technology is extremely complex …

1 Research project: Rationalisation and mechanisation → Internet research, p. 260
Do some research on rationalisation and mechanisation in the past. Here are some aspects you might want to consider:
- Which technology was introduced?
- What was the effect on the labour market?
- How did people react at that time?
- How is this development seen today?

2 Research project: Stem cell research → Internet research, p. 260
Find out more about stem cell research. Make sure that you include the following aspects in your presentation: pros and cons of stem cell research, arguments of supporters and opponents, government positions, current projects. Feel free to add any aspects you have strong opinions about.

3 Project: Organ donation → Projects and group work, p. 261

a) In groups of about four, do one of the following tasks:
- Design a brochure or poster informing people about organ transplants and trying to persuade them to give their consent to being a potential donor.
- Design a brochure or poster against organ donations, pointing out dangers and ethical concerns, and trying to get people to withhold their consent to being a potential donor.

b) Present your results in class and discuss your own attitudes towards organ donation.

Finding information

Check the websites of the following organizations and institutions:
Deutsche Stiftung Organtransplantation • Organspende (Bundeszentrale für gesundheitliche Aufklärung) • UK Transplant • The BBC (Health section) • The US Government of Organ & Tissue Donation and Transplantation

4 Project: The home of tomorrow → Projects and group work, p. 261
You have been asked to design the "home of tomorrow" as part of an international architecture competition. Think about the features the house would have and what it might look like. Prepare a poster or an information flyer and present your ideas to the class.

5 Project: Panel discussion → Projects and group work, p. 261
Prepare a panel discussion of the question: "Have we become dependent on technology in our lives?" Before you start, decide on roles that should be included in your discussion. Then collect arguments to prepare for the roles.

6 Research project: HIV / AIDS
Work in small groups. Create an information leaflet about AIDS/HIV including the following information: Definition of the illness, ways of contraction and symptoms, protection and treatment, research on possible cures, etc.

A 2.37

0 **fluorescent** – glowing
0 **feline** – cat
0 **to aid** – to support
0 **kitten** – young cat
1 **rite of passage** – ritual performed for change of status
2 **sufficiently** – enough for a particular purpose
23 **jellyfish** – a sea creature with a jelly-like, bell-shaped body that is typically transparent and has stinging tentacles around the edge
25 **to illuminate** – to light up
28 **to monitor** – to observe
29 **refinement** – improvement

theguardian

News | Sport | Comment | Culture | Business | Money | Life&Style | Travel | Environment

Comment is free > Research > Search GO

Glow cat: fluorescent green felines could help study of HIV

Scientists hope cloning technique that produced genetically modified cats will aid human and feline medical research

A 'glow in the dark' kitten viewed under a special blue light. The fur looks normal under regular light.

It is a rite of passage for any sufficiently advanced genetically modified animal: at some point scientists will insert a gene that makes you glow green. The latest addition to this ever-growing list – which includes fruit flies, mice, rabbits and pigs – is the domestic cat.

US researcher Eric Poeschla has produced three glowing GM cats by using a virus to carry a gene, called green fluorescent protein (GFP), into the eggs from which the animals eventually grew.

This method of genetic modification is simpler and more efficient than traditional cloning techniques, and results in fewer animals being needed in the process.

The GFP gene, which has its origins in jellyfish, expresses proteins that fluoresce when illuminated with certain frequencies of light. Poeschla, of the Mayo Clinic in Rochester, Minnesota, reported his results in the journal *Nature Methods*.

This function is regularly used by scientists to monitor the activity of individual genes or cells in a wide variety of animals. The development and refinement of the GFP technique earned its scientific pioneers the Nobel Prize for chemistry in 2008. In the case of the glowing cats, the scientists hope to use the GM animals in the study of HIV/Aids.

"Cats are susceptible to feline immunodeficiency virus [FIV], a close relative of HIV, the cause of Aids," said professors Helen Sang and Bruce Whitelaw of the Roslin Institute at the University of Edinburgh, where scientists cloned Dolly the sheep in 1996.

"The application of the new technology suggested in this paper is to develop the use of genetically-modified cats for the study of FIV, providing valuable information for the study of Aids."

"This is potentially valuable but the uses of genetically modified cats as models for human diseases are likely to be limited and only justified if other models – for example in more commonly used laboratory animals, like mice and rats – are not suitable."

Dr Robin Lovell-Badge, head of developmental genetics at the Medical Research Council's national institute for medical research, said: "Cats are one of the few animal species that are normally susceptible to such viruses, and indeed they are subject to a pandemic, with symptoms as devastating to cats as they are to humans." "Understanding how to confer resistance is … of equal importance to cat health and human health." (406 words)

33 **susceptible to** – prone to
33 **immunodeficiency** – immune system defect
38 **valuable** – very important
41 **justified** – legitimate
42 **commonly** – often
43 **suitable** – appropriate
47 **pandemic** – worldwide epidemic
47 **devastating** – very harmful
48 **to confer** – to transfer

1 Comprehension

a) Outline the process that creates a 'glow cat'.

b) Describe why cats could be useful in the study of HIV.

2 Analysis → Describing cartoons, p. 242

Describe and analyse the cartoon.

3 Comment

"This method of genetic modification […] results in fewer animals being needed in the process." (ll. 16–21) Many medical, pharmaceutical and cosmetic studies use animal testing. Do you think it is acceptable to use animals for research in this way? Discuss.

4 Research project

→ Hotspot 6, p. 85

Topic 6

ep5225

The impact of change

A

B

C

D

Getting started

1 **Study the words in the word bank and check their meanings.**

2 **Describe the pictures. What do they stand for? Relate the words in the word bank to the pictures. What have they got to do with the impact of change?**
→ Describing pictures, p. 241

3 **Work in small groups. Agree on five terms which you consider very important when talking about change. For each term, start and complete a word web.**
→ Word webs, p. 251

4 **The table on p. 89 shows some groundbreaking inventions and innovations.**

a) For each of them, say why it stands for change. Use words from your word web to help you.

b) Which inventions or innovations should be added to the list, and which should be removed? Give reasons.

Word bank

automation • shiftwork • mass production • progress • working conditions • rationalisation • work-life balance • demographic change • virtual reality • 24-hour society • machines • impact • online

Invention / Innovation	Year	Invention / Innovation	Year
wheelchair	1595	non-figurative art	1910
art auction	late 17th century	assemby line	1913
ball bearing	1794	stainless steel	1914
battery, electricity storage	1800	television	1923 / 1927
food canning	1809	frozen food	1924
kindergarten	1837	blood bank	late 1930s
refrigerator	1842	credit card	1950
jeans	1873	cardiac pacemaker	1952
shift work	large scale after the invention of the light bulb in 1879	botox	1967
airconditioning	1902	Internet	1969
decaffeinated coffee	1905	mobile phone	1973
convenience food	1905	virtual reality	1989
electric washing machine	1907	eBay	1995

5 a) List five things that you believe really made the world a better place. Explain your choice.

b) List five things which have at least as many negative as positive effects. Give reasons.

08 △ **6** **Describe and analyse the cartoon.**
→ Describing cartoons, p. 242

7 **Project** → Hotspot 1, p. 101

A Convenience food

1 Before you read → Questionnaires and surveys, p. 262
What type of convenience food (i.e. food that has been industrially prepared so that it requires very little preparation time) do you consume and how often? Interview at least three students about their eating habits and report back to the class.

theguardian

News | Sport | Comment | Culture | Business | Money | Life&Style | Travel | Environment

Comment is free > Society > Search GO

The rise and rise of convenience food

The news that Heinz is developing ready-made beans on toast has sent Britain reeling. But is it with horror – or delight? What is it about ready meals, dinner in a can and tea granules that keeps us coming back for more? Tim Dowling reports

This was the gist of the news: baked beans on toast, Britain's most popular convenience food, was about to get even more convenient. "Instant" baked beans on toast, a frozen, fused sandwich that goes in the toaster, is to be tested by Heinz in New Zealand and if successful, launched in the UK. It's the subject that everyone is talking about, but you have to ask: why are they doing it? [...]

A classic TV Dinner of fried chicken, mashed potatoes and corn.

Once upon a time convenience foods consisted largely of ready-made or at least easy-to-make versions of foodstuffs which had a reputation for being difficult to produce from scratch. Instant gravy and custard powder were nothing like their real-life counterparts, but they came out roughly the right colour. Baked beans were introduced to the UK in 1905; the first frozen foods appeared in 1937. The US company Swanson paved the way for the modern-day ready meal when it introduced the TV dinner in 1954, selling 10 million the first year the product went national. The next year saw the introduction of the fish finger to Britain. Certain popular dishes from the heyday of convenience food, such as faggots in gravy, blancmange and chicken kiev, are now best known in their frozen, tinned or reconstituted form.

Britain was meant to have turned a corner in terms of its attitude to food. Farmers' markets are springing up everywhere. A chastened Jamie Oliver has brought the woeful state of the nation's school dinners to public attention. Manufacturers have been pressured into reducing the salt content of processed foods, and everybody is meant to understand the importance of fresh, healthy, simply prepared meals. And yet Britain now spends £900m in a year on ready meals, with 31,000 more of them bought every month than a year ago.

0 **convenience food** – Fertiggerichte
1 **to send sb. reeling** – *hier:* jmdn in Aufruhr bringen
8 **fused** – schmelzflüssig
11 **to launch** – *hier:* auf den Markt bringen
18 **from scratch** – grundlegend
18 **instant gravy** – Fertigsoße
18 **custard powder** – Pulver für Vanillesoße
20 **to pave the way** – den Weg bereiten
22 **fish finger** – Fischstäbchen
23 **heyday** – Blütezeit, Hochzeit
23 **faggot** – Frikadelle
24 **blancmange** [blə'mɒnʒ] – Pudding, Flammeri
24 **to reconstitute** – wiederherstellen
25 **to turn a corner** – über den Berg kommen / sein
26 **to chasten** – züchtigen
26 **woeful** – traurig, elend
28 **processed foods** – industriell verarbeitetes Lebensmittel

Sales of baked beans, meanwhile, have risen by 13% since 2001 and are expected to increase by another 30% in the next five years. Spam is enjoying an unlikely resurgence in sales, as is canned pasta and tinned corned beef. Roast beef and yorkshire pudding, steak and kidney pie, even omelette and chips - there's almost nothing you can't get in a can. Sales of tinned food have risen 10% in the past year, to reach £660m. Perhaps it's a mark of patriotism: it was a British merchant, Peter Durand, who patented the tin can in 1810, and two Britons, John Hall and Bryan Dorkin, who opened the first commercial canning factory three years later. [...]

But does the convenience outweigh the cost? How busy do you have to be to need precooked rice? What are you going to do with the extra nine minutes? Let's bear in mind that rice simmering on the stove does not require the sort of concentration that's going to spoil the last bit of EastEnders. The value added here, from the consumer's point of view, is virtually nil. The cost, however, is considerable. Ordinary, unadulterated, precooked rice sells at about £5 per kilo, as opposed to 84p for the normal, just-add-water-and-cook sort. [...]

Inevitably a lot of this stuff is targeted at children, and the lessons it presents are dreadful. For a start, it teaches them that cooking is a loathsome chore, and that time spent cooking is time wasted. It teaches them that unpackaged, perishable, non-value-added food is inherently undesirable, that cheese string is cheese and that a Pot Noodle with a bit less salt in it is some kind of healthy option. At a point when we are meant to be revamping our thinking about food, we are actually coming up with bizarre convenience versions of convenience foods. On my last trip to the supermarket I saw ready-made six packs of jelly which don't seem to require any form of refrigeration to stop them going gloopy. Few of us have the time or resources to produce gourmet meals from the finest, freshest ingredients every day of the week, but if you can't be bothered to make your own jelly you haven't got any business having a kitchen.

(726 words)

32 **spam** – Frühstücksfleisch
32 **resurgence** – Wiederauferstehung
37 **canning factory** – Konservenfabrik
40 **to simmer** – köcheln
40 **to spoil** – verderben
41 **EastEnders** – populäre britische Fernsehserie
42 **unadulterated** – unverfälscht
44 **to target at sb.** – auf jmdn gerichtet sein
45 **a loathsome chore** – eine mühselige Aufgabe
46 **perishable** – verderblich
46 **inherently** – an sich, von Natur aus
48 **to revamp** – aufpolieren
50 **jelly** – Götterspeise
51 **gloopy** – matschig

2 Comprehension

a) Summarise the history of convenience food as mentioned in the article.

b) Outline the basic facts the text provides about convenience food today.

c) In your own words, summarise the arguments against convenience food mentioned by the author.

3 Analysis → Text analysis, p. 228

Analyse the way the text is written (structure, choice of words) and show how Tim Dowling tries to influence the readers of his opinion about convenience food.

4 Text production: Writing a letter/an email → Writing an email, p. 231

"Few of us have the time or resources to produce gourmet meals from the finest, freshest ingredients every day of the week, but if you can't be bothered to make your own jelly you haven't got any business having a kitchen." (ll. 51 – 53)
Write a letter / an email to the editor in which you comment on the final sentence of the newspaper article.

5 Research project → Hotspot 2, p. 101

B Lifelong learning

1 Before you read → Brainstorming, p. 253

a) Brainstorm reasons why elderly people decide to attend a computer class. Which other classes do older people you know take?

b) Explain the title of the article "Lifelong learning is the secret to happiness in old age" in your own words.

c) In how far does learning in old and young age differ?

theguardian

News | Sport | Comment | Culture | Business | Money | Life&Style | Travel | Environment

Comment is free > Society   Search [ ] GO

Lifelong learning is the secret to happiness in old age

Not only can learning during the later stages of life bring happiness, wellbeing and a connection to the wider community for those studying, it can also reduce dependency on welfare. […]

McNair, a semi-retired National Institute of Adult Continuing Education research fellow, says that in all the guidance about wellbeing, education is central. "[It is] particularly important for those in the latter stages of life when one is less mobile and having to cope with the death of partners and friends: getting out of bed and feeling one has a purpose can be particularly challenging."

This is clearly not an issue for 84-year-old Jim Kelly, winner of an Adult Learners' Week award in 2010, who has in recent years dedicated himself to a wide range of study – everything from gardening to the 1688 "glorious revolution". After school days blighted by poverty and bullying teachers, the impetus to study came from his granddaughter Becky who, as a two-year-old, grew frustrated with his inability to answer her questions. "Don't you know anything granddad?" she would ask. Now, 14 years later, he tells the teenager he's pleased she asked that question.

Evidence of the benefits of learning during the latter stages of life is overwhelming, from research by the Alzheimer's Society showing delayed onset of the disease, to reduced dependency on welfare support.

Melissa March is executive director of Learning for the Fourth Age, a charity dedicated to bringing trained volunteers into care settings where they work with residents. "Our volunteers help people with everything from recovering piano-playing after strokes to wanting to tackle Welsh for the first time," she explains. "There is lots of interest too in IT and the connections that email can bring. Our work helps break down older people's fears about young people and opens our volunteers' eyes to the lives of older people with very different experiences from their own." […]

John Salinas, at 91, is also embracing IT. Each week he drives to his computing class and has progressed rapidly from not even knowing how to plug in his laptop, to using digital photography. "John is an inspiration in the learning group of over-60s participants by being an example of

5 **dependency** – Abhängigkeit
6 **semi-retired** – in Altersteilzeit
7 **research fellow** – Forschungsbeauftragte(r)
8 **guidance** – Anleitung, Beratung
10 **latter** – letztere(r/s)
15 **to dedicate oneself to sth.** – sich einer Sache widmen
16 **blighted** – vereitelt
17 **impetus** – Schwung, Elan
21 **onset** – *hier:* Ausbruch
25 **stroke** – Schlaganfall
25 **to tackle** – in Angriff nehmen
29 **to embrace** – belegen, einbeziehen

someone committed to learn, and not letting age or knowledge be a barrier to 'getting digital'," says Iona Gibbons, a community learning development worker with Bath and North East Somerset county council.

Sharing with friends

For John, the benefits of lifelong learning are clear – the weekly classes have given him a new zest for life. "I want to remain active in myself for my own health but also access all the information that is on computers, to benefit from community opportunities and to meet other people who are in the same boat as me," he says. "I see my computer learning as now firmly part of my life and can share what I learn with my family and show them what I can do."

For 84-year-old Len Street, a committed contributor to the University of the Third Age (U3A) since its creation 19 years ago, it is the companionship while learning that leads to a healthier life. He currently runs opera and art-history study groups. "When people leave work it is often the company of others they miss most – education in older age can be a lifesaver."

The value of learning is no exaggeration, says Fiona Aldridge, Niace programme director and author of a recent report into lifelong learning in care settings. "The benefits of ensuring that ongoing learning is a part of a care package is hard to deny when one learns of some of the best practice in this area. It has significant benefits in terms of improving people's mental health and reducing their reliance on medication." (629 words)

32 **committed** – entschlossen
36 **zest** – Eifer
43 **opera** – Oper
45 **exaggeration** – Übertreibung
46 **care** – Pflege
47 **best practice** – Positivbeispiel
48 **mental health** – geistige Gesundheit
49 **reliance** – Verlass
49 **medication** – Medikation, medizinische Behandlung

2 Comprehension

In your own words, summarise the benefits of lifelong learning according to the text.

209 △ **3 Analysis** → Text analysis, p. 228

Analyse the function of quotes in the text "Lifelong learning is the secret to happiness in old age."

4 Mediation → Mediation, p. 245

Summarise the following German text in about 130 words in English.

Lebenslanges Lernen: Studie bescheinigt Deutschland nur Mittelmaß

In Deutschland sind die Voraussetzungen für das lebenslange Lernen im Vergleich zu anderen europäischen Ländern nur mittelmäßig. Zu diesem Ergebnis kommt eine Studie der Bertelsmann Stiftung, die dem SPIEGEL exklusiv vorliegt. Der Grund: Investitionen in Schulen und Hochschulen seien zu gering.

Bei einer europäischen Bildungsstudie der Bertelsmann Stiftung hat Deutschland ein mittelmäßiges Ergebnis erreicht: Die Bundesrepublik bleibt bei einem Vergleich des „Lernklimas" deutlich hinter Dänemark, Schweden, den Niederlanden und Finnland zurück. Diese Länder hätten „in Europa bislang am besten die Idee vom lebenslangen Lernen in die Tat umgesetzt". […]

Aus den vielen Zahlen errechneten die Forscher mehrere Rankings. Deutschland erreicht dabei insgesamt einen Platz nur knapp über dem Durchschnitt. Das mäßige Abschneiden ergibt sich laut den Fachleuten vor allem daraus, dass die Bundesrepublik vergleichsweise wenig Geld in Schulen und Hochschulen investiere. […]

Die Forscher entdeckten zahlreiche Zusammenhänge zwischen einem guten Lernklima in einem Staat und dem Wohlstand oder dem Wohlergehen dort. Staaten mit einem hohen Wert auf der Bildungsskala zeichneten sich unter anderem dadurch aus, dass dort Korruption weniger verbreitet ist, mehr Vertrauen in politische Institutionen herrscht und die Gefahr der Armut niedriger liegt.

Ein Fazit der Studie: „Lernen macht reich, produktiv und wettbewerbsfähig". Außerdem würden der „gesellschaftliche Zusammenhalt" und das „gesellschaftliche Grundvertrauen" gefördert. […]

Weil sich Investitionen in Bildung nur langfristig auszahlten, würden ihre positiven Effekte allerdings häufig unterschätzt, beklagte die OECD. (228 Wörter)

5 Project → Hotspot 3, p. 101

C Health education

1 Before you read → Brainstorming, p. 253

a) Brainstorm important aspects that contribute to a healthy lifestyle. Agree on a definition of a "healthy lifestyle".

b) Collect ideas about how these aspects can be taught to children.

c) Do you live a healthy life? Explain why (not).

A 2.39

Life123 *Answer at the speed of life*

Search GO

Arts | Beauty | Career | Vehicles | Hobbies | Food | Health | Entertaining | Home

Teaching children about living a healthy lifestyle

Teaching children about living a healthy lifestyle is not as hard as you may think. As parents, you should model the lifestyles you want your child to follow. Living an active way of life and eating healthy foods will help your child stay fit. People joke about being a couch potato, but the truth is that a sedentary lifestyle leads to unhealthy habits. Jump off the couch and jumpstart your child's way to a healthy life. If you and your child spend a lot of time in front of the TV or computer screen, shut it off. One hour of activity each day is a good starting point. Introducing a variety of activities is important. It cuts down on the number of

2 **model** – *hier:* Vorbild
4 **sedentary** – bewegungsarm
5 **to jumpstart** – auf die Sprünge helfen

times you hear "I'm bored" and it develops a broader scope of skills. Take a walk, play a game, ride a bicycle. Participation in a team sport not only enhances physical development, it also builds self-esteem and teamwork. Being active as a family will also increase your child's activity level. If you find it difficult to keep your child engaged, consider motivation techniques. Reward charts and recognition of achievements provide evidence of your child's growth and development. Plus, your child can take ownership and track his improvements. [...] (216 words)

9 **scope** – Spektrum
10 **to enhance** – verbessern
13 **reward** – Belohnung
14 **evidence** – Beweis

2 Comprehension

a) In your own words summarise the advice given by the author on how to live a healthy life.

b) Outline the role of parents according to the text.

3 Listening comprehension: Healthy eating → Listening, p. 221

Listen to the second part of the text and answer the following questions:

a) What does a balanced diet include?

b) How much fruit and vegetables do young children and teenagers need?

c) What are examples of 'healthy snacks'?

d) Which drinks should be avoided and which are recommended?

4 Mediation → Describing diagrams, p. 243, Mediation, p. 245

Summarise and explain the two German diagrams below in a short English text.

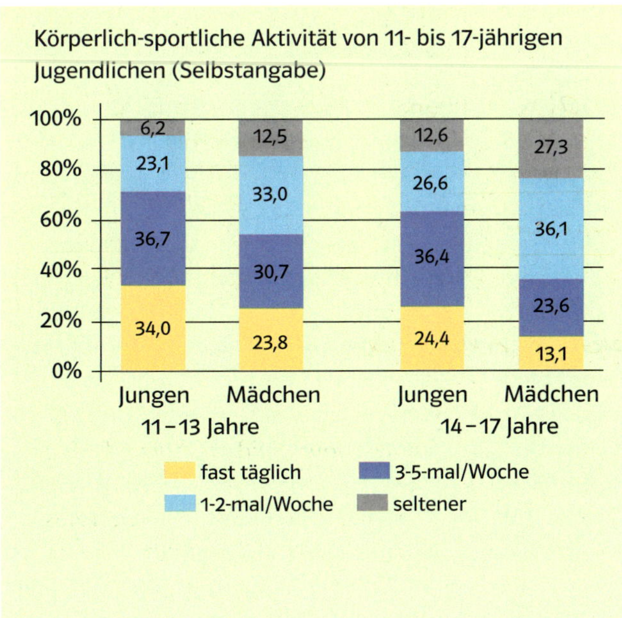

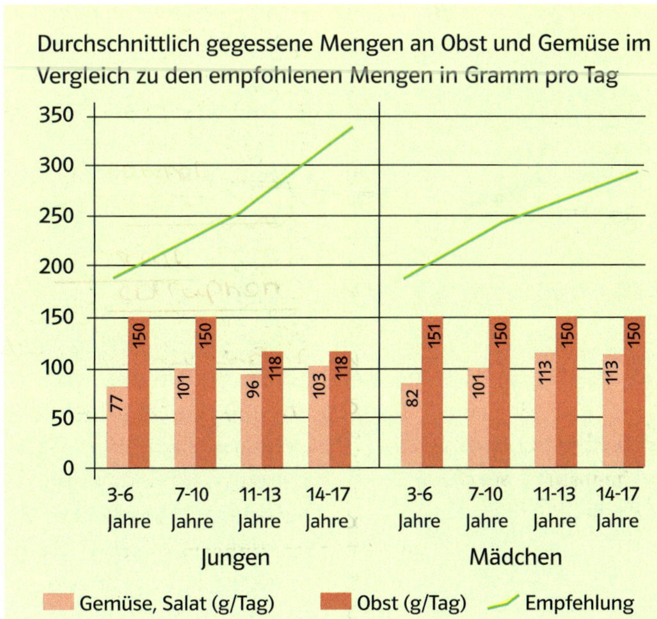

Source: Robert-Koch-Institut

D Digital media

1 Before you read → Brainstorming, p. 253
Compare your own use of media with that of your parents. Note down your ideas and share them with the class.

1 **native** – Ureinwohner(in)
9 **to transform** – umwandeln
18 **essential** – notwendig, wesentlich
23 **immigrant** – Einwanderer
24 **to come to terms with sth.** – mit etw. zurechtkommen
24 **to rule** – herrschen, regieren
36 **to indulge in** – sich etw. hingeben
39 **stimuli** *pl (sg* stimulus) – Anregung, (An-)Reiz
40 **scary** – Angst machend, erschreckend
42 **to chart** – vermessen, skizzieren
47 **attention span** – Aufmerksamkeitsspanne
48 **gnat** – Stechmücke

THE SUNDAY TI

The next step in brain evolution

Emily Feld is a native of a new planet. While the 20-year-old student may appear to live in London, she actually spends much of her time in another galaxy – out there, in the digital universe of websites, e-mails, text messages and mobile phone calls. **1** It may even be the next step in evolution, transforming brains and the way we think.

"The other day, I went to meet a friend in town, when I realised I'd left my mobile phone at home. I travelled the five miles back to collect it. I panicked. I need to have it on me at all times. I sound really sad, but everyone I know is the same. Technology is an essential part of my everyday social and academic life. I don't know where I'd be without it. I've never really been without it."

2 Her mother, Christine, on the other hand, is a 'digital immigrant', still coming to terms with a culture ruled by the ring of a mobile and the zip of e-mails. Though 55-year-old Christine happily shops online and e-mails friends, at heart she's still in the old world. "Children today are multi-tasking left, right and centre – downloading tracks, uploading photos, sending e-mails. It's nonstop," she says. "They find sitting down and reading, even watching TV, too slow and boring. I can't imagine many kids indulging in one particular hobby such as birdwatching, like they used to."

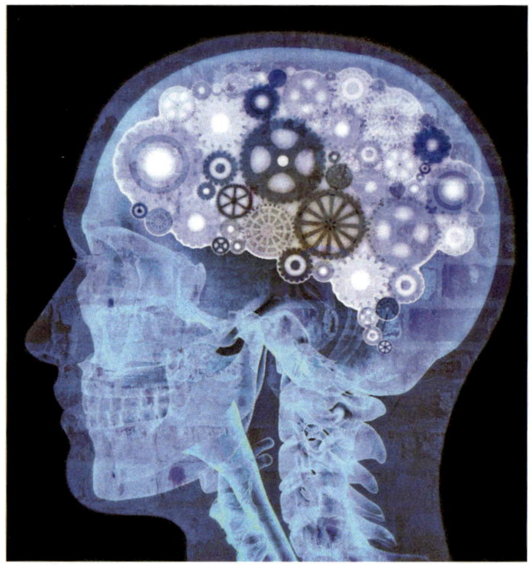

3 To some, a world flooded with endless info bits and constant stimuli is scary; to others it is full of possibility and fascinating questions. Are digital natives charting a new course for human intelligence? And if so, is it better, faster, smarter? Many parents still fear that children who spend hours glued to computer screens will end up nerdy zombies with the attention span of a gnat. But it need not be like that, say some experts.

4 "Is this a different way of thinking? Well, a bit. [...] People are becoming more visual than verbal." [...]
The mass of visual, auditory and verbal information in the modern world is forcing digital natives to make choices that those who grew up with only books and television did not. "Younger people filter more," says Helen Petrie, a professor of human-computer interaction at the University of York. "But I don't think attention spans are diminishing per se. If we find something that is engaging, then our attention span is just as long as it has always been." [...]
Where is it all leading? 5 [...] Faster broadband speeds, easier interfaces, smaller hardware – innovation is happening at such a pace that what was science fiction a few years ago is looming as fact. (538 words)

54 **auditory** – auditiv, mit dem Gehör wahrnehmbar
57 **to make choices** – Entscheidungen treffen
63 **to diminish** – kleiner werden
64 **per se** – an sich
65 **engaging** – einnehmend, faszinierend
69 **interface** – Schnittstelle
71 **pace** – Geschwindigkeit, Gangart
73 **to loom** – sich abzeichnen

2 Comprehension: Multiple matching

Read the text and choose from the sentences A – F the one which fits each gap (1-5). There is one extra sentence that you do not need to use.

A	This generational divide has been evident for a while, but only now is its impact becoming clear.
B	Only one thing seems clear: changes propelled by the digital world are just beginning.
C	Research shows that children between 7 and 11 spend up to five hours a day playing computer games.
D	"Computer games can improve some aspects of attention, such as the ability to quickly count objects," says Dr Anders Sandberg, who is researching "cognitive enhancement" at Oxford University.
E	The behaviour of Feld and her generation, say experts, is being shaped by digital technology as never before.
F	That's what makes Emily a 'digital native', one who has never known a world without instant communication.

evident – erwiesen, offensichtlich
impact – Auswirkung
cognitive enhancement – Wahrnehmungssteigerung
to shape – formen
instant – sofortig

3 Mediation → Mediation, p. 245

Erstellen Sie auf Deutsch eine Liste aller im Text genannten Auswirkungen, die die digitalen Medien auf die junge Generation haben. Schreiben Sie vollständige Sätze.

4 Comment: Choose one of the following tasks

a) "[...], innovation is happening at such a pace that what was science fiction a few years ago is looming as fact." (ll. 70 – 73)
Comment on this quotation from the text by giving examples of inventions for which this is true, and examples of inventions that still seem impossible today.

b) Explain how digital innovations have changed the world of work in the past decades.

5 Research project → Hotspot 4, p. 101

Ben Elton (English writer and comedian, born in 1959)

0 **contestant** – Teilnehmer(in) an einem Wettbewerb
0 **surveillance** – Überwachung
0 **to evict** – *hier:* ausschließen

1 **to drawl** – gedehnt sprechen
1 **distinguished** – angesehen, bedeutend
4 **baying crowd** – johlende Menge
5 **to vanquish** – bezwingen
6 **poll** – Umfrage
7 **to leech off** – sich wie ein Parasit von etw. ernähren
8 **loftily** – arrogant, von oben herab
11 **shadow minister for home affairs** – Schatteninnenminister
16 **to deny** – verweigern
17 **overwhelming** – überwältigend
19 **crucial** – entscheidend
22 **genuine** – echt, aufrichtig
25 **to grieve** – trauern

E New TV culture

1 Before you read

Many television viewers are obsessed with a new TV culture that focuses on reality and casting shows. Choose any reality or casting show you know and explain why it is popular among viewers. Why do people take part in such shows? Would you want to take part in them?

The following text is a passage from "Dead famous", a novel by Ben Elton. 'House Arrest' is a television show in which ten contestants are forced to live together under constant camera surveillance. In the course of the show, the contestants can nominate each other to be evicted from the show. One day, Kelly, one of the 'inmates', is found murdered on the toilet. The television producers decide to air a ninety-minute special edition including the lead-up to the murder, the murder itself and a live discussion programme "about the morality of their having continued to broadcast the show at all".

Murder on air

"Reality television, as it is called," drawled the distinguished broadcaster, "is a return to the gladiatorial arenas of ancient Rome. What we are watching is conflict, conflict between trapped and desperate antagonists who compete for the approval of the baying crowd. Like the plebeians of old, we raise and lower our thumbs to applaud the victor and condemn the vanquished. The only difference is that today we do it via a telephone poll."

Geraldine shifted in her seat. She hated the way supposed intellectuals leeched off popular culture while loftily condemning it.

"Personally," the distinguished broadcaster continued, "I am astonished that it has taken so long for murder to become a tactic in these entertainments."

"Yes, but does that justify its being broadcast?" the shadow minister for home affairs leapt in, angry that the discussion had been underway for two minutes and that he had yet to speak. "I say most definitely not. We have to ask ourselves what sort of country we wish to live in."

"And I would agree with you," said the distinguished poet, "but will you have the courage to deny the mob? The public must have its bread and circuses."

Geraldine swallowed an overwhelming desire to unleash a four-letter tirade and resolved to be reasonable. That was, after all, why she had come on the show. The last thing she needed at this crucial moment in her career was to be taken off the air.

"Look," she said. "I don't like what has happened here any more than you do."

"Really?" sniffed the poet. [...]

"There is a genuine public interest here in what is, after all is said and done, a major public event. The audience feel, I think legitimately, that they are part of this murder. In many ways they feel some responsibility for it. They have been shocked and traumatized. They are grieving and they need to heal. They need to remain connected to what is happening in order to begin that healing process. We cannot suddenly cut

2 Comprehension: Table completion
How does Geraldine, one of the show's producers, justify showing Kelly's murder on TV? What are her real reasons? Collect the relevant information from the text and complete the following table:

Reasons stated by Geraldine	Geraldine's real reasons
genuine public interest in major public event …	…

3 Analysis
Characterise Geraldine as she appears in this extract.

4 Projects → Hotspots 5 and 6, p. 101

them out of the loop. Kelly was much loved, an enormously popular contestant. She truly was the people's housemate, and in many ways this is the people's murder."

It was a brilliant, jaw-droppingly audacious gambit, and totally unexpected. Everybody knew that the real reason Geraldine and the channel wanted to continue broadcasting was money, pure and simple. The stark truth was that Kelly's murder had turned House Arrest from a moderately successful programme into a television colossus. Episode twenty-six, the last to be shown before the murder, had achieved a 17 per cent audience share. The episode that had just been broadcast, the one that included the murder, had been watched by almost 80 per cent of the viewing public. Almost half of the entire population. Thirty-second advert slots in one of the three commercial breaks had sold at fifteen times their normal price.

"To prevent further broadcasts would be entirely élitist," Geraldine continued. "What we would be saying is that we know what is good for the public. We, the high and mighty, the great and the good, will decide what the proles can be trusted to watch. That is totally unacceptable in a modern democracy. Besides which, let me remind you that this event has already been live on the Internet. It's already part of the culture. It is already out there. Do you condone the social disenfranchisement of people who do not own a computer? Are they to be denied their chance to grieve? To come to terms with Kelly's death just because they are not on-line?"

Even the distinguished poet and broadcaster was caught off balance by such a breathtaking display. […]

"As I believed I implied," he said, "in many ways this event crosses the Rubicon in the democratization of the human experience. Reality television has already shown us that privacy is a myth, an unwanted cloak which people eagerly discard like a heavy garment on a summer's day. Death was the last truly private event, but thanks to House Arrest it is private no longer. In our open, meritocratic age, no human experience need be seen as 'better' or more 'significant' than any other, and that includes the final one. If Kelly had the right to be seen living, then surely we must grant her the right to be seen dying."

(724 words)

27 **to be in the loop** – auf dem Laufenden sein
29 **jaw-droppingly** – umwerfend
29 **audacious** – kühn
29 **gambit** – Schachzug
43 **disenfranchisement** – Entrechtung
46 **to be caught off balance** – überrascht werden
50 **cloak** – Umhang
50 **to discard** – wegwerfen, abwerfen
52 **a meritocratic age** – ein Zeitalter, in dem Leistung belohnt wird

Improving your style

Complex structures are characteristic of written language. You can link different ideas by combining a main clause with subordinate clauses such as conditional clauses or relative clauses. Another way of forming complex sentences is by using gerund or participle constructions.
Gerunds and present participles are easy to confuse because they both look similar (-ing form). The basic difference is that a gerund functions as a noun while a participle describes another word in the sentence. The past participle is formed like the simple past in regular verbs, in irregular verbs it is the third form of the verb.

Examples:
The smart phone's most useful function is **connecting** its user to the Internet, anytime anywhere. → Here *connecting* is a gerund which has the function of a noun.

The smart phone started **uploading** my photos onto Facebook as soon as it connected to my laptop. → In this case, *uploading* is a (present) participle describing what the smart phone was doing.

The pictures **uploaded** by my smart phone are always of good quality. → The past participle *uploaded* is used here as a shortened relative clause (for "The pictures which are uploaded …").

a) Determine whether the -ing form in the following sentences is a gerund or a present participle construction, and identify the past participles.

1. In computer classes, elderly people learn new skills, allowing them to keep up with technological changes.
2. Designed by innovative developers, the smart phone is not only smart, but also stylish.
3. The *Volkshochschule* is one of the German institutions offering lifelong learning for everyone.
4. In the UK, an even wider range of convenience foods will soon be sold, making life easier for working mothers.
5. Living to the age of 100 will have become the norm by the year 2050.
6. The celebrity world depicted in the media is often based on gossip and rumours.

b) Rephrase the participle constructions (present and past participles) by changing them into subordinate clauses, or make two sentences out of the one sentence.

c) Rewrite the following sentences. Link the two ideas by using a gerund or a participle construction.

1. The new heating system heats your rooms automatically. It does not use much energy.
2. With your automated vacuum cleaner you don't have to clean the floor yourself anymore. You can relax instead.
3. My smart phone wakes me up every morning. I am very grateful.
4. Don't just press the 'start' button. You must always read the instructions first.
5. You can live longer. Just eat healthily.
6. The dinner party went well. My new food processor did everything for me.

1 Project: Songs about change → Projects and group work, p. 261
Work in groups of 4–6. There are many songs that are called "change" or which have got this word in their title.

a) Make a list of songs. Prepare to present these songs (lyrics, music, etc.) to the class.

b) Which topics that have to do with change do they deal with in particular?

c) Bring along pictures that represent the topics and the aspects mentioned in the songs.

d) Prepare posters that show your understanding and interpretation of these songs.

e) Present the posters to the class.

2 Research project: Change → Internet research, p. 260

a) Agree on one topic which in your opinion most strongly represents change (i.e. the Internet, working conditions, family structures, etc.)

b) Make a list of four to five sub-topics which are essential for the overall topic.

c) Go online and collect information about these sub-topics in the past and at present.

d) Compare and analyse your findings.

e) Forecast the importance of this topic for 2050 and explain your reasons.

Finding information

Look for information on the Internet. Use a search engine and try the following search words:
guardian.co.uk • mirror.co.uk • independent.co.uk • sundaymirror.co.uk • bigissue.com • sundaysun.co.uk • theherald.co.uk • British newspapers • American newspapers

3 Project: Further education classes → Projects and group work, p. 261
Make a flyer with the aim of attracting senior citizens to take part in further education classes. Include information from the texts in this topic and your own research results. Present your flyers to your classmates.

4 Research project: Mass media → Internet research, p. 260
Research the development of the mass media (books, newspapers, the cinema, radio, television, computer technology, the Internet) and draw up a timeline.
Make assumptions about the future of different forms of mass media.

5 Project: Panel discussion → Discussions, p. 246
Think of at least six interest groups that might have strong opinions on the question whether the show should have been stopped after Kelly's murder.
Form groups that represent each of these interest groups. Also nominate two chair-persons to lead the discussion.

6 Project: A new TV show → Projects and group work, p. 261
Create a concept for a new TV show, e.g. game show, reality show, talent show etc.
Present it to the class and explain why it is likely to become a huge success.

A 2.41

theguardian

News | Sport | Comment | Culture | Business | Money | Life&Style | Travel | Environment

Comment is free > Society Search GO

A shorter working week would benefit society

Ending compulsory retirement is a good idea – but we can do more to create a sensible and sustainable work-life balance

Phasing out compulsory retirement must be a sensible idea. Providing for a right to retire at an age pegged to rising life expectancy may be a sensible next step. No one should feel trapped in paid employment as the years advance beyond 70, but – who knows – it may not be long before 70 is the new 60.

The real problem lies with the whole idea of retirement as something that falls across our path like a tree in a storm. And that is because we have such fixed ideas about a "normal" working life. Why should everyone be expected to work at least eight hours a day, five days a week – and often much more? Why do we look upon the rise in "part-time" employment as some kind of aberration, instead of a step in the right direction?

The New Economics Foundation is calling for a move towards a much shorter working week, over a decade or more, with a goal of 21 hours as the new standard. Instead of settling for high rates of unemployment, why not share the work out, with shorter hours for all allowing more people to join the labour force? No one imagines this will be easy, but an incremental shift would leave time to put compensating measures in place – a higher minimum wage, more training, flexible working conditions and a gradual trade-off between pay increments and working time.

The benefits of a shorter working week could be very substantial. Think of it as a redistribution of paid and unpaid time. People who are currently out of work get a chance to earn a living. Everyone gets more discretionary time – so they have more

1 **compulsory** – obligatory
1 **retirement** – time when one no longer works after a certain age
2 **to peg** – *here:* to connect
9 **aberration** – abnormality
14 **incremental** – step-by-step
16 **increment** – level
18 **redistribution** – reallocation
19 **discretionary time** – free time

freedom to play their part as parents, carers, friends, neighbours and active citizens. It begins to make sense of the notion of "work-life balance", which has proved so elusive – especially for parents and carers – in a long-hours culture. It could even help to realise some of the more honourable intentions of the "big society" – how else, after all, are citizens and voluntary organisations to find the time to take more control over what happens to them at a local level?

There is evidence that people who work shorter hours are more productive hour-for-hour, so that's got to be good for business. And at the same time it helps to shift prevailing values away from high-rolling consumerism, where we work to earn, earn to consume and consume at the peril of our planet. We might give more careful thought to how much stuff we really need to buy and, therefore, why we need to work such long hours to earn the money to buy it.

It would help to promote equality, both by lowering unemployment rates and by sharing paid and unpaid labour more equally between women and men. There would be less mental and physical ill-health, since both are associated with long hours as well as with joblessness. And it would transform the way we deal with later life. People who work shorter hours throughout their lives are less likely to burn out by 65. Down-shifting for older workers could be a very gentle affair, with no great contrast between "normal" and pre-retirement patterns of work. Most people could go on working until well into their 70s, if they chose to do so, gradually reducing their time. The point is not to force people to work shorter – or longer – hours, but to change what we think of as the most sensible and sustainable way to lead our lives.

(613 words)

22 **elusive** – hard to achieve
28 **prevailing** – common
29 **peril** – risk
37 **down-shifting** – *here:* working fewer hours
37 **gentle** – smooth
41 **sensible** – reasonable

1 Comprehension
In your own words, summarise the text, focusing on the reasons why "a shorter working week would benefit society".

2 Analysis
Describe and analyse the diagram about total working time worldwide.

3 Comment
"[…] we work to earn, earn to consume and consume at the peril of our planet. We might give more careful thought to how much stuff we really need to buy […]" (ll. 28–30)
Working less and consuming less – would that be an option for you? Comment.

Total working time is lowest in Western Europe and highest outside Europe

Total minutes worked, paid and unpaid, per day

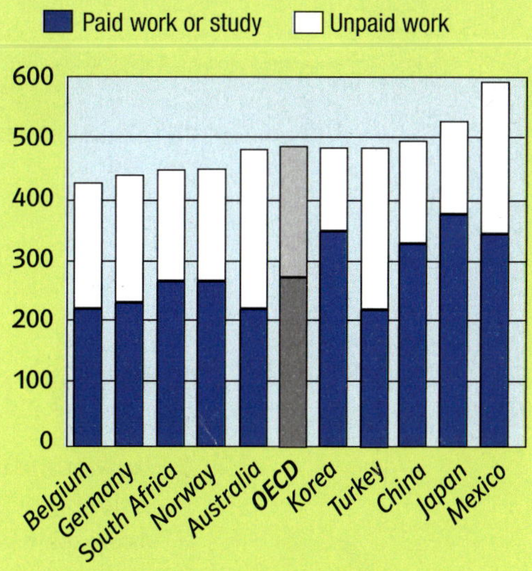

Population aged 15–64. Unpaid work is the production by family members of goods and services that are not sold on the market.

Source: OECD, 2011

Topic 7
Dreams and visions

py68st

Getting started

1 Look at the pictures above. Work with a partner and brainstorm what dreams and visions you think these pictures show. Create a list of at least five key words or expressions for each picture.

2 With the same partner, come up with three more images which show your dreams and visions for the future.

3 Share your ideas with the class and explain your choices.

In the year 2525

In the year 2525
If man is still alive
If woman can survive, they may find

In the year 3535
Ain't gonna need to tell the truth, tell no lies
Everything you think, do and say, is in the pill you took today

In the year 4545
Ain't gonna need your teeth, won't need your eyes
You won't find a thing to chew
Nobody's gonna look at you

In the year 5555
Your arms hanging limp at your sides
Your legs got nothing to do
Some machine doing that for you

In the year 6565
Ain't gonna need no husband, won't need no wife
You'll pick your son, pick your daughter too
From the bottom of a long glass tube

In the year 7510
If God's a-comin, he oughta make it by then
Maybe he'll look around himself and say
"Guess it's time for the judgment day"

In the year 8510
God is gonna shake his mighty head
He'll either say "I'm pleased where man has been"
Or tear it down and start again

In the year 9595
I'm kinda wonderin if man is gonna be alive
He's taken everything this old Earth can give
And he ain't put back nothing

Now it's been ten thousand years
Man has cried a billion tears
For what he never knew
Now man's reign is through

But through eternal night
The twinkling of starlight
So very far away
Maybe it's only yesterday

In the year 2525
If man is still alive
If woman can survive, they may find

In the year 3535

Words and music: Zager and Evans, 1969
In the Year 2525 K/T: Evans, Richard S © OV: Chelsea-Music Publ. / SV: Nordton Edition

4 **Read the lyrics of the song. What topics does the song deal with?**

5 **Analyse the song in detail. In your opinion, does it paint a more positive or negative vision of the future? Explain.**

Word bank

racism • prejudices • (violation of) human rights • pollution • clean environment • war • peace • old/young generation • mutual respect • helping each other • In my opinion, the song deals with the topic of … • I think the song is about … • rationalisation • genetic engineering • punishment • destruction of the planet • exploitation

A European issues

1 Before you read

The term the 'American Dream' is well-known. But what could be the 'European Dream'? Work with a partner and brainstorm some ideas.

2 **notion** – Konzept
4 **latterly** – in letzter Zeit
11 **upbeat** – optimistisch
11 **catchphrase** – Schlagwort
13 **to invoke** – anführen
14 **over-hasty** – übereilt
15 **delicate** – empfindlich
17 **to convey** – vermitteln
24 **assumption** – Annahme
25 **eager** – eifrig, willig
27 **vivid** – klar
29 **uncouth** – ungehobelt
29 **admiration** – Bewunderung
29 **to donate** – *hier:* schenken
31 **huddled** – zusammengedrängt
31 **to yearn** – sich sehnen
33 **dissenter** – Systemkritiker(in), Dissident(in)

theguardian

News | Sport | Comment | Culture | Business | Money | Life&Style | Travel | Environment

Comment is free > Politics > Search GO

Why national dream is a foreign concept

Confidence in a better tomorrow is a notion that comes more easily to Americans with a century of economic and, latterly, political dominance behind them than to the British.

Flags in front of the European Parliament in Brussels, Belgium

When Ed Miliband told Labour supporters in Gateshead about his fear that young people today were no longer sure of a better future than their parents had enjoyed he was careful to admit that Britain lacked an upbeat popular catchphrase to match "the American Dream". But when he invoked the idea of a broken "British promise" as over-hasty coalition spending cuts bite deep into the delicate fabric of society that was clearly what Miliband meant to convey: the chance of decent education and jobs for all, a secure environment, free healthcare and confidence in a better tomorrow. It is a notion that comes more easily to Americans with a century of economic and, latterly, political global dominance behind them, though the half century of rising living standards that followed the Great Depression and second world war has given way to far greater uncertainty for millions. Until recently postwar Europeans have made similar assumptions, but they started from a different, darker place. The US had been peopled for 400 years by immigrants – all of them eager volunteers apart from African slaves – determined to make a new and freer life in the New World.

By contrast most Europeans had vivid memories of war, tyranny and rigid class hierarchies. Mostly they admired America while also thinking Americans materialistic, uncouth and noisy. It was admiration which prompted France to donate Bartholdi's Statue of Liberty to New York in 1886, complete with Emma Lazarus's famous lines "Give me your tired, your poor, your huddled masses yearning to be free ..." Reality was not always like that in the sweat shops of New York or on the thin soil of Nebraska. But the dream of self-betterment had been powerful since religious dissenters sought to build their "shining city on a hill" in New England or make a fast buck growing tobacco in Virginia. The idea was embodied in the life, liberty and pursuit of happiness pledge of the constitution of 1776 when Americans overthrew the British rule they thought stood in the way of their goal. Millions crossed the Atlantic to join the pursuit. In the 19th century the fertile inventor Thomas Edison's rise to fame and fortune was said to embody the American Dream. In fact the phrase only attracted capital letters after James Truslow Adams, himself a wealthy writer, wrote about it expressing the idea of limitless success for the hard-working. It was as late as 1931.

Margaret Thatcher tried to foster a "British Dream" tradition, as did Tony Blair. Even the more prosaic Gordon Brown sought to blend European social democratic traditions of fairness with American entrepreneurial zeal. But Miliband gets it because the concept is in his blood. Like Emma Lazarus, a Jewish refugee from Russian pogroms, his own Jewish ancestors fled west to seek a better life. By 1940 they had reached Belgium where grandfather and his then-teenage father, Ralph, escaped to Britain from what would probably have been death in the camps. Britain gave them shelter, education and a chance to start afresh, he said – pure Americanism of the kind you do not hear in France, where patriotism is expressed in terms of republican virtue, though Nicholas Sarkozy, another child of Jewish refugees from Hungary, openly admires America as French leaders rarely do in public. The irony is that Ronald Reagan and Margaret Thatcher's response to emerging globalisation deliberately sought to create more risk-prone unequal societies, theoretically more meritocratic but in reality restoring the advantages of privilege which the mid-century shook off. Twenty-five years on, working- and middle-class skills and salaries are stagnant and declining while the wider world, which also admired the American Dream, decided they would build it at home in Shanghai or Bangalore rather than emigrate as their ancestors did. Dream or promise, both are under pressure in the west, regardless of who sits in No 10 or the Oval Office. (684 words)

34 **to make a fast buck** – schnelles Geld verdienen
35 **to embody** – verkörpern
35 **pursuit** – Streben
41 **limitless** – grenzenlos
42 **to foster** – fördern
43 **prosaic** – nüchtern
43 **to blend** – mischen
44 **zeal** – Eifer, Begeisterung
45 **refugee** – Flüchtling
50 **virtue** – Tugend
54 **risk-prone** – risikoanfällig
54 **meritocratic** – leistungsorientiert
55 **to restore** – wiederherstellen
56 **stagnant** – stagnierend

2 Mediation
A friend has to give a presentation on the American Dream and whether there is such thing as a 'European Dream'. He finds the article above in the Internet but has problems understanding it. Therefore, he asks you to sum up the main points for him in German.

3 Analysis → Describing cartoons, p. 242
Describe the cartoon, analyse it and relate it to the text.

10 **4 Comment** → Writing a comment, p. 229
"Ed Miliband told Labour supporters [...] about his fear that young people today were no longer sure of a better future than their parents had enjoyed [...]" (ll. 6–10)
As a European do you think your generation will have better future prospects than your parents' generation? Discuss.

5 Research project → Hotspot 1, p. 117

"I'M GLAD THE AMERICAN DREAM IS STILL ALIVE AND WELL SOMEWHERE."

B Global protests

1 Before you read

a) Describe the picture below.

b) What do people protest against? In Germany? Europe? Around the world? Work with a partner and make a list.

1 **to redefine** – neu definieren
3 **peak** – Höhepunkt
6 **battle-scarred** – kampf-erprobt
7 **lefty** – Linke(r)
10 **taxation** – Besteuerung
11 **to be held responsible for** – verantwortlich gemacht werden für
11 **due to** – auf Grund von
12 **greed** – Habgier
12 **trestle table** – Klapptisch
25 **uprising** – Aufstand
27 **shabby** – schäbig
28 **subsequent** – anschließend, nachträglich
30 **to be misplaced** – unan-gebracht sein
30 **to chime** – läuten

theguardian

News | Sport | Comment | Culture | Business | Money | Life&Style | Travel | Environment

Comment is free > Politics   Search [   ] GO

Global protests: Is 2011 a year that will change the world?

Will this year go down in history as one of those that redefined global politics? Just what are the parallels – if any – with 1968 and 1989?

Midway through last month, when the Occupy movement was at its peak and the New York police department was keeping its distance from Zuccotti Park, I was in Berkeley, California. Outside a branch of Bank of America, a compact local Occupy camp had sprung up, apparently drawing on a mixture of battle-scarred lefties, students from the University of California, and the sizeable local homeless population. Their line of argument was captured on A4 flyers that were pasted on to every available surface in the surrounding streets, the most direct of which read thus: "Are you pissed [off] yet? You should be! No taxation of the rich. Endless war. Bankers not held responsible. Corrupt politicians. Destruction of the planet due to politicians' and corporations' greed. Can it get any worse than this?" On a trestle table lay small piles of a leaflet credited to the "Bureau of Public Secrets", which quoted 69-year-old Kalle Lasn, the editor of the Canada-based countercultural magazine Adbusters: "We are not just inspired by what happened in the Arab spring recently. We are students of the situationist movement. Those are the people who gave birth to what many people think was the first global revolution back in 1968 when some uprisings in Paris suddenly inspired uprisings all over the world."

Looking at the shabby camp in front of me, any talk of Paris in 1968 seemed absurd – but then again, subsequent events in nearby Oakland, where thousands of Occupy supporters took to the streets on 3 November maybe suggested that such reference points were not completely misplaced. The 1968 reference also chimed with an article, not from any anarchist leaflet, but from the Financial Times, titled

2011: The Year of Global Indignation, and written by the paper's foreign affairs columnist, Gideon Rachman. "Many of the revolts of 2011 pit an internationally connected elite against ordinary citizens who feel excluded from the benefits of economic growth, and angered by corruption," he wrote. "The creation of a global mood is a mysterious thing. In 1968, before the word 'globalisation' or the internet were even invented, there were student rebellions around the world. The year 1989 saw not just the fall of the Berlin Wall but the Tiananmen Square revolt in China." And then a tentative question: "Perhaps 2011 will come to rank alongside 1968 and 1989 as a year of global revolt?"

This year has so far seen convulsive events in Tunisia, Egypt, Libya, Bahrain, Syria and Yemen. Mass protests against economic breakdown and austerity in Greece, Italy and Spain. Marches and protest camps in Chile and Israel. The arrival of Occupy Wall Street – which was cleared by police yesterday, though it will surely return in some form – and a movement-cum-meme which quickly arrived in London and beyond. And all the time, from Arab dictatorships, through to the world's banks and the Murdoch empire and now the vast edifice of the EU, the sense that interests and institutions, that once seemed invincible are either cracking or being questioned as never before, while mainstream politics is left looking bereft not just of answers, but even ideas. But what connects the crowds who are making all the noise? What could link a student camped outside St Paul's to Mohamed Bouazizi, the Tunisian vegetable seller who, having set himself on fire, died on 4 January, and thereby set in motion the events we now know as the Arab spring?

Sometimes, the answer seems to lie in actual links between the people at the centre of events. On 26 October, for example, Occupy Wall Street was visited by a group of activists drawn together by the Egyptian Facebook-based 6 April movement, who blessed the camp with the spirit of Tahrir Square; a fortnight ago, demonstrators outside St Paul's Cathedral conducted a live video linkup with pro-democracy activists in Syria. Such moments highlight the kind of people who have taken the lead in spreading the message of protest and dissent: a new political breed, unlike their politicised predecessors in some respects; but in others, remarkably similar.

(714 words)

- 32 **indignation** – Empörung
- 33 **to pit sth. against sth.** – etw. an etw. messen
- 34 **excluded** – ausgegrenzt
- 39 **tentative** – vorsichtig
- 41 **convulsive** – erschütternd
- 42 **austerity** – Einschränkung
- 45 **meme** – Gedankeneinheit, die sich durch Kommunikation weiterverbreitet
- 47 **edifice** – Gebäude
- 48 **invincible** – unbesiegbar
- 49 **bereft** – beraubt
- 57 **to bless** – segnen
- 57 **spirit** – Geist
- 57 **fortnight** – vierzehn Tage
- 58 **to conduct** – ausführen
- 59 **to take the lead** – die Führung übernehmen
- 60 **to spread** – verbreiten
- 60 **dissent** – Widerspruch
- 60 **breed** – *hier:* Generation
- 61 **predecessor** – Vorgänger(in)
- 61 **remarkably** – bemerkenswert

10 △ **2 Comprehension**

a) Sum up in your own words what, according to this article, people are protesting against.

b) Outline what happened in 1968 and 1989.

3 Presentation → Presentation, p. 264

Divide the class into two groups. The first group should focus on the "Occupy Movement" and the second group should focus on the "Arab Spring". Divide the two topics into sub-topics (i.e. background, locations, impact, timeline, etc.) and prepare a presentation for the class. Use the Internet to help you.

10 △ **4 Comment** → Writing a comment, p. 229

"Global protests: Is 2011 a year that will change the world?"

Do you think that the events of 2011 have changed the world? Discuss.

C Political speeches

1 Before you read

Which emblem represents the United Nations (UN) and what does it show? What are the other two? What do you know about the UN?

Ban Ki-moon, UN Secretary-General since 2007

2 **headquarters** – Hauptquartier
4 **remark** – Äußerung
4 **non-governmental organization (NGO)** – Nichtregierungsorganisation
6 **to appreciate** – (wert) schätzen
7 **commitment** – Engagement
11 **passion** – Leidenschaft
12 **crucial** – entscheidend, sehr wichtig
12 **to forge** – formen, schmieden
12 **sustainable** – nachhaltig
13 **prosperity** – Wohlstand
15 **summit** – Gipfel(treffen)
15 **landmark** – Meilenstein
16 **biodiversity** – Artenvielfalt
16 **awareness** – Bewusstsein
16 **to soar** – hochschnellen
18 **disarmament** – Abrüstung
20 **to dismiss sth. as** – etw. als ... abtun
20 **pie-in-the-sky ideal** – Luftschloss
23 **transition** – Übergang
23 **remarkable** – bemerkenswert
25 **to draft** – entwerfen
26 **judiciary** – Gerichtswesen

UN NEWS CENTRE

Search [ ] GO

Home | Press Room | Tools & Services | Resources | News Focus

Secretary-General Ban Ki-moon
UN Headquarters
26 October 2011

Remarks to Non-Governmental Organizations

Good morning, Ladies and Gentlemen,

It is a great pleasure to meet you today. Thank you very much for taking time and I appreciate your strong commitment and leadership and willingness to work together with the United Nations in addressing many important challenges which we are facing these days.

Perhaps the most important thing I wanted to tell you is to say is: thank you. Thank you very much for all you have been doing for humanity. Thank you for everything you do to support the United Nations. We simply could not do without your passion, your ideas – and your criticism, too. [...] Your voices and views are crucial. The world needs to forge a common agenda for sustainable peace, prosperity, freedom and justice.

I see three areas where your efforts will be especially important.

First, sustainable development. The first Earth Summit in 1992 was a landmark. It produced Agenda 21 and binding conventions on climate change and biodiversity. Global awareness soared. So did NGO engagement. Next year's Rio + 20 conference is a chance to build on that spirit.

The second area where NGOs can make a big difference is disarmament. We have seen encouraging progress in recent years, advanced in large measure by civil society and organizations such as yourselves. [...] Too many people dismiss disarmament as a pie-in-the-sky ideal. Let us work together to bring disarmament down to earth.

Ladies and Gentlemen,

The third major opportunity: helping countries in transition. This year has been a most remarkable year for all of us. Not only those countries in the Middle East and North Africa – Tunisia, Egypt and Libya – face major challenges organizing elections, drafting new constitutions, promoting democratic practices, building independent judiciaries and free media. There can be no success

2 Comprehension

a) Divide the speech into parts and give each part a heading.

b) Outline which goals Ban Ki-moon mentions in his speech and the suggestions he makes on achieving them.

3 Analysis

a) Analyse the language Ban Ki-moon uses to connect with and engage his audience.

b) Explain the following sentence in your own words: "Too many people dismiss disarmament as a pie-in-the-sky ideal." (ll. 20–21)

4 Mediation → Mediation, p. 245
Write a short German newspaper article in which you outline the challenges the world faces, according to Ban Ki-moon.

5 Project → Hotspot 2, p. 117

without a healthy civil society. Please, do your part. Help these women's groups, social media activists, human rights defenders and others to take their rightful place in society ... in government, in parliament, in every public institution.

Ladies and Gentlemen,

One of the most important lessons I have learned as Secretary-General is the power of partnerships. Governments cannot do it alone. We need support from business communities, civil societies, philanthropists, and faith leaders, and we need coalitions, we need alliances, multistakeholder platforms. This is our business model, and we know that it works. Thanks to the power of partnership, we are closing in on a day when we can eliminate deaths from malaria. Our target is 2015. By that time, we expect that there will be no malaria-related deaths. [...] Together, in close coordination and cooperation, we can achieve outsized results on virtually every aspect of our shared agenda. And we will continue.

Dear Friends,

These are difficult economic times. Tight budgets. Cutbacks. Belt tightening. You are living all of this, too. Everywhere, people are living in fear ... fear of losing their jobs, fear of being unable to feed their families, fear that governments and public institutions will fail them yet again. It is up to us – organizations like yours and mine – to help restore that faith. To deliver for people in need; to not forget people in need, especially now when times are so hard. [...] During this era of new austerity, I often say that we must learn to "do more with less." In fact, however, we must think and act in a deeper way. The austerity challenge is not merely about quantity; it is about quality. It is not merely about "doing more with less" but about "doing better with less". By that, I mean increasing the impact of our work ... making a bigger and measurable difference in the daily lives of real people. I know that we can do that with you by our side – as partners across the full spectrum of our work. That is the power of partnership.

Let me close on a more personal note. Many of you have told me, often more than once, that we do not see one another often enough. That we must do more to cement this partnership and amplify its potential power. [...] Let me say that I understand. And I am committed to doing what I can to nurture and deepen this UN-NGO relationship. In our modern world, so complex and fast-changing, no nation or institution can prosper alone. Only by working in concert, in strong partnership, can we advance our common goals.

Thank you very much for your strong support for United Nations goals and your own personal engagement and leadership. Thank you. (760 words)

33 **philanthropist** – Wohltäter, Menschenfreund
33 **multistakeholder** – Interessensvertreter
37 **outsized** – übergroß
40 **tight** – eng, knapp
40 **cutback** – Kürzung
43 **to restore** – wiederherstellen
45 **austerity** – Entbehrung, Einschränkung
46 **merely** – lediglich
48 **measurable** – messbar
52 **to amplify** – verstärken
55 **in concert** – gemeinsam

D Social responsibility

1 Before you read
Here is a definition of the word "entrepreneur":

> **entrepreneur (n)** [ˌɒn.trə.prəˈnɜː]: *a person who sets up a business or businesses, taking on financial risks in the hope of profit*

What do you think is the difference between an entrepreneur and a social entrepreneur? Share your ideas with the class.

2 Comprehension
Summarise each of the projects in your own words.

3 Analysis
Explain the phrase "tackling financial illiteracy" (l. 9) in your own words.

theguardian

News | Sport | Comment | Culture | Business | Money | Life&Style | Travel | Environment

Comment is free > Society   Search [ ] GO

The Guardian Social Entrepreneurship Awards

Elisabetta Lapana, London – Young People's Bank

The project will be a bank in secondary schools set up and run by students. Its objectives are to enable young people to become more enterprising and to develop a new approach to tackling financial illiteracy. The students will be able to invest and take out small loans for personal development and will also be empowered to improve the social and economic make-up of their communities. The students will learn valuable finance skills and schools could gain specialised status as financial literacy is high on the government agenda. An UnLtd award will cover the costs of computer equipment and volunteer expenses.

Jonathan Burr, Windsor – The Beam

This programme is targeted at 12 to 15-year-old boys who have a body mass index of over 30. It will cover nutrition, fitness, self-awareness and self-esteem. Jonathan hopes to run the programme for up to 15 teenagers and include their parents in at least one of the modules. He believes that weight issues are a major source of poor self-esteem and unhappiness in young British males and wants to

5 **objective** – Ziel
6 **to enable** – ermöglichen
7 **enterprising** – unternehmenslustig
9 **to tackle** – in Angriff nehmen, bekämpfen
9 **illiteracy** – Analphabetismus
12 **loan** – Darlehen, Kredit
13 **to empower** – befähigen
14 **valuable** – wertvoll
14 **to gain** – bekommen
16 **volunteer** – Freiwillige(r)
16 **expense** – Kosten
19 **nutrition** – Ernährung
19 **self-awareness** – Eigenwahrnehmung
19 **self-esteem** – Selbstwertgefühl
21 **weight** – Gewicht
21 **issue** – Frage, Problem
21 **major** – Haupt-

11 **4 Mediation** → Mediation, p. 245
Choose the two projects that interest you the most and sum up the key information in German.

5 Having a discussion → Discussions, p. 246
Which of the projects deserves to be given an award for social responsibility? Exchange arguments in class and take a vote.

6 Listening comprehension: Social entrepreneur of the year → Listening, p. 221
Listen to the recording and find out what a social entrepreneur is and what his/her main aims are. You do not have to write full sentences.

7 Research project → Hotspot 3, p. 117

provide participants with knowledge of alternative health choices. Project costs include venue hire, professional fees, travel and insurance.

Ben Ward, Bristol – World Jungle
This project aims to provide life-changing opportunities to young people and individuals in Ben's rural community through dance, music and art activities. World Jungle will give the young people a chance to learn about social and environmental issues facing other cultures. Ben already has links with Ghanaian, Indian and Moroccan dancers, drummers, speakers and relevant festival and carnivals organised to take young people to. Ben hopes this project will encourage the young people he is targeting to explore other cultures and challenge prejudices. Project costs include travel, venue hire, dancers, admin and publicity.

Jessica Sherlock, London – The Amoosi Project
This project will engage designers at the beginning of their careers to work with recycled clothing and textiles. Rather than see these materials go to landfills or be sold in developing countries, Jessica wants young fashion designers to develop their skills while using these materials. She strongly believes that these designers can influence the fashion industry as a whole. Project costs include: marketing materials, website hosting, sample production, company registration and advertising.

Helen Thomas, Cornwall – Film Kitchen
This will be a mobile film and food facility designed to enable films to be screened in a variety of locations including village halls, schools and outdoor locations. The aim of the project is to promote healthy food to the local community, introducing themed/multicultural food, while bringing a variety of films to people who would otherwise not be able to travel to their nearest cinema. The project will offer the local community a facility that educates, inspires and encourages them to get together. Project costs include a projector, speakers, sound mixer and further technical equipment. (482 words)

23 **to provide** – geben, bieten
24 **venue** – Veranstaltungsort
24 **fee** – Gebühr
24 **insurance** – Versicherung
27 **rural** – ländlich
32 **to explore** – erkunden
32 **to challenge** – herausfordern
32 **prejudice** – Vorurteil
33 **admin** – Verwaltung
35 **to engage** – involvieren
36 **landfill** – Deponie
39 **website hosting** – Bereitstellen von Speicherplatz für eine Webseite
40 **sample** – Muster
42 **facility** – Einrichtung
42 **to screen** – vorführen
44 **to promote** – fördern
46 **otherwise** – ansonsten
48 **projector** – Beamer

E Future living

1 Before you read

a) How do you think your hometown will change in the next thirty years? Discuss with a partner what you believe will change for the better and what you fear will change for the worse. Report back to the class.

b) Brainstorm ideas which express what your hometown would ideally look like in thirty years' time.

c) Discuss in class what you believe are aspects of an imaginary ideal place to live in.

Utopia and dystopia

Utopia is derived from the Greek words for 'good' and 'place', which sums up what utopias are all about: imaginary societies, set in a different place or the future, which are better than our current society. Technological progress was largely viewed with optimism until well into the 19th century, and positive utopian visions of the future were therefore common. Towards the turn of the century and in the early 20th century, however, the speed and transformative power of industrialisation and of scientific progress also created anxiety and resistance. In the following decades, the experience of the two World Wars, of totalitarian states and terrifying weapons, intensified this feeling. Pessimistic visions of the future (so-called 'anti-utopias', or more commonly 'dystopias') were understood as warnings against inhuman totalitarian states that dominate or enslave their citizens.
The main aim of both utopian and dystopian art is to portray alternative societies, implicitly criticising tendencies in contemporary society either by offering a better society or by projecting a dangerous contemporary development into a future where it has gotten out of hand. Technological progress does not have to play a role in this, but it often does because new technologies have such a significant impact on the structure of society. For example, the emergence of mass media and surveillance technology gave rise to dystopian visions of totalitarian regimes that control every aspect of citizens' lives, and advances in biotechnology inspired dystopias of genetic caste systems. (277 words)

1 **utopia** – Utopie
1 **dystopia** – Antiutopie, Dystopie
2 **to derive from** – sich ableiten von
3 **imaginary** – erfunden
4 **current** – aktuell
4 **progress** – Fortschritt
6 **transformative** – umgestaltend
7 **anxiety** – Angst
7 **resistance** – Widerstand
8 **decade** – Jahrzehnt
9 **terrifying** – furchterregend
9 **to intensify** – verstärken
10 **inhuman** – unmenschlich
11 **to enslave** – versklaven
11 **citizen** – Bürger
12 **to portray** – abbilden
13 **implicitly** – implizit
14 **to project** – projektieren
14 **contemporary** – gegenwärtig
14 **to get out of hand** – außer Kontrolle geraten
16 **significant** – bedeutend
16 **impact** – Auswirkung
17 **emergence** – Aufkommen
17 **surveillance** – Überwachung
17 **to give rise to** – etw. entstehen lassen
18 **advance** – Vorstoß
19 **caste system** – Kastenordnung

2 Comprehension

a) In your own words, outline the difference between utopia and dystopia.

b) Sum up what triggered the vision of the dystopia.

3 Vocabulary → Working with a dictionary, p. 255

Find the German equivalents of the following words in the text on page 115:

renewable energies • researcher • breakthrough • emission-free • inventors • emissions • solar power • sun collector • solar power station • fertiliser • car-free transport system • railway lines • solar-fuelled • cabin • evaporated

p. 211

4 Mediation → Mediation, p. 245

Summarise the main points of the article on the next page in English.

Hightech für die Umwelt: Die Stadt der Zukunft

Magnetschwebekapseln statt Autos, Photovoltaik statt Erdöl: Abu Dhabi plant im Rahmen der Masdar-Initiative eine „Grüne Stadt". An wichtigen Forschungsprojekten sind deutsche Institute federführend beteiligt.

Abu Dhabi nennt sein ehrgeiziges Projekt zur Entwicklung erneuerbarer Energien „Masdar" („Quelle"). Denn das Projekt will Quelle sein für Erfindungen, Innovationen und Unternehmergeist. Es will die besten Forscher zusammenführen und ausstatten, es will diesen Forschern Unternehmer an die Seite stellen, die ihre Erfindungen umsetzen. Masdar wird damit ein nachhaltiger Impuls, um den erneuerbaren Energien zum großen Durchbruch zu verhelfen und um das Zeitalter, in dem das Erdöl versiegen wird, in die weite Zukunft zu verschieben. Im Mai 2007 stellte das Emirat sein Projekt erstmals vor. Sein sichtbarster Teil wird die emissionsfreie „Grüne Stadt" sein, ein sechs Millionen Quadratmeter großer Komplex, der stadtplanerisch von dem britischen Architekturbüro Foster and Partners betreut wird. Abu Dhabi will für das Projekt die besten Forscher bündeln. Wo bei erneuerbaren Energien Exzellenz gefragt ist, sind deutsche Institutionen dabei. Ein wichtiger Baustein von Masdar ist das Research Network. In dieses hat Masdar sechs der führenden Forschungseinrichtungen der Welt eingeladen, zwei von ihnen kommen aus Deutschland: die Rheinisch-Westfälische Technische Universität (RWTH) Aachen und das Deutsche Zentrum für Luft- und Raumfahrt (DLR).

Um den Austausch zwischen Forschung und Industrie zu erleichtern, richtet Abu Dhabi eine Sonderwirtschaftszone ein, die „Grüne Stadt". In ihr werden die Institute und die Unternehmen angesiedelt, in ihr werden die Erfinder und Innovatoren leben und arbeiten. Diese neue Stadt am Rand des heutigen Abu Dhabi ist das für Außenstehende spektakulärste Projekt von Masdar. Die Stadt soll auf sechs Quadratkilometern Pilotprojekt und Modell zugleich sein. Sie soll nichts Geringeres werden als das Silicon Valley für erneuerbare Energien. In ihr wird kein Auto fahren und es wird keine Emissionen von Kohlendioxid geben. Sie wird mit Solarstrom auskommen, der aus Sonnenkollektoren auf den Dächern gewonnen wird und von einem benachbarten Solarkraftwerk. Der Müll wird zu Düngemitteln verarbeitet, und in der autofreien Stadt wird ein Transportsystem die Beförderung der Menschen sicherstellen: Auf Trassen werden solarbetriebene Kabinen verkehren, die jeden Einzelnen mindestens bis zu 200 Meter an jeden Punkt innerhalb der Stadt steuern. Ein „intelligentes" Dach wird Schatten spenden und mit verdunstetem Wasser die Temperatur in den Straßen regeln – trotz der extremen klimatischen Bedingungen in Abu Dhabi mit Außentemperaturen bis zu 50°C. (374 words)

12 △ **5 Analysis** → Describing pictures, p. 241
Describe the picture on the right in detail and compare its vision of a city of the future with that of the Masdar project.

12 △ **6 Comment: Choose one of the following tasks**

a) Imagine you have been offered the chance to spend one year living in the "Green City". Discuss whether you would accept the offer or not, outlining arguments for and against.

b) If you had to paint a picture of the future in, say, 2150, would it be more utopian or dystopian? Give reasons.

7 Research project → Hotspot 4, p. 117

Paraphrasing

Paraphrasing means putting information into your own words. When you answer questions on a text, write a summary or otherwise refer to a particular text, you should not copy the exact sentences but use your own words as much as possible.
Use introductory phrases (e.g. *The author says/claims that … / According to the text/author …*) if the ideas you are writing about are not yours.
If you use synonyms, remember to change the sentence structure, if necessary (e.g. *For politicians, being informed about current events is very much a part of daily life.* → *For politicians, being informed about current events is very important in daily life.*).

a) Read the following sentences and choose the paraphrase which you consider better. Give reasons for your choice.

Examples:

1. Although people around the world are protesting against a variety of things, these issues are not completely independent from one another.
   - People around the globe have many reasons for protesting but these do not exist independently from each other.
   - Although people all over the world are protesting about different issues, they are not completely independent from one another.

2. Instead, different protests are often connected by feelings of powerlessness and anger.
   - Instead, feelings of anger and powerlessness often connect different protests.
   - Instead, protests are often connected by the anger and powerlessness felt by the people protesting.

b) Now paraphrase the following sentences yourself. You can use an English-English dictionary or a thesaurus for help.

1. The year 1989 saw not just the fall of the Berlin Wall but the Tiananmen Square revolt in China.
2. The Occupy movement is an international protest movement primarily directed against economic and social inequality.
3. The Occupy Wall Street movement was initiated by the Canadian activist group Adbusters.
4. Just after midnight on November 9 in Ontario, police evicted protesters from the city's Victoria Park.
5. Later, on the night of November 14, authorities forcefully closed down camps around the world in cities such as New York, Oakland and Zurich.
6. However, protestors immediately regrouped and vowed to continue protesting.
7. The series of demonstrations and protests across the Middle East and North Africa has been labeled the "Arab Spring".
8. As of February 2012, governments in four countries have been overthrown.

1 Research project: The American Dream → Presentation, p. 264

a) Go online and find a definition of the American Dream.

b) Find Emma Lazarus's poem "The New Colossus", analyse it and relate it to the concept of the American Dream.

c) Come up with a definition for a "European Dream". Present your results to the class.

2 Project: The role of the UN → Presentation, p. 264
In groups do some research and find some United Nations peacekeeping missions. Who is at conflict? Since when? Over what? What are the chances of a peaceful solution? How is the UN involved? Present your findings to the class.

3 Research project: Social entrepreneurship in Germany → Internet research, p. 260
Do you know of any social entrepreneurship in Germany? Use the Internet to gather information about German projects that have innovative business ideas aimed at tackling society's most pressing social problems. Choose a project that interests you and prepare a 3-minute talk to introduce the project to your classmates.

4 Research project: Cities of the future → Internet research, p. 260
Go online and look for information about projects similar to the Masdar project, e.g. green cities, sustainable cities, zero emission cities, etc. Prepare a short talk in which you outline the most important details and the aims of the project.

A 3.3

1 **glittering** – sparkling
1 **to bristle** – to stand upright
2 **to straddle** – to extend across
2 **metropolis** – city
3 **entirely** – completely
3 **Perspex** – acrylic glass
5 **painstaking** – done with great care
5 **grave** – severe
6 **understatement** – the presentation of sth. as being smaller or less good or important than it really is
7 **to comprise** – to make up
8 **urban** – city
9 **meticulously** – exactly
9 **crafted to scale** – made in proportion
12 **faithfully** – in detail
15 **mere** – only
15 **indulgence** – luxury
15 **purpose** – reason
16 **alongside** – together with
17 **planning permission** – allowance to build sth.
17 **to date** – up to now
18 **to cast** – to spread
19 **blueprint** – plan
19 **at a glance** – with one quick look
20 **dwarfed** – made to look very small
23 **casual observer** – normal person
23 **striking** – surprising
27 **despite** – in spite of
28 **barely** – just
28 **inch** – 2.54 cm

BBC NEWS EDUCATION & FAMILY Search GO

Home | UK | Africa | Asia-Pac | Europe | Latin America | Mid-East | South Asia

London 2030: Modelling the future

A forest of glittering new skyscrapers bristles from the City of London, the completed Olympic Park transforms the East End and the £17bn Crossrail line straddles the metropolis at last. This is London 2030. But made entirely of Perspex.

To describe the construction of this model as painstaking is a grave understatement. Some 50,000 individual buildings or blocks comprise the urban landscape, each meticulously crafted to scale [...]. Every street and park – not to mention the familiar curve of the Thames – has been faithfully reproduced [...]. And a total of 5,000 hours of labour by model-making firm Pipers has gone into the 12-metre-long (36ft) result. But this is no mere indulgence – there is a definite purpose behind the creation of the model. For alongside the familiar structures – Buckingham Palace, the London Eye and the Houses of Parliament – sits every major development given planning permission to date. Some 500 unborn buildings are cast across the landscape, reproduced from architects' plans and blueprints. Thus, at a glance, the observer can see London in two decades' time.

Canary Wharf dwarfed

Nick McKeogh, director of Pipers, explained: "The model was first made in 2005, in the middle of a huge building boom. Not since Victorian times had London seen such development." [...] To the casual observer, the number of new skyscrapers is particularly striking. In London's financial district the Gherkin – designed by Norman Foster – has six new partners among the clouds. And four buildings across the miniature landscape dwarf the UK's current tallest skyscraper, Canary Wharf – despite being barely half an inch high in the model. Observers are left in no doubt: the skyline of 2030 will be a very different sight. But Mr McKeogh said: "It's not Shanghai-on-Thames. There are still a huge amount of low buildings, [...]. A few years ago people thought everything old and low was being knocked down to make way for big towers." [...]

Model makers used plans of future buildings such as The Shard, under construction at London Bridge

"Blank canvas"

While the proliferation of skyscrapers points firmly towards the future, the mark of history is still writ large, with clues to how developments of the past were carried out. Debbie Whitfield, director of New London Architecture, in whose galleries off Tottenham Court Road the model resides, said: "Although the model is quite simplified it's incredible what it reveals. It shows how the [historically] Roman walled City of London was largely built over the medieval street plan just as it was before the Great Fire of London. The medieval street plan informed the shape of developments that were built later."

Ms Whitfield continued: "Architects building there (the City) had to respond to very different circumstances than elsewhere in London. For instance you have Canary Wharf, which was a blank canvas. When you come out of the Tube there you could be in Tokyo – the complexity of London is its beauty." The city's complexity can be confusing for new inhabitants. Many new Londoners experience the epiphany of turning the corner to recognise a whole other district of London they had no idea was so close. And for those wanting to connect up the mental jigsaw the model provides a strong rival to peering through clouds from an aeroplane window.

"It's amazing to get a feel for where things are in relation to each other," Ms Whitfield said. [...] "It highlights that the distance between Stratford and the Square Mile is roughly equidistant to that from the Square Mile to Paddington. Most people tend to think of Stratford as being much further out." The model, built to a 1:1,500 scale, is constantly updated as new developments are approved. But will the London of 2030 be a better place? Or are developers putting profit over civic improvement? While his pride in the model is evident, Mr McKeogh retains a healthy cynicism. "I would not say all of these things will contribute to a better London," [...]. (655 words)

[39] **blank** – empty
[39] **canvas** – strong cloth
[40] **proliferation** – increase in number
[41] **writ large** – clear, obvious
[43] **to reside** – to live
[44] **to reveal** – to disclose, to show
[46] **to inform** – *here:* to influence
[51] **epiphany** – eye-opening experience
[53] **jigsaw** – puzzle
[53] **rival** – competitor
[53] **to peer** – to look
[57] **equidistant** – of the same distance
[58] **scale** – size
[59] **to approve** – to give permission
[60] **civic** – community
[61] **evident** – clear
[61] **to retain** – to keep
[61] **cynicism** – scepticism

1 Comprehension

a) Outline in your own words what the model shows and what its purpose is.

b) Describe how, according to the model, the London skyline will change over the next two decades.

2 Analysis

a) Explain what the following statement says about London: "Many new Londoners experience the epiphany of turning the corner to recognise a whole other district of London they had no idea was so close." (ll. 50–52)

b) Interpret McKeogh's statement: "I would not say all of these things will contribute to a better London." (ll. 61–62)

3 Comment

'Your town 2030'. What will your hometown look like in 2030? What changes will have taken place and how will they affect the people living there? Write a text explaining your vision of your hometown in the future.

Topic 8
Cross-cultural issues

u25ye8

In my country

Walking by the waters
down where an honest river
shakes hands with the sea,
a woman passed round me
in a slow watchful circle,
as if I were a superstition;

or the worst dregs of her
  imagination,
so when she finally spoke
her words spliced into bars
of an old wheel. A segment of air.
Where do you come from?
'Here,' I said, 'Here. These parts.'

Jackie Kay

Jackie Kay

Pat Mora

Legal alien

Bi-lingual, Bi-cultural,
able to slip from "How's life?"
to "Me están volviendo loca",
able to sit in a paneled office
drafting memos in smooth English,
able to order in fluent Spanish
at a Mexican restaurant,
American but hyphenated,
viewed by Anglos as perhaps exotic,
perhaps inferior; definitely different,
viewed by Mexicans as alien,
(their eyes say, "You may speak
Spanish but you're not like me")
an American to Mexicans
a Mexican to Americans
a handy token
sliding back and forth
between the fringes of both worlds
by smiling
by masking the discomfort
of being pre-judged
Bi-laterally.

Pat Mora

6 **superstition** – Aberglaube
7 **dregs** *(pl)* – Bodensatz
10 **to splice** – *hier:* aufsplittern

3 **me estan volviendo loca** *(Spanish)* – Sie machen mich verrückt
4 **paneled** – getäfelt
5 **to draft** – schreiben
5 **smooth** – *hier:* fließend (Sprache)
8 **hyphenated** – mit einem Bindestrich verbunden
10 **inferior** – minderwertig
16 **token** – *hier:* Spielstein
18 **fringe** – Rand
20 **to mask** – verbergen

Getting started

You are going to read three poems which all deal with living between different cultures. The poets are Jackie Kay, a black Scottish poet, who was adopted at birth by a white couple; Pat Mora, born in Texas to a Mexican family; and John Agard, a Caribbean poet who moved to Britain from Guyana in 1977.

A 3.7 **1 Listen to and read the first poem. Then answer the following questions.**

a) Who is the speaker of the poem and what experience does the poem describe? How does the title relate to the message of the poem?

b) Explain how the metaphor of the river and the sea relates to a society with ethnic minorities.

A 3.8 **2 Listen to and read the second poem. Then answer the following questions.**

a) What do you understand by the term "legal alien", and how does it relate to the situation described in the poem?

b) What does the speaker mean by the phrase "American but hyphenated" (l. 8)?

c) The speaker talks about "sliding back and forth between the fringes of both worlds" (ll. 17–18). How is this idea emphasised by the structure of the poem?

Windrush child

Behind you
Windrush child
palm trees wave goodbye

above you
Windrush child
seabirds asking why

around you
Windrush child
blue water rolling by

beside you
Windrush child
your Windrush mum and dad

think of storytime yard
and mango mornings
and new beginnings
doors closing and opening

will things turn out right?
At least the ship will arrive
in midsummer light

and you Windrush child
think of grandmother
telling you don't forget to write
and with one last hug
walk good walk good
and the sea's wheel carries on
spinning

and from that place England
you tell her in a letter
of your Windrush adventure
stepping in a big ship
not knowing how long the journey
or that you're stepping into history

bringing your Caribbean eye
to another horizon
grandmother's words your shining
beacon

learning how to fly
the kite of your dreams
in an English sky

Windrush child
walking good walking good
in a mind-opening
meeting of snow and sun

John Agard

John Agard

3 Compare the two poems on page 120 → Dealing with poetry, p. 226

a) To what extent are the experiences described in both poems similar, to what extent are they different?

b) How do the speakers feel about their experience? How is this expressed in the two poems?

9 **4 Listen to and read the third poem. Then answer the following questions.**

a) Who is the "Windrush child" addressed in this poem? What situation is being described here?

b) The poem contains references to the past and what has been left behind, the present and the future of the addressee. Copy this table into your exercise book and add similar references. Summarise each column of the table in one sentence.

Past	Present	Future
palm trees storytime yard …	seabirds blue water …	new beginnings doors opening …

0 **windrush** – *Empire Windrush* ist der Name des Schiffes, auf dem im Jahr 1948 die erste große Gruppe von Einwanderern aus der Karibik nach England kam.

36 **beacon** – Leuchtfeuer

38 **kite** – Drachen

Word bank

The writer wants to express … • The message of the poem is … • The person in the poem feels … • The choice of words suggests that … • In my opinion, … • … is a metaphor for …

A Racial stereotypes

1 Before you read → Describing cartoons, p. 242

a) Discuss what stereotypes of ethnic or other groups you know of. To what extent does your personal experience confirm or contradict these stereotypes?

b) Describe the cartoon. Who or what is the target of the cartoon? How is irony used to emphasise the point being made?

to spot – entdecken
split second – der Bruchteil einer Sekunde

Racial stereotypes can be unconscious but reversible

Negative stereotypes about various racial groups bombard us every day in the mass media and deposit their residue deep into our minds, often without our realizing it, says Brian Lowery. Even among the most well intentioned and consciously egalitarian people, says the associate professor of organizational behavior, non-conscious associations about ethnic groups still have a pernicious effect on behavior and attitudes.

The good news, he says, is that we can also be influenced for the better, particularly by social relationships with people who strongly value egalitarian ideals. Lowery's work moves the dialogue on racism beyond simple dichotomies that divide people into categories of "good" and "bad" according to their views on people of a different race or ethnicity. "The situation is much more complex," he says. Even people who consciously disavow prejudice can fall into racist traps.

In one study, for example, Lowery demonstrated how racial stereotypes subtly operate in the penal system. Los Angeles police and probation officers were asked to make judgments about a hypothetical adolescent (whose race was not identified) who had allegedly either shoplifted or assaulted a peer. Certain officers were first subliminally exposed to words commonly associated with African Americans (such as ghetto, homeboy, dreadlocks, etc.) on a rapidly flashing computer screen so that they took in the information subconsciously. In contrast to subjects who did not receive this "priming", officers with the subconscious messaging attributed more negative traits and greater culpability to the hypothetical offenders, and they endorsed harsher punishment – all typical responses to black as opposed to white offenders.

In other words, by simply unconsciously thinking about black people, officers suddenly began seeing a neutral situation in racially stereotypical terms – without even knowing it. The subliminal priming was all it took to activate the entire program of material these officers held about African Americans. The phenomenon held sway even for officers who reported – and truly believed – they were tolerant and non-biased toward non-whites. "What's particularly interesting is that many of the officers were African Americans themselves," Lowery notes. "This shows the degree to which even African Americans can be affected by the negative associations in the environment." When participants who

2 **residue** – Rückstand, Rest
3 **egalitarian** – egalitär, auf politische oder soziale Gleichheit ausgerichtet
4 **pernicious** – schädlich
8 **dichotomy** – Zweiteilung
10 **to disavow** – verleugnen, von etw. abrücken
11 **subtly** – fast unmerklich
11 **penal system** – Strafvollzug
12 **probation officer** – Bewährungshelfer
13 **allegedly** – angeblich
13 **to assault** – angreifen
14 **subliminal** – unterschwellig
17 **priming** – Grundierung; Vorbereitung
17 **trait** – Eigenschaft
18 **culpability** – Strafbarkeit
18 **offender** – Straftäter(in)
18 **to endorse** – billigen, unterstützen
24 **biased** – voreingenommen

had received the subliminal priming were later debriefed and told about the results, Lowery reports, they were extremely uncomfortable. "People are very reluctant to believe their scores reflect anything about their attitudes, and they instead try to invalidate the measures," he says.

In other research, Lowery examined just how readily people associate particular social groups with certain kinds of feelings. In a subliminal word-association exercise, black people's faces were more quickly associated with negative words, while white faces were linked with positive words.

Lowery found, however, that such associations would change when subjects were exposed to someone who displayed egalitarian attitudes (as evidenced by wearing a T-shirt with an anti-racism message). The presence of an egalitarian African American person or white person who was friendly and appealing was enough to shift participants' unconscious racial associations to become less negative about blacks. Interestingly, the presence of an unfriendly though egalitarian researcher did not result in such a shift. "When we like or identify with people, we're more likely to emulate their attitudes and behaviors," Lowery explains. His research also confirms that children who identify strongly with parental figures tend to pick up their parents' racial views.

What's hopeful about these latter results, Lowery says, is that a change in viewpoint toward another ethnic group can come from within a social group through positive and appealing role models who exhibit justice-minded attitudes – an important factor given that widespread segregation often makes it difficult for various groups to interact. By exploring such possibilities, Lowery's work is helping to expand the research on ethnic stereotyping in new directions. In addition, by working with participants in live settings such as the juvenile justice system – and not relying exclusively on student subjects as researchers in the laboratory typically do – he is also helping to demonstrate how racism operates in populations where such issues can literally be a matter of life and death.

(685 words)

27 **to debrief** – eingehend befragen
28 **reluctant** – widerwillig, widerstrebend
28 **score** – *hier:* Ergebnis
29 **to invalidate** – für nichtig erklären, entkräften
34 **to evidence** – ausdrücken, zeigen
38 **to emulate** – nachahmen
46 **juvenile** – Jugend-

2 Comprehension: True or false?

Read the statements below and decide whether they are true or false. Quote or paraphrase words from the text which confirm or disprove the ideas in the statements.

a) There is no clear division between people who are racists and people who aren't.

b) The officers who were shown the words on a flashing computer screen were not aware that they thought the offender was black.

c) Officers who said they weren't racists did not associate negative qualities with the offender, although they had received the "priming".

d) Negative stereotypes are subconscious and cannot be changed.

e) Lowery's research is important because it shows the influence of racial stereotypes on people who make important decisions about the lives of many others.

13

3 Comment → Writing a comment, p. 229

Discuss how both individuals and society as a whole can try to challenge and overcome racial stereotyping.

4 Group discussion → Discussions, p. 246

In your multicultural neighbourhood in Germany, some people are not quite happy with how little contact there is between the different ethnic groups. Some say that they don't feel welcome, while others say that some ethnic groups don't really want to mix and integrate. In your community centre, representatives of the different ethnic groups come together and discuss what can be done to improve the situation. Form groups to represent different ethnic groups and prepare arguments for a class discussion. Talk about how you perceive the situation, explain your reasons for behaving as you do, and then discuss plans to change things.

B National identity

1 Before you read

a) Which recent events can you remember that are connected to religious radicalism? Discuss with a partner.

b) In your opinion, what drives people to join extremist organisations?

A 3.10

Reflections of a former British Muslim extremist

The following interview with Ed Husain, a former Muslim extremist and author of the controversial book The Islamist *(2007), was recorded in February 2008.*

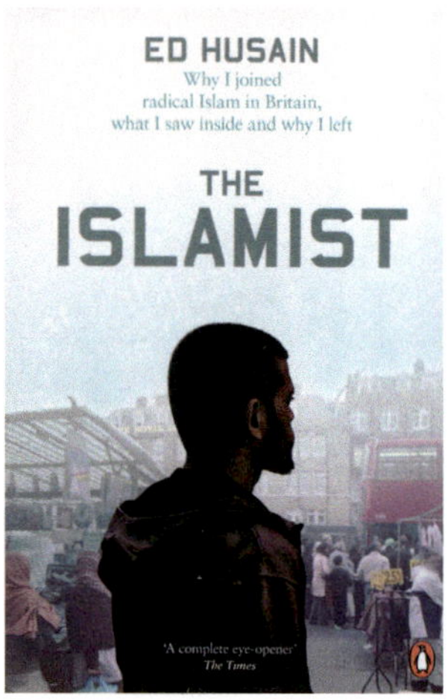

Ms Tippett: You were born and raised in Britain. You were not an immigrant. You were perhaps living in a culture that was defined by immigrants but, you know, talk to me a little bit about your British identity and why your link to that was susceptible or vulnerable or tenuous so that you were captured by some of these ideas.

Ed Husain: We have a real problem in Britain. It was the case when I was growing up and it's still the case now in that it's extremely difficult to define Britishness. Whereas in America it's different. You have a very clear sense of national identity. We don't have that here. There's the Welsh issue, the Scottish issue, and the Irish issue that compounds this problem. And then bring into the mix people who arrived in Britain in the 1960s after the winding up of the British Empire in the West Indies and in India. You have a group of people who arrived here, you know, my parents' generation, initially for economic purposes with some hope of, you know, going back as it were one day. That going back never happened. So my generation, born and raised here, we're confused as to where our parents stood. At home we were exposed to one culture; at school we were exposed to another. So Britishness was never clearly defined for my generation growing up. And the fact that we've got communities up and down the country that live totally separate lives – I mean, in the name of multiculturalism we've created these monocultural ghettos in Bradford, Birmingham, Burnley, parts of London where there is no interaction between, you know, native white English communities and the children of immigrants. And so it's very much a live problem here in Britain.

Ms Tippett: And I have a sense that when you first became attracted to a kind of politicized Islam, initially not necessarily extremist, but just that some of the words you used to describe what you found worthy in what you were experiencing was that, you know, it sounds like it almost seemed to bridge some of these different aspects of your identity that weren't bridged in the culture. You said it was English-speaking, educated, rooted in faith.

Ed Husain: You see, when we went to mosques – when I went to mosques – most of the imams came from Pakistan, Bangladesh, India. They spoke about an Islam that was very much village-based, a folkloric Islam. It wasn't something that people like myself, born and raised here in Britain in a different cultural-social-political setup, could easily relate to. We were always given Islam in a second language, the language of our parents – Urdu, Bengali, whatever. But suddenly when I reached my teens, there were these young people who spoke Islam in the language that I easily identified with, i.e., English. So it took me a while to cotton on to the fact that the sort of Islam they were trying to sell to people like myself was an Islam that was at odds with my parents' more Sufistic,traditional orthodox Islam. But the English-speaking radicals were trying to promote a sense … a type of Islam that was, you know, Islamist, politicized.

5 **susceptible** – anfällig, beeinflussbar
5 **vulnerable** – angreifbar, verwundbar
5 **tenuous** – schwach
10 **to compound** – verschlimmern
11 **to wind up** – enden
16 **to be exposed to sth.** – etw. ausgesetzt sein
30 **to relate to sth.** – sich mit etw. identifizieren
33 **to cotton on to sth.** – anfangen, etw. zu verstehen
34 **to be at odds with sth.** – zu etw. im Widerspruch stehen
35 **Sufistic** – sufistisch

But against that, there was something else going on in the early 1990s here in Europe that people often forget. And that was the entire Balkan crisis.

Ms Tippett: Right.

Ed Husain: Between '91 and '94, you had large numbers of Muslims in Bosnia, who were white, blond, blue-eyed, being slaughtered in their thousands. And when people from, you know, Arab countries who had taken political refuge in Britain – Omar Bakri and others – came and said to us that, 'Look, two hours away from London's Heathrow Airport, you've got people who are being slaughtered in their thousands despite being European Muslims for 600 years. What chance do people like you and I, who are brown-skinned, black-haired, got in the long term here in Britain?' So for a 16 year-old who is not entirely comfortable in being in Britain, that message, you know, has a strong resonance. [...] And I think the same thing is going today with Iraq with lots of young people, but most certainly Bosnia politicized me. Yes. [...]

Ms Tippett: Right. And over the years I've spoken with a number of people who – and not just Muslims – who as young people, you know, tends to be the rule became drawn into extremist movements. And, you know, one of the things they've talked about to me is the intoxication and the power that comes with that that meets something in adolescence and young adulthood, where one's identity is fragile, where one is looking for a cause and identity. Was that your experience too, I mean, could you talk about the appeal of this idea to you at that point in your life and in this milieu, you know, you really describe British universities and schools where these kinds of ideas were everywhere. [...] (872 words)

51 **intoxication** – Rausch
53 **fragile** – zerbrechlich, schwach

2 Comprehension

a) Summarise in your own words why, according to Ed Husain, his generation has had problems establishing a British identity.

b) Outline the reasons Husain and Tippet give for young Muslims being drawn into extremist movements.

3 Discussion

Work with a partner. Having read the first part of the interview with Ed Husain, which other things would you like to know about him? Write down at least five questions.

2 13

4 Listening comprehension → Listening, p. 221

Listen to the second part of the interview and answer the questions.

a) What impressed Husain about his Muslim scholars such as Iman Hamza and Yusuf Hanson?

b) What does Husain say about Muslims in America?

c) In which year did the 7th July terror attack in London take place, and how many people were killed?

d) Why, according to Husain, was this attack a kind of "wake-up call" for the UK?

e) What is, in the political far right's view, responsible for extremist movements in the UK?

5 Research project → Hotspot 1, p. 133

C Cross-cultural attitudes

Chris Cleave (British writer and journalist, born in 1973)

1 Before you read
What do you think are the problems that asylum seekers face when they come to a new country? Make a list and report back to the class.

"Little Bee", written by British author Chris Cleave in 2008, is a story about a Nigerian asylum seeker in Britain. It focuses on the treatment of refugees by the asylum system.

1 **coin** – Münze
3 **fickle** – flatterhaft
4 **corner shop** – Tante-Emma-Laden
9 **gunfire** – Schüsse
9 **thatch** – Dachstroh
14 **to disguise oneself** – sich verkleiden
15 **property** – Eigentum
16 **to trap sth.** – etw. einfangen
18 **sorcerer** – Zauberer
18 **to pursue** – verfolgen
18 **to shed** – abwerfen
18 **tail** – Schwanz
19 **to seize** – packen
25 **to leap** – springen
25 **turnstile** – Drehkreuz
26 **to dodge** – ausweichen
26 **tackle** – Angriff

Little Bee

MOST DAYS I WISH I was a British pound coin instead of an African girl. Everyone would be pleased to see me coming. Maybe I would visit with you for the weekend and then suddenly, because I am fickle like that, I would visit with the man from the corner shop instead – but you would not be sad because you would be eating a cinnamon bun, or drinking a cold Coca-Cola from the can, and you would never think of me again.

We would be happy, like lovers who met on holiday and forgot each other's names. A pound coin can go wherever it thinks it will be safest. It can cross deserts and oceans and leave the sound of gunfire and the bitter smell of burning thatch behind. When it feels warm and secure it will turn around and smile at you, the way my big sister Nkiruka used to smile at the men in our village in the short summer after she was a girl but before she was really a woman, and certainly before the evening my mother took her to a quiet place for a serious talk.

Of course a pound coin can be serious too. It can disguise itself as power, or property, and there is nothing more serious when you are a girl who has neither. You must try to catch the pound, and trap it in your pocket, so that it cannot reach a safe country unless it takes you with it. But a pound has all the tricks of a sorcerer. When pursued I have seen it shed its tail like a lizard so that you are left holding only pence. And when you finally go to seize it, the British pound can perform the greatest magic of all, and this is to transform itself into not one, but two, identical green American dollar bills. Your fingers will close on empty air, I am telling you.

How I would love to be a British pound. A pound is free to travel to safety, and we are free to watch it go. This is the human triumph. This is called, *globalization*. A girl like me gets stopped at immigration, but a pound can leap the turnstiles, and dodge the tackles of those big men with their uniform caps, and jump straight into a waiting airport taxi. *Where to, sir?* Western Civilization, my good man, and make it snappy.

13 **2 Comprehension** → Understanding fictional texts, p. 224

a) What do we learn about Little Bee? Summarise the information given in the text.

b) Outline why, according to Little Bee, it is so desirable to be able to speak the Queen's English.

13 **3 Analysis** → Text analysis, p. 228

a) Analyse how the author illustrates Little Bee's feelings and experiences.

b) Explain the phrase "Learning the Queen's English is like scrubbing off the bright red varnish from your toenails, the morning after a dance." (ll. 51–52)

4 Research project → Hotspot 2, p. 133

See how nicely a British pound coin talks? It speaks with the voice of Queen Elizabeth the Second of England. Her face is stamped upon it, and sometimes when I look very closely I can see her lips moving. I hold her up to my ear. What is she saying? *Put me down this minute, young lady, or I shall call my guards.*

If the Queen spoke to you in such a voice, do you suppose it would be possible to disobey? I have read that the people around her – even kings and prime ministers – they find their bodies responding to her orders before their brains can even think why not. Let me tell you, it is not the crown and the scepter that have this effect. Me, I could pin a tiara on my short fuzzy hair, and I could hold up a scepter in one hand, like this, and police officers would still walk up to me in their big shoes and say, *Love the ensemble, madam, now let's have a quick look at your ID, shall we?* No, it is not the Queen's crown and scepter that rule in your land. It is her grammar and her voice. That is why it is desirable to speak the way she does. That way you can say to police officers, in a voice as clear as the Cullinan diamond, *My goodness, how dare you?*

I am only alive at all because I learned the Queen's English. Maybe you are thinking, that isn't so hard. After all, English is the official language of my country, Nigeria. Yes, but the trouble is that back home we speak it so much better than you. To talk the Queen's English, I had to forget all the best tricks of my mother tongue. For example, the Queen could never say, *There was plenty wahala, that girl done use her bottom power to engage my number one son and anyone could see she would end in the bad bush.* Instead the Queen must say, *My late daughter-in-law used her feminine charms to become engaged to my heir, and one might have foreseen that it wouldn't end well.* It is all a little sad, don't you think?

Learning the Queen's English is like scrubbing off the bright red varnish from your toenails, the morning after a dance. It takes a long time and there is always a little bit left at the end, a stain of red along the growing edges to remind you of the good time you had. So, you can see that learning came slowly to me. On the other hand, I had plenty of time. I learned your language in an immigration detention center, in Essex, in the southeastern part of the United Kingdom. Two years, they locked me in there. Time was all I had. (967 words)

30 **stamped** – geprägt
32 **guard** – Wache
34 **to disobey** – nicht gehorchen
37 **tiara** – Diadem
37 **fuzzy** – kraus
39 **ensemble** – *hier:* Outfit
41 **desirable** – erstrebenswert
46 **mother tongue** – Muttersprache
48 **engaged** – verlobt
49 **heir** – Erbe
51 **varnish** – Lack
53 **stain** – Fleck
55 **immigration detention center** – Auffanglager für Einwanderer

D Immigration

1 Before you read → Brainstorming, p. 253
For what reasons do people leave their home country and start a life somewhere else? Make a list and compare it with your partner.

A 3.13

7 **niece** – Nichte
7 **nephew** – Neffe
14 **raspberry** – Himbeere
17 **to keep track of sth.** – über etw. Aufzeichnungen machen
21 **agricultural** – landwirtschaftlich
25 **papers** – offizielle Unterlagen, z. B. Aufenthaltserlaubnis
27 **resident** – Bewohner(in)
27 **permanent residency** – Daueraufenthalt
29 **green card** – Wohnsitznachweis für Ausländer(innen) in den USA
33 **to mind one's own business** – sich um seinen eigenen Kram kümmern
34 **jealousy** – Eifersucht

Migrant fruit pickers at work

An immigrant's long journey

Armando and his family

What aspects of your life in Mexico made you leave your home?
It wasn't me … it was my mom's decision. I was still young. My mom wanted more opportunities for a more successful life for her kids – all seven of us plus some of her nieces and nephews who counted more on her for support than on their own mother.

Was it easy to find jobs? What were they and how much did you earn?
I was only 13 when I arrived in the US, but I did work in the fields with my mom during the summer and after school. I worked in the raspberry fields where my mom worked. She earned about $2 per can (about the size of a large coffee can) of firm raspberries and $1 per can of softer raspberries, used for jams and juices. On good days, we would pick about 40 cans full of raspberries per day, three people (my mom, my sister and I) working for 14 hours on my mom's ticket. Each worker has a ticket that keeps track of how many cans they've collected. That's basically what they use to calculate your pay check for the week. The raspberry season is only about half the year and the good days are only about half of that time. Needless to say, the pay was minimal and sporadic. There was no future planning with agricultural jobs. The only non-agricultural job I was able to get without papers was at a fast food restaurant that paid me $4.50 per hour.

How did you go from being an illegal immigrant to becoming a US citizen? Was your story typical of the other immigrants you know?
Actually, all of my brothers and sisters now have their papers, thanks to the people they married. My route was faster because I married a US citizen, whereas they all married permanent residents. I was able to earn my permanent residency within one year of getting married, whereas they have had to wait at least 5 years for their green card. The only way I know of people getting their green cards is through marriage. What I've noticed about people who come to this country is that the relationship with their families is easily broken. It wasn't that way back home. In Mexico, there's more respect passed on to children. Children are looked after by all the neighbors when they play in the streets. Here everyone is expected to just mind their own business. With more money it seems that more jealousy and many more problems come. People are so busy working all day long, sometimes working two or three jobs. While in Mexico, life is lived day by day. We were poor in Mexico and we still gave to those who had less than we did.

How did you meet your wife?

Mimi came to Watsonville, California, as a volunteer. She used to pick up the kids at the labor camp where I lived and take them to the Penny Club for after-school activities. At first I thought she was too serious, but I think that was her reaction because she had never seen people living in such poor conditions. After she finished her volunteer year, we began dating and got married civilly about a year later. The only people who were present were two of my sisters and my mom. Mimi didn't tell her parents until after we were married.

I wouldn't say that her family immediately welcomed me, but slowly I grew on them. I think in part it was because they didn't expect such a commitment so soon.

How would you describe your present situation?

I am very thankful to my family and Mimi's family for where I am today. I'm also thankful for our two beautiful and healthy boys, Luis and Rafa. I try to live simply and work hard every day. I make time to play soccer with my two sons. I'm fortunate to be able to help my mom in California and my aunt in Mexico financially. This is due in part to the fact that Mimi's parents "gave" us one of their houses so we don't have a mortgage to pay. As a laboratory technician and a teacher, we do not earn a lot of money, but we make enough to provide for our family and save a little for the future. (738 words)

Interview with Uli Nürnberger

39 **volunteer** – Freiwillige(r)
40 **labor camp** – Arbeitslager
43 **to marry civilly** – standesamtlich heiraten
47 **commitment** – *hier:* Bindung
51 **fortunate** – glücklich
54 **mortgage** – Hypothek
55 **to provide for** – sorgen für, versorgen

14 **2 Comprehension**
Armando is representative of many immigrants from Latin America. Make a list of these typical aspects.

3 Analysis
Explain what elements of his story are not very typical of an immigrant's story.

4 14 **4 Listening comprehension** → Listening, p. 221
Listen to the second part of the interview and complete the sentences.

a) For Armando Perez, the *American Dream* is …

b) The first attempt to cross the border failed because …

c) They were eventually able to cross the border because …

d) In the USA they were helped by …

e) Illegal immigrants often work as …

f) The two things taken away from immigrants' paychecks are …

g) The government doesn't want to legalise undocumented workers because …

h) Many American citizens wouldn't do the jobs that illegal immigrants do because …

14 **5 Text production: A letter** → Writing a personal letter, p. 233
Write a letter to Armando in which you comment on his story. Include information about the situation of migrant workers in Germany.

6 Research projects → Hotspots 3 and 4, p. 133

E Patriotism

1 Before you read – Think-pair-share

a) What does patriotism mean to you? Write down five key words or expressions that you associate with this term.

b) Compare your list with that of a partner and agree on five words/expressions between you.

c) Share your results with another pair and agree on five words/expressions. Which of your words have negative or positive connotations? Discuss with the class.

2 **to spoil** – verderben
4 **to reinforce** – verstärken
4 **notion** – Idee
5 **to avoid** – vermeiden
7 **Aussie** – *(ugs.)* Australier(in)
7 **despite** – trotz
8 **to commemorate** – gedenken, feiern
8 **to found** – gründen
8 **penal colony** – Strafkolonie
8 **downtrodden** – unterdrückt
9 **to sentence** – verurteilen
9 **punishment** – Bestrafung
10 **loaf of bread** – Brotlaib
11 **over the top** – übertrieben
11 **reverence** – Verehrung
12 **sheepish** – kleinlaut
14 **to gather** – zusammenkommen
15 **sacred** – heilig
16 **to stage** – veranstalten
16 **fundraiser** – Benefizveranstaltung
20 **to highlight** – hervorheben
21 **invidious** – gehässig
23 **to witness** – beobachten
24 **spectator** – Zuschauer(in)
25 **peninsular** – Halbinsel
25 **coachload** – Busladung

theguardian

News | Sport | Comment | Culture | Business | Money | Life&Style | Travel | Environment

Comment is free > Australia   Search [ ] GO

It's Australia Day. Don't let the 'we grew here, you flew here' crew spoil it

Australians do patriotism much better than Brits – but some are using our national day to reinforce notions of us and them.

One of the many things Australia does particularly well – apart from sport and avoiding the global financial crisis – is patriotism. And never more so than today, Australia Day.

There have never been any flies on us Aussies as we celebrate our national day, despite the fact that it commemorates the founding 223 years ago of a penal colony for downtrodden Brits, who could find themselves sentenced to seven years' transportation as punishment for as little as stealing a loaf of bread.

Not for us, the over-the-top religious reverence of the United States (Australians never ask God to bless their country) nor the slightly sheepish British patriotism (because you always have to feel guilty about the empire). Instead, Australians today enjoy a day off work and gather for their most sacred ritual – the backyard BBQ (this year staged as fundraisers for the Queensland flood victims).

At least, that's what I thought. But a shadow is falling over the sunburnt country and its patriotic celebrations, highlighted by the growing use of an invidious new phrase: "We grew here, you flew here."

I have always thought Australian patriotism left British patriotism for dead. I once witnessed two Australian spectators at a tennis tournament show more support for the Aussie player than the rest of the British arena. When Australians visit the Gallipoli peninsular in Turkey in their coach-

2 Comprehension

a) Describe in your own words why, according to the author, Australia does patriotism "particularly well" as opposed to the USA and the UK. Give examples from the text.

b) Outline the recent developments in Australian patriotism the author has noticed, and how he feels about them.

3 Analysis

Explain the statement "We grew here, you flew here." (ll. 1–2)

4 Comment

Football players are often criticized for not singing the national anthem before international matches as this is seen to be unpatriotic. Do you agree with this criticism? Discuss.

loads, they alight at the little cove that marked the landing site of that disastrous first world war military action and cry.

I think the moment it hit home that Britain had a lot to learn from its former colony about national pride was when London won the 2012 Olympics. The contrast 12 years earlier when Sydney won the 2000 Olympics was total. Then thousands of Aussies stayed up until 3am, walked over the Harbour Bridge to Circular Quay to watch Sydney announced the winner on giant TV screens. Everyone expected Beijing to win so the place went wild. Twelve years later, Guardian colleagues gathered around the office TV for the 2012 announcement. Everyone thought Paris would win. When London was announced only one person leapt out of their chair in excitement – me.

One of the best aspects of Australianess, for me at least, is its elasticity. This is not to deny problems of racism but you can become Australian, by and large, because you want to. Thus over the years Australians have claimed as their own people as diverse as the late heart surgeon Victor Chang (born in China), Tony Grieg (born in South Africa, England cricket captain), Russell Crowe (born in New Zealand), Mel Gibson (born in New York) and Nicole Kidman (born in Hawaii).

It is a tradition pleasingly maintained by the man the nation awarded the honour of delivering this year's Australia Day address – Michael Parkinson.

But in recent years Australia Day is being used by some to reinforce notions of us and them. I first heard about this two years ago from friends who visited Australia's nicest and dullest city, Adelaide, and were shocked by how blonde and blue-eyed Australians gave their patriotic celebrations an aggressive, anti-ethnic edge.

Now David Koch, the avuncular breakfast presenter, has zeroed in on this problem with a provocative column for national opinion website The Punch, entitled "What I hate about Australia Day". His answer:

"I hate blonde-haired, blue-eyed yobbos prancing about in the Australian flag who intimidate people who don't look like them."

He recounted how he was haunted by not confronting racist sentiments when he came across them and urged readers to "let's not politely ignore derogatory race-related comments from friends and relatives".

In a way, it is because Australia has done so much to tackle racism that the growing divisiveness of Australia Day is so depressing.

Like Koch, I am proud of Australia and don't believe it a racist country. But yes, some of its residents are. (680 words)

26 **to alight** – aussteigen
26 **cove** – Bucht
28 **to hit home** – *hier:* klar werden
34 **to leap** – springen
35 **elasticity** – Anpassungsfähigkeit
35 **to deny** – abstreiten
37 **heart surgeon** – Herzchirurg(in)
40 **to maintain** – aufrechterhalten
43 **dull** – langweilig
45 **edge** – *hier:* Ton
46 **avuncular** – onkelhaft
46 **to zero in on sth.** – auf etw. fokussieren
49 **yobbo** – Rowdy
49 **to prance about** – herumtanzen
49 **to intimidate** – einschüchtern
51 **to recount** – erzählen
51 **to haunt** – verfolgen
51 **sentiment** – Ansicht
52 **to urge** – ermahnen
52 **derogatory** – abschätzig, abwertend
54 **to tackle** – bekämpfen
54 **divisiveness** – Gespaltenheit
57 **resident** – Einwohner(in)

Avoiding mistakes: German-English interference

In the following exercises, you are asked to identify some of the mistakes often made by German learners of English.

a) Read the sentences and then decide which answer is correct. Give a reason for your choice.

Pablo Jamirez **1** in San Diego for three years now.	lives	has lived
He **2** from Ecuador three years ago.	came	has come
In Ecuador, Pablo Jamirez studied to be **3**.	dentist	a dentist
In San Diego, however, he works as **4**.	fruit picker	a fruit picker
He **5** his family in Ecuador because the trip is too expensive, …	visits never	never visits
… but he writes letters and explains **6** why he can't come.	them	to them
Some days ago, his cousin called him and asked him about life in the USA. He gladly gave her the **7** she had asked for.	information	informations
He told her that in the USA **8** a lot of jobs for people who are willing to work hard.	are	there are
There are **9** Americans who are willing to pick raspberries all day long in the summer heat.	few	a few
Once they have a work permit, **10** people find better-paid jobs and don't pick fruit any more.	most	the most

b) Error-spotting: Read the following sentences and correct the mistakes.

The Notting Hill Carnival

1. The society has changed a great deal over the last decades, becoming much more multicultural.
2. In England live people from many different countries such as India, Pakistan and the Caribbean.
3. In the 1950s there have been fights between white youth gangs and the Caribbean immigrants.
4. As a response, a Caribbean street festival was celebrated during which people enjoyed to dance in the streets and to eat Caribbean food.
5. The Notting Hill Carnival is celebrated every summer in August since 1966.
6. Some people complain themselves about the noise and all the rubbish that is left in the streets.
7. However, the most people think it is a great symbol of the new multicultural Britain.
8. Seeing the costumes and hearing the steel drums is a good thing because many British people do not have enough informations about other cultures.

1 Research project: Writers and their roots → Internet research, p. 260
Work in small groups. Choose one of the following writers:

Pat Mora • John Agard • Ed Husain • Jackie Kay

Collect information on their ethnic background, their work, and how cross-cultural issues such as ethnic diversity, immigration, prejudice, and racism influence their writing.

2 Research project: Ethnic minorities → Internet research, p. 260
Divide the class into three groups, one for the United States, one for Britain and one for Germany. Within your group, research the main ethnic minorities living in that country and form small subgroups. Prepare a short presentation about the minority group you have researched, including information about their history within the new country:
- When and why did members of that ethnic group immigrate?
- Is immigration still going on?
- What is the situation of that ethnic group in the country (legal, social, etc.)?

3 Research project: Traces of German immigrants in the USA → Presentation, p. 264
The influence of German immigrants was very strong in the United States especially during the 19th century, and many traces can be observed to this day. Form different groups and find out about:
- **German place names in the US:** Select three or four cities which have German names and read up on their histories. Why were they given their names?
- **German words in the English language:** Use the Internet to find German words that have been adopted into the English language (you call this "borrowing"). Explain why these specific words were borrowed.
- **German food in the US:** Look for German restaurants in US cities on the Internet. Where are many of them located? Find out what specialties they offer.
- **German culture:** Find out about the Goethe-Schiller monument in Weimar. There are copies of this monument in four US cities. This is only one example of the influence of German culture in the US. Explain this and/or find further examples. One way to go about this is to type the name of a famous German person (Goethe, Schiller, Heine, etc.) plus "USA" into the search engine and see what results you get.
- **Famous German immigrants or descendants of German immigrants:** These are easy to find on the Internet. Choose a few prominent examples and present their stories.
- **In 2010, a German-American museum opened in Washington, D.C.:** Introduce this museum to the class.

Present your findings to the class in the form of a poster, a short presentation, an interactive mini-lesson, etc. It is possible to divide some of the topics between two groups.

4 Project: Immigration to Germany
Which ethnic groups are represented in your class? Interview your classmates with ethnic backgrounds and find out the reasons why their families immigrated to Germany. Present your results to the class.

A 3.16

Julian Baggini (British author, born in 1968)

1 **to point the finger** – to accuse
2 **Mail (Daily Mail)** – a British newspaper
2 **editorial** – a newspaper article that expresses the editor's opinion
3 **impact** – a strong effect
4 **to eschew** – to avoid
5 **to walk on eggshells** – to be very careful
13 **perception** – awareness of how sth. is
15 **to dilute** – *here:* to make weaker
22 **incarceration** – to put or keep sb. in prison

It's no use pointing the finger at ethnic minorities

The Mail expressed the dominant view of multiculturalism in an editorial on 17 July: "[The] malign impact of multiculturalism and political correctness has for years seen Britain segregated into inward-looking communities that eschew British values while the forces of law and order walk on eggshells, desperate not to offend." Put more positively, and in pub terms, it's that people "don't mind who lives here, whether they're black, white or green, as long as they follow our way of life." Interestingly, although we're not a particularly religious country, most people do think our values are in some important way Christian ones. A BBC poll reported that 61 % believe that "our laws should respect and be influenced by UK religious values", with even 49 % of those with no religion agreeing.

Antipathy towards British Asians in particular is thus based largely on the perception that they do not wish to adopt the 'British way of life' or that their numbers are getting so large that the English way is being diluted too much by their mere presence. […] The generally accepted solution is simple: live like the English or get out. Again it should not be presumed that this is racism in disguise. The mainstream wants to expel from society, through enforced emigration or incarceration, all sorts of people who refuse to conform, and the fact that the majority of those they currently want out have different coloured skins is a historical accident.

1 Comprehension

a) Using the text, outline what British people expect of ethnic minorities in their country.

b) In your own words, summarise the reasons why different cultural and ethnic groups in England hardly mix.

2 Analysis → Describing cartoons, p. 242

a) Explain the author's view on the lack of mixing between the minority groups mentioned in the text.

b) Decribe the cartoon, analyse it and relate it to the text.

The argument may be flawed but it is based on several truths that we would be foolish to ignore. The first is that it is true that many minorities do not fully integrate into mainstream English culture. This is plain fact. Ethnic minority populations do concentrate in particular areas. […] Although mixed race marriages are on the rise, they still comprise only 2% of all marriages. Only 6% of British Indians, 4% of Pakistanis and 3% of Bangladeshis have married a non-Asian. In contrast 29% of black Caribbean men and 48% of other black men have married non-black women. For the most part, people mix and marry with people mainly of their own cultural background, as determined by a combination of country, family origin or religion. This is the same the world over. For instance, while in Spain I saw a newspaper report on a study which showed that 75% of immigrants there did not have a Spanish friend.

The key point, however, is that every sector of society does this. It's no use pointing the finger at ethnic minorities. England is a patchwork of almost hermetically sealed sub-worlds, in which class as much as race is a crucial factor. […] We all like to feel that we're open-minded people who can be friends with anyone, and we also can probably come up with a few examples of friends who do not match our demographic profile to prove our lack of insularity. […] But if we are honest, the vast majority live, work and socialize overwhelmingly with people of a similar social type. […]

The point about multiculturalism is therefore a red herring. All sorts of social groups don't mix very much, yet we don't chastise them for it. The trouble is not caused by not mixing, but refusing to do so in ways which seem to threaten other groups. As long as staying apart isn't threatening, it is not only accepted, it is actually what people want. (588 words)

From: Julian Baggini, Welcome to Everytown

27 **flawed** – having mistakes

40 **patchwork** – sth. that is made up of different things

41 **crucial** – very important

44 **insularity** – interested only in your own country or group

47 **red herring** – a wrong track

48 **to chastise** – to punish

3 Comment

→ Writing a comment, p. 229

"As long as staying apart isn't threatening, it is not only accepted, it is actually what people want." (ll. 50–51). Discuss to what extent you agree with this statement. Choose examples from what you have learned about minorities in the US or Britain, or from your own experience.

Topic 9
The global challenge

7mz39c

A

B

C

D

E

F

Getting started

1 **a)** Identify seven different personal objects in the classroom (clothes, watches, etc.) that originated from seven different countries by checking the labels. Find the countries on a world map. Make a grid.

Object	Produced in	What you know about the country
mobile	…	…
trainers	…	…

b) Which of these findings surprised you most? Why?

c) How did the objects that were not made in Germany get into the classroom?

d) Why were none of these objects produced in Germany?

e) Were they ever made here? When? Where? How?

Globalization Blues

You can't hide in your bed;
You can't hide in your head.
They'll run over you; you'll be worse off than dead.
I'm talkin' globalization, globalization.
Drug-dealing, money-stealing globalization blues.

They say forget your suspicions;
Work in sweatshop conditions.
Sew some more sneakers and guard these munitions.
It's globalization, globalization.
People-bashing, job-smashing globalization blues.

They say your country's in debt
And you've got to pay.
If you want to eat, then do what we say.
That's globalization, globalization.
Slave-made, world-trade globalization blues.

Since you can't get away,
Better fight them today.
From Seattle to Prague, Manila Bay to LA,
It's globalization, globalization.
On the street, we're gonna beat the globalization blues.

Words and music: Ray Korona

3 **to be worse off than sb./sth.** – schlechter dran sein als jmd/etw.
8 **suspicion** – Misstrauen
9 **sweatshop** – Ausbeuterbetrieb
10 **to sew** – nähen
10 **sneakers** – Turnschuhe, Sportschuhe
11 **munitions** – Munition
13 **to bash** – schlagen, schlechtmachen
15 **debt** – Schuld
19 **slave** – Sklave, Sklavin

2 With a partner, make a word web and then write a definition for globalisation as you understand it now. → Word webs, p. 251

3 Listening comprehension → Dealing with songs, p. 227

a) Make a list of the aspects of globalisation that the song "Globalization Blues" focuses on.

b) Write a headline for each of the four verses.

c) Analyse the choice of words used in this song. What is their effect on the listener?

d) Which of the pictures (A – F) can be linked to the song, and why?

e) Which aspects of globalisation are illustrated by the other pictures?

4 Projects → Hotspots 1 and 2, p. 149

Word bank

developing / developed country • global player • with a highly developed / deficient infrastructure • a free market economy • an exporter / importer of … • raw materials • manufactured goods • state-of-the-art technology

A Discovering globalisation

1 Before you read

a) When do you think globalisation really started? Collect your ideas in class.

b) Look at the photos. The heading of the text states three eras of globalisation. From what is shown on the photos, try to guess what these three eras could be.

2 Comprehension: Table completion → Taking notes, p. 254
Make a three-column table and fill in the main features describing each of the three great eras of globalisation. Use your own words as far as possible.

The three eras of globalization

There have been three great eras of globalization. The first lasted from 1492 – when Columbus set sail, opening trade between the Old World and the New World – until around 1800. I would call this era **Globalization 1.0**. It shrank the world from a size large to a size medium. [...] In this era, countries and governments (often inspired by religion or imperialism or a combination of both) led the way in breaking down walls and knitting the world together, driving global integration.

The second great era, Globalization 2.0, lasted roughly from 1800 to 2000, interrupted by the Great Depression and World Wars I and II. This era shrank the world from a size medium to a size small. In **Globalization 2.0**, the key agent of change, the dynamic force driving global integration, was multinational companies. These multinationals went global for markets and labor, spearheaded first by the expansion of the Dutch and English joint-stock companies and the Industrial Revolution. In the first half of this era, global integration was powered by falling transportation costs, thanks to the steam engine and the railroad, and in the second half by falling telecommunication costs – thanks to the diffusion of the telegraph, telephones, the PC, satellites, fiber-optic cable, and the early version of the World Wide Web. It was during this era that we really saw the birth and maturation of a global economy, in the sense that there was enough movement of goods and information from

4 **to shrink** – schrumpfen
6 **to knit sth. together** – etw. verknüpfen
8 **roughly** – ungefähr
13 **to spearhead** – anführen
13 **joint-stock company** – Aktiengesellschaft
17 **diffusion** – Verbreitung
18 **fiber-optic cable** – Glasfaserkabel
19 **maturation** – Reifung

3 Presentation → Presentation, p. 264
Read the quotation by Byron Dorgan and prepare a 3-minute talk to explain to your class what he might have meant when he said it.
"I am not someone who believes we should build fences around our country but I do believe there ought to be some fairness with respect to the rules of this globalization."
Byron Dorgan (former United States Senator from North Dakota)

4 Analysis → Describing cartoons, p. 242

215 **a)** "Globalization 3.0 is shrinking the world from a size small to a size tiny […]." (l. 24). Explain this quote in your own words.

b) Explain the term "[…] to plug in and play." (l. 38).

c) Examine the author's attitude towards globalisation.

d) Describe the cartoon, analyse it and relate it to the text.

5 Comment
"Where do I as an individual fit into the global competition and opportunities of the day […]" (ll. 32–33)
Discuss to what extent you feel fit for the global market.

continent to continent for there to be a global market, with global arbitrage in products and labor. […]

Right around the year 2000 we entered a whole new era: **Globalization 3.0.** Globalization 3.0 is shrinking the world from a size small to a size tiny […]. The dynamic force in Globalization 3.0 – the force that gives it its unique character – is the newfound power for individuals to collaborate and compete globally. […] People all over the world started waking up and realizing that they had more power than ever to go global as individuals, they needed more than ever to think of themselves as individuals competing against other individuals all over the planet, and they had more opportunities to work with those other individuals, not just compete with them. As a result, every person now must, and can, ask: Where do I as an individual fit into the global competition and opportunities of the day, and how can I, on my own, collaborate with others globally? […] Globalization 1.0 and 2.0 were driven primarily by European and American individuals and businesses. […] Globalization 3.0 is going to be more and more driven not only by individuals but also by much more diverse – non-Western, non-white – groups of individuals. […] Globalization 3.0 makes it possible for so many people to plug in and play, and you are going to see every color of the human rainbow take part. (490 words)

from: "The World is flat" by Thomas L. Friedman

Thomas L. Friedman (American journalist, born in 1953)

21 **arbitrage** – Arbitrage, Nutzung der Kursunterschiede an verschiedenen Börsen

25 **unique** – einzigartig

26 **to collaborate** – zusammenarbeiten

26 **to compete** – konkurrieren

34 **primarily** – hauptsächlich, vornehmlich

B A fair world?

1 Before you read

a) Go online and find the official English *Fairtrade* homepage. Use the online information to come up with a definition of Fairtrade.

b) Do you know any Fairtrade shops or supermarkets that sell Fairtrade products in your area? Have you ever been there? What did you buy? If you do not know anything about Fairtrade shops in your area, find out if there are any and give a short presentation to introduce them to your class.

2 Comprehension → Understanding non-fictional texts, p. 222
Work with a partner. One of you reads the leaflet on the left, the other reads the one on the right. Summarise the texts for each other.

FAIRTRADE INTERNATIONAL

Fairtrade International

HOME | ABOUT US | ABOUT FAIRTRADE | STANDARDS | PRODUCT

TRADING UP

THE FAIRTRADE MARK GIVES SMALL FARMERS A STRONGER POSITION IN WORLD MARKETS

In the Windward Islands, in the Caribbean, thousands of families make their living growing bananas on small, hilly farms. During the 1990s, many of them were forced out of business by large-scale Latin American banana plantations where labour is cheaper and costs are lower.

"When prices dropped, the economy went down to zero because bananas are the heartbeat of the country," explains Amos Wiltshire, National Fairtrade Coordinator for Dominica, one of the Windward Islands.

Amos joined forces with other farmers who saw Fairtrade as the only way to survive in a cut-throat market. Through Fairtrade, producers learn how best to sell their products and what the international market and consumers want. Today, nearly 100% of Dominica's banana farmers are members of Fairtrade groups.

> "FAIRTRADE HAS BEEN THE SAVIOUR OF THE FARMERS IN DOMINICA – OF AGRICULTURE AND THE WHOLE ECONOMY. WITH FAIRTRADE, SMALL FARMERS HAVE BEEN TRANSFORMED FROM MARGINALISED FARMERS INTO BUSINESSMEN.
> AMOS WILTSHIRE, BANANA FARMER, DOMINICA"

0 **to trade sth. up** – mit etwas Hochwertigerem ersetzen
0 **mark** – *hier:* Zeichen
2 **to make a living** – seinen Lebensunterhalt verdienen
2 **to grow** – anbauen
4 **to be forced out of business** – gezwungen werden, den Betrieb einzustellen
5 **large-scale** – *hier:* riesig
6 **labour** – Arbeitskräfte
12 **to join forces** – zusammenarbeiten, sich zusammenschließen
13 **to survive** – überleben
13 **cut-throat** – Verdrängungs-
saviour – Retter(in)
to marginalise – ins Abseits drängen

3 Listening comprehension: Making globalisation work → Listening, p. 221

Listen to the thoughts of American economist and university professor Joseph Stiglitz on globalisation. Take notes in English and answer the following questions:

- Which problems and anomalies of globalisation does Stiglitz mention at the beginning of the text?
- How have French workers been affected by globalisation?
- Contrast the USA's and Scandinavia's approach to remaining competitive and efficient in a globalised world. What have been the results?
- Which solutions to the current issues of globalisation does he suggest?

4 Project → Hotspot 3, p. 149

TACKLING POVERTY AND EMPOWERING PRODUCERS THROUGH TRADE

PRODUCERS | RESOURCES | NEWS   Search [ ] GO

A BETTER DEAL

THE FAIRTRADE MARK MEANS A CLOSER LINK BETWEEN SHOPPERS AND PRODUCERS

FAIRTRADE INTERNATIONAL

More and more of us want to know where our shopping comes from and that the people who produce it have received a fair deal. Fairtrade encourages more direct trading relationships so that producers get a bigger share of the export price.

Sweet rewards

In Ghana, liberalisation of the internal cocoa market created big challenges for small farmers; they responded by forming Kuapa Kokoo, a farmer-owned business. Their decision proved wise: Kuapa Kokoo now owns a one-third share in a UK-based company selling Fairtrade chocolate. As well as supplying the cocoa, they have a direct share in the company's success.

"I WANT TO BE SURE THAT FARMERS GET A FAIR PRICE AND BENEFIT DIRECTLY FROM MY PURCHASE. AS THE DAUGHTER OF A GHANAIAN FATHER, I KNOW HOW IMPORTANT FAIRTRADE IS TO SMALL PRODUCERS. WITH MORE SHOPS STOCKING MORE GREAT QUALITY PRODUCTS CARRYING THE FAIRTRADE MARK, IT'S A WIN-WIN SITUATION. WE CAN EAT AND DRINK IN GOOD HEALTH AND GOOD CONSCIENCE." **ADJOA ANDOH, ACTRESS (PICTURED TOP RIGHT)**

(351 words)

21 **to encourage** – ermutigen
22 **share** – Anteil
24 **reward** – Belohnung
25 **liberalisation** – Liberalisierung
26 **challenge** – Herausforderung
26 **to respond** – reagieren
28 **to prove wise** – sich als klug erweisen
30 **to supply** – liefern
33 **to stock** – führen
35 **conscience** – Gewissen

C Global players

1 Before you read
If corporations were persons, which characteristics would you give the following ones?

BÖRSE ▸ ONLINE Search GO

GLOBAL PLAYER: Auf der ganzen Welt zu Hause

Wenn Unternehmen die Vorzüge der internationalen Expansion anpreisen, dann fällt oft der Begriff Abhängigkeit von bestimmten Märkten. Global agierende Konzerne machen Einbußen auf dem Heimatmarkt im internationalen Geschäft wett.

Irgendwo ist immer Wachstum – auch wenn Südeuropa mit einer Schuldenkrise kämpft oder die US-Konjunktur auf der Kippe steht. Für Anleger sollte es sich daher lohnen, nach Aktien weltweit präsenter Unternehmen zu fahnden.

„Wo Firmen ihr Geld verdienen, wird für Investoren immer relevanter", erklärt HSBC-Stratege Garry Evans. So kommt den global agierenden Konzernen derzeit entgegen, dass die Konjunktur in Fernost brummt. „Für den Export sieht es weiter gut aus. Wir profitieren vom Boom in Asien", sagt WestLB-Volkswirt Jörg Lüschow. Der Ländermix hilft den Unternehmen, günstige Währungseffekte auszunutzen und Ertragsrisiken zu streuen.

Ein klassisches Beispiel für eine Weltaktie ist Coca-Cola. Mit einem Markenwert von 58 Mrd. Dollar zählt der Name zu den top drei weltweit. Beinahe überall wird die Brause getrunken – in New York und Peking, auf Grönland und in Kapstadt. Allein in Europa setzte der Softdrinkhersteller aus Atlanta 2009 ein Drittel um.

Boeing 787 Dreamliner

Auch der Flugzeughersteller Boeing gibt wieder eine gute Figur ab. Die peinliche Serie von Entwicklungspannen beim neuen Langstreckenflieger Dreamliner ist passé. Der Supervogel soll in den kommenden Tagen auf der Flugschau in Farnborough vorgestellt werden. Der dickste Auftragsbrocken wartet aber zu Hause: Die US-Luftwaffe will insgesamt 534 Tankflugzeuge ordern. Der Auftrag ist 100 Mrd. Dollar schwer. Um den Zuschlag für die fliegenden Zapfsäulen buhlt auch der Rivale EADS. Doch Brancheninsider rechnen dem US-Unternehmen bessere Chancen aus.

Eine deutsche Weltaktie kommt aus Ludwigshafen. Dort hat BASF die Idee des Verbundstandorts entwickelt: Die Produktionsanlagen sind so miteinander verknüpft, dass sich effiziente Wertschöpfungsketten ergeben. Die Nebenprodukte einer Fabrik dienen an anderer Stelle als Einsatzstoff. Das führt zu Synergien und senkt die Herstellungskosten. BASF hat das Konzept in die Welt exportiert: in die USA nach Freeport und Geismar, in Asien nach Nanjing (China) und Kuantan (Malaysia). Diese Globalisierung der Produktion machte BASF zum führenden Chemiekonzern. Immerhin 16 Prozent der Erlöse erwirtschaftet der Konzern in der Region Asien/Pazifik, in Nordamerika sind es 18 Prozent. Bis 2020 will der Chemieriese den Gesamtumsatz auf mehr als 90 Mrd. Euro fast verdoppeln. Dabei soll das Branchenwachstum jährlich um zwei Prozentpunkte übertroffen werden. (373 words)

2 Vocabulary → Working with a dictionary, p. 255
Find the German equivalents of the following words in the text:

advantages • to praise • dependency • losses • domestic market • growth • debt crisis • economic cycle • shares • Far East • to boom • currency • effects • yield risk • to spread • brand value • to turn over • long-distance aircraft • contract • production facilities • value-added chain • byproducts • production material • production costs • total turnover • to exceed

3 Mediation → Mediation, p. 245
Sum up the main points of the text for an English youth magazine.

4 Analysis → Describing diagrams, p. 243
Describe the table and analyse it.

5 Research projects
→ Hotspots 4 and 5, p. 149

Rank	Previous Rank	Brand	Region/Land	Sector	Brand Value ($m)	Change in Brand Value
1	1	Coca-Cola	United States	Beverages	77,839	8%
2	8	Apple	United States	Electronics	76,568	129%
3	2	IBM	United States	Business Services	75,532	8%
4	4	Google	United States	Internet Services	69,726	26%
5	3	Microsoft	United States	Computer Software	57,853	-2%
6	5	GE	United States	Diversified	43,682	2%
7	6	McDonald's	United States	Restaurants	40,062	13%
8	7	intel	United States	Electronics	39,385	12%
9	–	SAMSUNG	South Korea	Electronics	32,893	40%
10	11	Toyota	Japan	Automotive	30,280	9%
11	12	Mercedes-Benz	Germany	Automotive	30,097	10%
12	–	BMW	Germany	Automotive	29,052	18%

Source: Interbrand 2012

D Corporate power

Max Barry (Australian writer, born in 1973)

1 Before you read → Brainstorming, p. 253
Look at the following quote from the novel *Jennifer Government*:
"But now America has all the best companies and all the money because everyone works and the Government can't spend money on stupid things like advertising and elections and making new laws. They just stop people stealing or hurting each other and everything else is taken care of by the private sector, which everyone knows is more efficient." Brainstorm pros and cons of this vision of the future.

2 Comprehension
In your own words, outline the world that Hayley lives in.

The following text is an extract from Jennifer Government, *a novel written by Max Barry. The story is set in a dystopian alternate reality, in which most countries (now controlled by the USA) are dominated by large profit-seeking corporations.*

3 **to hotfoot (it)** – hasten
9 **to suck** – ätzend sein
11 **to jot** – schnell notieren
13 **arch** – Bogen
14 **to abolish** – abschaffen
18 **crack-up** – etw. zum Totlachen
26 **a smattering of sth.** – ein bisschen
26 **to guess** – glauben, schätzen
27 **to work up enthusiasm for** – Begeisterung aufbringen für
27 **to head for sth.** – etw. ansteuern

McDonald's

Until she stood in front of them, Hayley didn't realize how many of her classmates were blond. It was like a beach out there. She'd missed the trend. Hayley would have to hotfoot it to a hairdresser after school.

"When you're ready," the teacher said.

She looked at her note cards and took a breath. "Why I Love America, by Hayley McDonald's. America is the greatest group of countries in the world because we have freedom. In countries like France, where the Government isn't privatized, they still have to pay tax and do whatever the Government says, which would really suck. In USA countries, we respect individual rights and let people do whatever they want."

The teacher jotted something in his folder. McDonald's-sponsored schools were cheap like that: at Pepsi schools, everyone had notebook computers. Also their uniforms were much better. It was so hard to be cool with the Golden Arches on your back. "Before USA countries abolished tax, if you didn't have a job, the Government took money from working people and gave it to you. So, like, the more useless you were, the more money you got." No response from her classmates. Even the teacher didn't smile. Hayley was surprised: she'd thought that one was a crack-up.

"But now America has all the best companies and all the money because everyone works and the Government can't spend money on stupid things like advertising and elections and making new laws. They just stop people stealing or hurting each other and everything else is taken care of by the private sector, which everyone knows is more efficient." She looked at her notes: yep, that was it. "Finally I would like to say that America is the greatest group of countries in the world and I am proud to live in the Australian Territories of the USA!"

A smattering of applause. It was the eighth talk this period: she guessed it was getting harder to work up enthusiasm for capitalism. Hayley headed for her seat.

3 Analysis → Text analysis, p. 228

a) Analyse Hayley's attitude towards the world she lives in. Include quotes from the text to support your answer.

16 △ **b)** Illustrate Hayley's character. Once again, use quotes from the text to support your answer.

c) Examine the emotions that Hayley goes through during her presentation, and show how the writer puts these across to the reader.

d) Analyse the teacher's attitude towards Hayley's presentation.

16 △ **4 Comment** → Writing a comment, p. 229
"McDonald's-sponsored schools were cheap like that: at Pepsi schools, everyone had notebook computers. Also their uniforms were much better. It was so hard to be cool with the Golden Arches on your back." (ll. 11 – 14) Some people claim that major companies and their brands have too much influence on modern society. Do you agree? Discuss.

"Hold it," the teacher said. "I have questions."
"Oh," Hayley said.
"Are there any positive aspects to tax?"
She relaxed: a gimme question. "Some people say tax is good because it gives money to people who don't have any. But those people must be lazy or stupid, so why should they get other people's money? Obviously the answer is no."
The teacher blinked. He made a note. That must have been an impressive answer, Hayley thought. "What about social justice?"
"What?"
"Is it fair that some people should be rich while others have nothing?"
She shifted from one foot to the other. She was just remembering: this teacher had a thing about poor people. He was always bringing them up. "Um, yeah, it's fair. Because if I study really hard for a test and get an A and Emily doesn't and fails" – renewed interest from the class; Emily raised blond eyebrows – "then it's not fair to take some of my marks and give them to her, is it?"
The teacher frowned. Hayley felt a flash of panic. "Another thing, in non-USA countries they want everyone to be the same, so if your sister is born blind, then they blind you, too, to make it even. But how unfair is that? I would much rather be an American than a European Union … person." She gave the class a big smile. They clapped, much more enthusiastically than before. She added hopefully, "Is that all?"
"Yes. Thank you."
Relief! She started walking. A cute boy in the third row winked at her.
The teacher said, "Although, Hayley, they don't really blind people in non-USA countries."
Hayley stopped. "Well, that's kind of hypocritical, isn't it?"
The class cheered. The teacher opened his mouth, then shut it. Hayley took her seat. Kick ass, she thought. She had aced this test. (628 words)

31 **gimme** *(coll.)* – gib mir
33 **obviously** – offensichtlich
34 **to blink** – blinzeln
34 **impressive** – beeindruckend
35 **justice** – Gerechtigkeit
38 **to shift** – wechseln
41 **renewed** – erneut
43 **to frown** – die Stirn runzeln
43 **flash** – *hier:* Anflug
50 **relief** – Erleichterung
50 **cute** – süß
50 **to wink at sb.** – jmdm zuzwinkern
53 **hypocritical** – scheinheilig, heuchlerisch
54 **to cheer** – jubeln
55 **to ace** – *hier:* die Note 1 bekommen

E Water poverty

1 Before you read

a) Describe the picture and relate it to the title of the article.

b) How do you think limited access to clean drinking water would affect your everyday life? Discuss with a partner and report back to the class.

2 Comprehension: Short answer questions

Read the text and answer the following questions in 5–20 words.

a) What did the United Nations say about the consequences of a lack of access to clean water?

b) What effects does a lack of access to clean water have on women and girls?

c) What is GWC?

GWC **GLOBAL WATER CHALLENGE** Search GO

1 IN 8 PEOPLE LACK ACCESS TO SAFE WATER

Around the globe, nearly 800 million people lack access to water and over 2.5 billion lack access to sanitation. The scope and impact of this crisis are staggering. The United Nations has reported that more people die from water- and sanitation-related disease than from all forms of violence, including war. According to the United Nations Development Program, every US$1 spent on water and sanitation generates a return of US$9 in saved time, increased productivity and reduced health costs in Africa.

Beyond loss of life, water poverty and inadequate sanitation cripple all development efforts. A lack of adequate water and sanitation facilities keeps children, especially girls, from attending school. Women spend an average of 3-5 hours each day fetching water, missing out on opportunities to perform other tasks or engage in economically productive activity. Parents miss work due to water-related illness or caring for sick family members. Existing medical conditions, such as HIV/AIDS, are exacerbated because of unsafe water and inadequate sanitation. Climate change, population growth, industrialization and urbanization all threaten to make the global WASH [Water Sanitation and Hygiene] crisis much worse.

Fortunately, there is room for hope. Waterborne illness is preventable and lasting water supply and sanitation solutions exist. Through concerted efforts by governments, corporations, foundations and nongovernmental organizations, roughly 200 million people have gained access to clean water during the past decade. However, even with these efforts, many countries are unlikely to meet the Millennium Development Goal (MDG) for water and even fewer will reach the MDG for sanitation. Unprecedented collaboration between all sectors of society is needed in order to achieve sustainable solutions to this challenge. [...]

Founded in 2006, Global Water Challenge (GWC) is a nonprofit [...] coalition of leading organizations committed to addressing water and sanitation issues. Drawing upon the experience, expertise and assets of its members, GWC is able to create partnerships that achieve far greater results

0 **access** – Zugriff
2 **sanitation** – sanitäre Einrichtungen
2 **scope** – Ausmaß
3 **staggering** – überwältigend
12 **facility** – Einrichtung
18 **to exacerbate** – verschlimmern
19 **urbanization** – Verstädterung
21 **waterborne** – durch Wasser übertragen
21 **preventable** – vermeidbar
22 **concerted** – gemeinsam
26 **unprecedented** – beispiellos
26 **sustainable** – nachhaltig
30 **asset** – Vermögen

d) In which countries has GWC invested in school programs?

e) How have the students in these schools benefitted?

f) How successful are the GWC's water and sanitation projects?

g) What makes a water and sanitation project 'sustainable'?

3 Analysis
Describe and analyse the cartoon.

4 Presentation → Presentation, p. 264
Access to safe water is not something to take for granted and those in the developed world must learn to use water more responsibly – but how? Work in a small group and create a poster that gives 5–10 tips on how people can save water every day. Present your posters to the class.

5 Research project → Hotspot 6, p. 149

than any one organization could by itself. Since its inception, GWC is a powerful catalyst for fostering collective action in the water sector. GWC serves three core functions:

CONNECTING.
GWC is a platform for collaboration that unites corporations, implementing nonprofits, research institutes, and governmental agencies in partnerships that leverage their unique resources and expertise. In addition, GWC connects citizens with policymakers to increase the priority placed on water and sanitation globally.

INVESTING.
GWC has invested in and collaborated with members on innovative programs and campaigns globally. Some examples include:
Schools Programs: GWC's investment in schools programs has benefited nearly 500,000 students in Kenya, El Salvador, Guatemala, Honduras, Nicaragua, Tanzania, and Mexico. These programs have enhanced children's health and education, paving the way for more opportunities for the students, their families and their countries. [...]

LEARNING.
GWC is committed to improving the long-term impact of investments in the sector by working with its members and other partners to identify and share important lessons and best practices. [...]
To achieve our goal of universal access to clean water and safe sanitation, all GWC projects are sustainable, replicable and scalable by local communities and national governments. GWC is committed to learning from past projects, connecting those who can help each other, and investing and leveraging financial or policy support for innovative projects.

Sustainable
All projects must have long-term plans. It is estimated that half of all water and sanitation projects fail after 5 years. Sustainable projects maintain the local water source and build local capacity in order to maintain and operate a water system. This requires the involvement of the local community, local government, and local businesses. For each system that doesn't have to be replaced, more resources will be available in the future for new projects.

Replicable
GWC measures impacts and benefits consistently, communicating these clearly throughout the project. Monitoring programs and sharing information helps communities, governments, local entrepreneurs, and non-profits working in this sector. Having access to results allows leaders in the field to replicate the program on their own.

Scalable
GWC invests in successful models with the potential to expand beyond a particular area. These models should be flexible enough to meet the demands of individual localities. (676 words)

31 **inception** – Gründung
31 **catalyst** – Beschleuniger
31 **to foster** – fördern
32 **core** – Kern-, Haupt-
34 **to implement** – einführen
35 **to leverage** – etw. wirksam einsetzen
43 **to enhance** – steigern
43 **to pave the way for sth.** – den Weg ebnen für etw. *(fig.)*
47 **best practice** – beste Vorgehensweise
49 **replicable** – replizierbar
49 **scalable** – anpassbar
54 **to maintain** – aufrechterhalten
60 **to monitor** – überwachen
64 **to expand** – ausdehnen

Mastering assignments

How to write a comment about positive or negative aspects/effects, pros and cons, advantages and disadvantages:

Topic: Many large fashion retailers have their goods produced in Asian countries like India or Bangladesh, where production is cheap. Discuss the pros and cons of this trend.

a) Write an introduction to the topic. There are several ways of writing a good introduction:
- You can start with a rhetorical question, or one that people might ask in relation to the topic.
- You can use a quote that is related to your topic.
- You can begin with an interesting fact that is related to the topic.
- You can use an analogy or a paradox, but make sure that it is easy to understand.
- You can use examples from your own experience.

Example: Have you ever looked at the labels in your clothes? Do you know where your new jacket was made? Do you care? Many high street fashion chains have their clothing produced in Asian countries like India or Bangladesh, where production is cheap. This trend has advantages and disadvantages and there are winners and losers.

Which of the above listed methods were used to write this introduction?

b) Brainstorm pros and cons in relation to the topic. Here is a list of pros and cons of producing clothes in Asian countries. Make a table and sort them into the correct column.

pros	cons

many jobs in industrialised countries are lost • companies can save money because labour is cheap • companies are exploiting workers in developing countries • local shops and small family-owned businesses can't compete with global players • low cost = clothing companies can update clothing range more often • brings jobs to poorer countries • harms the environment because of global transport • poor quality • keeps prices low for consumers • poor working conditions • possible use of child labour • wide range of products due to low production costs • avoiding strict European environmental regulations (e.g. waste disposal)

c) Now you need to choose the pros and cons which you think are the most important. But make sure that you have something to say about each of them. Look at the table and choose the three or four most important arguments on each side.

d) The next step is to write the main part of your comment. Use connectives (see the list at the back of your book) to connect your thoughts. Don't make the mistake of just listing your arguments in one sentence. Elaborate by giving details and examples. If you are more inclined to support production of clothing in Asian countries, start with the cons, and vice versa. Write the main part of the comment.

e) The last part is the conclusion. Sum up the arguments above and draw conclusions from them. Finally, state your point of view. Don't forget to use connectives. Write a conclusion to the comment.

1 Project: Songs about globalisation → Presentation, p. 264
Go online and find the song "My Global Mind" by Queensrÿche. Listen to the song and complete the following activities:

a) In your own words outline the singer's state of mind.

b) Compare the music and the message of this song to those of "Globalization Blues" at the beginning of this topic.

c) Find the metaphors in the song and explain their effect on the listener.

d) Now find another song about globalisation and collect additional information such as facts about the artist or video clips and prepare a short presentation. Is it a protest song or is it in favour of globalisation? Give your presentation to the class.

2 Research project: How products are made → Internet research, p. 260
Work in small groups. Choose one of the objects from exercise 1a) on page 136. Go online and find out how your chosen object is made, explaining the production process from the raw materials to the finished product. Create a collage that illustrates this process and present it to the class.

3 Project: A talk show on globalisation → Discussions, p. 246
Organise a serious TV discussion on the topic "Globalisation – blessing or curse?" First decide who will be the talk show host / guests. Give your guests different roles e.g. local food producer, African coffee farmer, restaurant owner, representative of large discount supermarket chain, etc. Discuss the following topics:

- food miles
- prices
- competition
- exploitation
- etc.

4 Research project: A case study → Internet research, p. 260
Go online and find an example of a German company that has outsourced parts of its business (services or the manufacturing of products) to another country. Collect information on the reasons behind the decision. If possible, also outline the effects it has had on the company itself, the customers, and the country it has outsourced to.

5 Research project: German global players → Internet research, p. 260

a) With the help of the Internet, create a ranking of Germany's biggest companies by turnover/revenues or profit. Compare your group's ranking to another group's. Did you get the same results?

b) Chose one of the companies in your ranking that interests you and collect background information on it, e.g. the company history, its key products or services, the number of employees, its future prospects, etc. Present your findings to the class.

6 Research project: Virtual/embedded water → Internet research, p. 260
Work in small groups and research the concept of 'virtual/embedded water' on the Internet. Find out what this concept is, give some examples, outline the impact it has on water supplies around the globe, and explain who the winners and losers are.

A 3.25

1 **gloomy** – dark, depressing
1 **prospect** – outlook
2 **bleak** – poor
3 **downturn** – decline
5 **beyond** – over and above
6 **to reshape** – to change
7 **root** – origin
7 **abject** – pitiful
7 **failure** – mistake
7 **governance** – ruling
8 **neglect** – ignorance
9 **to reveal** – to show
11 **lack of sth.** – sth. missing
13 **prosperous** – wealthy
14 **to ensure** – to make sure
14 **to gain** – to profit
15 **to expose** – to uncover
16 **unprecedented** – never seen before
19 **to prevent** – to keep from happening
20 **legitimate** – rightful
22 **to affect** – to influence
23 **urgent** – pressing
24 **multilateral** – varied
27 **welfare** – well-being
28 **equity** – justice
28 **afterthought** – second thought

No country, no matter how powerful … can control the forces of globalisation on its own

[…] The world looks a gloomy and uncertain place. Every day the prospects for the global economy look bleaker. We don't know how deep or long-lasting the downturn will be. But we do know there is plenty of pain to come.

In every crisis, however, there is opportunity. If we have the courage to learn the lessons of the past […] and put them into practice beyond the economic sphere, we can put in place new foundations to reshape our world for the better.

For the roots of this crisis go beyond an abject failure of financial governance and neglect of warnings of the risks being run. Connections between economies have been revealed which were clearly not fully understood, let alone regulated. There may have been endless talk of globalisation. But it is very clear there has been a lack of recognition of what this means for us all.

We have now learnt decisively that no country, no matter how powerful or prosperous, can control the forces of globalisation on its own. The lack of inclusive processes and institutions needed to manage the risks and ensure all gain from the benefits has also been exposed.

The present crisis has already led to unprecedented international co-operation. There has been co-ordinated action to protect the financial system from collapse, to try to stimulate the global economy and find new rules and structures to prevent this disaster being repeated. But while the G20, combining rich nations with emerging market countries, is a better and more legitimate forum than the G8, it does not go far enough to give the poor and excluded a voice. After all, they are the ones most affected by the decisions made.

The real lesson of the past year is the urgent need to build on and extend this multilateral approach. It means accepting that the rich and powerful alone can no longer rule the world.

It means, too, recognising that the only lasting and effective solutions to the challenges we face will be those which have the security, opportunity and welfare of all at their heart. Fairness and equity can no longer be an afterthought. No

1 Comprehension

a) Using your own words, sum up the global issues Annan addresses in his speech.

b) Outline the solutions he suggests to solve these issues.

2 Analysis → Text analysis, p. 228

Point out the rhetorical devices that Annan uses to get his message across, and the effects they have. Give examples from the text.

one's stability, security and prosperity can be guaranteed unless we strive to tackle the gross inequality of wealth, opportunity and influence in our world.

What is needed is a fundamental change of mindset. Solutions to the financial crisis must look beyond the impact on the market, financial institutions and developed countries. They must also focus on jobs, family incomes and the effect of the slowdown on the poorest countries. Market forces are the engine for economic growth. But they need to be well regulated to ensure fairness and equal opportunity for all.

The present crisis has underlined the importance of government in effective regulation of the market. But governments must also look beyond their borders and at the long-term picture. Richer countries cannot use the excuse of tighter finances to renege on their aid promises to the poorest on the planet. As global trade contracts and protectionist instincts are emboldened, the danger is that those least responsible for the present crisis will be hardest hit. [...]

We can waste no time. Only by working together can we hand over a healthy and sustainable planet to future generations. [...] There must be a radical, effective and universal agreement at Copenhagen this year based on climate justice and the principle that the polluter pays.

The developed economies must accept their responsibilities to our planet and future generations. They must take the lead in cutting their emissions. They must also fund the transfer of knowledge needed to help the rest of the world to grow their economies sustainably and to adapt to the inevitable change in our climate already underway. No other approach will work.

The consequences for our children if we fail to rise to this challenge are immense. Breaking our addiction to fossil fuels and investing in green technologies will also help us to deliver energy security, jobs, prosperity and sustainable economic growth.

This will, however, require robust and inclusive global economic, financial and political institutions. We need fundamental reform to involve a far wider range of countries and voices meaningfully in decision-making.

(720 words)

Kofi A. Annan (Secretary-General of the United Nations from 1997 to 2006)

29 **to strive to do sth.** – to try hard to achieve sth.
29 **to tackle** – to fight
31 **mindset** – opinion
32 **impact** – effect
34 **engine** – driving force
40 **to renege** – to withdraw
41 **to embolden** – to encourage
48 **to take the lead** – to be in control
50 **inevitable** – unavoidable

3 Comment → Writing a comment, p. 229
"We can waste no time. Only by working together can we hand over a healthy and sustainable planet to future generations." (ll. 43–44) How can you as an individual contribute to solving the global problems mentioned in Annan's speech?

Topic 10
Marketing and media

3fc22h

A

> Advertising is the greatest art form of the twentieth century.
>
> Marshall McLuhan, Canadian social scientist (1911–1980)

> You can tell the ideals of a nation by its advertisements.
>
> Norman Douglas, Scottish author (1868–1952)

> What is the difference between unethical and ethical advertising? Unethical advertising uses falsehoods to deceive the public; ethical advertising uses truth to deceive the public.
>
> Vilhjalmur Stefansson, Canadian explorer & ethnologist (1879–1962)

B

Getting started

1 Describe the different forms of advertising shown above and say what you think of them.

2 Which forms of advertising do you regularly encounter? How do you react to them?

3 Which other forms of advertising are part of our daily lives? Think of some examples.

“Many a small thing has been made large by the right kind of advertising.”

Mark Twain, US humorist and novelist (1835–1910)

“Advertising is legalised lying.”

H.G. Wells, British author (1866–1946)

“Advertising is the modern substitute for argument; its function is to make the worse appear the better.”

George Santayana, US (Spanish-born) philosopher (1863–1952)

“Advertising may be described as the science of arresting the human intelligence long enough to get money from it.”

Steven Leacock, Canadian economist & humorist (1869–1944)

Word bank

sponsorship • billboard • neon signs • merchandising • to receive spam • text message • to target • to bombard • to convey a message • campaign • to deceive • to persuade • to place an ad • brand

4 **Explain what you understand by each of the quotations above and then give your opinion on how true you think each statement is.**

5 **What is advertising in your opinion? Collect statements of your classmates which begin with "Advertising is . . .".** → Brainstorming, p. 253

A The influence of advertising

1 Before you read → Brainstorming, p. 253

a) When you think about TV ads, what is the first ad that comes to your mind? Write down what the ad is for, what happens in it, and what made you remember it.

b) Has this ad affected the way you think about the product or service advertised? How? Why?

c) Share your ideas with a partner and report back to the class.

theguardian

News | Sport | Comment | Culture | Business | Money | Life&Style | Travel | Environment

Comment is free > Society   Search [ ] GO

Can brands make consumers see sustainable behaviour as desirable?

Well, with one campaign (and a pig in an armpit) they managed to change the routines of Russian women

In Russia, in 2007, most women used deodorant only on special occasions. They would spritz their armpits with the sweet-smelling stuff to party, but not every day. As a result, Russians got through less than one pack of deodorant each per year, compared with five in the UK. For obvious reasons, this was not a habit that pleased Russian deodorant brand Rexona or its makers Unilever, so they set about changing it.

To do this they enlisted the help of cultural analyst Greg Rowland, who identified some key cultural themes in Russia to draw on, including "an obsession with glamour and beauty" and "a culture of embarrassment". In the resultant advert, a seemingly glamorous woman raises her arm in a lift only to find – to her horror – that the smell makes the guy next to her dash for the exit. In case the viewer doesn't get it, there's also a drawing of a pig on her underarm. The advert helped significantly increase deodorant use in Russia.

By playing on cultural anxieties and desires, Rexona managed to change Russians' morning routines. This is not unique; brands and businesses have influenced the way we live for decades, in a bid to sell us more stuff. But as

0 **sustainable** – nachhaltig
0 **behaviour** – Verhalten
0 **desirable** – wünschenswert, erstrebenswert
1 **armpit** – Achsel
8 **obvious** – offensichtlich
10 **habit** – Gewohnheit, Angewohnheit
12 **brand** – Marke
15 **to enlist** – *hier:* in Anspruch nehmen
19 **to draw on sth.** – an etw. anknüpfen
19 **obsession** – Besessenheit
20 **embarrassment** – Beschämung, Peinlichkeit
22 **to dash for** – losstürzen, rasen
25 **anxiety** – Angst
25 **desire** – Wunsch, Verlangen
26 **unique** – einzigartig
27 **decade** – Jahrzehnt

the burgeoning corporate sustainability movement has matured some firms have started using these well-honed tools to a different end. Companies such as Unilever have realised that for some products the biggest environmental impact comes from their customers' behaviour – people using soaps and shampoos in a hot shower, for example – and have begun trying to promote more sustainable choices and habits. […]

One of the most obvious tools at their disposal for this is marketing. "Brands have the ability to make sustainable behaviours aspirational," says Madden. This can take the form of a campaign like Sainsbury's Love your Leftovers, which tries to change the way people see food waste, or Ariel's Turn to 30, which plays on the idea that the detergent is so powerful that washing at high temperatures is unnecessary, and is credited with increasing the number of people washing at 30°C.

More subtle marketing can also help combat the fact that sustainable behaviours are often perceived as "not attractive and not normal" says Lucy Shea, CEO of sustainable communications agency Futerra. A green version of product placement – adverts featuring recycling bins or people cycling instead of driving, for instance – could be an interesting way of making those behaviours more normal and desirable, says Shea. […]

Some firms' business models already coincide with environmental aims – bus companies trying to get people out of cars and on to buses, for example. The car-sharing companies Streetcar and Zipcar, for example, offer their customers mobility when they need it (in the form of a car on a street near them to hire when they want) without the need for everyone to own their own car. […] (726 words)

28 **burgeoning** – aufkeimend
28 **corporate** – Unternehmens-
28 **sustainability** – Nachhaltigkeit
28 **to mature** – reifen
29 **well-honed** – gut geschliffen
29 **to use sth. to an end** – etw. für einen Zweck einsetzen
31 **impact** – Auswirkung
34 **at one's disposal** – *hier:* zur Verfügung
35 **aspirational** – erstrebenswert
36 **leftovers** – Reste
38 **detergent** – Waschmittel
39 **to credit sb. with sth.** – jmdm etw. zuschreiben
41 **subtle** – dezent
41 **to combat** – bekämpfen
42 **to perceive** – wahrnehmen
44 **to feature** – *hier:* zeigen
47 **to coincide** – übereinstimmen

2 Comprehension

a) Summarise in your own words the problem faced by deodorant companies in Russia, what Unilever did to combat this, and what the result was.

b) Aside from selling products, outline what aim businesses have become more interested in recently and what the key to achieving this is.

c) Table completion: Collect all the pieces of information the text gives you about the following companies regarding sustainable consumer behaviour:

Sainsbury's	Ariel	Streetcar/Zipcar

3 Analysis → Analysing advertisements, p. 244

a) Explain how product placement can be used to make sustainable behaviour more attractive.

b) Find an advertisement that appeals to you. Analyse it in detail and present the results to the class.

4 Projects → Hotspots 1 and 2, p. 165

B New media and infotainment

1 Before you read: News media → Questionnaires and surveys, p. 262
→ Describing diagrams, p. 243

a) Draw up a class survey about where your classmates get their daily news from.

b) Present your results in a suitable graph.

2 Comprehension → Scanning, p. 221

a) What information can you find in the text about the following numbers:

20 • 28 • 49 • 62 • 64 • 72 • 87 • 1000

b) With the help of the information in the text, draw two bar graphs. The first should show the most frequently used news media in Australia. The second graph should display people's trust in different forms of media.

smh.com.au

The Sydney Morning Herald

Search GO

NSW | World | Business | Sport | Environment | National Times

New media fail to click on the reliability scale

Australians trust the ABC more than its commercial rivals, while supposed "old" media such as newspapers, television, and radio fare much better than the internet, a survey of attitudes to media has found. An Essential Research survey of 1000 people showed that despite the recent protestations of web media proprietors, traditional media is still the dominant source for information on news and current affairs, and is also more highly trusted than its internet counterparts.

The survey found commercial TV news and current affairs is the most frequently consumed news media, with 87 per cent of people saying they watched at least once a week. Daily newspapers came second, with 72 per cent reading at least weekly. In contrast, just 28 per cent of people said they accessed blogs at least once a week, but in results that will give some comfort to the mainstream media proprietors behind major news websites, 62 per cent of people said they accessed them at least weekly. The consumption habits also reflected people's trust of different forms of media. Asked the extent to which they trusted commercial TV news and current affairs, 64 per cent said "a lot" or "some", with daily newspapers closely behind on 62 per cent. The affiliation with a major media outlet appeared to bolster the trust in news and opinion websites, which sat at 49 per cent, but internet blogs, which are usually independently run, were trusted by just 20 per cent.

Essential Research's director, Peter Lewis, said the figures showed consumers sought a distinction between news and opinion, which was more prevalent in newspapers than online.

"It gives some encouragement to professional journalists that there is in the public's mind a difference between news and opinion, and as long as that separation remains in the public's eyes, there's always going to be a place for quality journalists," he said. [...] (355 words)

0 **to fail** – scheitern
0 **reliability** – Glaubwürdigkeit, Vertrauenswürdigkeit
1 **ABC (Australian Broadcasting Corperation)** – öffentlich-rechtliche Rundfunkgesellschaft in Australien
1 **rival** – Konkurrent(in)
2 **to fare better** – besser abschneiden
3 **protestations** – Beteuerungen
4 **proprietor** – Besitzer(in), Eigner(in)
5 **current affairs** – aktuelle Nachrichten, Zeitgeschehen
5 **counterpart** – Gegenüber
18 **affiliation** – Verbindung, Zugehörigkeit
19 **to bolster** – stärken
22 **prevalent** – verbreitet
23 **encouragement** – Ermutigung
24 **separation** – Trennung

c) Taking into account the information you collected in tasks a) and b), sum up the most important information of the article in your own words.

217 △ **3 Mediation** → Mediation, p. 245

Prepare an English summary of the following text for your email pen pal in Australia, who is very interested in cars and technology.

WinFuture
WINDOWS ONLINE MAGAZIN

Search [ ] GO

Software | Hardware | Spiele | Internet | Sicherheit | Mobiles

Infotainment-Systeme im Auto immer beliebter

Glaubt man diversen Marktforschern, werden integrierte GPS-Navigationsgeräte sowie Kameras und Sensoren für leichteres Einparken schon bald zur Grundausstattung von Autos gehören. Stattdessen werden neue Technologien die entscheidenden Kaufargumente darstellen. Nachdem die Automobilindustrie 2008 und 2009 einige Probleme zu bewältigen hatte, scheint sie nun das Internet als Wachstumsfaktor für sich entdeckt zu haben. Laut Instant Research werden bereits in diesem Jahr rund 15 Millionen so genannte In-Vehicle Infotainment-Systeme (IVI) verkauft. Bis 2015 soll diese Zahl auf über 35 Millionen anwachsen. Die Analystin Stephanie Ethier erklärt, dass die Automobilindustrie in diesem Jahr mit den Innovationen der Unterhaltungselektronik mithalten muss, um wettbewerbsfähig zu sein.
Gab es 2009 nur etwa eine Million Fahrzeuge, die mit dem Internet verbunden waren, so werden es 2017 bereits mehr als 42 Millionen sein, prophezeien die Marktforscher aus dem Hause iSuppli. Man hat erkannt, dass das Internet für die Menschen inzwischen das wichtigste Medium ist, um verschiedene Inhalte zu konsumieren. Diese Möglichkeiten auch in Autos anzubieten, ist ein logischer Schritt, der erfolgversprechend ist.
„Die Leute wollen Erfahrungen, die sie bereits von zu Hause oder von ihren mobilen Geräten kennen", erklärt Joe Pitarresi, Forscher bei den Intel Labs. „Sie wollen Unterhaltung und Zugriff auf Online-Dienste, die sie bereits von außerhalb des Fahrzeugs kennen." Die Produkte für Autos müssen so entwickelt werden, dass sie ein sicheres Fahren ermöglichen, erklärt Pitarresi, der bei Intel nach Möglichkeiten forscht, das Internet in Autos auf sichere Art und Weise zu integrieren.
Der Wunsch nach Infotainment-Systemen kann bei Fahrzeugbastlern bereits seit mehreren Jahren beobachtet werden. (254 words)

17 △ **4 Analysis**
→ Describing cartoons, p. 242
Describe and analyse the cartoon, and relate it to the above text.

"It's the new iPed. It's a pedometer, a GPS, and it has apps that show you the nearest ice cream parlors and dessert shops."

5 Group discussion → Discussions, p. 246
If you had to invent the ultimate news medium for people your age, what would it look like?

6 Project → Hotspot 3, p. 165

C Consumer protection

1 Before you read → Brainstorming, p. 253

a) What do you think targeted advertising is?

b) How good is your Internet English? Match the terms with their definitions.

1. cookie	a) The program people use to access the World Wide Web.
2. spyware	b) An add-on for a program that adds functionality to it.
3. browser	c) A small amount of data generated by a website and saved by your web browser. Its purpose is to remember information about you.
4. plug-in	d) Software that can capture information like web browsing habits, usernames and passwords, etc.

NETWORKWORLD

Search GO

Security | Wans & Lans | UC/VoIP | Cloud Computing | Infrastructure Mgmt

Privacy groups rip Google's targeted advertising plan

Two online privacy groups slammed Google for launching a behavioral advertising program, with one advocate calling Google's plan a privacy "disaster."

Google's proposal would bring user tracking to the world's largest ad network, said Marc Rotenberg, executive director of the Electronic Privacy Information Center. "It's a disaster," he said. "It's about whether the most dominant Internet media firm should be able to exploit its access to Internet user data for advertising purposes. Google long maintained it would not do this type of advertising. Indeed, they claimed they didn't need to and they went after others who did." Google privacy officials, as recently as early 2008, said they had no plans to engage in behavioral advertising. Behavioral advertising doesn't work, Google officials said then.

Rotenberg called on the U.S. Federal Trade Commission to halt Google's plans.

The plan, announced Wednesday on Google's official blog and its public policy blog does allow people using Google's AdSense network and YouTube to change their advertising preferences and to opt out of being targeted at all. Google solicited advice from several groups before launching the behavioral advertising beta, wrote Nicole Wong, Google's deputy general counsel. "We talked to many users, privacy advocates and government experts," she said. "By listening to them and by relying on the creativity of our engineers, we built a product that's not only consistent with industry groups' privacy principles, but also goes beyond their requirements."

Google is one of the first Internet companies to allow users to see and to change their advertising profile, according to some privacy advocates. The Google plan got a mixed review from

0 **targeted advertising** – gezielte Werbung
1 **to slam** – scharf kritisieren
1 **to launch** – auf den Markt bringen
1 **behavioral advertising** – verhaltensbezogene Werbung
2 **advocate** – Befürworter(in)
3 **proposal** – Vorschlag
3 **user tracking** – Benutzerverfolgung
5 **to exploit** – ausbeuten, ausnutzen
6 **to maintain** – behaupten
11 **to engage in sth.** – sich an etw. beteiligen
18 **to opt out of sth.** – sich abmelden, aussteigen
19 **to solicit** – erbitten
20 **beta (software)** – Testsoftware
20 **deputy** – Stellvertreter(in)
21 **to rely on sb./sth.** – sich auf jmdn/etw. verlassen
22 **consistent with** – übereinstimmend mit
23 **beyond sth.** – über etw. hinaus
23 **requirement** – Anforderung

Ari Schwartz, vice president and chief operating officer of digital rights group the Center for Democracy and Technology. While he praised Google for allowing users to change their advertising profiles, he criticized the difficulty of opting out. Schwartz is also disappointed that the Internet advertising industry has not gotten together to come up with better ways for Web surfers to control their advertising experiences, he said. Google chose a flawed way of honoring opt-out requests – by putting a cookie on users' machines, similar to a frequently criticized model offered by the Network Advertising Initiative.

Many users and spyware software programs frequently delete cookies, Schwartz noted, although Google has offered a browser plug-in that will prevent the Google opt-out cookie from being deleted. "The cookie opt-out doesn't work, it's a bad idea," he said. "People who care about their privacy enough to opt out also are the same people who delete their cookies."

(497 words)

30 **flawed** – fehlerhaft
30 **to honor** – anerkennen
31 **frequently** – häufig
34 **to prevent** – verhindern

2 Comprehension: True or false? → Comprehension questions, p. 228
Read the statements below and decide whether they are true or false. Quote or paraphrase words from the text which confirm or disprove the ideas in the statements.

a) Marc Rotenberg works for Google and supports the use of targeted advertising.

b) In 2008, Google said they wouldn't use advertising based on consumer behaviour.

c) People who use Google's AdSense network and YouTube cannot influence which ads they are exposed to.

d) Google claims that their new tracking software agrees with privacy standards.

e) Ari Schwartz sees no positive aspects to Google's behavioural advertising program.

f) Users can "opt out" of Google's targeted advertising by deleting their cookies.

3 Analysis → Describing cartoons, p. 242
Describe the cartoon, analyse it and relate it to the text.

4 Listening comprehension: Too much choice
→ Listening, p. 221
Write down short answers only.
- Where and when does this scene take place?
- What did the narrator want to do?
- What was typical of the coffee stand he went to?
- What did listening to the other customers' orders make the narrator want to do?
- How does he describe the other customers' orders?
- What did he order himself?
- Name three details the salesperson asks the narrator.
- What time is it now and how long has the narrator been in line for the coffee?
- How does he threaten the salesperson?
- How does the narrator characterise himself?

5 Research project → Hotspot 4, p. 165

D Food consumption: We are what we eat

1 Before you read → Brainstorming, p. 253

a) What is your favourite food? Where does it come from and how is it produced?

b) How do you interpret the statement "You are what you eat"? Do you agree with the statement. Discuss with a partner.

THE INDEPENDENT

Search GO

Opinion | Environment | Sport | Life & Style | Arts & Ents | Travel | Money | Indy Best

Organic movement split over air-freighted food

For the conscientious, food shopping poses many ethical dilemmas: are organic bananas better than FairTrade or English tomatoes preferable to imports?

Britain's booming organic movement has been wrestling with one such dilemma for years and the debate has become so heated it can no longer be ignored. From today, the country's organic farmers, suppliers and shoppers are being asked for an answer to an awkward question: is it acceptable to air-freight organic food?

On this one question could hinge the prosperity of thousands of African farmers, fruit and vegetable importers, the integrity of the organic movement and, to some extent, the health of the planet itself.

If the body which certifies three-quarters of organic food (in Great Britain), the Soil Association, rules that the climate change pollution cannot be justified, it may ban all flown-in food.

A ban might split the organic movement: one side with strict environmental standards and another with looser standards that factor in the development of the Third World. The argument arises from the rapid rise of the UK organic movement, which has burgeoned into a £1.6bn-a-year business.

Farmers have struggled to grow enough food and in 2005 supermarkets imported one-third of their organic range, mostly by air.

Nationally "food miles" are at a record high, with air-freighting up 136 per cent between 1992 and 2002. Yet flying food thousands of miles from poor farmers to wealthy Westerners generates substantial amounts of CO_2 just as climate change is being recognised as an emergency. Shoppers find the dissonance uncomfortable: a Soil Association survey found that eight out of 10 would prefer to buy conventional local food rather than an organic import.

0 **to be split over** – geteilter Meinung sein über
0 **air-freighted** – per Luftfracht
1 **conscientious** – die Bewussten
2 **to pose** – darstellen
12 **awkward** – seltsam
14 **to hinge** – abhängen
22 **to rule** – *hier:* entscheiden
28 **to factor in** – berücksichtigen, einbeziehen
31 **to burgeon** – entwickeln
44 **dissonance** – Unstimmigkeit

At Britain's biggest vegetable box supplier, Riverford Farm in Devon, air-freighted food is banned. The self-imposed ban is sometimes difficult but Guy Watson, its founder, believes the environment must take priority. He tells customers: "Most out-of-season vegetables imported to the UK are flown in from Africa and South America causing horrendous emissions, or trucked from southern Europe with less, but still substantial, environmental impact." About 80 per cent of the company's 35,000 customers' food comes from the UK, with the rest arriving by road or ship.

By contrast, the importer Blue Skies in Northamptonshire buys fresh pineapple, mango and coconuts from Ghana, where it employs 1,500 people. "We would see any change to the rules as unfair to us and unfair to Africa," said the founder, Anthony Pile. "The carbon emissions for air-freighted food is something like 1 per cent of the total emissions. Why hit farmers who have a tiny carbon footprint and often live without electricity?" he asked. In its consultation, the Soil Association is setting out the case for five options. Maintaining the status quo would help faraway producers but might damage the organisation's credibility. A gradual or total ban would damage exporters but help tackle climate change and encourage more sustainable agriculture. Warning stickers or offsetting flights would be a compromise.

Anna Bradley, of the Soil Association's Standards Board, explained that the rules had to evolve over time and the time had come for a definitive answer on aviation. "It's quite clear right now that these issues of climate change and CO_2 are much more important than they were 10 years ago and it feels much more pertinent to talk about them," she said. But Britain's organic trailblazer could lose business by raising its standards, just as it did when it tightened its rules on poultry farms. "That cost us licensees but it has … retained the integrity of the standard," she said. (598 words)

51 **self-imposed** – selbst auferlegt
58 **horrendous** – übermäßig, horrend
72 **to hit** – *hier:* benachteiligen
76 **to set out** – *hier:* (im Detail) darlegen
81 **to tackle** – bewältigen
82 **sustainable** – nachhaltig
83 **to offset (offsetting)** – ausgleichen, *hier:* CO_2-Emissionsausgleich tätigen
93 **pertinent** – relevant
94 **trailblazer** – Wegbereiter
96 **poultry** – Geflügel
97 **licensees** – Lizenznehmer
98 **to retain** – behalten

2 Comprehension: Table completion → Taking notes, p. 254

a) Collect all the pieces of information the text gives you about the arguments for and against air-freighted food in the view of the people listed below:

Guy Watson, Riverford Farm	Anthony Pile, Blue Skies	Anna Bradley, Soil Association	Kenyan organic farmer	British conventional farmer	British shopper

b) Choose the three arguments you find most convincing. Give reasons.

3 Comment

"Food miles are at a record high." (ll. 37–38) Food miles are part of our carbon footprint. Discuss several ways you can reduce your individual carbon footprint.

4 Presentation → Presentation, p. 264

Some time ago, a "slow food movement" came into existence. Find out where it started and what its advantages and disadvantages are. Write down the most important cue-words on a transparency and use this to present your findings in class.

E The art world

1 Before you read
Which pieces of art do you know? Why do people spend a fortune on buying art for private collections? Discuss with a partner and report back to the class.

2 Comprehension → Understanding fictional texts, p. 224

a) Outline where Lacey and her companion are, what they are doing, and why.

b) Summarise in your own words how the art world is presented in the text, and how this contrasts with the reality of a young person working in this world.

c) After reading the text, what do you think the title of the book might refer to?

Steve Martin (American actor, comedian and writer, born in 1945)

Steve Martin is a renowned comedian and actor who has starred in many Hollywood films. His book, An Object of Beauty, *is a story set in the Manhattan art world.*

3 **offshore** – vor der Küste
4 **exploit** – große Tat
12 **a class act** – *hier:* eine Person, die sehr schick und eindrucksvoll erscheint
12 **to blare** – plärren
12 **to zero in on** – auf etw. abzielen
13 **to wince** – zusammenzucken
14 **to deter** – abschrecken
15 **to zip up** – den Reißverschluss zumachen
15 **to emerge** – herauskommen
17 **cleavage** – Ausschnitt, Dekolleté
18 **to mutter** – murmeln
19 **barrette** – Haarspange
20 **instantly** – sofort
20 **to mature** – reifen
21 **broke** – pleite

An Object of Beauty

LACEY'S LIFE AND MINE have paralleled each other for a long while. When we were twenty-three, our interest in art as a profession landed us both in New York City at a time when the art world was building offshore like a developing hurricane. Our periodic lunches caught me up with her exploits. Sometimes she showed up at a Manhattan cafe with a new boyfriend who was required to tolerate my unexplained presence, and when she excused herself to the restroom, the boyfriend and I would struggle for conversation while he tried to discover if I was an ex-lover, as he soon would be. [...]

"Come with me," she said after coffee. "Where to?" "I'm buying a dress. I'm interviewing at Sotheby's tomorrow and I have to look like a class act." The New York heat baked us till we found the inside of a moderately cooler downtown dress shop that featured recycled class-act clothing. Music blared as Lacey zeroed in on a dark blue tight skirt and matching jacket. She winced at the price, but it did not deter her. She pulled the curtain of the changing room, and I could hear the rustle of clothes. I pictured the skirt being pulled on and zipped up. She emerged wearing the jacket loosely opened, with nothing on underneath – which created a sideways cleavage – and started buttoning it up in front of the mirror, surveying herself. "I've got a blouse at home I can wear with this," she muttered to me. She straightened up and pulled the barrette from her hair, causing the blond mix of yellows and browns to fall to her shoulders, and she instantly matured.

"They're going to love you," I said. "They goddamn better because I'm broke. I'm down to seven thousand." "Last week you said you had three thousand." "Well,

3 Analysis → Text analysis, p. 228

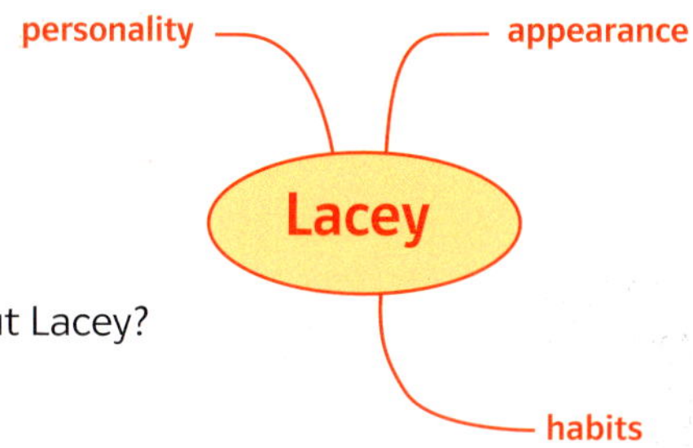

a) What sort of person is Lacey? Use the word web to collect information about her. You should also include extracts from the text to support your answer.

b) What does the extract tell us about the narrator? How does he feel about Lacey?

c) Analyse the language the author uses to show the youthfulness of the characters. Collect relevant words and passages from the text. Indicate the lines as well.

d) Explain the phrase "And so Lacey joined the spice rack of girls at Sotheby's." (l. 27) in your own words.

e) Using your results from a), b), c) and d), characterise Lacey as she appears in this extract.

18 △ **4 Comment** → Writing a comment, p. 229
"To those that have, shall be given." Many people believe that being beautiful makes it easier for you to be successful in life. Do you agree? Comment.

if I've got three, I'm fucked. So let's call it seven." Lacey turned from the mirror for the first time and struck a pose in the preowned Donna Karan, "You look great. A lot of people our age don't know how to go in and apply for a job," I said. Lacey stared at me and said, "I don't go in and apply for a job. I go in and get a job." And so Lacey joined the spice rack of girls at Sotheby's. Sotheby's and Christie's, the two premier auction houses in New York, drew young, crisp talent from Harvard and its look-alikes. Majors in art history were welcomed over majors in art making, and pretty was preferred in either sex. The houses wanted the staff to look swell as they crisscrossed the busy galleries on exhibition days, holding in their arms files, faxes, and transparencies.

Because the pay was low, the young staff was generally financed from home. Parents thought well of it because their children were at respectable firms, working in a glamorous business, with money of all nations charging the atmosphere. The auction houses seemed not as dull as their financial counterparts on Wall Street, where parents of daughters imagined glass ceilings and bottom patting. Sotheby's was an institution that implied European accents and grand thoughts about art and aesthetics coexisting with old and new money in sharp suits and silk ties. This was a fresh and clean New York, where you dressed nicely every day and worked in a soaring, smoke-free, drug-less architectural building filled with busts, bronzes, and billionaires. What the parents forgot about were the weekends and evenings when their children left the Cezannes and Matisses and crept underground, traveling back to shared downtown spaces where they did exactly the same things they would have done if they had joined a rock band.

(681 words)

24 **to strike a pose** – eine Pose einnehmen
24 **preowned** – gebraucht
27 **spice rack** – Gewürzregal
28 **crisp** – *hier:* frisch
30 **major** – Studiengang, Hauptfach
31 **staff** – Angestellte(r), Personal
31 **swell** – großartig
31 **to crisscross** – durchkreuzen
31 **exhibition** – Ausstellung
32 **file** – Akte
35 **to charge** – aufladen
36 **dull** – langweilig
37 **glass ceiling** – unsichtbare Decke, an die Frauen auf der Karriereleiter stoßen
37 **bottom patting** – Klaps auf den Hintern
38 **to imply** – implizieren
39 **sharp** – *hier:* schick
40 **silk tie** – Seidenkrawatte
41 **soaring** – hoch aufragend
42 **bust** – Büste
44 **to creep** – kriechen

Word families – word building

a) Read the sentences and fill the gaps with a word belonging to the same word family as the word given on the right.

Teachers call for a ban on **1** of all unhealthy food and drink on all TV channels before the 9 pm watershed.	advertise
Teachers should not be **2** into using commercial materials in the classroom.	pressure
Will most of the seafood stocks really be **3** by the year 2048?	depletion
Unethical advertising uses falsehoods to **4** the public.	deception
Advertising is **5** lying.	legal
Online advertising is constantly **6** and developing itself.	innovation
Television was **7** developed without advertising in mind, whereas online developments were driven by advertising revenues.	initial
The favoured method of advertising online is through paid-for search, which is **8** by Google.	domination

b) You can link two words with a hyphen and so get a new word or part of speech.
Example: hi + tech = hi-tech

Make more new words like this by combining the following words:

ad-	consumer-	paid-	owned	cal	based
cut-	peanut-	medium-	range	sized	week
job-	UK-	farmer-	related	consuming	scale
large-	two-	time-	tech	friendly	for
low-	free-	hi-	related	like	throat

Make a meaningful sentence with each of your word combinations.

c) What preposition normally follows each of these words?

- opinion, ban, based, spending, impact
- amounted, addicted, intended, linked, lead
- account, in return, advertising, inappropriate, substitute

Make a meaningful sentence with each of the words plus their prepositions.

d) Write a text of at least 150 words on the topic of marketing. Include at least five of the following words:

consumerism • advertising • target • sexploitation • ban • addiction • fair • fairtrade • choice • campaign

1 Project: Creating an ad campaign → Analysing advertisements, p. 244
Work in groups. You work for an advertising agency and have been asked to create an ad campaign for one of the following products:

smart phone • energy drink • perfume/aftershave • pain killer • car • product/service of your choice

Design an ad (poster, power point presentation, script for TV/radio ad etc.) for it. Think about the name of the product, its design and packaging, the target group, the image, the price, where it will be sold and the slogan. Use the AIDA formula (see Skills files, p. 244) to help you. Present your ideas to the class.

2 Project: Scandalous advertising → Presentation, p. 264

a) Can you think of any scandalous advertising campaigns? What were they about and why were they considered scandalous?

b) Search the Internet for examples of scandalous advertising. Use a search engine for images, enter "scandalous advertising" and choose three of your findings to present to your class: Describe the ad image, say what makes it scandalous and add your own impression and reaction to the image.

3 Project: Media preference → Describing diagrams, p. 243
The graph on the right shows people's preference of news media around the globe. Work in groups. Analyse the graph and find a new way of presenting the information shown (e.g. pie chart, bar graph, written report, word cloud). Use a transparency or poster to present your results.

Media preference when gathering news and background information

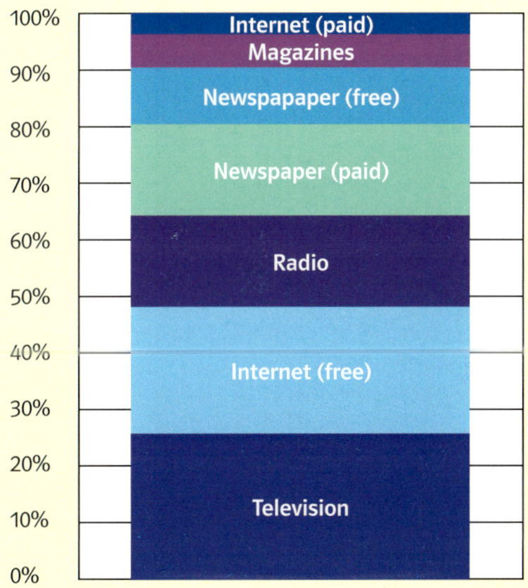

4 Research project: ASA → Internet research, p. 260

a) When carrying out advertising campaigns in the UK, advertisers may come into contact with the ASA. Check the web to find out more about the ASA and to answer the following questions:
- What is ASA short for?
- What does the ASA do?
- What role does the ASA play in ad regulation in Europe?

b) Find out about advertising campaigns that had to be withdrawn. You may use a search engine or the websites of newspapers such as *USA Today* and *The Independent*. You can enter key words such as "ad campaign" and "withdraw". The ASA website also lists controversial ad campaigns. Present your findings to the class after considering the following points:
- a description of the campaign
- reactions to it
- consequences for the advertisers / company.

c) Find out what "greenwash" is. Look for examples to illustrate this advertising technique.

A 3.30

1 **to demand** – to ask authoritatively
4 **to call for** – to publicly ask for
6 **9 pm watershed** – a time each evening after which certain material may be shown, e.g. sex and violence
8 **union** – association
10 **unashamedly** – without shame
10 **to target** – to aim at
11 **to exploit sb.** – to take unfair advantage of sb.
11 **to pester sb.** – *here:* continually asking sb. for sth. until you get it
16 **treats** – an event or item that is out of the ordinary and gives great pleasure
19 **to cite** – to quote
29 **pole-dancing kit** – equipment needed for pole dancing
30 **lace lingerie** – erotic underwear

THE INDEPENDENT

Search GO

Opinion | Environment | Sport | Life & Style | Arts & Ents | Travel | Money | Indy Best

Teachers' call for "sexploitation" of children to end

Teachers' leaders have demanded an end to the "sexploitation" of children through commercial marketing. They also called for a ban on the advertising of all "unhealthy" food and drink on all TV channels before the 9 pm watershed.

A report published by Britain's biggest teachers' union, the National Union of Teachers (NUT), warned: "Companies are unashamedly targeting their campaigns to exploit children's 'pester power'."

"Growing up in a Material World"

The report – "Growing up in a Material World" – argued that this included targeting "day to day purchases of food and drink, through treats, such as meals out, to clothes and toys which can include expensive electronic equipment".

The report cited figures from Ofcom, the television regulator, which showed that products with high sugar, salt or fat content accounted for between 82 per cent and 92 per cent of all food and drink advertising before the 9 pm watershed.

It also cited examples of what Steve Sinnott, the union's general secretary, described as the "sexploitation of young children" – such as Tesco marketing a pole-dancing kit on the toys section of its website, Asda selling pink and black lace lingerie to children and Next being forced

to remove T-shirts for young girls with the slogan "so many young boys, so little time" and BHS selling padded bras with a "Little Miss Naughty" logo.

It also warned teachers "not to be pressurised into using commercial materials in the classroom or take part in schemes such as voucher schemes".

"Parents are collecting vouchers for chocolates with Cadbury's and for crisps with Walkers in return for books," said Mr Sinnott. "We need to change the culture of this country in this regard."

New regulations introduced this week will mean all children's TV channels have to ban advertising for junk food by January 2009. They will also be extended to other channels covering children's programmes by January 2008.

"We need to change the culture of this country in this regard."

However, the NUT said this did not go far enough and demanded a ban on all junk food advertising before the 9 pm watershed. It also wants the ban extended to cover "sponsorship, celebrity endorsement, mobile phone, internet, e-mail and publications aimed at children". Asda said it had stopped the sale of its lace knickers, while Tesco said the pole-dancing kit was not sexually orientated and was "clearly aimed at adults who wanted to improve their fitness".

However, Mr Sinnott argued: "All of this sexualisation of childhood is inappropriate for youngsters."

(425 words)

32 **to remove** – to take away
34 **padded** – stuffed
34 **bra** – women's underwear
35 **naughty** – indecent
37 **to be pressurised** – to be put under pressure
39 **schemes** – program
39 **voucher scheme** – coupon system
41 **crisps** – potato chips
44 **in this regard** – in this respect
48 **to be extended to** – *here:* to be applied to
49 **to cover** – *here:* to broadcast, to air on TV
57 **celebrity endorsement** – advertising with celebrities
61 **lace knickers** – erotic underpants
67 **inappropriate** – unsuitable

1 Comprehension

a) In your own words, summarise which marketing strategies are criticised by the NUT, and why.

b) Outline which further demands the NUT has.

2 Analysis

→ Describing cartoons, p. 242
Describe the cartoon, analyse it and relate it to the text.

3 Comment

→ Writing an email, p. 231
A famous saying about advertising is that "sex sells". Considering advertising today, do you think that some companies are taking this too far? Write an email to the NUT, in which you state your opinion.

"Your vital signs are all healthy..."

1 If … Cloning Could Cure Us

Topic 5

BBC Motion Gallery

Stem cells have the potential to develop into many different cell types in the body. They can also serve as an internal repair system, dividing limitlessly to replenish other cells. When a stem cell divides, each new cell can either remain a stem cell or become another type of cell with a more specialized function, such as a muscle cell, a red blood cell, or even a brain cell.

Scientists all over the world are working on methods to infuse stem cells into a patient where – once they are integrated into the tissue – they ideally divide, growing more and more of the surrounding tissue and thus regenerating damaged cells.

Based on a fictionalised case, this film deals with the controversial subject of cloning and stem-cell research.

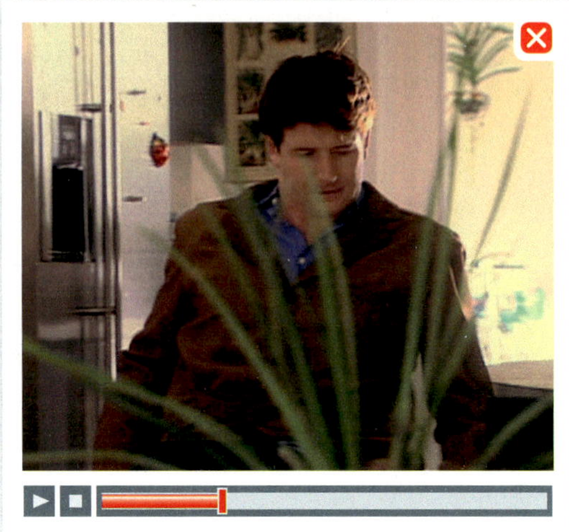

Before watching

a) Work with a partner. Agree on five sentences beginning with "If cloning could cure us …".

b) Collect pros and cons of therapeutic cloning.

c) Find out more about the ethical and social issues of stem cell research and therapeutical cloning.

d) Take a class vote: Who is in favour of therapeutic cloning?

While watching

Watch the film and collect phrases in the word field of "therapeutic cloning". Divide the class into two groups and watch the film again.
Group A: Collect arguments in favour of therapeutic cloning.
Group B: Collect arguments against therapeutic cloning.

After watching

a) Collect information about the legal status of stem cell research in five countries of your choice including GB / the USA.

b) Search the Internet and collect information about the main arguments of those strictly in favour / against stem cell research. Present the results to the class.

c) Form groups, each with at least two people from group A and two from group B. Discuss the pros and cons of therapeutic cloning using the notes you made. Then take a second vote: Who is still in favour of therapeutic cloning? Why have you (not) changed your mind?

2 A Brit in Berlin

Topic 6

BBC Motion Gallery

Seema Prabhu is a 26-year-old English journalist who is living in Berlin at the moment. In the video, she talks about her life in the city and her ideas about Europe.

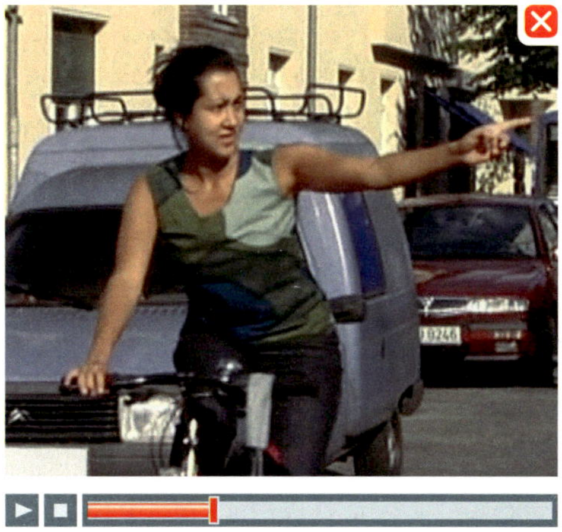

Before watching

Look at the vocabulary in the box and complete the sentences.

a) I was supposed to go to New York but I changed **1** and went to Washington DC.
b) When you fly, you are allowed to take 20 kg of baggage. Your **2** is 20 kg.
c) At the weekend, I often **3** my friends in town.
d) The sea is within **4** of the town and in summer everyone **5** to the beach.
e) The first thing I did when I arrived in London was to **6** at a language school.
f) They had nothing when they arrived in the new country. They had to **7** from **8** .
g) However, they worked hard, made friends and slowly they got it **9** .
h) There's a Mc Donald's in **10** every city in the world now.
i) The **11** from being a student to having a job and working isn't always easy. People often have to do some **12** .
j) Have you found an apprenticeship yet? – No, but I'm **13** it!
k) Life in modern Europe is really interesting. There's **14** exciting **15** .

1. **I was supposed (to do)** *ich sollte (etwas tun)*
2. **I changed my mind** *ich habe es mir anders überlegt*
3. **be within easy reach** *leicht erreichbar sein*
4. **decamp (to)** *aufbrechen (nach)*
5. **transition** *Übergang*
6. **baggage allowance** *Freigepäck(menge)*
7. **start from scratch** *bei Null anfangen*
8. **get it together** *sein Leben in den Griff bekommen*
9. **enrol** *sich anmelden*
10. **work on (doing sth.)** *dabei sein (etw. zu tun)*
11. **Soho** *Stadtteil Londons*
12. **sign from God** *Zeichen Gottes*
13. **serve a purpose** *einen Zweck erfüllen*
14. **do some readjusting** *sich neu einstellen*
15. **pretty much** *so ziemlich*
16. **hang out (with someone)** *(mit jmdm) herumhängen*
17. **there is sth. going on** *es passiert etwas*

While watching

Take notes and answer the following questions. Short answers will do.

1. Why did Seema come to Berlin?
2. What did she do on her first weekend in Berlin?
3. How did she find her first couple of weeks there?
4. What did she find in a street in Soho in London? How did this help her?
5. Why is the language school in Berlin good for Seema?
6. How do Seema's parents feel about her decision to go to Berlin?
7. What does Seema say at the end about Europe and living in Europe?

After watching

Listen one more time and write a short text for your school newspaper's "English page" about Seema Prabhu in Berlin.

3 American Immigration

Topic 8

BBC Motion Gallery

This film shows the situation at the US-Mexican border. Every day, many Mexicans try to enter the US illegally. The film portrays both illegal immigrants and those who try to defend the border.

Before watching

a) In many cases, emigration seems to be the only solution for people who want to make a better life for themselves. Due to strict border controls in both the countries of origin and some potential host countries, migrants have to take the risk of crossing borders illegally. Make a list of how people try to do this and also consider the dangers involved.

b) Collect information about the US-Mexican border.

c) Estimates say that there are between 10 and 15 million illegal immigrants living in the US, more than half of them from Mexico. Brainstorm reasons why these people leave their home country to come to the USA illegally.

While watching

Take notes on the following questions.

1. How do most illegal immigrants cross the border? What risks do they take? Why do they do it?
2. What is being done about illegal immigration? How do US residents view illegal immigration?
3. What is said about the scale of illegal immigration?

After watching

a) Using the information above as a starting point, prepare a report on illegal immigration in the US. Find out how many immigrants cross the border from Mexico every year, how many illegal immigrants live in the US, what the chances of being granted permanent residence are, and how the government plans to deal with the situation. Work in groups and, using statistics where necessary, present your results as an oral report to the class.

b) Research arguments for and against a permanent wall along the US-Mexican border.

c) Search the Internet for information about the novel "Tortilla Curtain" by T.C. Boyle (plot, characters, setting, topics, etc.). Present the results to the class.

d) Search the Internet for information about the film "Sugar" (storyline, characters, setting, topics, etc.) It shows the story of a young baseball player from the Dominican Republic who comes to the USA. Present your findings to the class.

e) Compare the fictional stories of Tortilla Curtain and Sugar. Which one do you like better? Why?

4 Cocoa Children

Topic 9

BBC Motion Gallery

The Ivory Coast in West Africa supplies half the world's cocoa. This video tells the story of Marc, a young boy who is one of the country's 'Cocoa Children'.

Before watching

Look through the English expressions below and match them with the German translation.

1. stagnation (economics)	a) ausrotten
2. belt	b) Machete (Buschmesser)
3. barely	c) (sich) hacken
4. poverty	d) (Wirtschafts)Flaute
5. to eradicate	e) kaum
6. to set out	f) Armut
7. machete	g) *(hier:)* Region
8. to hack (oneself)	h) kaum

While watching

a) Why do so many farmers in this region of Africa grow cocoa?

b) Why do so many children work on the farms?

c) What important 'protocol' was signed in 2001?

d) Who did the BBC reporters meet in the bush?

e) What did they find in the village? (WARNING! Shocking images!)

f) The reporters meet Marc again when they leave the village. Summarise what Marc tells them.

g) What question does the video ask at the end? What do you think is the answer?

After watching

Write a summary of the video in English. Begin like this:
In this video called 'Cocoa Children', a reporter from the BBC visits the Ivory Coast, the West African country which supplies half the world's cocoa. He wants to find out about …

1 **ceiling** – the upper interior surface of a room

2 **piece of kit** – equipment

6 **incandescent** – emitting light as a result of being heated

7 **to sap** – to drain

7 **orb** – a round object or shape

11 **humble** – modest

16 **inconvenient** – difficult, causing trouble

21 **array** – a number of

22 **to resemble** – to be similar to

28 **to phase out** – to gradually withdraw

31 **diode** – a semiconductor device with two terminals, typically allowing the flow of current in one direction only

32 **anode** – the positively charged electrode by which the electrons leave an electrical device, the opposite of cathode

32 **cathode** – the negatively charged electrode by which electrons enter an electrical device, the opposite of anode

36 **to deposit** – to place

36 **semiconductor** – a solid substance that has a conductivity between that of an insulator and that of most metals

37 **to impregnate** – to fill

38 **impurity** – substance inside a confined amount of liquid, gas or solid

41 **to emit** – to produce and discharge

42 **property** – specification

49 **predictable** – foreseeable

65 **fortuitous** – lucky

BBC NEWS Technology

Search GO

Home | UK | Africa | Asia-Pac | Europe | Latin America | Mid-East | South Asia

LED bulbs: The end of the lightbulb as we know it?

Look up at the ceiling above you, and chances are there is a centuries-old piece of kit swinging from a cord. The light bulb has been hanging around for more than 150 years. […]

But now the days of the traditional incandescent bulb look numbered. These electricity-sapping glass orbs have fallen out of favour with environmentally-conscious governments and consumers. And waiting in the wings is a new breed of hi-tech light based on the humble LED (light-emitting diode), the small lights found in everything from TV remote controls to bike lights. […]

Already, the efficiency and long life of LEDs is making them a popular – if costly – option in places where changing bulbs is inconvenient or expensive, such as in motorway lights, traffic signals, airport runways or on large buildings and bridges. […]

But the real hope of the LED industry is that arrays of these tiny twinklers packed into something that resembles a bulb will become the light of choice in your bedroom, bathroom or study, allowing them to grab a slice of a global lighting market that was worth an estimated €52bn in 2010. Their cause is helped by the numerous governments around the world which have chosen to phase out the sale of incandescent bulbs. […]

As their name suggests, LEDs consist of a simple diode. In traditional electronics these are two metal posts – an anode and a cathode – placed very close to one another, through which power can only flow in one direction.

In LEDs, the anode and cathode are formed by depositing two areas of semiconductor that have been "doped" – impregnated with impurities – next to one another. As power flows through the junction between these two patches, some of it is unable to make it through and is instead emitted as photons of light. The colour of the light is dictated by the properties and structure of the semiconductor used to make the LED. […] Although this may sound complicated, the manufacturing process to create LEDs is well understood.

And – like all processes involving semi-conductors – it is coming down in cost all the time, and at predictable rates. In fact, the rates are so predictable that there is even a law – called Haitz's law – that describes the fall. This states that every decade, the cost of producing useful light will fall by a factor of 10, whilst the amount of light generated increases by a factor of 20. This is crucial for LEDs, which are currently around ten times more expensive than incandescent bulbs. Yet decreasing costs are only one part of the excitement.

In traditional incandescent bulbs, only about 5% of the electricity used is converted into light, while the rest is wasted as heat – the bulbs are therefore little more than tiny electric heaters which give out light as a fortuitous side-effect. But LEDs can be up to ten times as efficient. […]

And LEDs have another environmental trick up their sleeve: they last far longer than most other light sources. Incandescent bulbs last around 1,000 hours before burning out. LEDs do not burn out in the same way but simply get dimmer over time, and when they fall to 70% of their initial brightness their useful life is considered over. A good LED light should have a useful life of between 30,000 and 50,000 hours, and maybe up to 70,000 in the future, meaning less are thrown away and less are made.

But LEDs do not have it all their own way. One of the biggest challenges they face is the quality of the light that they produce. LED bulbs tend to generate a stark, cold light – a world away from the warm, yellowish light we are used to from incandescent bulbs. […] To get around this, scientists and manufacturers are now working on using a combination of blue LEDs and less efficient red ones to create a warmer glow. […]

Since white light is made up of a spectrum of different colours, the possibility of manipulating the light spectrum emitted by LED lights offers some of the most intriguing possibilities. For example, it should be possible to tune lights to give out a dose of near-violet light that would have antiseptic-like qualities. These could be used to keep countertops in kitchens clean, or to help maintain sanitary conditions in washrooms. It may be possible to design lamps that emit tailored light for students to use, to help them study more effectively, or ones that counter natural circadian rhythms to help night workers to stay awake. […]

(757 words)

82 **stark** – severe or bare
92 **intriguing** – interesting
97 **countertop** – work surface
98 **to maintain** – to keep
98 **sanitary conditions** – cleanliness
100 **tailored** – customised
102 **circadian rhythm** – biological clock

1 Comprehension: Short answer questions

Read the text and answer the following questions in 5–20 words.

a) What does the LED industry hope will happen, and why?

b) What determines the colour of the LED light?

c) What is Haitz's Law?

d) How much electricity is wasted as heat in a traditional lightbulb?

e) When is an LED's 'useful life' over?

f) What is currently one of the LED bulb's biggest disadvantages?

g) What could an LED emitting near-violet light be used for in the future?

2 Analysis

Describe and analyse the graph and link it to the text.

3 Comment

"[…] LEDs […] are currently around ten times more expensive than incandescent bulbs." (ll. 56–57). Many 'environmentally-friendly' products are more expensive than the alternative. Are you as an individual prepared to pay extra for such products? Explain your answer.

Energy Saving vs. Energy Consumption

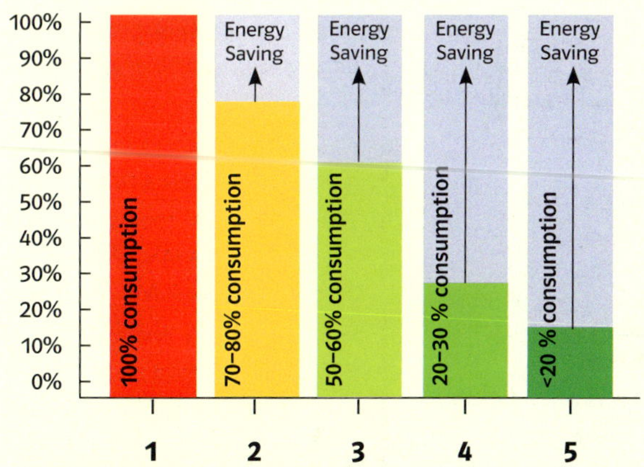

1 – Conventional incandescent bulbs
2 – Improved incandescent bulbs (class C of the energy label, halogen lamp with xenon gas filling)
3 – Improved incandescent bulbs (class B of the energy label, halogen lamp with infrared coating)
4 – Compact fluorescent lamps (CFLs)
5 – Light-emitting diodes (LEDs)

Source: European Commission, 2009

BBC NEWS Technology

Search GO

Home | UK | Africa | Asia-Pac | Europe | Latin America | Mid-East | South Asia

Wireless highway charges electric cars as they go

Researchers are close to developing a system that allows electric cars to recharge while they are moving ... via a recharging road.

Road works. Inconsiderate drivers. Congestion. Today's drivers have their fair share of stress already. But now there is a new malaise for the modern motorist: range anxiety.

That is the term given to drivers of electric cars that are struck by the sudden fear that their vehicle does not have enough charge to reach its destination. Most of us have experienced that sinking feeling when the little orange indicator light comes on to tell us we are low on petrol, but there is not a gas station in sight. Imagine that, combined with the feeling that you get when your cellphone starts beeping because the battery is low, and you are nowhere near a plug. That gets you close to the feeling of range anxiety.

It is an interesting phenomenon, particularly when you begin to look at how many of us actually use our cars. According to the US Bureau of Transportation Studies, 78% of drivers do less than 40 miles (65km) a day – a trivial distance for many of today's electric cars. In fact, the poster child of electric cars – the Tesla – has a range of 300 miles (485km) using some batteries.

According to Dr Richard Sassoon, of Stanford University, there are "three main reasons" that many of us choose the internal combustion engine over its cleaner, quieter alternative.

"One is the short range that an electric vehicle can travel between charges, and that's based on the size of the battery," he said. "The second is the lack of a sufficient charging infrastructure, and the third is that even if you can charge, it takes a long time to charge – several hours. That means you're going to have to take a break in your trip in order to charge your vehicle."

Researchers and firms are trying to tackle all of these problems. Firms, such as Better Place, have started building battery "switching stations" that allow drivers to pull in and swap their batteries as easily as filling up with gas, whilst countless researchers are developing more efficient batteries.

But Dr Sasson believes there may be another answer: recharging roads.

Engineers in his lab are developing a way to wirelessly charge electric cars from magnetic coils embedded into the road. The car would pick up the power via another coil, meaning – in theory – that you would never have to make a charging stop again.

The system works using a technique called "magnetic resonance coupling". You can think about resonance as the phenomenon that allows an opera singer to smash a glass using only the power of their voice. In that case, when the singer hits a note that has the same resonant frequency as the glass, they couple and energy begins to build up in the glass, eventually causing it to smash.

3 **inconsiderate** – selfish
3 **congestion** – traffic jam, heavy traffic
4 **malaise** – problem
4 **range** – distance
4 **anxiety** – fear
5 **to strike** – to hit
20 **poster child** – role model, example
23 **internal combustion engine** – engine which generates motive power by the burning of petrol, oil, or another fuel
32 **coil** – a length of something wound in a joined sequence of rings
32 **embedded** – built-in
35 **coupling** – joining together

Instead of using acoustic resonance, the Stanford team use the resonance of electromagnetic waves. A coil in the road that is connected to a power line is made to vibrate with the same resonance frequency as the coil on the bottom of the car, allowing energy to flow between them. […]

They have come up with designs of coil that allow 97% efficient transmission of power over a distance of about 2m (6ft). Using models, they estimate they can transfer up to 10kW of power.

"That number is about the number we'd probably want to transfer to vehicles" says Dr Sasoon.

And to turn this principle into a practical "recharging road" is not as difficult as it seems, he says.

"Road beds are made of asphalt or concrete, but there is often a lot of steel in the roads – a lot of rebar, a lot of ties between the segments of the road and so on," he said. "What we want to do is use that to our advantage."

He believes they could use much of the metal in the roadbed as part of the transmitter, and then the receiver would use the metal of the car body, again avoiding too many extra structural components.

It may take years, if not decades, until roads are retrofitted in this way. But various firms, including an MIT spin-out called WiTricity, are already taking the first steps by building charging stations for car parks, garages and beyond. […]

Dr Sasoon believes electric cars will become the technology of choice, displacing our current love of gas guzzlers and banishing the concept of range anxiety forever.

"You never need to worry about stopping and filling up," he said. […] (773 words)

46 **concrete** – cement

46 **rebar** – reinforcing steel used as rods in concrete

49 **roadbed** – the material laid down to form a road

51 **to retrofit** – to add a component to something that did not have it when manufactured

52 **spin-out** – subsidiary

54 **to displace** – to replace

54 **gas guzzler** – car that uses a lot of petrol

55 **to banish** – to get rid of permanently

1 Comprehension

a) In your own words, outline why people still prefer petrol cars to electric cars.

b) Outline how researchers have tried to tackle the problems connected to electric cars.

c) Describe how the 'recharging road' (l. 31) works.

2 Analysis

a) Explain the term 'range anxiety' (l. 4).

b) Describe and analyse the bar graph and relate it to the text.

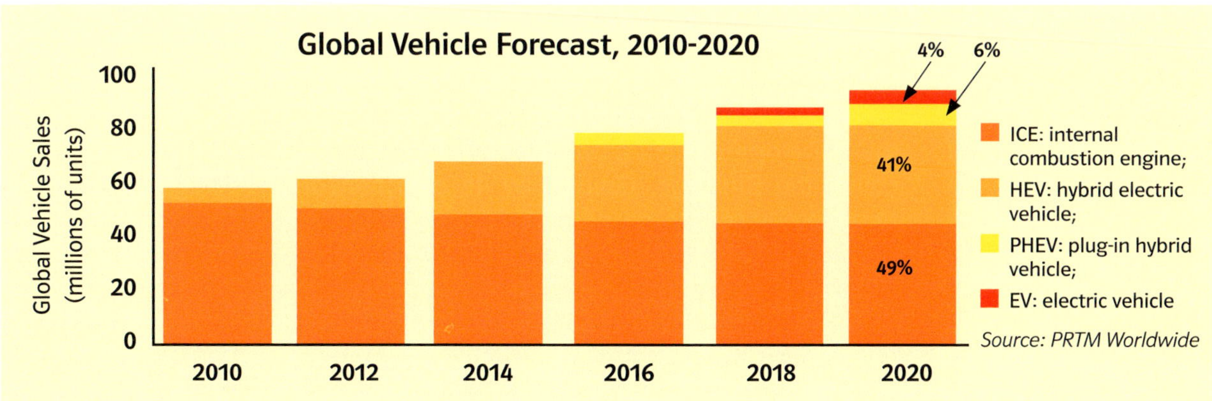

3 Comment

"[…] electric cars will become the technology of choice, displacing our current love of gas guzzlers […] forever." (ll. 54–55) Do you think people will be prepared to give up their petrol cars for electric cars in the near future? Discuss.

theguardian

News | Sport | Comment | Culture | Business | Money | Life&Style | Travel | Environment

Comment is free > Work   Search [ ] GO

Dawn of the age of the robot

The robots are coming. The second decade of the 21st century will see the rise of a mechanised army that will revolutionise private and public life just as radically as the internet and social media have shaken up the past 10 years. Or so says Marina Gorbis, futurologist and head of Californian think tank *The Institute for the Future*. [...]

Gorbis says robots will increasingly dominate everything from the way we fight wars to our work lives and even how we organise our kitchens.

Robots are likely to prompt a political storm to equal the row over immigration as they increasingly replace workers, says Gorbis. But it's not all bad news. "When IBM's Deep Blue became the first computer to beat chess grand master Gary Kasparov, people said, that's it, computers are smarter than people," she says. "But it didn't mean that at all. It means they are processing things faster, not that they are thinking better." Working together, she believes, robots and humans will be able to create a world of new possibilities impossible before our new industrial revolution.

Gorbis says the robots are already here. The US military is backing the development of a four legged, mechanical, pack-carrying robot, called the BigDogs. Guided by its own sensors, BigDog can navigate treacherous terrain carrying 150 kg on its back. In the air, robot drones are stalking targets in Afghanistan, remote controlled helicopters are ferrying supplies.

0 **dawn** – Morgendämmerung, Beginn

5 **think tank** – Expertenkommission

8 **to prompt** – hervorrufen

8 **to equal** – gleich sein, an etw. herankommen

8 **row** – Streit

17 **to back** – unterstützen

20 **drone** – Drohne (männliche Biene), *hier:* kleiner Flugkörper

21 **to stalk** – sich an jmdn/etw. heranpirschen

22 **to ferry** – befördern

22 **supplies** *(pl)* – Vorräte

Military technology from the Roman road to the internet has a habit of hitting the mainstream, and robots are already spreading their influence. Robots may soon do building work. The University of Southern California has developed a system called Contour Crafting that allows machines to construct buildings in layers, guided by computers. The system can reduce construction times and costs by 75%, according to USC.

In South Korea robots assist teachers in language classes, repeating words and phrases over and over and assessing how well they are parroted back. Google is working on cars that drive themselves. "What is that other than a robot," says Gorbis. Amazon and shoe retailer Zappos' huge warehouses are organised by an army of squat orange robots designed by Kiva Systems.

Inevitably the rise of the robots will put people out of work. Gorbis believes that this and other trends will mean unemployment will remain around 10% in many parts of the developed world over the coming years. "We are in transition. It is similar to when we mechanised agriculture. After that we went through a period of high unemployment as people transitioned to new kinds of jobs. People learned to do other things," she says.

There is potential for a huge backlash. "But once a technology is invented, it is very rare that it disappears. You can delay the introduction but it is going to be used. If someone can produce something cheaper and faster, you are competing in that environment." [...]

We too are likely to become more robotic, she believes. "We have been modifying ourselves with technology forever, with eyeglasses, cochlear implants. We are going to see more of that. Sensors are going to be on our bodies, in our bodies, letting us and others know what we are doing, what is going on with our health. All kinds of applications we haven't even thought of yet."

Gorbis says she is often asked if the future is arriving faster than ever. "I'm not sure that it is," she says. "We know more, we have access to more information, but if you lived during the period of electrification or the building of railroads, I'm sure you really felt the pace of change too. It's all relative."

With all this information being bombarded at us it is no wonder that people worry, she said. "I feel schizophrenic myself. Half the time I feel really depressed when I look at, say, climate change or the potential to misuse technology. But then I get really excited about how we are reinventing ourselves through technology." (672 words)

23 **habit** – Gewohnheit
27 **layer** – Schicht
30 **to assess** – beurteilen
31 **to parrot** – nachplappern
33 **squat** – gedrungen
35 **inevitably** – zwangsläufig
38 **transition** – Übergang
38 **agriculture** – Landwirtschaft
40 **to transition to** – wechseln zu
42 **backlash** – Gegenreaktion
43 **to delay** – hinauszögern
47 **cochlear implant** – Innenohrprothese
50 **application** – Anwendung
53 **access** – Zugang
55 **pace** – Geschwindigkeit
61 **to reinvent oneself** – sich neu definieren

Mediation

You are a member of the school newspaper team. The newspaper's editor would like to publish an article about the growing influence of robots, and has found the above text. He asks you to sum up the most important information for him in German.

4 **unfathomable** – impossible to understand

5 **to spawn** – to produce a large number of sth.

5 **merchandise** – official goods

8 **amenities** – facilities

11 **gender** – sex

21 **launch** – an occasion where something new is introduced

22 **pitch** – sales talk

24 **to savour** – to enjoy

29 **corporate** – business

30 **wireframe** – an image which displays

33 **brief** – a set of instructions

34 **straightforward** – simple

theguardian

News | Sport | Comment | Culture | Business | Money | Life&Style | Travel | Environment

Comment is free > Work   Search [ ] GO

A working life: The app developer

Many of those familiar with the world of smartphones and other handheld computers will have daydreamed of inventing a killer app, one of the simple and often brilliantly useful little programs that run on touchscreen phones and tablet computers like the iPad. Perhaps we imagine our idea will become part of the zeitgeist, be downloaded millions of times and generate unfathomable profits, spawning lucrative toys, T-shirts and other merchandise.

As I stroll along Oxford Street to the head offices of Grapple Mobile, I think of a couple of my own money-spinning ideas: a football stadium app telling you where in the ground your seat is, local amenities and the ability to message other fans. Or how about an app that could tell you the real-time gender mix in a bar or club? But it doesn't take much time chatting to Justin James, head of development at Grapple, for me to realise I have no chance of turning my app fantasies into reality. […]

Justin James, head of development at Grapple.

James impressed the Grapple bosses enough to become head of development after just four and a half months, having worked on successful launches such as a multi-platform app for wine magazine *Decanter*, as well as client pitches. "We often get asked to build something speculatively for a client and it's great fun to let your imagination run wild, especially if the app ends up being given the green light," he explains. It is the experimentation that James clearly savours. […]

James tells me what his job is all about. "It often involves taking large chunks of data and making it work for the user. It's about coming up with different solutions to the same problems. You're building on stuff all the time, taking what has worked with something else and applying it to a new app."

Most often, a corporate client will approach Grapple with what they want from an app, Grapple will take that idea, cost it out, produce wireframes (walkthroughs of how the app will work) and a design aesthetic (if needed) and build the app for as many different types of mobile platform as the client needs. […]

James's job is to take a brief from the client, create the app and deliver it on time and on budget. It is easier said than done: "It can be straightforward or it can be difficult. With the Decanter wine app, we had a huge database of wines and regions that the user had to be able to access. We had to find a way of displaying that information quickly and we decided to force the app to access the internet to do it. Even then, that's a large chunk of data for a mobile phone to process so we had to find ways to slow the user down and stop them getting angry if it took too long to find what they wanted."

James calls the solution to these problems "the twist", as in: "The client owns the app, but we bring the twist." And clients pay handsomely for it, too. Apps can cost a corporate client around £30,000, even more for a quick turnaround. [...] Grapple has in-house testers to ensure the finished product ticks all the boxes and, most importantly, is exactly what the client wanted.

I leave James with his colleagues as they discuss their work schedules for the week and as I saunter along Oxford Street once again, my head quickly becomes full of more app possibilities. It's not long before I've got another cracking idea – the one that could make me a fortune. All I need is £30,000 and someone like James to build it for me. (609 words)

41 **to pay handsomely** – to pay well

45 **to saunter** – to walk casually

46 **a cracking idea** – an excellent idea

1 Comprehension

a) Summarise the information given in the text about Justin James and his career at Grapple.

b) Describe James' role in developing apps at Grapple.

2 Analysis

Describe and analyse the bar graph below, and give possible reasons for the figures shown.

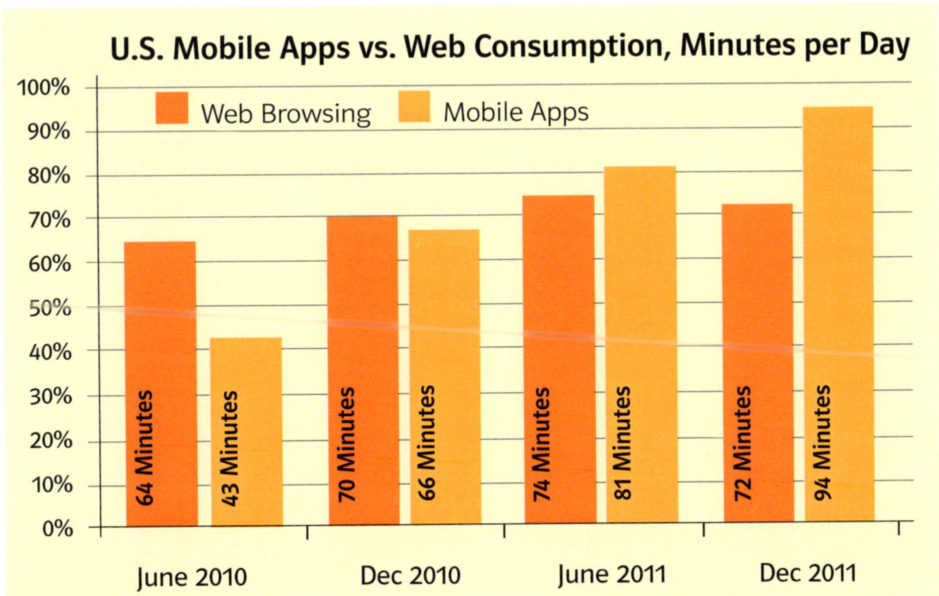

Source: Flurry Analytics

3 Comment

"Many of those familiar with the world of smartphones and other handheld computers will have daydreamed of inventing a killer app [...]" (ll. 1–2). If you were asked by Grapple to develop an app, what would it be? Explain your choice, thinking about your own experiences with apps.

3 **bunch** – *hier:* Völkchen

4 **to stride** – große Schritte machen

5 **stiff upper lip** – kontrollierte Emotionen

5 **old school tie** – alte Seilschaft aus der gleichen Schule

10 **reserve** – Scheu, Förmlichkeit

10 **to crumble** – zerfallen, sich auflösen

17 **born-and-bred** – einheimisch

19 **to fumble around** – herumfummeln

22 **chit-chat** – Geplauder

27 **at the outset** – am Anfang

The Economist

World politics | Business & finance | Economics | Science & technology | Culture | Blogs

Doing business in London

London is not a difficult place to do business. Forget the stereotypes you might have heard elsewhere: in general terms, the transport systems work, the weather is okay and the British are a tolerant bunch. These tips below should help you to stride into meetings with that extra bit of confidence. Stiff upper lips and old school ties are much rarer than they used to be, but Londoners are still relatively shy. Buy a round of drinks in the pub later in the day, though, and you'll find the reserve starts to crumble.

Meeting and greeting

London is a multicultural city. It is worth finding out where your contact is from. You are quite as likely to be dealing with an Indian or an Australian as you are with a born-and-bred Londoner. Business cards are typically exchanged at the end of a meeting. But it is not unusual for a Brit to forget about them entirely. If your contact fumbles around for his card, or fails to produce one, don't take it personally.

The British tend to be punctual, and meetings generally follow the Anglo-Saxon norm, with brief chit-chat swiftly followed by a focused, action-oriented discussion.

Working habits

E-mails perfectly suit the famous British reserve. In general, they are promptly responded to and are often the preferred method of communication, at least at the outset. As a relationship strengthens, and certainly if complex negotiations are involved, expect face-to-face meetings and telephone conversations. The strongest relationships are forged after

work – be that in a pub or at an informal evening meal. The line between work and private life is not as clearly delineated as in America, and the British tend to socialise with colleagues quite regularly. Drunken behaviour on a Friday evening will be laughed off the following Monday, and in some cases is quite the norm. The woes of public transport are a sure-fire way of reviving flagging conversation. London's motorists have to pay a congestion charge to drive into the city. Your contacts will be sure to have an opinion on whether the experiment is working.

Eating and drinking

A business lunch can just as easily mean a quick sandwich and coffee as a slap-up meal in a smart restaurant. Breakfast meetings are rare. Most Brits subscribe to Oscar Wilde's claim that "only dull people are interesting at breakfast." Midday drinking has declined, but it is still normal to have a glass of wine or a beer, with food or without.

Likewise, smoking has fallen off dramatically. Smoking was banned in all public spaces (including restaurants and bars) from July 2007 and the smoky haze that used to be a feature of many pubs is but a memory. If you want to smoke, you have to be outside. When in a pub, do not expect table service, unless you are seated in the restaurant area. And don't tip the bar staff unless they bring the drinks and bill over to you.

Table manners are keenly observed as a subtle sign of good breeding. Never talk with your mouth full; never reach across the table; do not wave cutlery around or yell "I'm done" to the waiter. London's top restaurants are expensive (£100 a head is not unheard of). Furthermore, an increasing number insist on taking credit card details before accepting a booking. The British are less politically correct than their American counterparts. Wittiness can still mean an agility with sexual innuendo, with a pint in one hand and a cigarette in the other. (589 words)

35 **delineated** – abgegrenzt
43 **woes** – Leiden, Probleme
43 **sure-fire** – todsicher
43 **to revive a flagging conversation** – ein erschlaffendes Gespräch beleben
44 **congestion charge** – Staugebühr
50 **to subscribe to a claim** – sich einer Behauptung anschließen
50 **dull** – langweilig
55 **smoky haze** – rauchiger Schleier
59 **good breeding** – gute Erziehung
64 **counterpart** – Gegenstück, Pendant
65 **wittiness** – Witzigkeit
65 **agility** – Gewandtheit
65 **innuendo** – Anspielung

Mediation

You are doing a work placement at a German marketing company. The company has just acquired an important English client based in London, and some of your company's representatives are about to travel there for the first round of meetings. The head of your department has found the above information online and has asked you to put together an information sheet on 'Doing Business in London' in German.

theguardian

News | Sport | Comment | Culture | Business | Money | Life&Style | Travel | Environment

Comment is free > Business Search [ ] GO

Top tips for web startups

Are you curious about starting up online, but concerned about the legalities? Olivia Perrott and Nick Atkins give some key advice for internet startups.

Web-based businesses can in theory be set up overnight with a very limited budget. However, the following legal issues are worth bearing in mind to minimise risk and optimise the value of investment.

Prepare for success

Consider how your business should be structured to provide the flexibility to bring in investment and grow.

1

Compared with operating as a sole trader, a limited company has the key advantage of limiting your personal liability. Your company can then borrow – although most lenders and some suppliers will ask for personal guarantees – and enter into contracts in its own right. UK corporation tax rates are currently low. Ordinarily, the advantages of incorporating will outweigh the administrative burdens of running a company, which include annual accounts and other filings.

As it grows, a company provides you with a platform to issue shares to investors in return for important growth capital. As is particularly common in the IT industry, share schemes can also be put in place to incentivise and help retain talent in your business. […]

As well as companies limited by shares, there are other types of legal entity, such as limited liability partnerships, but in our experience private limited companies by shares are the most popular for web-based businesses. […]

Domain names and trade marks

2

Carrying out some basic searches will help you rule out potentially problematic domain names, and more sophisticated clearance searches can be carried out by trade mark agents.

1 **legality** – level of accordance with the law

10 **sole trader** – a business owned and run by one person

10 **limited company** – a private company whose owners are legally responsible for its debts only to the extent of the amount of capital they invested

11 **liabililty** – the state of being legally responsible for sth.

13 **incorporating** – joining together

15 **filing** – bookkeeping

16 **to issue** – to give out

18 **to incentivise** – to make sth. appealing

18 **to retain** – to keep

19 **entity** – a thing with distinct and independent existence

22 **domain** – a distinct part of the Internet

22 **trademark** – brand

24 **to rule out** – to exclude

25 **sophisticated** – *here:* thorough

1 Comprehension: Multiple matching

Read the text and choose from the sentences A–F the one which fits each gap (1–5). There is one extra sentence that you do not need to use.

A	Important details to consider include ensuring that the deadlines which the parties will work towards are set out in writing.
B	Having the benefit of the experience of someone who has gone through the process themselves can be invaluable to a new business.
C	User-generated content can enhance your site, but entails certain risks.
D	In most cases this will mean setting up a limited company in which you, your business partners and investors can hold shares.
E	Advertising your products online can be very lucrative if you choose the right site.
F	When naming your site, you should avoid using a name which is the same, or similar to the trade mark or name of another business.

You may wish to register your business name as a trade mark, which means you can prevent others from using the mark or a similar mark for the same kind of goods or services. Doing this at an early stage is a good idea as your business name will not otherwise be protected until you have established a reputation in the market. It will also provide you with a valuable asset which can be attractive to investors.

Website and software development

If you use independent website developers you should review the terms of their contract carefully.

3

Also, that the developers are required to provide some support to you once the site goes live; and that the obligation to pay for the services does not arise until you have had the opportunity to test and accept the site. [...]

If you are creating your own software, make sure you check that any code which appears to be open-source – so free to download – has no awkward conditions attached to its use.

Third party material

If you plan to use third party copyright material on your site, such as music, video or text, you risk being liable for copyright infringement unless permission has been obtained for its use, or other limited circumstances exist.

4

The content may be infringing because it contains third party copyright material, defamatory or illegal and as website operator you may be liable for it in certain circumstances. It is therefore important to include a prohibition in your site's terms and conditions against the use or uploading of illegal, infringing or defamatory content and reserve the right to remove this content at your discretion. [...]

Information about users

New regulations provide that any website which uses cookies must provide users with clear and comprehensive information about their use on the site and the purpose, and in most circumstances obtain consent from each user to use them.

Many web-based businesses will process users' personal data in some way. Personal data is essentially any information from which an individual can be identified. [...]

Learn from others

Talk to a trusted mentor from an early stage so they can guide you through the startup process.

5

(724 words)

29 **reputation** – beliefs or opinions that are generally held about someone or sth.
29 **asset** – sth. of value
35 **obligation** – responsibility
35 **to arise** – to appear
38 **awkward** – *here:* complex
41 **infringement** – violation
to entail – to include
44 **defamatory** – damaging the good reputation of someone
46 **prohibition** – ban
47 **at one's discretion** – based on one's own decision/judgement
invaluable – very valuable

2 Analysis

Describe and analyse the cartoon and link it to the text.

3 Comment

Internet shopping has changed the face of retail forever. Discuss the pros and cons of shopping on-line.

"Honey, look how cute ... The kids have started their own little business."

0 **holistic** – comprehensive

0 **approach** – way of doing sth.

3 **to tackle** – to try to stop

6 **to forge a link** – to make a connection

11 **denial** – refusal to admit sth. is true

12 **to ease out** – to help out

17 **sustainable** – can be kept at a constant level

17 **paediatric** – branch of medicine dealing with children

18 **dietician** – nutrition expert

20 **hands on approach** – a practical approach

theguardian

News | Sport | Comment | Culture | Business | Money | Life&Style | Travel | Environment

Comment is free > Health — Search GO

New holistic approach to treat child obesity

Clinical team joins forces with community services to tackle child obesity

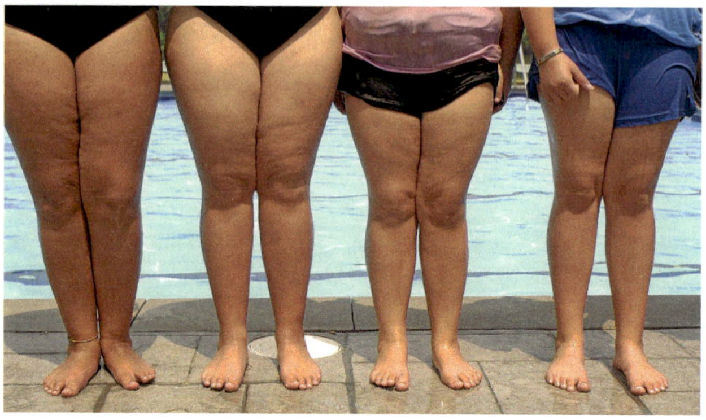

Mary Haddow is a specialist nurse working on a new scheme that forges links between healthcare professionals and community services to tackle obesity. The most enjoyable part of her job is helping children and families, but her task is not an easy one.

"Denial, guilt and low self-esteem are linked to obesity so it can be a real challenge getting children and families to attend appointments," says Mary. "So we try to find ways to ease children out of their comfort zone. A walk along the beach with our exercise instructor can be a crucial first step."

The new scheme brings together a range of healthcare professionals and services to offer personalised care and support for children with obesity problems. It is based on a local, holistic and sustainable approach and brings together a multi-disciplinary 'paediatric healthy weight team' – consisting of doctors, nurses, a dietician, psychologist and physical instructor – providing medical assessment, dietary advice, exercise programmes and nursing support. Children and parents also work with community services offering a hands on approach to empower them to improve diet, physical activity and confidence. Services include cooking classes, exercise programmes and fun activities.

1 Comprehension: Multiple choice

Read the text and choose the answer (1., 2. or 3.) which you think fits best according to the text.

a) Obese children and their families
1. are keen to meet with healthcare professionals.
2. have difficulty getting appointments with healthcare professionals.
3. do not often initiate meetings with healthcare professionals.

b) Parents of obese children
1. have an active part in the scheme to help their children.
2. are not involved in the new scheme.
3. are required to pay a fee for their children to attend the scheme.

c) Since its launch seven months ago, the scheme
1. has been heavily criticized.
2. has cost the government a lot of money.
3. has proven to be successful.

"By getting out into the community, children can make new friends, develop new skills and more confidence," says Mary, adding that it is, ultimately, a lifestyle choice that the scheme is aiming to change. And this is where community services play a crucial role.

Around 110 children have been referred to the scheme from paediatric services, school nurses, health visitors and GPs. There have been positive results since its launch seven months ago and an evaluation will be undertaken by the University of East Anglia.

Mary was responsible for setting up the day-to-day running of the scheme, and has developed a range of managerial and organisational skills with the experience of setting up a whole new scheme, coordinating services and working closely with community services.

"It has been a fascinating role, a good challenge and a huge learning curve," says Mary. "Many people, even health professionals, do not know what is available in the community," she says. There are good services in place but effective co-ordination is needed to bring these together. While the extra workload has been a struggle, good communication and a supportive team with a "can do" attitude has helped to deliver the comprehensive service, she explains. Every child and family is unique, and with a range of services on offer, it is important to think creatively and outside of the box to deliver personalised care and support and to ensure no child or family slips through the net, she explains.

Hilary Class, president of the paediatric and child health royal society, praised the scheme: "The biggest challenge in overcoming a problem like childhood obesity is that there isn't a single solution; there are multiple factors at play. So any solution must necessarily draw on a range of people if it's to really work."

"This kind of innovative approach rightly sees obesity as a complex problem; but one that with joined-up working and interventions from healthcare professionals and parents alike, can be overcome."

"We need to monitor the success of such services carefully; and where they're seen to work well, look to replicate elsewhere," she added.

But while these community services have been shown to work, with some recommended by NICE as a front line treatment to obesity, less than 5% of overweight and obese children have access to these type of programmes, says Paul Sacher, chief research and development officer at MEND. "Obesity is widely considered as one of the most serious public health threats facing our society, but there is a lack of funding for such treatments and programmes," says Sacher. [...]

Meanwhile, Mary is enthusiastic: "This is a new service and as long as everyone pulls together and are keen to try different things, we have an opportunity to make it work." (666 words)

24 **ultimately** – put simply
37 **unique** – one of a kind
48 **to replicate** – to copy
49 **to recommend** – to strongly suggest
49 **NICE** – National Institute for Health and Clinical Excellence
51 **MEND** – healthy-lifestyle program for 7–13 year-olds who are overweight
52 **threat** – danger
53 **lack of** – the state of being without or not having enough of sth.
53 **funding** – financial support

d) Despite obesity being one of the most serious health problems today,
1. there is not enough financial support available to tackle it.
2. there is still a lack of physical activity in schools.
3. parents still do not pay enough attention to what their children are eating.

2 Analysis

Describe and analyse the cartoon and link it to the text.

3 Comment

"Obesity is widely considered as one of the most serious public health threats facing our society [...]" (l. 52). Give reasons as to why more and more children are becoming obese and suggest what could be done to tackle this problem. Use the text to help you.

theguardian

News | Sport | Comment | Culture | Business | Money | Life&Style | Travel | Environment

Comment is free > Society   Search [ ] GO

Just another day in court as a social worker

Aggressive cross-examinations, a lack of privacy and tense confrontations with angry parents are all part of the process – one social worker in Ireland shares their experience.

Depending on your cases, court can be a big or a small part of the job of a social worker, but it is always part of the job at some stage; each trip to court filled with waiting, nervous tension and more waiting. Most of it is hidden from the world by the confidentiality rules of family law.

Each day in court begins with everyone crowding into a small hall with no windows, no ventilation and no seating – at least that's my experience – and the day spent standing around in this small hall outside the actual courtroom waiting. First, we wait for the judge to arrive and get proceedings under way, then we wait for lawyers and barristers to negotiate, and finally waiting for your case to be heard.

There is no clear timetable for cases, so you could be done in two minutes, or wait around several hours before being heard. This is just one of the many things that makes a day at court so unpredictable, time-consuming and ultimately frustrating.

It's not just the social workers in this corridor, the families are all here, waiting around endlessly too. They are waiting to have a judge take their child away,

0 **court** – building where legal cases happen

1 **cross-examination** – questioning of a witness called by the other party in court to challenge or extend testimony already given

1 **tense** – strained

7 **confidentiality** – discretion

20 **barrister** – a lawyer who specializes in courtroom advocacy, drafting legal pleadings and giving expert legal opinions

20 **to negotiate** – to agree on terms

24 **unpredictable** – uncertain

1 Comprehension

a) In your own words, describe a day in court for a social worker.

b) Outline what could make a social worker's job easier.

2 Analysis

Describe the picture and relate it to the text.

waiting for access to be refused, waiting for the worst to happen. Standing there in front of them are the social workers, the people who are inflicting this on them, adding tension to the already stuffy atmosphere.

The clients usually end up hating us, undermining any relationship, which has been so carefully built up. Running around among this crowd are lawyers and barristers from both sides – arguing, negotiating, and doing their best to fit social work's shades of grey into the black and white world of law.

And still we wait thinking about all the work you need to do but can't. No matter what is happening in your other cases, everything is dropped while you are in court. Without access to a room of our own with adequate privacy, even simple phone calls prove difficult, and anything more complex, such as case notes or referrals, is never going to happen.

Eventually you wind up in the courtroom itself in front of a judge. The courtrooms are often the complete opposite of the corridor we wait in. Earlier in the day you don't have any idea which judge you will be in front of, but this can really matter. It is worrying how much a judge's personality can actually impact a case, and it's hard to know if you and the child at the centre of the case will win or lose this judicial lottery.

I try and remember it's not personal. When the lawyers verbally assault me during cross-examination, they are just doing their job; when judges shout at me, they are just doing theirs.

At the end of the day there is a child, or sometimes several children, whose future depends on this spectacle. That is the worst part, and the most stressful part. We as social workers try to do our best, but if the court doesn't agree for whatever reason that can have real and serious consequences. These are the cases where you can easily be haunted by the personal doubt of "did I do enough?"

Is there anything that can make this better? Simple things like giving the social workers some office space, maybe even with a computer hooked up to our case database, or just some privacy to allow work to be done would help. This separation can also reduce the tension with parents.

On a deeper level, a complete overhaul of how the courts work would make a significant difference, replacing the combative nature of common law with an inquisitorial system that is not acting as referee between two sides. This, however, is a huge change to our legal system and not without controversy. (676 words)

29 **to inflict sth. on sb.** – to cause sth. to happen to sb.
30 **stuffy** – unfriendly
31 **to undermine** – to ruin
39 **referral** – an act of referring someone or sth. for consultation, review, or further action
45 **judicial** – relating to the administration of justice
46 **to assault** – to attack
53 **to be haunted by sth.** – to be plagued by sth.
58 **overhaul** – major changes
59 **combative** – aggressive
60 **referee** – person who mediates/judges

3 Comment

Your school requires you to complete a four-week internship in the social work field. The local council is offering internships as a social worker. Based on your knowledge of social work and what you have read in the text, would you be interested in this opportunity? Explain your answer.

0 **vocational** – beruflich, Berufs-

3 **to kit out** – ausrüsten

3 **safety goggles** – Schutzbrille

17 **peak** – Höchststand

19 **aborted** – abgebrochen

20 **to be on a par with sth.** – sich mit jdm./etw. messen können

20 **casualty** – Opfer

21 **humanities** – Geisteswissenschaften

22 **to abandon** – *hier:* aufgeben

30 **to investigate** – erforschen, untersuchen

theguardian

News | Sport | Comment | Culture | Business | Money | Life&Style | Travel | Environment

Comment is free > Education > Search GO

Has England finally found the formula for vocational education?

It's an unusual sight in a British school. Michael Micallef is kitted out in safety goggles and blue overalls, expertly operating machinery that wouldn't look out of place on the workshop floor of one of Europe's top manufacturers.

The 18-year-old says – with considerable pride – that what he does feels more like working for a company than going to school. He is one of a growing number of teenagers to attend a new kind of school in England known as a university technical school or UTC.

Pupils, parents, employers and government ministers have high hopes that these schools will reduce youth unemployment – at a near 20-year peak – by equipping youngsters with the sorts of skills the country's engineering and manufacturing firms have long cried out for.

In the past 30 years, there have been a number of aborted attempts at introducing a vocational education system on a par with Germany's. […] The latest casualty has been "academic diplomas" in humanities, languages and science, which were to combine work-based training and traditional study. They were abandoned in 2010, a year before they were to be officially introduced.

UTCs, however, herald a promising fresh start.

Micallef's UTC in Rocester, Staffordshire, is named after the world's third-largest construction equipment manufacturer – JCB – whose headquarters are down the road. […]

The schools have a specialism, which tends to be engineering but for some will be construction, digital media or anything that requires practical skills and specialised equipment. […]

Pupils at UTCs, who are aged 14 to 19, are set real workplace tasks, such as designing a pump for a jet engine or investigating the materials needed to help trains change direction.

During the year, students at Micallef's school are assigned five eight-week projects. After each task, they present their findings to a panel of employees from companies that work with the school and help design the projects. [...]

The schools are state-funded. Neither the companies nor the university provide extra cash – just their employees' time. [...]

Micallef believes he has improved his job prospects by going to a UTC. "In interviews, I can talk about the practical side of things," he says. "I can show them I know how to use a lathe and I've got a portfolio of work for them to view. In a community school, you learn a subject and then you sit a test."

Jim Wade, the headteacher, says there are more companies interested in becoming involved in the JCB academy than he has space for. Pupils know these firms are under no compulsion to hire them, but, as Charlie Crawshaw, 14, says, "at least we have the sense that we have a foot in the right door".

More than 100 senior engineers come to the school each year to help pupils with their work. Will Wainwright, 18, who hopes to study engineering at university, says these visits are "the greatest way to learn". "You just listen to what they say – they've had 20-plus years of experience in their field."

The first cohort of pupils will leave the JCB academy this summer and, so far, their prospects are looking rosy. Half have offers to study engineering at university and the other half are waiting to hear whether they have been successful in interviews for apprenticeships.

Wade says at most of England's schools, pupils very often move between lessons – and therefore subjects – every 50 minutes and this makes it harder for them to acquire the skills they need for the workplace.

"By spending that much longer with our students because of the project work we do, we can help them develop team-building and communication skills," he says. Pupils are more likely to see the relevance of what they are learning because it is set in the context of the "real world", he argues.

But, while some politicians hope for at least 100 UTCs to be open by 2015, Wade is not getting carried away. UTCs are probably suitable for about 10% of the school population, he says. "If you want to be a dancer, for example, you wouldn't come here."

There is another problem that is likely to prevent UTCs from opening up in great numbers across the country in the near future: British snobbery.

"We're still at the stage where if someone asks a young person what they are studying and they say Latin, we reply 'how fantastic'," Wade says. "If they say they are doing a diploma in engineering, we say 'oh, right'."

"As a country, we still make value judgments about technical education, but at least there's now clearly a recognition that we need to do something about that." (773 words)

32 **panel** – Gremium
37 **lathe** – Drehbank
41 **compulsion** – Zwang
42 **to hire** – einstellen
48 **cohort** – Gruppe
50 **apprenticeship** – Berufsausbildung, Lehre
62 **snobbery** – Snobismus
66 **value judgment** – Werturteil
67 **recognition** – *hier:* Erkenntnis

Mediation

You have recently completed school in Germany and are interested in studying engineering at a UTC in England. As your parents are a little sceptical about the idea, you need to convince them. In German, summarise the key information about UTCs and how students learn there to persuade them that it is a good idea.

Self-assessment – Selbsteinschätzung

Nachdem Sie die Aufgaben (Seite 194–199) bearbeitet haben, können Sie die Ergebnisse mit den Lösungen vergleichen. Schätzen Sie dann bitte Ihre Leistung in den folgenden Kategorien selbst ein: Leseverstehen, Hörverstehen, Schreibfertigkeit und Sprechfertigkeit. Bitte beurteilen Sie für jede Kategorie, ob Sie die einzelnen Stufen „überhaupt nicht erreicht", „voll erreicht" oder Ihrer Meinung nach „deutlich überschritten" haben.

In den danach folgenden Kategorien Wortschatz, grammatische Strukturen, Aussprache und Flüssigkeit sowie Aufbau und Gedankenführung wählen Sie die Kategorie, die Ihre Leistung am besten beschreibt.

Leseverstehen

Stufe 1
Wenn ich einen unbekannten englischen Text lese, kann ich oft die wesentlichen Punkte erfassen. Die Texte sollten nicht zu kompliziert und nicht zu lang sein, es ist leichter, wenn sie ein Thema behandeln, bei dem ich mich gut auskenne. Die Informationen, die ich benötige, finde ich dann schnell. Mit dem vorliegenden Text hatte ich nach wiederholtem Lesen keine großen Schwierigkeiten, ich habe alle gesuchten Informationen ohne sehr große Probleme gefunden.

Stufe 2
Ich lese englische Texte insgesamt sehr selbstständig und verstehe auch dann vieles, wenn ich Fachartikel lese. Längere Texte machen mir meistens keine Schwierigkeiten, Zeitungsartikel zu aktuellen Fragen verstehe ich zum größten Teil. Den vorliegenden Text habe ich schnell auch im Detail verstanden, nur wenige Sätze musste ich mehrfach lesen.

Stufe 3
Ich verstehe fast alle englischen Texte. Ich kann lange, komplexe Texte im Detail verstehen, auch wenn sie ein Thema behandeln, mit dem ich mich nicht gut auskenne. Manchmal lese ich komplizierte Passagen mehrmals, aber ich fühle mich im Lesen von englischen Texten insgesamt sehr sicher. Den vorliegenden Text fand ich insgesamt leicht, er hat mir keine Probleme bereitet. Alle Details habe ich sehr schnell gefunden.

Hörverstehen

Stufe 1
Ich verstehe die Hauptaspekte in Redebeiträgen zu alltäglichen oder vertrauten Themen. Das Hörverstehen fällt mir leichter, wenn die Sprecher(innen) deutlich artikulieren. Die Beiträge sollten aber nicht sehr lang sein.

Stufe 2
Ich verstehe die Hauptaussagen in Redebeiträgen auch zu komplexeren Themen. Wenn der Akzent vertraut ist und deutlich gesprochen wird, verstehe ich auch Fachdiskussionen zu weniger vertrauten Themen. Das Hörverstehen fällt mir leicht, wenn die Sprecher(innen) deutlich artikulieren.

Stufe 3
Wenn ich einen längeren englischen Redebeitrag höre, kann ich meist die wesentlichen Punkte erfassen. Die Texte können auch fremde und komplexe Themen behandeln. Ich verstehe auch Unterhaltungen mit zwei oder mehr Sprecher(inne)n ohne Probleme, leichte Probleme habe ich eigentlich nur bei fremdem Akzent.

Texte verfassen

Stufe 1
Ich kann zu bekannten oder alltäglichen Themen zusammenhängende Texte verfassen, in denen eine klare Struktur zu finden ist.

Stufe 2
Ich kann in strukturierten, zusammenhängenden Texten Vor- und Nachteile von bestimmten Standpunkten darlegen und meine Meinung besonders zu vertrauten Themen aus meinem Interessengebiet darlegen. Hier kann ich auch Detailinformationen klar und überzeugend präsentieren.

Stufe 3
Ich kann klar, flüssig und gut strukturiert über komplexe Themen schreiben, es fällt mir nicht schwer, bestimmte Punkte besonders hervorzuheben. Mein gedanklicher Aufbau ist mit Standpunkt(en), Beispielen und klarem Ende gut nachzuvollziehen.

An Gesprächen teilnehmen

Stufe 1
Die meisten vorhersehbaren Situationen kann ich in Gesprächen so lösen, dass mein(e) Gesprächspartner(in) versteht, was ich sagen möchte. Ich kann Informationen austauschen, meine Meinung darlegen und Argumente für vertraute Sachverhalte vorbringen.

Stufe 2
Ich kann mich soweit fließend und spontan verständigen, dass ein normales Gespräch über verschiedene Freizeit-, aber auch berufliche Themen möglich ist, ohne dass mein(e) Gesprächspartner(in) sich anstrengen muss, mich zu verstehen. Ich kann mich auch über einen längeren Zeitraum an Gesprächen beteiligen und habe keine Mühe, ein Gespräch durch meine Initiative aufrechtzuerhalten.

Stufe 3
Ich kann mich fast mühelos spontan und fließend ausdrücken. Mein Wortschatz ist groß genug, um immer auch Umschreibungen für das zu finden, was ich sagen möchte. Schwierigkeiten habe ich nur bei Fachthemen, bei denen mir zum Teil Begriffe unbekannt sind. Ich kann flexibel auf Gesprächspartner(innen) eingehen und eigentlich immer alles ausdrücken, was ich sagen möchte, dies schließt auch z. B. Scherze, Emotionen usw. ein.

Wortschatz

	... sehr differenziert, d.h. ich kann fast alles sagen, was ich möchte, bei vielen Wörter kenne ich auch andere Wörter mit gleicher oder ähnlicher Bedeutung oder die jeweiligen Gegenteile; die Wörter kann ich auch alle korrekt schreiben.
	... differenziert, ich kann vieles sagen, was ich möchte, manchmal kenne ich Wörter mit gleicher oder ähnlicher Bedeutung; ich mache sehr wenige Rechtschreibfehler.
Ich denke, mein Allgemein- und Fachwortschatz ist ...	... weniger differenziert, d.h. manchmal fehlen mir auch alltägliche Wörter; für viele Aspekte kenne ich nur jeweils ein Wort. Insgesamt kann ich aber vieles sagen, was ich sagen möchte, auch wenn ich ab und zu Rechtschreibfehler mache.
	... begrenzt, d.h. häufig fehlen mir auch alltägliche Wörter; nicht immer kann ich sagen, was ich sagen möchte; die Zahl der Rechtschreibfehler ist insgesamt hoch.
	... deutlich begrenzt, ich weiß viele Wörter nicht, die ich schon vor Jahren gelernt habe; häufig muss ich im Wörterbuch nachsehen, ich mache auch bei einfachen Wörtern sehr viele Rechtschreibfehler.
	... stark begrenzt; ich kann sehr vieles (auch Alltägliches) nicht sagen; die Wörter, die ich dann im Wörterbuch finde, habe ich häufig noch nie gehört; die Grundregeln der englischen Rechtschreibung kenne ich nicht.

Grammatische Strukturen

	... haben einen sehr hohen Grad an Korrektheit, ich weiß, dass ich kaum Grammatikfehler mache; gelegentliche Fehler kann ich als Fehler erkennen und entsprechend schnell korrigieren.
	... haben einen hohen Grad an Korrektheit, ich mache nur gelegentlich Grammatikfehler, diese kann ich selbst erkennen und korrigieren, wenn ich in einer Grammatik nachschlage.
Ich denke, die von mir benutzten grammatischen Strukturen ...	... zeigen, dass ich eigentlich die englische Grammatik beherrsche, obwohl ich vermehrt Fehler mache; ich kenne die wichtigsten grammatischen Regeln, sie sind nur im Sprachgebrauch nicht immer selbstverständlich für mich.
	... sind bei einer ziemlich hohen Fehlerzahl noch im Rahmen; ich weiß, dass ich einige Regeln im Detail wiederholen müsste, aber ich habe von den wichtigsten Regeln schon gehört und kann sie eigentlich auch anwenden, wenn ich sie wiederholt habe.
	... zeigen, dass ich im Bereich Grammatik ziemliche Lücken habe; ich mache sehr viele Fehler und weiß auch oft nicht, was an meinen Sätzen von der Grammatik her falsch ist.
	... zeigen, dass ich die englische Grammatik kaum beherrsche; ich kenne auch sehr elementare Regeln nicht und bin auch nicht in der Lage, meine Fehler ohne Hilfe zu korrigieren.

Aussprache und Flüssigkeit

Ich denke, meine Aussprache ist …	… klar, korrekt, flüssig; die Zuhörer(innen) können immer sofort verstehen, was ich sagen möchte, meine Sprechgeschwindigkeit ist recht hoch.
	… weitgehend klar, korrekt, flüssig; manchmal zögere ich kurz, wenn ich ein Wort nicht sofort weiß, aber das bedeutet keine langen Pausen.
	… so, dass die Zuhörer(innen) mich eigentlich schon verstehen, auch wenn ich manchmal recht langsam spreche; die Aussprache bei einigen Wörtern fällt mir manchmal schwer und ich weiß nicht alle Wörter sofort.
	… ist bei einer ziemlich hohen Fehlerzahl noch im Rahmen; ich weiß, dass ich Wörter falsch ausspreche, aber meine Beiträge sind weitgehend zu verstehen, auch wenn ich manchmal Pausen mache.
	… geprägt von einigen Aussprachefehlern, ich zögere vielfach, manchmal sind die Pausen auch länger.
	… geprägt von vermehrten Aussprachefehlern, das Verständnis ist nicht gesichert, für die Zuhörer(innen) ist eine Unterhaltung mit mir insgesamt anstrengend.

Aufbau und Gedankenführung

Meine Gedankenführung halte ich für …	… stringent, komplex und differenziert; ich kann einzelne Aspekte und die gedanklichen Verbindungen zwischen Aspekten sehr gut darstellen.
	… klar, stringent und nachvollziehbar.
	… angemessen, da ich immer eine Gliederung habe und meine Ausführungen nachvollziehbar sind.
	… verbesserungswürdig, da ich oft Schwächen im logischen Aufbau habe; ich schaffe es trotzdem, eine grundsätzliche Gliederung zu erstellen.
	… häufig zusammenhanglos; ich weiß, dass ich mir oft widerspreche und dass man eine Gliederung kaum erkennen kann.
	… sehr unzureichend, da mir eine Strukturierung und Gliederung dessen, was ich sagen möchte, fast nie gelingt.

Assessment test 1 – Diagnose

A 3.33

1 Listening comprehension: A news report → Listening, p. 221
Listen to the recording and complete the sentences with information from the listening text.

a) Immigrants represented more than …

b) People entering Britain from outside Europe and the Commonwealth …

c) Immigrant communities make up …

d) The largest groups came from …

e) There were major increases in immigration from countries such as …

f) Nearly 20 per cent of people born in India …

g) Fewer than half of new immigrants from Bangladesh …

h) The expansion of the European Union is resulting in …

2 Comprehension: True or false? → Comprehension questions, p. 228
Read the statements below and decide whether they are true or false. Quote or paraphrase words from the text which confirm or disprove the ideas in the statements.

a) The percentage of ethnic minorities in the British population is expected to grow from 8% to 20% in the course of 50 years.

b) The trend of ethnic groups to concentrate in certain places will continue.

c) Many of the immigrants coming to Britain in the coming years are expected to be white.

theguardian

News | Sport | Comment | Culture | Business | Money | Life&Style | Travel | Environment

Comment is free > Society Search GO

Ethnic minorities to make up 20% of UK population by 2051

Projection of British population over 40 years shows sharp growth in ethnic groups outside of white British majority

Ethnic minorities will make up a fifth of Britain's population by 2051, compared with 8% in 2001, according to new projections published today by the University of Leeds. The figures, which show Britain's total population growing to 77.7 million, also indicate that the UK will become far less segregated as ethnic groups disperse throughout the country. In October, the Office for National Statistics predicted the population would exceed 70m by 2029. Researchers found striking differences in the respective growth rates of the 16 ethnic groups studied. White British and Irish groups are expected to grow the most slowly, while the so-called other white group is projected to grow the fastest, driven by immigration from Europe, the US and Australasia. Traditional immigrant groups of south Asian origin (Indian, Pakistani and Bangladeshi) will also grow rapidly. The initial findings of the three-year study include population projections for 352 local authorities in England, as well as projections for Wales, Scotland and Northern Ireland, for each year until 2051.

"The ethnic makeup of the UK's population is evolving significantly," said Professor Philip Rees of Leeds University. "Groups outside the white British majority are increasing in size and share, not just in the

6 **to disperse** – to spread out over a larger area

7 **to exceed** – to be more than a specific number or amount

7 **respective** – belonging to each of the different items that are mentioned

14 **to evolve** – to go through a development gradually

d) Asian and African groups will remain in poorer areas.

e) Trends in demographic change can be predicted with great accuracy.

f) The British government considers the regulation of immigration a necessary measure.

3 Text production: Blog entry → Writing a blog entry, p. 232
Write a blog entry in which you comment on the question whether it is OK to restrict migration into Germany, allowing only skilled people with the qualifications needed and shutting out others.

4 Role play: Immigration to Germany → Discussions, p. 246
Now prepare for a role play. There are four roles. Work on your own and collect arguments to prepare for the discussion.

a) You are a politician who is strictly in favour of limiting the numbers of unskilled immigrants. You fear that the state can no longer afford to finance them if they do not find a job.

b) You are a Pakistani who runs a small shop in a large German town. You believe that Germany is no longer as attractive as other European states like, for example, Spain, but also think that Germany needs immigrants.

c) You are a politician who is strictly against immigration restrictions. You think it is time to officially acknowledge that Germany is a multi-cultural country.

d) You are a social worker who sees the danger of ghettos in larger German towns. You fear that many immigrants do not want to assimilate, while at the same time many immigrants feel excluded.

areas of initial migration, but throughout the country, and our projections suggest that this trend is set to continue through to 2051." He added: "At a regional level, ethnic minorities will shift out of deprived inner-city areas to more affluent areas, which echoes the way white groups have migrated in the past. In particular black and Asian populations in the least deprived local authorities will increase significantly."
The research team investigated ethnic population trends on a local scale in the UK and built a computer model to project those trends under a variety of scenarios. They used existing data on the 16 ethnic groups recognised in the 2001 census, along with demographic factors such as immigration, emigration, fertility and mortality.
The research shows the white British population shrinking from 87.1% to 67.1% and the white Irish group shrinking from 2.5% to 2.1%. The other white group's share grows from 2.5% to 9.9% – the greatest gain. Asian groups increase their share by three percentage points, black groups by two percentage points and Chinese and other ethnic groups by 2.6 percentage points. The researchers said their data generated five different scenarios for population makeup for each year until 2051, with each of the five projections yielding different absolute figures for ethnic groups and the population size as a whole. This, they cautioned, highlighted the difficulty in predicting trends such as migration.
"It is impossible to predict exactly how people will move into, out of and within the country in the coming decades as all of these trends are influenced by a whole range of socio-economic factors," said Rees. "However, our results suggest that overall we can look forward to being not only a more diverse nation, but one that is far more spatially integrated than at present." The immigration minister, Damian Green, said Britain had always benefited from being outwardlooking and having a population with diverse back-grounds, but added: "Problems arise in periods when the population changes too fast for comfort. That's why the government wants to control the level of immigration so that we can benefit from the arrival of talented people from all over the world without putting pressure on our public services." (582 words)

17 **to shift** – to move from one position to another
17 **deprived** – poor
18 **affluent** – wealthy
27 **to generate** – to cause sth. to exist
34 **spatially** – relating to space
36 **too fast for comfort** *(idiomatic)* – so fast that one doesn't feel good about it

Assessment test 2 – Diagnose

A 3.34

1 Listening comprehension: The situation of women in Chile → Listening, p. 221
Listen to the report about women agricultural workers in Chile. Take notes and answer the questions.

a) Why doesn't it help that there are more temporary jobs now in Chile?

b) Where does the money for exported products end up?

c) In what three senses are the women workers poorer than before?

d) Why can't the agricultural labourers take holidays?

e) How does Rosa Paleres feel about her situation?

f) What does she want from the government?

g) How many free trade agreements has Chile signed?

h) What is the price of a container of grapes?

i) Name three important export products in Chile's agricultural industry.

2 Comprehension → Comprehension questions, p. 228

a) Complete these sentences with information from the text.
1. Diets in China and India have changed as prosperity has grown, creating …
2. With the price of crude oil high, farmers are …
3. There is a war for resources between …

THE TIMES

To eat … or to drive?

Finishing her bag of Karu cheese-flavoured snacks, Shoko Taketani blushes and admits that she still feels oddly peckish. It is not her imagination: Japanese crisp packets contain 10 per cent fewer crisps than they did a month ago. In Munich, beer at this year's Oktoberfest will be the most expensive in the festival's history. […]
In Kuala Lumpur, Rhosdi is mulling a decision he thought would always be beyond him: whether to trade in his motor scooter for his first car. He is one of the 1.2 million Malaysian civil servants who have just received a windfall pay increase – their first in 15 years. Though geographically diverse and apparently unrelated, these developments are in fact connected, symptoms of a new global trend. Stomachs and petrol tanks are for the first time in competition and farmers everywhere are asking themselves a novel question: am I planting food or energy? There is no single source for the revolution sweeping across every continent. But one starting point is Jim Curl's 350-acre farm in Brahman, Oklahoma. This year he planted a third of it with genetically modified corn instead of the area's traditional crop of wheat. This amounts to 100 acres or so, a mere flap of a butterfly's wings in the great scheme of things. But by the time the impact of Mr Curl's decision has made its way to the other side of the world, the results are seismic. The economics of food – what is affordable, what it costs, and what that money buys – are creating unprecedented waves through all continents. From nut plantations in Indonesia to barley fields along the Rhine, farmers are all adjusting to this new world. Part of the result is tortilla riots in Mexico, the astonishing leap in Brazilian chicken leg prices and mayonnaise price spikes in Western Europe. These, say industry insiders, are the first skirmishes of a conflict that could soon dominate geopolitics: the war for resources between the world's 800 million cars and

1 **to blush** – to turn red
2 **peckish** – feeling slightly hungry; having an appetite
5 **to mull a decision** – to think about a decision long and hard
7 **windfall** – *here:* an expected event that brings good fortune
10 **novel** – *here:* new
11 **to sweep** – to move fast
13 **crop** – agricultural produce, such as grain, vegetables, or fruit
13 **wheat** – type of corn *(Weizen)*
13 **flap of a butterfly's wings** – *Flügelschlag eines Schmetterlings* – represents the idea in Chaos Theory that a very small event can have global consequences
15 **seismic** – relating to or caused by earthquakes
16 **unprecedented** – unparalleled
17 **barley** – type of corn *(Gerste)*
18 **leap** – jump
19 **price spike** – sudden and dramatic rise in prices
19 **skirmish** – a short fight

4. The war centres largely on global demand for "green" replacements …
5. Farmers are making a …

b) Put these statements into a logical order.

1. there is not enough of the crop on the market
2. soya oil prices have risen
3. much more corn will be grown in the near future
4. price was 50 per cent higher in 2007 than in 2006
5. the US wants to increase the use of ethanol
6. increase in corn production has already led to a cut in soya cultivation

3 Comment → Writing a comment, p. 229

Write a comment in which you outline what you think about the war for resources between the world's 800 million cars and its six billion stomachs. In your opinion, what is more important: fuel or food?

4 Role play: Fair trade or cheap products? → Discussions, p. 246

Now prepare for a role play. There are four roles. Work on your own and collect arguments to prepare for the discussion.

a) You are a teenager and do not have much money for expensive alternatives to cheaper products.

b) You are a parent and are concerned about your children growing up in a world of abundance.

c) You are a retail manager and justify low prices in developing countries.

d) You work for a fair trade organisation which tries to secure higher prices for Kenyan coffee farmers.

its six billion stomachs. In the developed world, the war will come down to price and choice; in the developing world it could come down to survival. The war centres largely on global demand for biofuels – "green" replacements for petrol, such as ethanol, that can be produced from sugar, corn and other agricultural products rather than fossil fuels.

Farmers are making a perfectly rational economic choice. With the price of crude oil high, they are planting crops to meet demand for cheaper biofuels. But converting more crops into energy means there is less to go into foodstuffs. And so the prices of those foodstuffs rise. The price increases for German beer, for instance, arise from replacing barley fields with ethanol feedstocks. […]

The US is a driving force in such change. In January President Bush called for a massive increase in the use of ethanol over the next decade – a move regarded by traders as setting the battle lines of the future conflict. This decision has momentous consequences. Planting more corn for ethanol has meant a 15 per cent cut in the amount of land devoted to soya. So soya oil prices are rising. That in turn has opened the door to cheaper palm oil – 90 per cent of which comes from Malaysia and Indonesia.

That surge in sales of palm oil is, in Malaysia in particular, creating dramatic social change overnight. Government coffers are so full that last month all civil servants were given pay rises of between 7.5 per cent and 42 per cent. […] Diets in China and India have (also) changed as prosperity has grown, creating greater demands for meat and, as a consequence, the crops that feed livestock. […] But it is corn – global inventories are at a record low and the price of the crop is 50 per cent higher than it was last year – and edible oils where the greatest impact is being felt. […] Within a year, say economists, China could reach the hugely significant point of becoming a net importer of corn. Oils give food a sophistication that more and more Chinese and Indians are getting a taste for. Shoko Taketani, with her empty crisp packet in Tokyo, knows this to her cost. (715 words)

25 **crude oil** – unrefined oil

36 **surge** – sudden increase

41 **edible** – which can be eaten

43 **sophistication** – having a good knowledge of others and their culture

Assessment test 3 – Diagnose

A 3.35 **1 Listening comprehension: Is shopping your drug of choice?** → Listening, p. 221
Listen to the recording and complete the table with information from the listening text.

Characteristics of compulsive shopping	Shopping addiction as a vicious circle	Indications that shopping is an addiction

2 Comprehension

a) In your own words, describe what FarmVille is and how Lady Gaga uses it to promote herself.

b) Summarise in your own words why advertising through online games is attractive to bands and musicians.

2 **casual** – *here:* occasional
3 **to reap** – to collect
3 **bumper crop** – large crop
11 **to partner with sb.** – to work together with sb.
14 **unicorn** – mythical horse-like creature with a horn on its forehead
16 **roughly** – approximately
17 **demographic** – relating to the structure of populations
17 **appeal** – attraction
17 **broad** – far-reaching
18 **leek** – a type of vegetable
19 **to harvest** – to collect

theguardian

News | Sport | Comment | Culture | Business | Money | Life&Style | Travel | Environment

Comment is free > Society   Search [ ] GO

Get down on the FarmVille

Aimed at older women and 'casual gamers', FarmVille has reaped a bumper crop of 60 million global users. No wonder Lady Gaga wants in.

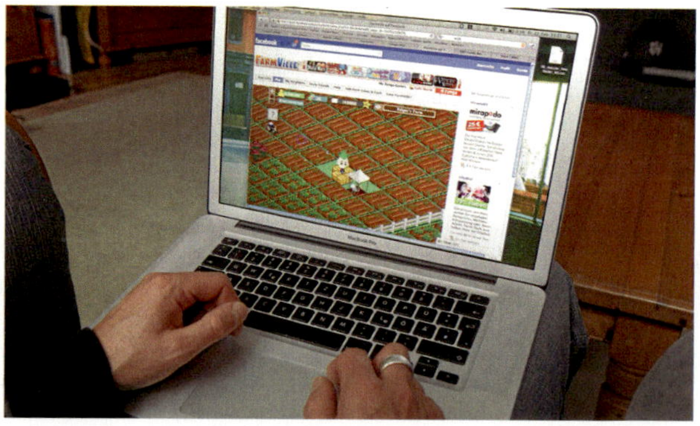

Lady Gaga, pop supremo, wearer of meat dresses, the star who has sold more than 15m albums worldwide, announced on Wednesday that she is partnering with games company Zynga to release exclusive songs through their Facebook game, FarmVille. The singer's fans will be able to visit GagaVille, a specially designed farm inside the virtual farming simulation game, which will contain unicorns and crystals.

Lady Gaga's choice of FarmVille makes sense: it's an enormous market. The game has around 60 million players worldwide – that's roughly the same size as the population of the UK. And FarmVille's demographic appeal is broad.

In FarmVille, players plant virtual crops – strawberries, bell peppers and leeks are just some of the many choices – wait a few hours, and then harvest them to receive coins that allow them to buy more farming supplies. Of course, the best farming goods can't be bought with ingame

3 Comment → Writing a comment, p. 229
Comment on the fact that websites primarily designed for entertainment or games are increasingly used for marketing purposes.

4 Role play: Pressure by advertising → Discussions, p. 246
Now prepare for a role play. There are four roles. Work on your own and collect arguments to prepare for the discussion.

a) You are a social worker and witness an increasing pressure among teenagers to buy. Mobile phones, clothes, shoes – very soon teenagers will fear becoming an outsider if they cannot keep up with the others.

b) You are a parent and are concerned about your children growing up in a material world. The advertising industry is responsible for the enormous pressure teenagers face today. Why is a cool pair of sneakers more important than character traits?

c) You work for an advertising agency and reject the criticism that you are responsible for people becoming shopping addicts or getting into debt.

d) You work for a debt councelling agency. More and more people face bankruptcy because they buy more than they can afford.

coins, but need real money, with items ranging from a few pence to a few pounds. As the New York Times pointed out in a profile of FarmVille's founder Mark Pincus last year, "the sums are small, but add up quickly when multiplied by millions of users".

But the genius of the game is that players advance much more quickly if they rope their friends in too. My Facebook account is littered with requests such as: "I'm trying to nourish my baby lamb! Could you send me a bottle?" Some find these requests hard to turn down and by exerting this social pressure FarmVille has consolidated a solid user-base. Lady Gaga's not the first to spot the business potential of a tie-in with such a popular brand: the last time I entered FarmVille's virtual space I was offered a "free windmill from American Express". They've also partnered with McDonald's in the past, as well as raising money for earthquake victims in Haiti. The growth of FarmVille is just the latest and most obvious expression of a change in gaming demographics over recent years. The media's image of a "gamer" might still be of a man in his teens or 20s sitting in front of Call of Duty for six-hour stretches, but that stereotype is now more inaccurate than ever.

FarmVille, of course, is unashamed about being a game. It's partly that playful style that makes it a good partner for Lady Gaga, an artist famed for antics and experimentation. Gaga has also used social media to develop a deep connection with her fans – she surpassed Britney Spears last year as the most-followed user on Twitter, and topped a survey of the most popular musical artists in online social media.

But Gaga isn't the only musician tapping into the increasing reach of games. Adrian Hon, CCO of Six to Start, a games company, […] says: "Games are a good way for bands to connect with their younger fans, to engage with the sort of people who buy music and go to concerts. Labels and publishers have seen the internet primarily as a place to advertise and a source of worrying piracy, but artists tend to be much more interested in the creative possibilities."

The games industry is growing by somewhere between 10% and 20% a year, a figure that the film and the music industry could only dream of. We might not all be wearing meat dresses in 10 years' time, but in hooking up with an online game, Lady Gaga is likely to be a forerunner of things to come. (743 words)

24 **to rope in** – *here:* to involve
25 **littered** – full of
25 **to nourish** – to feed
27 **to exert** – to apply
27 **to consolidate** – to build up
28 **tie-in** – combination
30 **earthquake victim** – sb. who has suffered because of an earthquake
33 **stretch** – *here:* length of time
33 **stereotype** – popular assumption
34 **inaccurate** – false
35 **unashamed** – not embarrassed
36 **to be famed for sth.** – to be well known for sth.
36 **antics** – fooling around
37 **to surpass** – to outdo
40 **to tap into sth.** – to take advantage of sth.
47 **forerunner** – pioneer

Helping hand – Differenzierung

Topic 1

B3 Mediation → p. 13

Here are some aspects which you might want to use in your text:

- Abkommen zwischen dem britischen *Specialist Schools and Academies Trust* als Vertreter von 90% aller britischen staatlichen Sprachschulen und der chinesischen Regierung.
- 200 Lehrer nach England.
- Mandarin als verpflichtende strategische Weltsprache der Zukunft.
- Europäische Sprachen aus dem Lehrplan verdrängen.

B4 Analysis → p. 13

The following aspects might help you with your analysis:

- All the people who are quoted or referred to in indirect speech are experts and support the idea of introducing Mandarin and other Asian languages in language teaching.
- Direct speech gives the impression of closeness and authenticity, the reader gets the impression that Richard Garner, the author of the article, was very close to Sir Cyril Taylor.
- Reported speech gives the impression of knowledge about people in the background, they are not that important but support the same idea.
- No personal opinion of the author is found in the text.

D2 Listening comprehension: Schoolchildren now speak "The Queen's Hinglish" → p. 16

The following facts are mentioned in the listening text:

- Queen's Hinglish is a mixture of English and South Asian languages such as Hindi, Urdu and Punjabi in South Asia.
- Modern blend of standard English, Indian English and South Asian languages.
- Hinglish has already moved into the mainstream and is used on musical channels and in advertising.
- In the UK, Hinglish has appeared in TV programmes.
- Hinglish is used increasingly throughout the United Kingdom, particularly in playgrounds.
- Collision of languages has produced colourful phrases.
- People are becoming more and more comfortable with mixing words from languages such as Hindi, Urdu and Punjabi with English.
- Hinglish could soon become the most widely spoken form of English on earth.

D4 Analysis → p. 16

The following sentences might help you to analyse the cartoon:

- English class for immigrants, students look foreign (turban, headscarf, moustache etc.).
- Teacher in front looking at one angry student holding up a sign saying "I have tried telling you several times my name is Ken and I am from Glasgow".
- Cartoon makes fun of the fact that immigrants have to take English classes where they are taught how to speak English.
- English consists of so many varieties and dialects that not all native speakers of English can communicate with each other.
- The student from Scotland surely has told his English teacher several times that he speaks English, still the teacher has not been able to understand him or has not accepted this as English. That's the reason why he is attending / has been made attend this class.

Topic 2

E3 Having a discussion → p. 35

Here are some arguments to help you plan your panel discussion:

Option 1

For	Against
• strengthened patriotism amongst Americans • America doing its duty / helping the world • world becomes a more peaceful place • standing up for human rights • new democracies need military support • tyrants must be stopped	• Americans fear for their safety • America a target for others • many societies reject US's view of democracy / human rights • opens the US up for international criticism • other political systems must be respected • democracy cannot be enforced

Option 2

For	Against
• no room for idealism in world unstable with global terrorism / economic competition • necessary to engage with world pragmatically / selectively to promote US interests • US interests often require friendly relations with undemocratic governments	• acting without regard for other nations' interests leads to resentment, international violence, undermines international cooperation • relationship with dictators may endanger worldwide movement towards democracy • cooperation with undemocratic leaders = possible acceptance of genocide, ethnic cleansing, etc.

Option 3

For	Against
• global problems (environmental pollution, financial crises, refugees, AIDS, nuclear proliferation) require international cooperation • USA has power and influence to bring nations together • US cooperation with EU, UN, NATO cannot be criticised	• handing over power to international institutions: loss of international influence • American values in conflict with those of large parts of the world – therefore cooperation may not work / could be dangerous • USA can no longer respond flexibly / quickly to international changes.

Option 4

For	Against
• 9/11 has shown vulnerable USA – security at home is top priority • USA has wasted money on allies and should concentrate on domestic threats • military action / spending should be concentrated on defense • international action only brings criticism / anti-US feeling • US's first priority = protect its residents	• foolish to pretend the rest of the world does not matter • in the US's interest to promote democracy / human rights around the world • best way to protect the US homeland is through a wise foreign policy • many countries need the US's help

E4 Comment → p. 35

Here are some ideas to help you write your newspaper article:

- Western world needs to understand what it is fighting against
- must learn exactly what al-Qaeda / other extremists stand for
- change foreign policy – avoid alienating the majority of Muslims (war of hearts and minds)
- perhaps be less aggressive in conflicts around the world
- Germany: should support the rest of the world in the methods mentioned, should be consistent in its approach, but should not put itself in unnecessary danger.

Topic 3

A3 Analysis → p. 43

The following bullet points might help you to analyse the cartoon:

- the cartoon depicts a tired and injured old lion covered in flies, wearing a battered crown
- the lion is standing against a setting sun whose rays form the stripes of the Union Jack
- the exhausted, dying lion stands for Britain and the end of the British Empire
- the cartoon is making the point that with the loss of Hong Kong, the British Empire is now a thing of the past
- the sun has finally set on it; allusion to the saying "The sun never sets on the British Empire"
- the British lion is now too weak to rule over an empire

B2 a) Comprehension → p. 45

Here are some points to help you:

- the union between England and Scotland is 304 years old (2011)
- in 2007, 9% of Welsh voters felt "British not Welsh"
- now (2011), 16% feel "British not Welsh"
- in 2010, 37% of Northern Irish people saw themselves as "British"
- in 2007, 51% of Northern Irish people saw themselves as "British"
- last year (2010), 52% of English people described themselves as British

D4 Comment → p. 49

You might want to include the following points:

For	Against
• British monarchy is famous all over the world, iconic • British monarchy is a tourist attraction • thus it brings money into the country • the Queen has a very high status, can use her international influence and popularity to help Britain • thanks to the monarchy, old traditions are continued • the monarchy is a political institution and stands for political stability • the royals do a lot of charity work • part of British national identity	• British monarchy and its traditions can be regarded as being archaic • the monarchy costs the British tax payer a lot of money (£32 million in 2011) • some members of the royal family don't really behave very "royal", image is crumbling, embarrassment for Britain • fancy lifestyle of the royals; makes them more celebrities than representatives of an old and honored institution

Topic 4

A3 Mediation → p. 59

Here are some points you might want to include:

- Ringordner für Dokumente; Inhaltsverzeichnis; Trennblätter
- Zielformulierung; Zusammenfassung und Dokumentation der Arbeitserfahrung; Dokumente über bestimmte Fachkenntnisse; Charaktereigenschaften; Zeugnisse; Bescheinigungen über besuchte Fortbildungen
- eingescannte Version des Job Skills Portfolios; manche Firmen nehmen Bewerbungen digital in Empfang; Einpflegung in Systeme
- nur relevante Arbeitsproben integrieren; Abhebung durch Berichte, Projekte, PowerPointPräsentationen etc.; keine vertraulichen oder geschützten Informationen und Daten
- besondere Leistungen sollten ersichtlich werden; Auszeichnungen; Empfehlungsschreiben oder positives Kundenfeedback; Entfernung von persönlichen Daten
- Portfolio nicht überladen, Gefahr der Unübersichtlichkeit
- Portfolio auf digitales Medium kopieren und beifügen

B2 a) Comprehension → p. 61

Here are some arguments to start you off:

Pros	Cons
• The money raised by "selling" internships is often donated to charity. • More students are gaining work experience abroad.	• Young people already have enough debts from their time as students. • Families with more money or "powerful" friends may have an advantage over less wealthy or influential families.

C4 Analysis → p. 63

Here are some sentences which you might want to include in the description and analysis of the cartoon:

- A boy is lying on his bed looking out of the window with a pair of binoculars.
- The cartoonist uses the double meaning of "looking for sth." in his cartoon. On the one hand this means … On the other hand, however, looking for a job …
- I think the cartoon is funny because the cartoonist makes the point that some teenagers simply …
- I do not really like the cartoon because the cartoonist is clearly exaggerating. In today's world, no teenager…
- In my opinion the cartoon works because it addresses a topic …

D3 a) Analysis → p. 65

Here are some quotes to start you off:

Positive	Negative
• "Most of us liked most everyone […]" (l. 6) • "We loved free bagels in the morning." (ll. 11–12) • "Our benefits were astonishing in comprehensiveness and quality of care." (ll. 12–13)	• "Our mornings lacked promise." (ll. 2–3) • "We thought moving to India might be better, or going back to nursing school. Doing something with handicapped or working with our hands. No one ever acted on these impulses, despite their daily, sometimes hourly contractions. Instead we met in conference rooms […]." (ll. 14–17) • "Our boredom was ongoing, a collective boredom, and it would never die because we would never die." (ll. 26–27)

D4 Comment → p. 65

Here are some arguments to start you off:

Reasons for wanting to work at the company:

- The pay is good.
- Most people liked one another.
- Advertising work may be interesting.

Reasons for not wanting to work at the company:

- The work sounds boring.
- Some of the colleagues are a little strange.
- It seems as if there is often a bad working atmosphere.

E3 Comment → p. 67

Here are some arguments to start you off:

Arguments for the statement:

- A high salary is an indication of the importance of the job.
- You are respected if you earn a lot of money.
- Having a lot of money can make you happy.

Arguments against the statement:

- The amount of money you are paid cannot influence how much you enjoy your daily tasks.
- A job should be rewarding in itself.
- Working just for the money is a short-term outlook.

Topic 5

A 3 Mediation → p. 75

The following notes might help you with the German summary of the text:

- Beispiel Professor Pete Coffey vom University College in London
- aktuelle Forschungen und medizinische Entwicklungen im Bereich der Stammzellentechnologie
- Professor Coffey: mit Hilfe von aus Embryonen gewonnenen Stammzellen Behandlungsmöglichkeiten zur Augenkrankheit Makuladegeneration entwickeln
- Positivsignal der britischen Genehmigungsbehörde
- Regierungswechsel in den USA
- Stammzellenforschung hofft auf mehr an Genehmigungen für die Forschung aus Fruchtbarkeitsbehandlungen gewonnenen Stammzellen
- Professor Coffey: Stammzellentechnologie wird Medizin in die Lage versetzen Leber- und Herzerkrankungen und möglicherwiese Diabetes, langfristig auch Alzheimer und Parkinson zu behandeln.

A 4 Analysis → p. 75

The following aspects will only serve as starting point for your analysis, you need to go into more detail and of course support this by quoting from the text:

- positive picture of Pete Coffey
- calls the USA the world's powerhouse of biomedical research
- more detailed account of Coffey's project
- no opponent of stem cell research mentioned
- positive aspects and hopes are dealt with
- author never includes his personal opinion

D2 b) Comprehension → p. 81

Here are some ideas to start you off:

Features	Benefits
• voice recognition for household functions such as doors, windows, lights, …	• no need to have keys for doors • can turn on / off lights when hands are full • children or disabled / elderly / blind people will find it easier to get around the house
• automated cleaning, recognises when something is dirty / dusty, cleans automatically	• no need to do the cleaning yourself • house always looks clean and tidy, even when guests arrive unannounced
• waste disposal system that automatically separates waste and arranges for it to be picked up and taken away	• more efficient waste separation • no need to keep so much waste in the house
• adjustable modes, for example, holiday mode, party mode, etc.	• you will be able to set your house to do certain things automatically • different modes have different benefits
• heated driveway	• no need to shovel the driveway clear
• smart fridge that orders food when things run out	• no need to go to the supermarket

E3 Analysis → p. 83

The following aspects will only serve as starting point for your analysis, you need to go into more detail and, of course, support this with quotations from the text:

- includes himself when talking about the future
- adjectives or exclamations which very clearly express his opinion
- rhetorical questions
- presentation of possible negative developments as something factual and irrevocable

Topic 6

6 Describe and analyse the cartoon → p. 89

Below is a list of words and sentences which you might need to describe and explain the cartoon:

- to make a confession
- to confess
- to commit a sin
- to repent
- words of forgiveness
- to contradict the idea of sth.
- value of a face-to-face conversation
- active listening

- The cartoon consists of an illustration of an elderly woman in a confessional.
- In the partition wall of the confession box there is an intercom; in a normal confessional there would be the priest on the other side of the wall listening to the person making the confession.
- The text in the speech bubble next to the intercom says: "Thank you for choosing our automated service, for venial sins, press one …"
- The elderly woman looks startled and surprised by this recorded voice.
- The elderly woman is a stereotype of an elderly churchgoer.

A 4 Text production: Writing a letter / an email → p. 91

This is how you could start your letter / email to the editor:

- In the newspaper article *The rise and rise of convenience food*, which was published in the online edition of the Guardian, the author Tim Dowling …
- He concludes by …
- His final remark in his report …

The following phrases for expressing your opinion might be helpful for your letter:

- I believe that …
- I strongly doubt if …
- I wonder whether …
- I think …
- I feel …
- I don't think …
- In my opinion, …
- If you ask me, …

B 3 Analysis → p. 93

The following ideas might help you to get started with your analysis. Make sure that you give them a logical structure before you start writing your text:

- two active participants: John Salinas, 91, and 84-year-old Len Street
- all just point out the extremely positive aspects of adult learning; no word of criticism
- experts underline positive aspect of lifelong learning; no need for the author to include his opinion
- experts quoted: McNair, a semi-retired National Institute of Adult Continuing Education research fellow; Melissa March is executive director of Learning for the Fourth Age; Iona Gibbons, a community learning development worker and Fiona Aldridge, Niace programme director and author
- other quotes are by two senior learners who at the age of 84 and 91 are active participants
- almost all quotes in the text are by either scientists or those in charge of adult education programmes, all are experts

C 4 Mediation → p. 95

The following results will surely help you with your text about the two diagrams:

- two diagrams showing levels of physical activity and consumption of fruits and vegetables of 11 - 17 year olds
- diagram 1: physical activity; boys and girls, two age groups 11 - 13 and 14 - 17
- more than 1 / 3 of younger boys do sports almost daily, 37% 3 - 5 times a week: nearly 70% in that age group are physically active;
- 1 / 4 of the boys in that age group are physically active 1 - 2 times a week, only 6% say that they rarely do sports;
- girls are not that active, only 1 / 4 report daily physical activity, 30% say that they do sports 3 - 5 times a week; slightly more than 50% are physically very active;
- 30% report occasional physical activity, 12% say that they rarely do sports
- slightly different trend for age group 14 - 17, slight decrease in physical activity for boys (2 - 3% less), major change for girls: only 13% are physically active every day, just above 20% 3 - 5 times a week: more than 60% do sports only 1 - 2 times a week or even less than that
- diagram 2: consumption of vegetables / fruits compared to daily recommendations
- four age groups; youngest age group closest to recommendations; the older the boys get, the less they consume in terms of fruits / vegetables; age group of 14 - 17 year old boys: only one third of recommended amount; girls half of the daily recommendations, consumption remains unchanged but the recommended quantities rise

Topic 7

A4 Comment → p. 107

Here are some points to help you write the comment:

Yes	No
• no major war involving Europe • open borders between EU member states = more international job opportunities • higher standard of living • higher mobility through improved transportation • women have more career choices nowadays	• more opportunities = increased competition • younger people under more pressure to succeed • European economy unstable (problems with the Euro currency) • environmental damage / climate change / unpredictable weather

B 2 a) Comprehension → p. 109

Here is some information to get you started:

- higher tax for rich
- war
- irresponsible / greedy behaviour by bankers
- corrupt politicians
- climate change / global warming
- globalisation being out of control
- people being exploited
- people feel excluded from decision-making

B 4 Comment → p. 109

Here are some arguments to help you write the comment:

Yes	No
• Arab Spring / Occupy Movement have shown that people will stand up for themselves if pushed too far • people will no longer be threatened • people no longer scared of government violence • the events of 2011 brought global struggles to the eyes of the world – more people aware of what goes on and quicker to support those protesting • political world showed support for the people in undemocratic states (Libya) • 2011 demonstrated an increased willingness to go onto the streets and be more active • the use of social media was revolutionary	• it takes more than protests to change the world long term • more important to see how the affected parties / countries react • Arab Spring may have changed the world in terms of the scale of the protests, but how will they change the fate of North Africa and the Middle East? • Occupy Movement only small victories for the man on the street against upper classes • small number of successful protests compared to unsuccessful protests

D4 Mediation → p. 113

Here is some help for your mediation:

Young People's Bank
- Schüler eröffnen und führen eine Bank in der Schule.
- Fähigkeit der Schüler, mit Geld umzugehen und finanzielle Transaktionen durchzuführen soll verbessert werden.
- Motivation zu unternehmerischer Aktivität.
- Schüler können investieren und kleine Kredite erhalten.

The Beam
- Zielgruppe: Jungen im Alter von zwölf bis 15 Jahren mit BMI von 30 und mehr.
- Inhalte des Projekts: Ernährung, Fitness, Selbstwahrnehmung, Selbstvertrauen.
- Eltern sollen integriert werden.
- Wissen um eine gesunde Ernährung soll gesteigert werden.

World Jungle
- Ziel dieses Projekts: jungen Menschen kulturelle Möglichkeiten bieten.
- Aktivitäten: Tanz, Musik und Kunst.
- Fokus auf soziale und wirtschaftliche Probleme anderer Kulturen.
- z. B. indische, marokkanische und ghanaische Tänzer, Trommler und Sprecher, die bei Festivals auftreten.
- Vorurteile sollen abgebaut werden.

The Amoosi Project
- Designer, die am Anfang ihrer Karriere stehen sollen Möglichkeit erhalten, mit recycelten Kleidern und Textilien zu arbeiten.
- Fähigkeiten sollen entwickelt werden.
- Es soll vermieden werden, dass die Materialen auf Müllhalden landen.
- Designer sollen Modeindustrie mit ihren Kreationen beeinflussen.

Film Kitchen
- Mobile Filmvorführ- und Essenszubereitungseinrichtung.
- Filme sollen an verschiedenen Orten wie Gemeindehallen, Schulen und im Freien gezeigt werden.
- Ziele des Projektes: 1. Gemeinden gesundes und multikulturelles Essen vorstellen; 2. Menschen, die ansonsten keine Möglichkeiten haben, ein Kino zu besuchen, Filme anbieten; 3. Gemeindemitglieder inspirieren und zur Zusammenkunft motivieren.

E4 Mediation → p. 114

Here are some points you might want to include in your mediation:

- Abu Dhabi planning "green city"
- two German institutes involved in project
- project named *Masdar*: means "source", "fountain"
- project aim: to promote renewable energy resources
- size of city: approximately six million square meters
- Abu Dhabi to enlist scientists from the world's leading research institutes
- aim: to create ecological equivalent of Silicon Valley in the USA
- the city will rely totally on renewable energy

E5 Analysis → p. 115

The following ideas might help you to describe the picture and link it to the text:

- painting
- very colourful
- scene of a futuristic looking city
- foreground: people standing in front of a tall golden building → people appear to be staring up at building
- people are wearing multi-coloured clothing → do not look human
- golden building = temple of some kind?
- background: other high buildings of different colours → smoke coming from the buildings
- sky: large planet → looks like Saturn
- sky is a dark blue: impression of being in space

Connection to Masdar vision of the future:

- picture can be linked to the text in that it shows how cities of the future could look
- may be a utopian vision of the future
- alternatively: may show a more dystopian image → what can happen when development does not work as planned
- perhaps picture shows what may happen when there are too many people → "green" energy is not sufficient / war breaks out, etc. for instance → lot of pollution in this city
- it is possible that the city in the picture started out with utopian ideals, like Masdar, but things did not progress in the right way

E6 a) Comment → p. 115

You might want to consider the following points in your comment:

Arguments for spending one year in Masdar	Arguments against spending one year in Masdar
• wonderful opportunity to be a part of the experiment • chance to live in another part of the world • opportunity to experience renewable energy first hand • learn a lot about using renewable energy • see if such utopian visions can work • Masdar: safe and healthy place to live – no cars, pollution • life would be more convenient and comfortable – new transport system, controlled climate	• miss your family / friends • if you go alone → lonely • Masdar has no natural beauty – mountains, lakes, forests, etc. • if no sense of community, (then) it will not be a pleasant place to live • feeling of claustrophobia could set in after some time • city surrounded by desert • no guarantee everything will function as planned • due to international interest in project, it may be like living in a fish bowl – i.e. under constant observation

Topic 8

A 3 Comment → p. 123

You might want to consider the following points:

- important for people to be open-minded and tolerant
- people should try to get to know members of other cultures and races and try and understand their traditions and way of life → visit cultural events
- people could join sports or social clubs → meet new people
- parents should be good role models for their children
- children must understand that people cannot be judged on their colour / race / gender / religion
- children must be taught to speak up against racism / prejudice
- encourage mixed-race pre-school → children learn to mix at an early age
- governments / administrations can hire more ethnic minorities

B 4 Listening comprehension → p. 125

The following words and phrases might help you with the listening comprehension:

- intelligent, spoke English, embodied compassion, justice and love – showed him the spiritual side of Islam
- US Muslims are patriotic / proud to be American and Muslim
- 2005, 52 killed
- after the attack, Britain realised: violent extremist movements exist
- far right blames immigration

C 2 a) Comprehension → p. 127

Here are some key words to help you answer the question:

- African girl from Nigeria
- has experienced war → talks about "the sound of gunfire and the bitter smell of burning thatch behind"
- has a mother and an older sister called Nkiruka
- experienced problems at immigration at the airport
- speaks English; but not "the Queen's English"
- previous experiences with the police
- two years in an immigration detention centre

C 3 a) Analysis → p. 127

The following sentences might help you to analyse the text:

- author uses an analogy with a pound coin
- pound coin represents life Little Bee would like to lead, and the experiences she would like to have → this is contrasted with her actual experiences and feelings

Examples:
- "Most days I wish I was a British pound coin instead of an African girl. Everyone would be pleased to see me coming." (ll. 1–2) → pound coin welcome everywhere, but immigrants are not
- "It can cross deserts and oceans and leave the sound of gunfire and the bitter smell of burning thatch behind." (ll. 8–10) → pound coin can go wherever it wants and can escape danger. She, however, was not always safe in Nigeria – needed to find a way to escape

D2 Comprehension → p. 129

Here are some points to help you:

- economic reasons causing immigration
- immigrants crossing the border illegally on foot
- illegal immigration often needs several attempts to succeed
- working as fruit pickers
- low pay for work
- Armando now has papers; feels integrated into US society

D4 Listening comprehension → p. 129

The following words and phrases might help you with the listening comprehension:

- work, house, comfortable life
- group too large, were discovered
- change of guards
- strangers: gave them money for food; Mexican family: shower in their home, fed them, gave them clothes; Mexican restaurant: food; hotel: stay overnight; Armando's cousin: plane ticket to San Francisco
- fruit pickers, canneries, poultry farms, other agricultural areas
- taxes, social security
- refund the workers tax and social security taken from their wages; also, difficult to find people to do the low-paid work if immigrants had the necessary papers to work in better jobs
- hard work, low pay – slave labour

D5 Text production: A letter → p. 129

The following points will help you write the letter:

- just listened to your interview; wanted to write a letter
- interested in your story
- can imagine that it was tough for you – starting work aged 13, picking fruit for low pay
- also difficult for migrant workers in Germany – many from Turkey, Poland, Italy, etc.
- main problems for migrant workers: splitting up of families, language problems, integration, working conditions, insurance.
- some are successful – start a new life for themselves / their families.
- your story is an inspiration

Topic 9

A4 a) Analysis → p. 139

Here are some useful keywords to help you explain the quote:

- trade, telecommunications and internet had already "shrunk" the world
- more global companies = more people connected around the world
- technological innovations: faster information, 24/7 news
- low-cost travel: go anywhere, anytime

B3 Listening comprehension: Making globalisation work → p. 141

Use the following points to answer the listening comprehension:

- Problems and anomalies of globalisation: unfair trade regime (blocking development), unstable financial systems, expensive medication not available to places that need it the most, flow of money from poor to rich.
- Effect on French workers: lower wages, less job protection.
- USA's approach: tax cut for rich, reduce welfare state. Results: USA = rich country with poor people.
- Scandanavia's approach: invest in education, research, strong social security system for poor. Result: more productive/competitive economy + higher living standards for majority.
- Solutions to current issue: understand global problems more, look for causes of problems, implement policies that benefit the most people.

C3 Mediation → p. 143

Here are some points to help you with your mediation:

- One advantage of having presence in foreign markets = "brand dependency".
- Global players: offset losses in domestic markets with lucrative international business operations.
- Always growth somewhere in the world.
- Global companies attractive to investors.
- Acting globally = companies can exploit currency exchange rates/spread risk.
- Coca Cola is prime example of globally-active business: brand worth 72 billion US dollars.
- Boeing recovered from setbacks concerning the 'Dreamliner' to receive huge contracts all over the world.
- BASF business model: production facilities are connected – byproducts from one factory used as production materials in another.
- BASF exports production worldwide (China, Malaysia).
- BASF is leading pharmaceutical company: aims to have total turnover of more than 90 billion euros.

D3 b) Analysis → p. 145

Here are some ideas to get you started:

- she is easily distracted – "Until she stood in front of them, Hayley didn't realize how many of her classmates were blond." (ll. 1–2)
- wants to "fit in" – "She'd missed the trend." (l. 2)
- not well educated? – "Before USA countries abolished tax, if you didn't have a job, the Government took money from working people and gave it to you." (ll. 14–15); "Some people say tax is good because it gives money to people who don't have any. But those people must be lazy or stupid, …" (ll. 31–32)
- does not question the state of the world – "Finally I would like to say that America is the greatest group of countries in the world …" (ll. 23–24)

D4 Comment → p. 145

Here are some arguments to help you write the comment:

Agree	Disagree
• Everyday life invaded by brands. • Sponsorship (major sporting events, football teams and television programs, etc.) brings brand names into the home. • People (mostly younger people) can become addicted to brands. • Children bullied in school if they do not wear the "fashionable"/"cool" brands. • Brand consciousness at young age = peer pressure. • Brand names becoming more important than quality products. • People get into debt spending too much money on clothes, electronic devices, etc. that they do not need. • Wearing brand names = walking advertisements for companies. • Result of brand influence: people associate quality with high prices.	• Nothing wrong with brands influencing consumers' buying decisions. • Brands are powerful because products are highest quality. • People not as easily influenced as quote suggests. • Big brands and big companies = more competition amongst businesses = good news for consumers. • Brand names help people choose – for example, if you want to buy a laptop, you can use Apple as a reference point. You know the Apple costs €X, so you can see how good value Brand Y is when it costs €Z. • Influential brand is result of successful company or product – surely the goal of running a business. • Influential brand helps the consumer make the right choice.

Topic 10

A2 a) Comprehension → p. 155

Here are some keywords to help you answer the question:

- Russian women: deodorant for special occasions only
- consequence: low sales for deodorant companies
- solution: funny ad campaign
- idea behind campaign: use cultural attitudes towards beauty, glamour and embarrassment
- result: successful ad; increased deodorant sales in Russia

B3 Mediation → p. 157

The following keywords might help you with your mediation:

- new technologies in cars will become decisive in choosing a car
- automobile industry sees internet as opportunity for growth
- in 2011 around 15 million IVIs sold
- 35 million IVIs by 2015
- car makers need to keep up with the latest consumer electronics to remain competitive
- more than 42 million cars connected to the Internet by 2017 – approximately one million in 2009
- people want the same connectivity and entertainment in their cars as they enjoy at home

B4 Analysis → p. 157

The following sentences might help you to analyse the cartoon:

- cartoon shows two women jogging
- one of the women is carrying a small handheld device
- device is called iPed and is clearly inspired by Apple products
- woman is explaining that it has many different functions
- one function is an application that points out the nearest ice cream parlor and cake shops
- what makes the situation funny is the fact that the two women are obviously trying to be healthy; however, they seem to be using the new iPed to locate places where you can buy unhealthy food
- cartoon relates to the text as it shows people's desire to be connected, entertained and informed anytime, anywhere
- iPed demonstrates our desire for new "gadgets" that we believe make our life more interesting or easier

C3 Analysis → p. 159

The following sentences might help you to analyse the cartoon:

- three people standing at a bus stop, waiting for the bus
- people are standing next to bus shelter, in the rain, and they all look very unhappy
- inside the bus shelter: speaker playing an advertisement, telling the people to buy things
- seems as if people would rather stand in the rain than listen to advertisement in bus shelter
- could suggest that people are tired of hearing / seeing ads everywhere
- relation to text: people being exposed to advertising more and more
- text suggests: people would be unhappy about being monitored and tracked; cartoon shows: people trying to get away from advertising

E4 Comment → p. 163

You might want to consider the following points:

Arguments for	Arguments against
• most Hollywood stars / music stars are good looking • for many (often highly-paid) jobs, attractiveness is a prerequisite • attractive people often use their good looks to get what they want • good-looking people are often more self-confident • attractive people often climb the career ladder more easily • by nature, humans are drawn to physical beauty • not so attractive people have to work harder to be noticed / have to distinguish themselves through their skills	• for the most important / influential jobs in the world looks are not as important • some of the most famous / successful actors and musicians are not good-looking in the classical sense • skills, knowledge and experience are more important in gaining success than good looks • charisma, sense of humour and intellect have no relation to physical appearance • not everybody is impressed or influenced by good looks • some attractive people might even have to work harder to prove that they are "more than just a pretty face"

Grading grid – Bewertungsbogen für Englisch (Vorschlag)

Aspekt	Gewicht	Note	sehr gut	gut	befriedigend	ausreichend	mangelhaft	ungenügend
		Punkte	15 14 13	12 11 10	9 8 7	6 5 4	3 2 1	0
Wortebene	**Allgemeiner Wortschatz**		sehr differenziert, treffsicher und umfangreich, sehr hoher Grad an Korrektheit	differenziert und meist treffend, hoher Grad an Korrektheit	weniger differenziert bei vermehrter Fehlerzahl	begrenzt, teils ungenau, recht hohe Fehlerzahl	deutlich begrenzt, Verständlichkeit beeinträchtigt, hohe Fehlerzahl	stark begrenzt, Verständlichkeit erheblich beeinträchtigt, sehr hohe Fehlerzahl
	Fachwortschatz, Funktionswortschatz		sehr differenziert, treffsicher und umfangreich, sehr hoher Grad an Korrektheit	differenziert und meist treffend, hoher Grad an Korrektheit	weniger differenziert bei vermehrter Fehlerzahl	begrenzt, teils ungenau, recht hohe Fehlerzahl	deutlich begrenzt, Verständlichkeit beeinträchtigt, hohe Fehlerzahl	stark begrenzt, Verständlichkeit erheblich beeinträchtigt, sehr hohe Fehlerzahl
Satzebene	**Grammatische Strukturen**		sehr hoher Grad an Korrektheit	hoher Grad an Korrektheit	grundlegende Beherrschung trotz vermehrter Fehlerzahl	noch angemessene Beherrschung, recht hohe Fehlerzahl	hohe Fehlerzahl, zum Teil auch bei elementaren Strukturen	durchgängige Verstöße, auch bei elementaren Strukturen
	Satzbau und Satzverknüpfungen, Idiomatik		sehr differenziert und variantenreich, treffsichere Verwendung auch von idiomatischen Konstruktionen	differenziert und variabel, gelegentliche Verwendung von idiomatischen Konstruktionen; meist treffende Verwendung von Konstruktionen	eher einfache Konstruktionen, erkennbare Variabilität	meist einfache Konstruktionen, kaum Variabilität, gelegentliche Stilbrüche	sehr einfacher Satzbau, keine Variabilität, Verständlichkeit beeinträchtigt auch durch unidiomatische Wendungen und zahlreiche Stilbrüche	durchgängig sprachuntypische Syntax, Text wirkt wie übersetzt, Verständlichkeit erheblich beeinträchtigt
Textebene	**Aufbau / Gedankenführung**		sehr stringent, komplex und differenziert, überzeugende Hervorhebung und Verbindung von Gedanken; sinnvoller und funktionaler Einsatz von Zitaten, in hohem Maße eigenständig, flüssig	klar, stringent, nachvollziehbare Schlussfolgerungen; überzeugende Darstellung von Aspekten; eigenständige Leistung, flüssig	Gliederung und gedankliche Zusammenhänge nachvollziehbar; zum Teil Anlehnung an Vorlage	Gliederungselemente und gedankliche Zusammenhänge erkennbar, Schwächen im logischen Aufbau, häufige Anlehnung an Vorlage	mangelnde oder widersprüchliche Gliederungselemente, teils zusammenhanglos, sehr enge Anlehnung an Vorlage	unzureichende Strukturierung, Aufbau und Gedankenführung zusammenhanglos, übernommene Passagen
	aufgabenformattypische Versprachlichung		souveräne Beherrschung des zu erstellenden Textformats; überzeugende Anwendung der entsprechenden sprachlichen Konventionen	sichere Beherrschung des zu erstellenden Textformats, sprachliche Konventionen getroffen	angemessene Beherrschung des zu erstellenden Textformats, sprachliche Konventionen weitgehend getroffen bzw. dem Zieltext angemessen	durch Aufgabenformat vorgegebene Textsorte erkennbar, formattypische Merkmale stellenweise vorhanden	nur Ansätze der Konventionen der zu erstellenden Textsorte erkennbar	Versprachlichung insgesamt nicht der Textsorte entsprechend, erforderliche sprachliche Konventionen nicht beherrscht

Listening

As with all comprehension, watch out for **key words** and try to get the gist.

When you are involved in a **conversation** (e.g. on the telephone) or asked to interpret for someone, you can always request the speaker to **repeat or explain** what you haven't understood. When you not only hear but also see people talk, their **body language** helps you to understand what they say.

Announcements contain important information, usually in clear, simple language. They are often **repeated** several times to make sure everyone understands them.

Following **radio programmes** is more difficult because the only help you can get is from the speakers' **intonation**.

Be aware of the most important differences between **British and American English**, and be prepared for other variations such as **regional pronunciation**.

When you listen to **longer speeches or interviews**, take notes in a systematic way, e.g. in a grid or a checklist.

Useful phrases

Excuse me, can you say that again, please? • Could you repeat that for me, please? • Sorry, I don't understand the word … • What does it mean? • Can you spell that for me, please? • Have I got that right? • Sorry, would you mind explaining that again, please?

Skimming

Skimming means finding the **main ideas in a text** in order to get an impression of its content.

- Read the title, the introduction or the first paragraph, the first sentence of every paragraph and any headings and sub-headings.
- Note any pictures, charts or graphs.
- Pay attention to any words or phrases in italics or bold print.
- Read the last paragraph, which often offers a short summary of the text.

Scanning

Scanning is useful for finding **specific information** quickly, e.g. you have a question in mind and read a passage to find the answer.

- Decide what **specific information** you are looking for. Ignore unrelated information.
- Look out for **relevant key words**. Stop when you find one and read that part of the text carefully. Make notes if necessary.
- How might the information be given in the text? For example, if you need a date, only look at the numbers in the text.
- **Headings** can help you to identify sections which might contain the information.
- **The first sentence** in a paragraph should indicate whether the information you need could be there, or not. Do not read the text in detail.

Understanding non-fictional texts

A **non-fictional text** is a text whose **content is based on facts**. The writer refers to people and places which really exist and incidents which really took place. Typical examples are **newspaper** or **magazine articles**, **essays**, **comments** or **advertisements**.

1 Reading a non-fictional text

- Read the text carefully.
- Look up unknown vocabulary if necessary, but try to concentrate only on key words that block your understanding of the text.
- Ask yourself the following questions and write notes:
  What type of text is it? • What is its central idea / main theme / message? Can you state it in a single sentence?
- Structure the text. Divide it into different units and underline important passages.

2 Understanding a non-fictional text

What kind of text is it?
- What kind of text is it? A newspaper / magazine article, an essay, etc.?
- Who is the author?
- When was it written?
- Where was it published? In a newspaper, on the Internet, etc.?
- Why was it written? What is the target group?

What is the text about?
- What is the central idea / main theme / message?
- What parts can it be divided into?
- What is the purpose of the text?
- What is the author's point of view / intention?
- What arguments or examples does the author use?
- What is special about the text?

Newspaper reports

We are confronted with a wide range of different newspapers from all around the world. On the one hand there are quality newspapers. They present the news in a neutral way and separate information from opinion so that the reader can form his /her own view. On the other hand, there are popular newspapers (tabloids). Their news reports are often sensational with big pictures and headlines. Popular newspapers often mix information and opinion, offering the reader a ready-made opinion.

Example:

quality newspaper **popular newspaper**

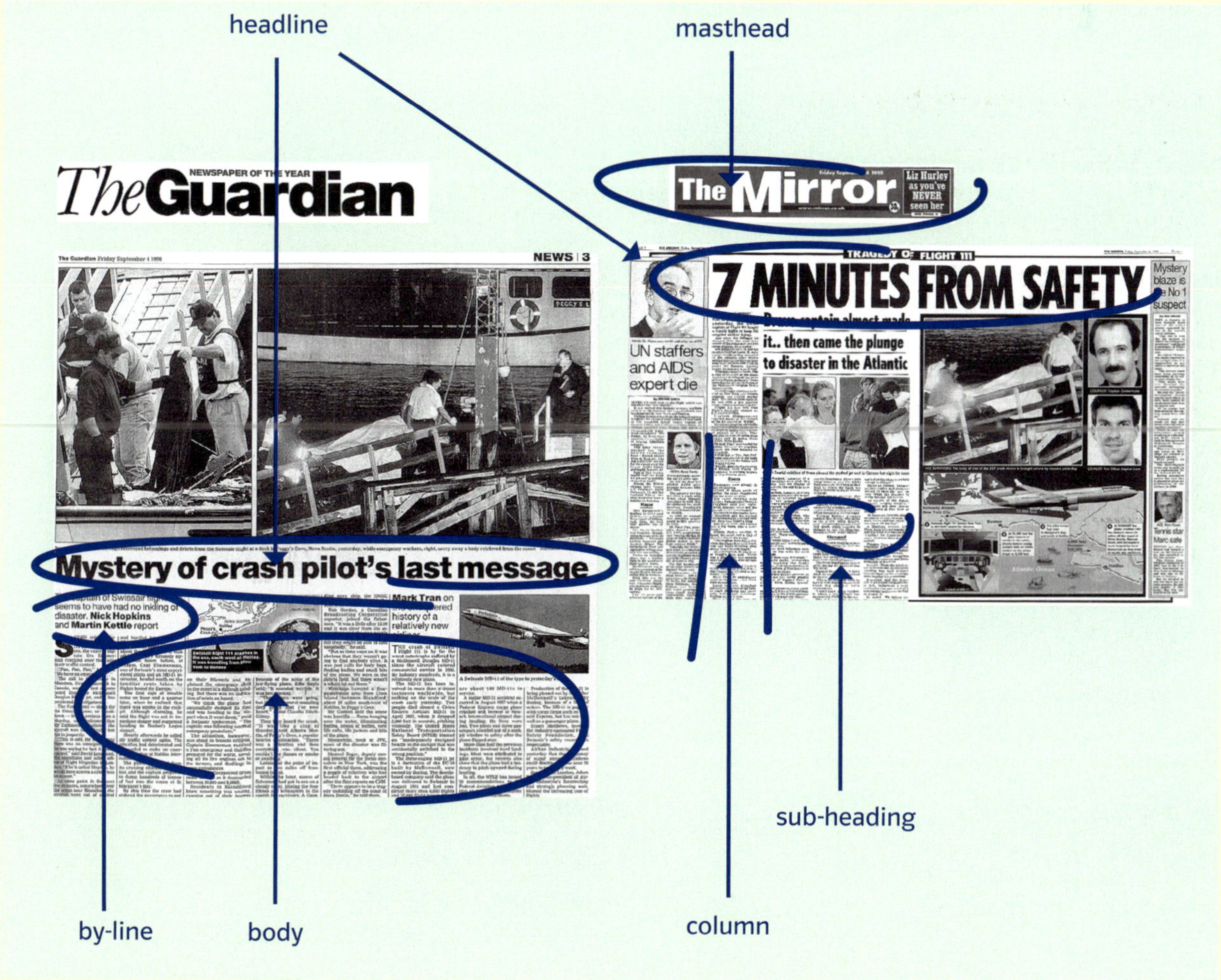

Understanding fictional texts

A **fictional text** is a literary work whose content is based on the **imagination of the author** and not necessarily on facts. There are three **literary genres: poetry** (poems, songs), **drama** (plays) and **fiction** (novels, short stories, fables, fairy tales, etc.).
By reading a fictional text, the reader is transferred into a different world and the author's intention is often a matter of interpretation. Pictures in the reader's mind are produced to create a new reality, and atmosphere and emotions are often more important than hard facts.

1 Reading a fictional text

- Read the text carefully.
- Look up unknown vocabulary if necessary, but try to concentrate only on key words that block your understanding of the text.
- Ask yourself the following questions and write notes:
  What is the story about? • What is its central idea/main theme / message? Can you state it in a single sentence?
- Structure the text. Divide it into different units and underline important passages.

2 Understanding a fictional text

When you analyse a text, you should follow these steps. Answer the questions and write notes.

What kind of text is it?
- What is the literary genre of the text? Poetry, drama or fiction?
- What kind of text is it (poem, song, short story, etc.)?
- Who is the author and when was it written?

What is the text about?
- What is the central idea / main theme / message?
- Who is the narrator?
- What is the setting?
- What is the plot?
- Who are the characters?

How we learn about the characters in a story:
- outward appearance
- language
- actions, behaviour, mood
- main traits
- motives, influences from the past
- roles, social background
- character's function in the constellation of characters

3 Character grid

outward appearance	*athletic, attractive, blond, elegant, fat, tall, young, …*
language	*excited, gentle, polite, rude, …*
actions, behaviour, mood	*angry, embarrassed, emotional, irresponsible, terrified, upset, …*
main traits	*honest, intelligent, jealous, kind, show-off, shy, sympathetic, violent, …*
roles, social background	*boss, daughter, girlfriend, broken home, criminal, lonely, married, rich, …*
function in the constellation of characters	*enemy, friend, rival, …*

4 Special features of the text

- What parts can it be divided into?
- Is there a turning point in the plot?
- What kind of language is used?
- What atmosphere is created and how?
- What else is special about the text?

The features of a short story

A **short story** is a short fictional prose text which is meant to be read in a single sitting. It can be as short as 500 and as long as 15,000 words. A lot of short stories follow different patterns but the following points apply to many of them.

- There may be one main **character** or a group of equally important characters.
- There is often only a single **setting** (i.e. the time and place of the action does not change). Longer short stories might have more than one setting.
- The setting helps to create a certain atmosphere.
- The reader may be led into the story through an **exposition**.
- In modern stories the action often starts in the first sentence.
- The action develops logically through **conflicts or crises**, reaching a climax or **turning-point** near or at the end (emphasis on action and suspense).
- Some stories concentrate on a decisive moment in the main character's life (emphasis on character and psychology).
- There is often a surprise **ending**, a happy / unhappy ending or an open ending.

The features of a play

Plays are very different from short stories or poems because they are not written to be read but to be **performed** and **watched**. Outside school or university, people do not normally sit down to read a play, unless they are planning a trip to the theatre. When a **playwright** or **dramatist** sits down to put pen to paper, he has **directors, stage managers** and **actresses / actors** in mind.

- A dramatic text usually consists of two parts: **dialogue** and **stage directions**. In a play, **dialogue** covers all the spoken language, not only the conversation of two characters.
- The **stage directions** give information about how to perform the play. This might refer to the setting, scenery, the characters' movements, tone of voice, etc.
- When you analyse a play, look at the **setting**, the **action** and the **characters** (→ Understanding fictional texts p. 224).
- Don't forget to describe the **atmosphere** of the play.
- Finally, give an **interpretation** of the play.

Dealing with poetry

Poetry may look shorter than other literary forms, but it can be more demanding. Here are some ideas on how to improve your feeling for and understanding of poetry.

- Read the poem and try to get the gist or message of the poem first. Then sum it up in your own words.
- Read the poem aloud to stress the relationship between certain words and ideas.
- Take a close look at structure and form:

  stanza: the way the lines of a poem are grouped together
  rhyme pattern: groups of words that rhyme
  repetition: when words or sounds are repeated

- Look for comparisons and contrasts (metaphors and similes). Identify images and symbols, and what impressions or ideas they give you.
- Find devices that are used to bring out certain feelings and to create an atmosphere, e.g. colours, sounds.
- Describe any characters who appear in the poem.
- Who is the speaker? What do we learn about the setting?

Example:

Films

Some films are sad – you watch them and cry. A
You know that the hero is going to die. A

Some films have spies – they fight, run and jump. B
When they crash their cars, there's a very big bump! B

Sometimes aliens come down from space. C
That often means trouble for the human race. C

And then there are ghost films – ghosts come out at night D
And give everybody an awful fright. D

But the worst films are love films where all the stars kiss. E
Those are the films that I want to miss! E

William Sears

stanza: five stanzas with two lines each
rhyme pattern: AABBCCDDEE
repetitions: some(times) (lines 1, 3, 5), you (lines 1, 2), films (lines 1, 3, 7, 9, 10)

Useful phrases

The poem consists of / is divided into … stanzas / sections / lines … • It has an unusual layout. • It follows a clear rhyme scheme. • It is an example of unrhymed verse. • The rrangement of the rhymes is … (e. g. aabb). • A number of lines do not rhyme at all. • Lines x and y rhyme. • The poet aims to express a certain message poetically. • The vocabulary is simple / difficult. • The words mainly belong to the word field of … • The repetition of the words '…' creates a … atmosphere. • There is a strong contrast between '…' and '…'. The tone of the poem is serious / calm / sad / ironical / cheerful / … This is heightened by words such as …

Dealing with songs

Songs are **similar to poems**, but they additionally contain a **musical aspect**, which is particularly important. It is always useful to look for background information on the songwriter and / or the artist performing the song, who shouldn't be confused as they aren't necessarily the same person. Look at all the information you have got. If something is missing that could help you to understand the song better, try to find out more. The Internet is probably the best source of information for you. You can follow these steps:

Background information
- What is the title of the song?
- Who is / are the singer(s) / the band?
- Who wrote the lyrics? Who wrote the music?
- When was the song written?
- Was the song a success?

Music
- What kind of music is it?
- What instruments are used?
- What does it sound like?
- Can you describe the rhythm?
- What feelings are created by the music?
- What is the structure of the song (verses, chorus)?

Lyrics
- Examine the song text (verses and chorus). Look at form, structure and the language which is used (→ Dealing with poetry p. 226).
- Do the lyrics tell a story? What happens and what is the setting?
- What feelings are expressed by the words?
- Is there a message?

Comprehension questions

There is no general rule for answering comprehension questions. However, the following guidelines can be helpful:

- If the task refers to the text, **scan** the text for points you want to use, **take notes** and order them.
- For an **introductory sentence** it can be useful to refer to the words used in the task.
- Sometimes it is unavoidable to use the words from the text but you should try to use **your own words** as much as possible.
- Use **linking words** or **connectives** to show the logical development of different points, ideas or arguments of your answer.
- If your text is longer, divide it into **paragraphs**.
- Find a sentence that **concludes** your answer adequately and has the form of a general statement.

Text analysis

For all texts
- text type
- author
- target group
- purpose
- (historical) context
- structure
- language, register, style and tone
- relationship between style and content
- atmosphere
- other remarkable features
- effect on the reader
- your personal impression (if asked for)

For literary texts
- literary genre
- narrator and point of view
- setting
- characters (direct / indirect characterisation)
- main theme
- plot
- exposition, climax, turning point, rising / falling action, dénouement
- narrative techniques (chronology, frame story, suspense, tone, descriptions, comments, etc.)

Tips
- Secure your comprehension of the text by looking for keywords and taking notes.
- Considering background information about the text, its historical context, and its author can be helpful.
- Answer questions on the text precisely and to the point. Watch out for the way questions are asked: Do exactly as you are told when you are asked to *analyse*, *examine*, *describe*, *discuss*, *compare*, *summarise*, *interpret* or *comment* on things.
- Don't forget to relate the individual points to each other, i.e. look for similarities or contrasts in the characters, the atmosphere, the language, and find reasons for the author's choice of genre and style for a particular content.
- Explain everything in your own words, but use quotations from the text to support your statements, marking them clearly as quotations and giving line references.
- Clearly distinguish between facts and your interpretation.
- Avoid repetition.
- Never state your opinion without giving reasons, and only if you are asked.
- When you write about a text, think of using connectives and structuring devices as well as suitable adjectives and adverbs to give precise descriptions of characters, action and circumstances.

Writing a comment

An comment is a **clearly structured** piece of writing in which important arguments on a topic are presented.

Comments are generally written in the **simple present**. When you are asked to write a comment, always read the task carefully.

1 Preparation

- **Define** the topic clearly.
- **Brainstorm ideas**. Write down what you know about the topic in a word web, diagram or table.
- If necessary, **collect facts, arguments and other information**.
- Formulate your **opinion** on the topic.

2 Arranging your material

- Decide on the **most important facts, arguments or pieces of information** that you want to include.
- For each main argument try to think of two **supporting arguments**.
- Put your facts or arguments in a **logical order**. For example, you could:
  - start with general ideas and then go on to talk about details.
  - put things into chronological order.
  - start by giving all the arguments in favour and then give all the counterarguments.
  - follow each argument in favour with a counter-argument.

3 Writing your comment

The introductory paragraph
- The introductory paragraph should **introduce your topic** and catch the reader's interest.
- In your introductory paragraph you should also:
  - say clearly what your comment is going to be about in one or two sentences.
  - ask a question or questions which you will answer in your text.
  - give a **brief outline** of the problem / topic.

The main paragraphs
- Start a **new paragraph for each new idea**.
- Begin each paragraph with a **main idea or argument**.
- Write simple sentences.
- Arrange sentences in a logical order.
- Join sentences using suitable **connectives**.
- Use adverbs to emphasise points.
- Use **examples** where possible.

The conclusion
- Do not introduce new ideas!
- Make a **brief concluding statement** summarising what you have said in your comment.

4 Checking your comment

- Check that all your **sentences are complete** and that they make sense.
- Check your comment for **grammar, spelling and punctuation** mistakes.

5 Writing a model comment

Expressing your opinion To be quite honest, I do not think that/I cannot (fully) agree with … / I am not convinced by … / I would like to question the view that … / I reject the idea that … • In my opinion / view this argument is wrong / weak / unconvincing because …	I do not think anyone would disagree • In fact / As a matter of fact, I believe it is fully justified to say that … • I am of exactly the same opinion as … • I share the view that … • To my mind, … • this argument is very strong / powerful / convincing / plausible
Making concessions To a certain extent, I can accept … • However, we shouldn't forget that … • Most of the arguments are hard to dismiss. • Yet there are experts who … • I agree in principle, but … • Personally, I would not go so far as to say that … • Although …, we should accept / must admit that … • In spite of all this, … • Admittedly, …, but …	**Giving arguments / reasons** One reason for my criticism / scepticism is that … • Another / A second / A further / An additional argument I would like to present is that … • I would also argue that … • Another point I would like to make is that … • The main reason, however, is that … • The most convincing argument is that … • That brings me neatly to my final and most important point: …
Your conclusion/summary To sum up, … • In short, … • Considering all these arguments, … • I would conclude that … • I have come to the conclusion that … • It is safe to say that … • I would support the view that … • My suggestion is that … • My appeal to … is: … • In conclusion … • Having weighed up all the arguments, I would like to	

Writing a newspaper / magazine article

The following steps can help you to write a newspaper or magazine article:

- Remember the **ABC of news writing**:
  Accuracy (be exact, all the facts have to be correct)
  Brevity (keep it short and to the point)
  Clarity (make sure everyone understands).
- Remember also the five Ws: **Who? What? When? Where? Why?** (sometimes How? and So what?)
- Give **answers** to these questions.
- Attract the **reader's attention** with the headline and the lead, which is usually the first word, sentence or paragraph of the story. The lead contains the most important, most exciting point and makes the reader go on reading.
- The **structure of a newspaper article** is basically an inverted pyramid: The most important thing is at the top, in the lead. More facts and additional details follow, the least important ones at the end, so that you can stop reading any time after the lead should you feel you have enough information. If the story is written well, however, or if you are interested in the details, you can read on till the end.
- Good news **style** is **active, informative, to the point**. Nothing is repeated and nothing is said that is not necessary. Everything must be logical and easy to understand.
- News articles often contain **anecdotes, examples and quotes**. If you use quotes when writing, make sure they express the speaker's intention. Without the right context, they may be misunderstood. Only use them when they make a point clearer.
- A **good ending** rewards the reader for finishing the article by making some kind of reference to the lead.

Writing an email

From:	r.moll@doppelsechssports…de
To:	purchasing@citysports.co…uk
Cc:	s.bauder@ doppelsechssports…de
Sent:	20…-12-04 13:34
Attachments:	Doppel Sechs Winter Specials.pdf
Subject:	Order Confirmation_15 May

Dear Mr Warren → *Salutation*

Thank you for your order of 21 February. I can herein confirm that 22 units of item number WSB554, 18 units of item number QPR414, and 16 units of item number MUX982 have been dispatched to the given delivery address. Please find attached our Winter Specials catalogue, with many special offers for the Christmas and New Year season. If you require any further information or have any queries, please do not hesitate to contact us. → *Body of email*

Kind regards → *Complimentary close*

Roman Moll → *Signature block*
Senior Export Clerk

Roman Moll → *Signature footer*
Doppel Sechs Sports
Hohe Straße 6
50667 Köln
Germany
Tel: + 49 221 4569…
Email: info@doppelsechssports…de
ww#.doppelsechssports…de

From:	The sender's email address will appear here automatically.
To:	Pay attention when writing the recipient's email address. One small typing mistake and the email will either be sent to the wrong person, or returned.
Cc:	This stands for 'carbon copy'. Here you enter the email address of anybody you would like to also receive the message.
Bcc:	This stands for 'blind carbon copy'. This has the same function as 'carbon copy' but the addresses under Bcc do not appear in the message header of the other recipients.
Sent:	This may also be labeled 'Date'. The correct date and time the message was sent will be added automatically.
Attachments:	Any kind of file, such as MS Word (.doc), MS Excel (.xls), PDF (.pdf) or pictures (.jpg) can be attached to an email.

Subject:	You should always mention the precise subject of your email. This will help all people involved deal with the mail, and will prevent it from being deleted.
Salutation:	Very formal salutations such as 'Dear Sirs' are not used in emails. Instead use 'Dear …' wherever possible. In the English-speaking world emails are personalised as often as possible – Dear Ms Dietrich, Dear Kevin, etc. To avoid 'Dear Sirs' you can use 'Dear East Slope Furnishings'.
Body of the email:	Begin the first word with a capital letter.
Compliment-ary close:	There are a number of expressions to choose from: Best/Kind regards Best wishes Regards Yours sincerely (considered very formal in emails)
Signature block:	Write your job title or department underneath your name.
Signature footer:	Write your company's full name, address and telephone number.

Writing a diary / blog entry

- When you write a diary or blog entry, it is often necessary to **slip into the role of a different character**.
- Try to put yourself into the character's situation (age, background, job, sex, etc.).
- Try to imagine **the character's thoughts, feelings and ideas**.
- Although in a diary entry the main focus is on the past, present emotions and dreams and hopes about the future may also play a role.
- Write your entry from the **first-person point of view**.

Writing a personal letter

A **personal letter** is a letter you write to someone you know well **on a personal basis**, e.g. a friend or relative. There are no special rules which you have to follow when you write to people you know well. The model letter below shows you what an informal letter generally looks like in English. You can use **informal language** in a personal letter, as if you were speaking to the person.

Thomas Reiter
Dinkelstr. 1
70183 Stuttgart
Germany

Your address goes in the top right hand corner.

May 3, 20...

Write the date under the address.

Start the letter: Dear + name

Dear Frank

Use a capital letter for the first word.

Just a few lines to let you know I'm still alive! Sorry for not having written for so long, but I've been very busy at college with exams.

How are things with you? What are you doing for the summer? Unfortunately my applications for jobs in the States have all been turned down so far. Oh well, I'll keep trying...

Group your news, etc. in paragraphs.

Please drop me a line when you have a minute. We really must keep in touch. Give my regards to the family.

Finish the letter with one of these phrases: All the best • Best wishes • Bye for now • Love • Lots of love

All the best

Thomas

P.S. If I do get to the States, I'll let you know my address. Maybe we'll be able to meet up!

Writing a formal letter

A formal letter can be **a letter of application, a reservation, a request for information**, etc. **Commercial correspondence** refers to formal letters written in a business context, i.e. from one company to another. There are different ways of layouting these types of letters. The model letter below is in 'block form', which is probably the best to use because it is accepted everywhere. The parts in **blue** are only necessary in **commercial correspondence**.

Writer's address. In commercial correspondence you should include the company name, telephone, email, Internet address and fax number.

Weltweit Services
Thomas Reiter
Dinkelstr. 1
70183 Stuttgart
Germany
Tel: 0711 7682...
Fax: 0711 7682...
Email:
ww#.

Punctuation: In 'block style' you don't use commas in the address, salutation or complimentary close.

Addressee, including name and position, if known.

Personnel Manager
Import Export
11270 White Blvd.
Los Angeles CA 91430
USA

In commercial correspondence include references. 'Our ref:' is usually the initials of the person who wrote the letter. (TR = Thomas Reiter)

Your ref:
Our ref: TR

Date: The British write day, month, year (11.1.200…). Americans write month, day, year (1.11.200…). So it is best to write the date in full to avoid confusion.

11 January 20...

Dear Mr ... / Ms ...

In commercial correspondence include a subject line beginning 'Re:'.

Re: Your advertisement in the Sun Times of April 28

Main part of letter: State your reason for writing in formal, polite language. Group your points in paragraphs.

With reference to your advertisement in the Sun Times of April 28, I would like to apply for the position of bilingual buying assistant.

I am particularly interested in this job as I would very much like to gain work experience abroad. As well as speaking fluent English and Spanish, I have a working knowledge of French. My mother tongue is of course German.

I can supply references from former employers if you wish.

I enclose my curriculum vitae. Please do not hesitate to contact me if you should require further information.

Complimentary close

Yours sincerely

Signature

Thomas Reiter

Name in full

Thomas Reiter

In commercial correspondence: Writer's position in company.

Trainee buyer

Enc.

Enc. = Enclosures: Indicates that additional material is being sent with the letter.

Salutation	When used	Complimentary close
Dear Sir or Madam	to a company and when you don't know the person's name or sex	Yours faithfully
Dear Madam	to a woman, when you don't know her name	Yours faithfully
Dear Sir	to a man, when you don't know his name	Yours faithfully
Dear Mr Brown	to a man, whose name you know	Yours sincerely
Dear Ms / Mrs Brown	to a woman, whose name you know	Yours sincerely
Note: Nowadays the use of *Yours faithfully* and *Yours sincerely* is not always divided up as strictly as given above.		

Useful phrases

Explaining the purpose of the letter
We are writing / I am writing … • in connection with … • … with reference / regard to … • … to advise you of … • … to confirm … • … to let you know … • … to tell you that … • … to ask / enquire (whether) … • …to inform you of … • … to request you to …

Stating a reference
Thank you for your mail of July 1st. • Many thanks for your letter dated 26th July. • We refer to your order for … • I have received your enquiry regarding … • Further to our telephone conversation today, … • With reference to your mail of June 5th, … • With regard to your enquiry of June 5th about …

Giving good news
I am delighted to tell you that … • You will be pleased to hear that …

Giving bad news
We regret to inform you that … • I am afraid that … • We are sorry to have to tell you that … • Unfortunately we are unable to …

Making a request
Please … • Please could you … ? • Could you possibly…? • We would be grateful if you could/would … • We would be much obliged if you could … • I would appreciate it if you could … • … would be very much appreciated.

Offering help
If you wish, we would be happy to … • Would you like us to …? • At your request we would gladly …

Giving information
We wish to advise you that … • We are pleased to inform you that … • For your information: …

Enclosing documents
I am enclosing … • Please find enclosed … • Please find attached … (= attachment / papers fixed to the letter with a paper clip / …)

Thanking
Thank you for sending me … • Many thanks for … • I am grateful to you for … • I am much obliged to you for sending me … (formal)

Useful phrases

Apologising
I am sorry about the delay in replying. • We were (very / extremely / most) sorry to hear about the problem. • We regret that this problem has occured. • We apologize for any inconvenience caused.

Assuring
Please rest assured that we will do our utmost to help you. • We assure you that we will do our best to put the matter right. • We promise to look into the matter immediately. • You can count on us to ensure smooth delivery in future.

Making concessions
We agree to reduce the price by (percentage / sum of money). • We are happy to grant you a discount of 3% on the goods. • We will let you have the goods at a reduced price of …

Closing remarks
If you have any questions, please do not hesitate to call me / us on (tel. no.). • Should you have any questions, feel free to contact me / us. • If you require further information, please do get in touch / ask. • Should you require further details, please contact us again. • If we can help in any way, we would be happy to be of assistance.

Referring to future contact
We look forward to hearing from you soon / meeting you next week / seeing you on the 29th. • We are looking forward to receiving your proposal / order.

Writing an enquiry

East Slope Furnishings
32 North Street
Brighton
BN1 2RG
Tel: + 44 1273 6307…
Email: purchasing@esfurnishings.co…uk
ww#.esfurnishings.co…uk

Möbelwelt GmbH
Gaußstraße 7
51503 Rösrath
Germany

Your ref:
Our ref: ELG/ag

17 November 20…

Dear Sir or Madam

Re: Product enquiry

Your address was passed on to us by a business partner who recommended your products. Our company, East Slope Furnishings, is a young and rapidly growing home furnishing company with outlets in six cities across the south of England. We supply affordable and stylish furniture and home accessories.

Source of address

Introduce your company

We have visited your website and were very impressed with your product range. Consequently, we are interested in adding a number of your products to our collection.

Reason for enquiry

Could you please send us a copy of your latest brochure and an up-to-date price list? Please also supply us with information regarding your terms of payment, delivery times, possible discounts, as well as the minimum quantity for a trial order.

Ask for further information – sales literature, terms and conditions, delivery times, etc.

Thank you in advance and we look forward to hearing from you.

Polite ending

Yours faithfully

E. Lloréns Gómez
Elisabet Lloréns Gómez
Purchasing manager

Writing an offer

Möbelwelt GmbH
Gaußstraße 7
51503 Rösrath
Germany
Tel: + 49 2205 4569…
Email: info@moebelwelt…de
ww#.moebelwelt…de

East Slope Furnishings
32 North Street
Brighton
BN1 2RG

Your ref: ELG/ag
Our ref: MD/jh

24 November 20…

Dear Ms Lloréns Gómez

Re: Your enquiry of 17 November 20...

Thank you very much for your enquiry of 17 November. We are pleased to hear of your interest in stocking our products in your store.

Reference to enquiry

Please find enclosed, as requested, a copy of our latest brochure as well as an up-to-date price list.

Respond to enquiry / make offer

Our prices are quoted DDP Brighton and Möbelwelt GmbH has a minimum order policy of 100 for deliveries to the United Kingdom. Nevertheless, trial orders can be arranged on an individual basis. Please also refer to our catalogue and website for special offers.

Our usual terms of payment are bank transfer to our account with the European Bank within 30 days from date of invoice. Regular customers are granted open account terms.

State terms of delivery and payment

Standard delivery times to the United Kingdom are 2-3 working days, although express overnight delivery is available on some orders.

Refer to the delivery time

Should you have any further questions or queries, please do not hesitate to contact us.

Polite ending / creating goodwill

Yours sincerely

M. Dietrich
Meike Dietrich
Senior Export Clerk

Enc.

Writing an order

East Slope Furnishings
32 North Street
Brighton
BN1 2RG
Tel: + 44 1273 6307…
Email: purchasing@esfurnishings.co…uk
ww#.esfurnishings.co…uk

Möbelwelt GmbH
Gaußstraße 7
51503 Rösrath
Germany

Your Ref: MD/jh
Our ref: ELG/ag

30 November 20…

Dear Ms Dietrich

Re: Your offer of 24 November 20...

Thank you very much for sending us your brochure and price list. We also appreciate you outlining your delivery terms and conditions.

Reference to offer / previous contacts

We have studied your catalogue and are very impressed with your products. We would like to order 16 units of item number AQW445 and 16 units of item number AQR457.

Place an order

As agreed, we will make payment by bank transfer to the previously named bank within 30 days from date of invoice. Delivery is to be made DDP Brighton.

Confirm method of payment / terms of delivery / delivery time

We look forward receiving the goods in time and to doing further business with you in the future.

Polite ending / creating goodwill

Yours sincerely

E. Lloréns Gómez
Elisabet Lloréns Gómez
Purchasing manager

Writing a CV

CV is short for 'Curriculum Vitae'. There are no rules about how to write a CV in English. Use the following 'Dos and Don'ts' and the model CV below as a guide.

Dos

Do include skills and interests which are relevant to the job, if possible.
Do give the English equivalents of German terms, where possible.

Don'ts

Don't write more than one page.
Don't necessarily include a photo, unless asked to.
Don't use handwriting for your CV.
Don't sign your name at the end.

Curriculum Vitae

Name:	Ute Braun
Address:	Musterstraße 1, 50400 Köln, Germany
Telephone:	0211 / 2345...
Email:	u.braun@e-mail...de
Date of birth:	6.5.1988
Nationality:	German
Schools attended:	2004 – 2006: Language College, Stuttgart 1997 – 2004: Pfeiffer Realschule (Comprehensive)
Qualifications:	Diploma course as a bilingual secretary (English, Spanish)
Work experience:	July 2005 – September 2005: kitchen work at McDougall's July 2004 – September 2004: office assistant in the export department of Bosch
Skills, Interests and Experience:	fluent English and Spanish, a working knowledge of French; good computer skills (Word, Excel); clean driving license; tennis and member of the local repertory company (latest role: the Nurse in Romeo and Juliet)

Describing pictures

1 Types of pictures

photo(graph) • print • transparency • slide • painting • drawing • sketch • picture • illustration • image • collage • electronic image • snapshot • skyline • panorama • close-up • action photo • still (from a film) • scene • sequence

2 Describing a picture

First impression
- Where is the image from?
- What type of image is it?
- What does the image (roughly) show?
- Who created it?
- When and why was it drawn / taken?

Description
- Describe in detail what can be seen in the picture.
- Talk about what you can see in the foreground and in the background, from the left to the right and from the top to the bottom.
- Don't forget to look at the details. Describe the setting or situation, the quality of the picture, the characters and their appearance and body language.

Interpretation
- What message is given by the picture?
- Is it aimed at a particular target group?
- Did the person who created the picture intend it to have a certain effect on the viewer? If so, how is this achieved?

Evaluation
- Do you think the picture has the intended effect?
- Which elements are responsible for its success or failure?
- If it is a historical picture, compare the effect it might have had in its original context with the one it has on a viewer now.

Useful phrases

First impression
This is a photo / an illustration of … • This photo was taken in … • The illustration shows … • In this illustration / photo you can see (that) … • My first thought when I saw the picture was … • The photograph is shocking/disgusting / amazing / spectacular / special … • The picture reminds me of … • It shows … • It was probably taken in / at … • The photograph looks as if it was staged to achieve a certain effect. • It is a realistic picture.

Description
on the right-hand / left-hand side of the picture • in the centre • in the foreground • in the background • at the top • at the bottom • in the upper right-hand corner • in the lower left-hand corner • The picture was painted by … • It is a portrait / cartoon / still life / landscape / an oil / watercolour painting. • In the middle /centre of the picture there is … • to the left / right of … • in the top left-hand / bottom right-hand corner • There is a contrast

Useful phrases

between … • … is clearly visible • The focus is on … • The field size is a close-up / medium shot / long shot • The colours are bright / dark. • … is seen from above / below / the front / the back • This creates a … atmosphere.

Interpretation
The person in the picture looks … (+ *adjective, e.g. happy*) • The photo / illustration supports the point made in the text that … • The photo / illustration gives you the impression that … • The illustration makes me feel … (+ *adjective: e.g. worried*) • The colours the artist has chosen make me feel … (+ *adjective: happy / sad / worried / …*) • In my opinion the illustration would be better, if … (+ *simple past: e.g. if it was more life-like*)

Evaluation
The artist aims to present … • The picture is (not) convincing because …

Describing cartoons

A cartoonist aims to be both **funny and critical**. When looking at a cartoon, the most important thing is to try to work out what point the cartoonist is making. Generally **the point is made by a combination of the text and the illustration**, so it is important to analyse and understand both. **Illustrations** generally show caricatures of **well-known people or particular stereotypes.** To understand a cartoon, you need to recognise and define the person or group of people illustrated.

To analyse a cartoon, you can follow the steps in the skill 'Describing pictures' → p. 241.

Useful phrases

Describing the cartoon
The cartoon consists of an illustration of … • The illustration shows … • There is a caption under the cartoon, which says "…". • In the (first) speech bubble it says "…". • The text in the speech bubble is spoken by … • The figure is a stereotype / caricature of … • The drawing is detailed / clear / sketchy / abstract.

Talking about the point
The cartoonist is making fun of … • The cartoonist is satirising … • The cartoon is funny because of the misunderstanding between …

Giving your opinion
I think / I don't think the cartoon is (very) funny because … • I get the joke / point. / I don't get the joke / point. • I think / I don't think the cartoon is easy to understand because … • I agree / I don't agree with the point the cartoonist is making because …

Describing diagrams

As you know, **diagrams sum up a lot of statistics or information in very little space** and can make information easier to understand. The kind of diagram you choose to use (bar chart, pie chart, flow chart, line graph, etc.) depends on what you want to show.

A pie chart shows percentages of 100 %:

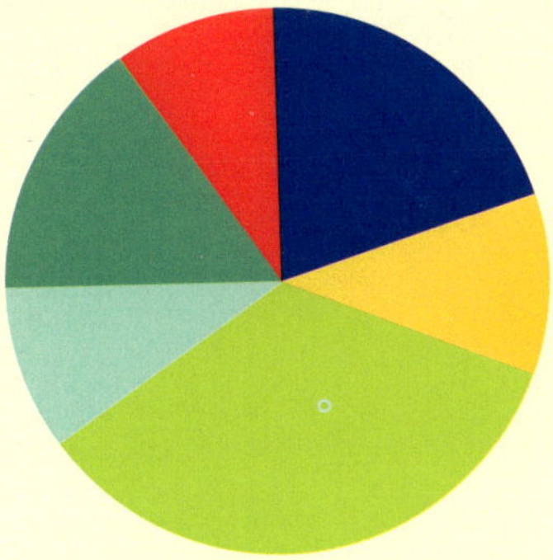

A bar chart is used to compare figures directly:

A line graph shows a development over a certain amount of time:

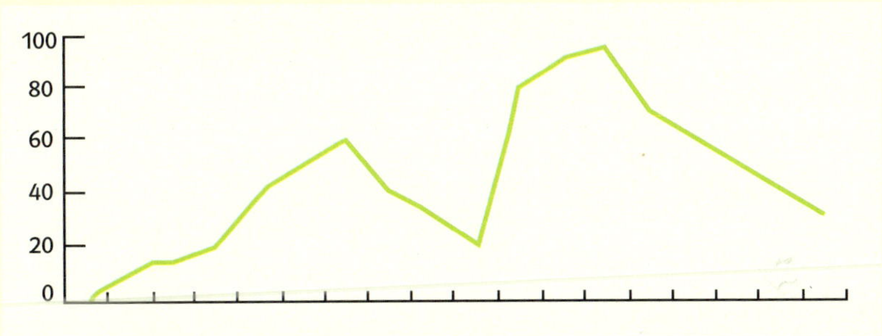

A flow chart shows the links between elements and their influence on each other. It is best used to describe processes that contain decisions at certain points, where alternatives need to be shown:

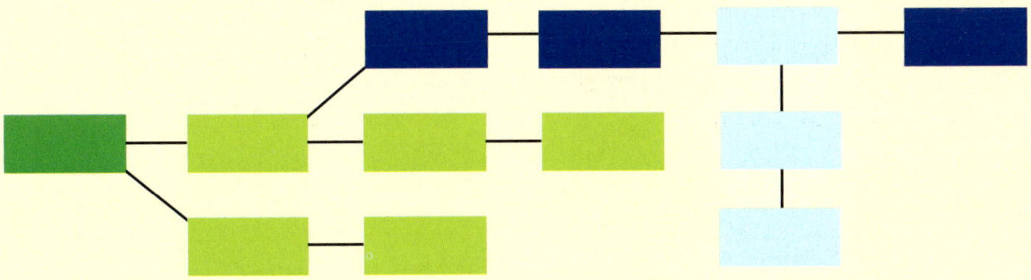

Useful phrases

Describing an increase
to rise • to increase • to have increased by • growth • an increase / a rise (in the number of …)

Describing a decrease
to decrease • to drop • to decline • a decrease • a decline • a drop (in the number of …) • a reduction (in the number of …)

Useful adjectives and adverbs
sharp(ly) • slow(ly) • steady / steadily • continuing / continual(ly) • gradual(ly) • significant(ly) • insignificant(ly) • negligible…negligibly • large • high • small

Expressing numbers & figures
the figures for the last year / the last month / … • the latest figures • the total number of … • a (significant/insignificant / …) number of … • a (high / …) percentage of … • the statistics • a majority / minority of …

Useful nouns
amount • proportion • sum • level • figure(s)

Useful verbs
to show that … • to indicate that … • to suggest that … • to give information about … • to make it clear that … • to illustrate … • to represent … • to depict

Qualifiers
a total of • over • under • nearly • more / less than • between • the same number as • the same amount of • from over / under … to just over / under • half • a third • two thirds • a quarter • (25) per cent • twice as many • three times as many • on average • averagely • roughly • exactly • precisely

Analysing advertisements

When you want to analyse an advertisement, you need to think of the following aspects:

- What is being advertised?
- What is the advertising medium (e.g. a poster, internet pop-up?)
- Who is the ad targeting? What is the product's target group? – men, women, older people, kids, etc.
- What image of the product does the ad try to give? – healthy, hi-tech, value-for-money, …
- How does it try to do this? What "devices" does it use? Think of pictures, text and layout. Ads can be complicated or simple, serious or funny, etc.
- What do you think of the ad? Do you think it is effective, entertaining, awful, clever, sexist, …?

Advertisers often use the AIDA formula to plan advertisements. Ads can also be analysed by using this formula:

Attention:	How does the ad attract your attention?
Interest:	How does the ad create interest in the product?
Desire:	How does the ad arouse desire?
Action:	How does the ad make you take action (i.e. buy the product)?

Useful phrases

Design
The advertisement is divided into … / consists of … • In the foreground / background … / On the left / right … • It features a … / It shows an image of … • The product is presented / depicted as a …

Impact
The design is colourful / simple / bold / … • It grabs / catches the reader's attention by … • The eye is drawn towards … • The arrangement of text and images has the effect of … • The most striking feature is … • The use of … conveys an impression of … • The choice of font creates a retro / modern look

Product and target market
The product / service being advertised is … • It might appeal to people who … • The advert seems to be directed / aimed at … • It appeals to the desire for status / prestige / security / …

Claim and message
The slogan / strapline promises the customer … • It claims to … • The claim is supported with statistics / endorsements / … • The hidden / underlying message seems to be that … • It makes fun of … / It plays with the idea of … • The language is flowery / plain / straightforward / … • It makes use of alliteration / pun / wordplay / irony … • It prompts / urges the reader to …

Mediation

Mediation means **communicating the main points of a text**, written in one language, **in another language.** For example, the text may be in English and you have to formulate the main points in German, or the text may be in German and the text you produce should be in English. Mediation is not a word-for-word translation. Instead, it is about **getting a message** or **the main points of a text** across in a different language.

Tips

- Read the **task description** carefully to understand what you are supposed to do.
- Read the text and **underline the words** you need to look up in a dictionary.
- Read the text again and **mark the most important points** based on the task description. You can also write **key words** in the margin.
- Pay attention to words such as 'but', 'however', and other signals which indicate a new point.
- You do not normally need to include examples in your mediation text as these usually only illustrate the main points in the original text.
- **Plan the structure** of your mediation text: Think of a good introduction to your text. Which points will you start with? Do you want to include a conclusion?
- Your mediation does not need to have the same structure as the original text.

Discussions

1 Rules for a discussion

- Always be polite!
- Look at the person / the people you are talking to but don't stare at them.
- Don't interrupt unless you feel it is really necessary.
- Listen carefully to what other people are saying.
- Keep to the point.
- Don't talk too much.

2 The role of a discussion leader

A discussion leader makes sure the **discussion is held in an orderly way** and that participants are always polite to each other. He / She always remains neutral (i.e. doesn't give his / her own opinion).

Useful phrases

Introducing the topic and the participants
(As you know,) our discussion today is about… • On my right / left I have … *(name of person or group)*, who is / are in favour of / against …

Choosing whose turn it is to speak
Who'd like to open the discussion? • … , would you like to open the discussion? • The next person to speak is … , followed by … and then …

Making sure everyone has an equal chance to speak, including people who are shy
Is there anything you'd like to say, …?

Making sure no one person monopolises the discussion
I'm sorry to interrupt you, but I'm afraid you'll have to stop there. • Sorry, but I must give the others a chance to put forward their arguments now.

Making sure that only one person speaks at a time
Please wait your turn, you'll have a chance to speak in a minute! • If you'd just let … finish, please.

Noting down the most important points and summarising the discussion at the end
Time is running out, so I'd like to sum up what we've been discussing. • We heard from … that …

Thanking everybody at the end
Thank you for taking part in the discussion! • And finally I'd like to thank all the participants for holding a fair / friendly / … discussion.

Making a suggestion
Let's consider … • I suggest/propose that you / we … • I suggest/propose (+ -ing form) • What do you think about …? • If I were you, I'd …

Responding to a suggestion
That's a good idea! / Fine! • OK / Yes, why not? • OK, if you want, I don't really mind. • I think it would be a better idea to talk about / consider … • Couldn't we look at this / do this another way? • What about …? • I'm not sure. How about …?

Useful phrases

Asking for an opinion
What do you think / feel about …? • What is your view / opinion on / about …? • What would you say? • I'd like to hear what you think about …

Giving an opinion
As far as I'm concerned … • I think / feel / believe / am of the opinion that … • To my mind … • In my opinion … • In my view …

Agreeing
You're (quite / absolutely) right. • That's a very good point! • Absolutely! / Exactly! • I agree (with you / Susie / …). • You have a point there. • You might / could be right. • I think you're right to a certain extent / up to a point.

Disagreeing
I disagree (entirely). • I'm sorry, but I completely disagree. • Stop exaggerating! • I think you're oversimplifying things. • That's an interesting point, but … • That's not the point. • You've missed the point (entirely).

Interrupting someone
Sorry to interrupt, but could you please explain / repeat the point you've just made. • Excuse me for interrupting, but I don't understand what you've just said. • Sorry for interrupting but …

Dealing with being interrupted
Can I just finish what I was saying, please? • Just a second. I haven't quite finished. • Would you let me / allow me to make my point, please. • You could at least let me finish my sentence!

Changing the subject
There is something else that I'd like to say … • Have you ever thought of / considered …? • On the other hand … • Try looking at things another way / from a different angle. • I'd like to bring up another point.

Returning to the original subject
Let's get back to what we were saying / discussing. • Let's get back to the point. • As I was saying before, … • Getting back to what we / you / … said earlier …

Asking for a further explanation
Did I get that right? • Do you really mean that …? • Did I understand correctly that you think …? • Could you explain what you just said / the point you just made / … again, please? • Could you give me / us a concrete example, please?

Saying that a point has been misunderstood
That's not what I meant to say (at all)! • You've got me (completely) wrong. • You've (completely) misunderstood me. • That's not what I was trying to say! • I didn't make myself clear. I'll try and explain again.

Tips for everyday conversation

Always make sure your **language and behaviour is appropriate for the situation** at hand. If it's a formal situation and you know what will be talked about, prepare by looking up useful words and facts.

When you are talking to older or more **experienced people or to your boss**, you should use more **polite phrases** and not be too direct. With **people of the same age or people you know really well**, you probably feel more at ease and can **be a little more direct**. In any case, always show that you are interested in what the person has to say and that you respect him / her.

Give **precise and clear information** and remember to **be tactful** when telling people something that affects them personally.

Always pick up on what your conversation partners have said to show that you **respect and sympathise** with them, that you are listening carefully and judging the content fairly. Use **supportive intonation and body language** as well as the following phrases, where appropriate.

Useful phrases

please • thank you • you're welcome • don't worry • not at all • Could I …? • Would you …? • May I …? • I'd like … • Yes, I will • No, I don't • Yes, that's true, but … • I agree, but … • It's just … • of course • I see • you know • I mean … • Really? • Are you sure? • What a pity. • That's very kind of you. • I appreciate that.

Small talk

Small talk is **light (casual) conversation**. It is a way of showing interest in others, communicating in a friendly way and avoiding conflict at all times! At a **social event**, such as a party, you might spend the whole time in casual conversation. At a **business meeting, on the phone, at an interview, etc.** you can start (and end) with **a little small talk**.

Topics for small talk

- The weather (especially popular in Britain!)
- A journey (to or from the place where you are)
- Where you live / Where your conversation partner lives
- Your family and / or your conversation partner's family (if you know them)
- A recent / well-known TV programme or film
- Tips about what to see and do in a certain town or city (i.e. cultural events, attractions, restaurants, local specialities, etc.)
- Sport (e.g. a current sports event)
- A vacation
- Where you / your conversation partner went to school or university
- What you do for a living / what your conversation partner does for a living
- Hobbies and interests
- An experience / event that you and your conversation partner are both currently involved in or have been involved in
- A non-controversial item in the news

Useful phrases

Starting a conversation
Hi! / Hello! • What are you up to? • Do you mind if I join you? • Nice to see you (again)! • How are you? • How are you doing? • How are things?

Finding a topic
Did you see … on TV last night / at the weekend / …? • Have you seen the new … film yet? • Did you read about … in the newspaper this morning? • Terrible / Beautiful weather, isn't it? • How was your journey? • How did you get here? • What made you decide to come here? • Have you ever been here before? • Who do you think is going to win … this evening?

Making plans
Shall I pick you up? • Let's arrange to meet at … • Sorry, I can't manage Friday. I'm meeting … then. • I've got an appointment with … at … • Thursday would suit me better / best. • That's no good, I'm afraid. What about …? • I've got a date with … on … • I'm seeing … then. • Shall we book seats / tickets / a table? • When does the performance start? • It starts at … • If there's a problem, call me.

Responding & showing surprise
Really? • I don't believe it! • That's incredible! • Well, I've never heard of anything like that before! • That's the funniest / most interesting / strangest thing I've heard in ages! • I've never thought of it like that before. • I couldn't agree more! • That's funny! Exactly the same thing happened to me the other day / two weeks ago / … .

Finishing a conversation
It was nice talking to you! • Goodness / Oh no, is that the time? • Excuse me, / What a shame, I've got to go now. • Hope to see you again soon. • Hope you get home safely. • Take care. • Give my regards to … . • Don't forget to say hello to … for me!

Making phone calls

1 Preparing a phone call

- **Prepare yourself** thoroughly. Make **notes in English** or write out a rough draft of the main things you want to say. This is especially important when making formal or business calls.
- If possible **find out the name and number** of a direct contact person in advance.
- **Think of things** the contact person is likely **to ask or say** and work out responses.
- **Be prepared to spell words**, especially people's names and names of places.

2 During the phone call

- **Speak clearly and slowly**. State your requests clearly and to the point.
- Don't worry about making mistakes.
- **Be polite!** Say *please* when you ask for information and *thank you* when you receive help.
  Remember: *please* = *bitte* • *you're welcome / not at all* = *bitte schön; gern geschehen*
- When making a social call, give your first name only.
- When making a formal / business call, give your first name and surname.

- **Address people** you know well by their first names. In a formal / business situation address people using *Mr, Mrs* or *Ms* [mz] + surname.
- **State telephone numbers** as single digits. When the same number occurs twice consecutively, you can say *double* (e.g. *33 = double 3*). *0 = Oh* (BE & AE) or *zero* (AE)
  Example: *07145 14406: Oh / zero – seven – one – four – five – one – double four – oh / zero – six*
- **Ask the caller to spell names**, etc. for you to avoid confusion.
- **Repeat important information** (times, names, addresses, prices, etc.) to be sure that you have understood everything correctly.
- Don't expect to understand every single word that is said.
- If you are not sure if you have understood something:
  - **Ask the person to repeat** what they have just said: *Could you repeat that, please?*
  - **Ask the person to explain** something in a different way: *So what you're saying is …?*
  - **Ask the person to speak more slowly**: *Could you speak a little more slowly, please?*
- If you can't hear the caller properly, **ask the caller to speak more loudly**.
- If you think you've got the wrong number, check and apologise. Don't just hang up.
- If the caller has got the wrong number, explain politely. **Don't just hang up**.

Useful phrases

The kind of things you may want to say

Hello. Is that Mr Brown speaking? • Could I speak to Mr Brown, please? • This is … I'm calling from Germany. • I'm calling about … • I'd like to enquire about … • I hope I'm not calling at an inconvenient time. • I've got a few questions/ a complaint about … • I'd like to make an appointment to see the doctor/ dentist / … • Shall I ring back later? • Could you take a message/ give him / her a message, please? • What time would be most convenient? • Could you repeat that, please? • I'm afraid the line's very bad/ we've got a bad connection.

What you may hear at the other end of the line

Brown and Wilson Car Rentals. Can I help you? • Speaking! • I'll just fetch him. Hang on a moment, please. • I'm afraid he's not available / he's in a meeting. I'm afraid the line is engaged at the moment. • Could you call back later? • Can I take a message? • I'll give you his extension. • I'll put you through to the … department… • I'll connect you. Please hold the line. • Sorry. I think you've dialled the wrong number. • The person you are calling is not available at the moment. Please leave a message afterthe tone. • If you wish to contact the sales… complaints…customer service department, please press ONE…TWO…

A job interview

If a company finds your letter of application and CV interesting, their human resource department may invite you for an interview. For the interviewee, the interview process starts beforehand with **good preparation**.

1 Preparation

- **Find out about the business or institution** where you will have your interview.
- **Think of questions** that you might be asked, and come up with **suitable answers**.
- Have a friend ask you the questions (plus some surprise ones) and give you a constructive feedback on how you answered them.
- **Think of questions to ask the interviewer** about the business or institution. You want to show that you already know something about them.
- **Dress nicely and arrive early** so that you can collect your thoughts before the interview.

2 During the interview

- **Smile and maintain eye contact** with your interviewer (although it isn't a good idea to stare).
- The interviewer knows that you are nervous, so he or she might try to lighten the atmosphere with **small talk** (→ Small talk p. 248). Be prepared to chat with him or her.
- **Speak clearly and not too quickly!** It is perfectly alright to pause for a moment and think about what you want to say.
- If necessary, ask the interviewer to repeat or explain a question. This also gives you more time to think!
- **Do not answer questions with only *yes, no,* or *I don't know*.** However, keep answers clear and concise. This is your chance to convince the interviewer that you are the right person for the job!
- If possible, **ask the question(s) about the business or institution** that you thought of.
- **Thank** your interviewer at the end.

3 After the interview

- After a short time, **send a short, follow-up mail** thanking your interviewer and expressing interest in the position again. If you haven't been told when the decision will be made, ask politely when you can expect a reply.
- **If you don't get the job, don't worry!** Think of what you can do better next time, and work on these points. As with any other skill, the more interviews you do, the better you will get!

Useful phrases

As you can see from my CV … • I trained in … • I graduated / will be graduating from school in … • I enjoy dealing with clients / working with people. • I have excellent … skills / good knowledge of … • I'm PC literate. • I'm accustomed to working hard. • I'm prepared to work overtime. • During my time at school I did internships at …

Word webs

Word webs are useful for **collecting and organising a large amount of information** about a certain topic. You can make a word web for yourself or as a group. The basic structure of a word web is always the same.

1 How to make a word web

- **Use a pencil** so that you can easily delete things or change their position, if necessary.
- Write your main topic in the middle of a page and draw a circle around the word or phrase. (Fig. 1)
- Think of **important things** directly related to the main topic. Write each idea (subtopic) in a **circle** around the outside of your first circle. **Draw lines** connecting the subtopics to the main topic. (Fig. 2)
- Now add more circles with related ideas around the subtopics. (Fig. 3) Instead of drawing circles you can use lines with 'branches' for subtopics. (Fig. 4)

2 Ways of using word webs

- To **brainstorm for ideas on a given topic:** Write the topic heading in the centre circle and add all new and related aspects.
- To **organise information from a text** (or other source): Start with the most important point in the text, add the main subtopics, then add relevant detailed information or quotations from the text.
- To **develop word fields**: Start with the generic term and add all related words.
- To **organise arguments**: Start with the topic of discussion. Add a branch or circle: 'for' and another one 'against'. Continue by adding further branches / circles with arguments 'for' and 'against'.

Fig. 1

Fig. 2

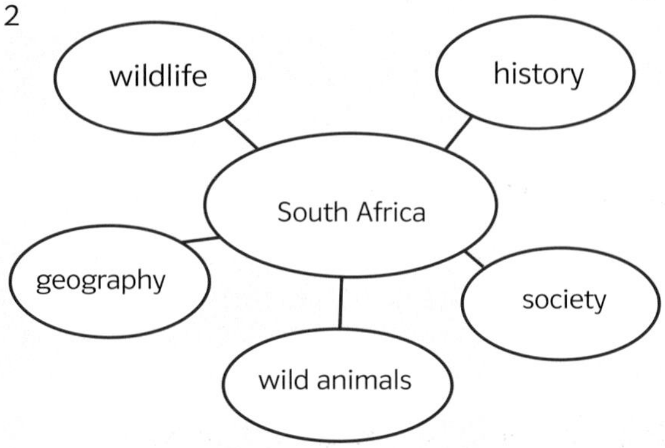

Fig. 3

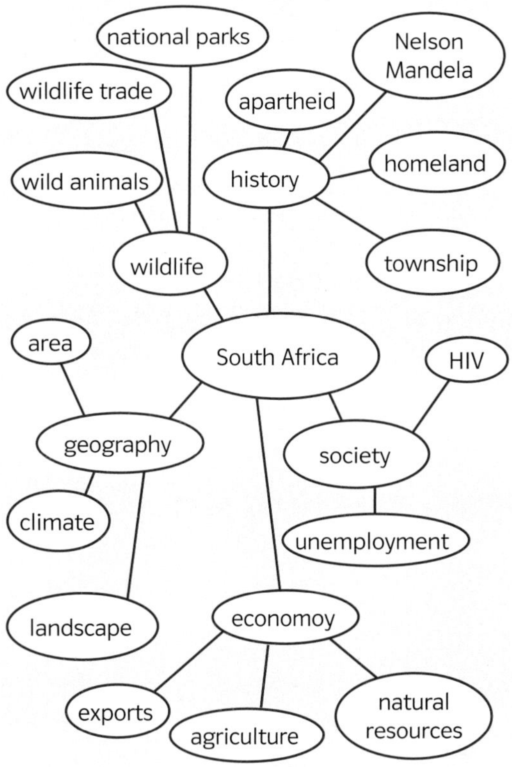

Fig. 4

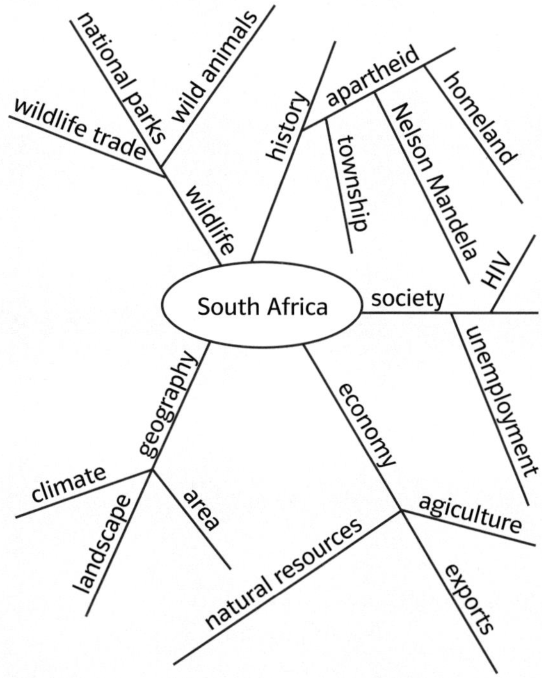

Brainstorming

Brainstorming is the first step when you want to **collect ideas on a specific topic**. You can brainstorm on your own, with a partner or in a group.

1 Individual brainstorming

- First write down **each idea that comes to mind** when you think of the topic.
- In a second step, go through your collection of ideas and choose those which you really want.
- **Structure** your ideas in a grid or a word web.

2 Brainstorming in a group (placemat)

- Form groups of four. Write down the topic in the middle of a big sheet of paper (placemat). Each of you works in one corner.
- Collect your ideas on the topic and write them down in your corner.
- Discuss all ideas and decide on the ones you find best or most important. Write them in the middle of your placemat.

Example:

- apartheid (blacks, whites, other ethnic groups)
- townships, homelands
- wildlife (national parks, wild animals, protection of wild animals)

- landscape (interior plateau, hills, narrow coastal plain
- agriculture (maize, wheat, wine)
- natural resources (gold, diamonds, metals, minerals)

South Africa
- apartheid (blacks, whites, townships, homelands)
-
-
-

- history (settlers, apartheid, democracy)
- HIV
- unemployment
- problems between blacks and whites

- national parks
- wild animals
- wildlife trade
- protection of animals
- safaris
- holiday

Taking notes

Taking notes means writing down information from a spoken source (speech, interview, etc.) in short form.

- Only write down the **most important information**. It is impossible to note down everything.
- Only write down **key words**, never complete sentences. Key words are often names, times, numbers and places.
- Try to order your notes systematically. If possible, use headings, sub-headings or grids.
- Use **symbols** for certain relationships, for example: = ≠ →
- Make sure that you can read your handwriting!

Marking up a text

When you read a text, it can be useful to mark up **information that you will need later** for answering questions, etc. Remember that you can only mark up texts **in photocopies or in books that belong to you**.

- When you read the text, keep in mind **which information** you are looking for.
- Mark relevant information by **underlining, circling or highlighting** the words or phrases.
- If you want to mark different kinds of information, choose **different colours**.
- You can also write down **key words in the margins**.
- When you read the text again later, you can **concentrate on the marked words** and phrases and on your notes in the margins.

Example:

The struggle against apartheid

Apartheid (meaning *separateness* in Afrikaans) was a system of legalised racial segregation in South Africa. Apartheid had its roots in the history of colonisation and settlement of southern Africa. *definition and roots*

The first Europeans who settled in South Africa were the Dutch in 1652. In 1806 the British arrived. The discovery of diamonds in 1867 and gold in 1886 led to increased immigration and brought wealth which, however, native Africans were denied. The Union of South Africa was formed in 1910 and racial segregation was generally accepted although the policy of apartheid didn't become official until 1948, when the National Party came to power. *first settlers*

Apartheid classified inhabitants and visitors into racial groups (black, white, coloured, and Indian or Asian). South African blacks had to move to small and economically unproductive areas of the country known as 'homelands'. Blacks who worked in factories and mines had to live in 'townships', i.e. poor and underdeveloped living areas which were built around the major cities. The government also segregated education, medical care and other public services. The services for black people were greatly inferior to those of whites and the black education system was designed to prepare blacks for life in the labouring class. *apartheid examples*

Guessing new words

Don't be afraid of texts containing new words. You already know many different ways of guessing their meanings. After applying your guessing technique there will still be some words you don't know, but don't worry, you will probably understand the most important points in the text.

Guessable words	**Examples:**
• Words that are used in a German context.	*bestseller, boycott, clown, laptop, track, …*
• Words that are similar to German words → but watch out for false friends!	*individuality, inner, install, parallel, to wander, …*
• Words that are similar to words you know from another foreign language (French, Latin, Spanish, Italian) → but watch out for false friends!	*academic, announcement, artificial, descendant, dignity, disrespect, individuality, junior, minor, pasta, phase, …*
• Compounds of words you already know.	*handwriting, heartfelt, mixed ability, single-sex, washing machine, wholeheartedly, …*
• Words from a word family you already know.	*adventurous, announcement, importation, to mirror, nationalism, relevance, …*
• Words you already know, but with a different meaning, the new meaning being guessable from the context.	*to admit, light, plain, pretty, to report sb…*
• Words whose meaning you can guess from the context.	*(he) dozed off (in his chair); (it's old-fashioned) out of date*

Working with a dictionary

1 English-German, German-English

When using an English-German or German-English dictionary, make sure to check the following information in your dictionary.

- What part of speech is the word?
- What does it go together with?
- What topic or word field does it belong to?
- How is it pronounced?
- Are there irregular forms?
- What translations are given?
- Which of the translations can only be used in a limited context (*AE, formal, slang*, etc.)?
- Which of the translations fits the context?

Example:

fo·cus['fəʊkəs] <*pl* **focuses, foci**> [*pl* 'fəʊsaɪ] *s* ❶ (MATH OPT) Brennpunkt *m* ❷ *(fig)* Brennpunkt, Herd *m*, Zentrum *nt*; ~ *(un)scharf eingestellt*; ~ scharf einstellen *vt* ❶ (OPT PHOT) einstellen *(on* auf) ❷ *(fig)* konzentrieren *(on* auf); **focus group** *s (in marketing)* [ausgewählte] Test-

2 English-English

This type of dictionary is best used for **writing an English text** when you are not quite sure which is the best word in a given context. The more English you read, the more you will improve your language! An English-English (monolingual) dictionary provides you with the following information:

- What part of speech is the word?
- What does it go together with?
- What topic or word field does it belong to?
- How is it pronounced?
- Are there irregular forms?
- What synonyms and / or definitions are given?
- Which of the given meanings fits the context?
- Examples show how the word is typically used.

Tips for using an English-English dictionary

- Before looking up a word identify whether it is a verb, noun, adjective, adverb, etc.
- When you have found the entry for the word, make sure you look at the meaning for the correct class of word.
- Read any additional information which the dictionary gives you about the word.
- Take your time to read the entry carefully.
- Make sure you find the entry which matches the use of the word in the given context.

Example:

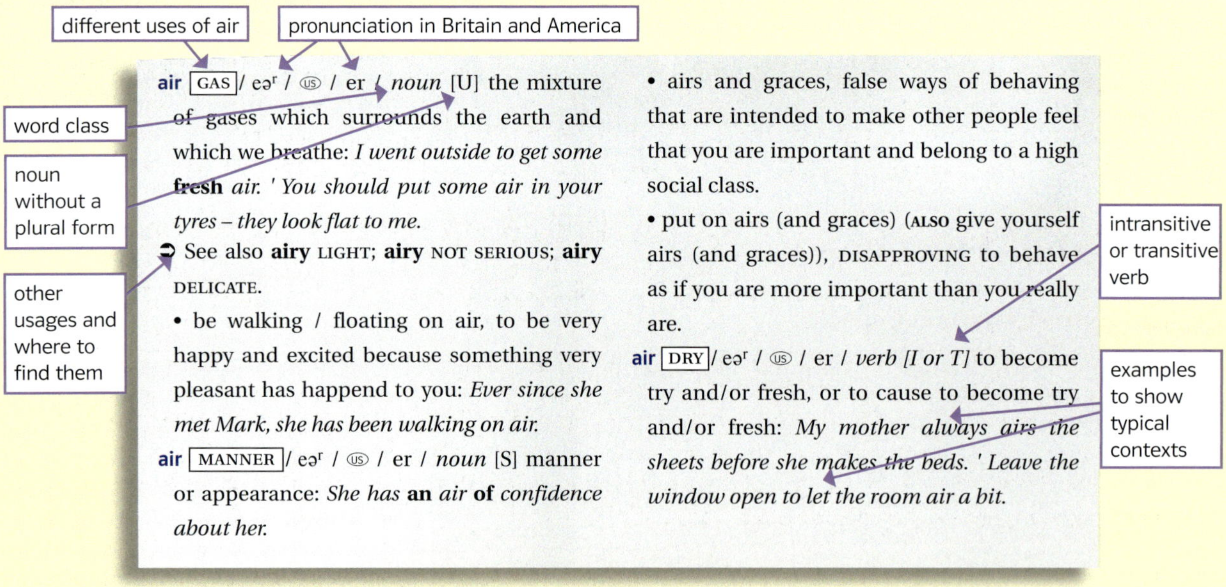

air GAS / eəʳ / US / er / *noun* [U] the mixture of gases which surrounds the earth and which we breathe: *I went outside to get some* **fresh** *air. ' You should put some air in your tyres – they look flat to me.*
➲ See also **airy** LIGHT; **airy** NOT SERIOUS; **airy** DELICATE.
• be walking / floating on air, to be very happy and excited because something very pleasant has happend to you: *Ever since she met Mark, she has been walking on air.*

air MANNER / eəʳ / US / er / *noun* [S] manner or appearance: *She has* **an** *air* **of** *confidence about her.*

• airs and graces, false ways of behaving that are intended to make other people feel that you are important and belong to a high social class.
• put on airs (and graces) (ALSO give yourself airs (and graces)), DISAPPROVING to behave as if you are more important than you really are.

air DRY / eəʳ / US / er / *verb [I or T]* to become try and/or fresh, or to cause to become try and/or fresh: *My mother always airs the sheets before she makes the beds. ' Leave the window open to let the room air a bit.*

Working with films

An interesting way of dealing with a specific topic is by watching and analysing related films. A film usually tells a story, so you **can analyse the plot, setting, characters and narrative techniques** exactly the way you do with a fictional text (→ Understanding fictional texts p. 224). In addition to the content, you can analyse the **audiovisual aspects** of the film.

1 Important film genres

action • adventure • comedy • crime • drama • epic / historical • horror • musical • science fiction • war • western • fantasy • romance • melodrama

2 Choosing a film

- If you are looking for a film that deals with a specific topic, you can search on the Internet. Use a search engine or check the *International Movie Database*.

3 Analysing a film

- **Choose a scene** from the film.
- Make a **list of the types of camera shots**.
- Say what effect each shot creates, e. g. it shows a character's emotions, it includes the viewer in the scene, it shows where the action is going to take place, etc.
- If you have access to **different versions of the film**, compare the same scene in both. What similarities / differences do you notice?
- If the film is **based on a novel, short story or play**: How much of the original plot has been used in the film? Have characters been cut out / added in? Why is this the case, do you think? Compare the message of the film with that of the original text. Which do you prefer – the book or the film? Why?
- Is the **music** memorable? Does it create a particular atmosphere? What effect does the music have on the scenes?
- If you have the film on DVD, also watch the **special features** (director's commentary, interviews, cut-out scenes, trailers, etc.)
- If you have got the **film script**, compare it to the film version, concentrating on one or two scenes. What changes were made in the film?
- Choose two actors / actresses from the film. Find out about other films they acted in. Then say whether you found them suitable in their role in the film you are analysing.
- Describe the **film poster and / or film trailer**. What aspects of the film does it emphasise? Most modern films have homepages which include the poster and trailer.
- Write a **review** of the film in which you **outline the plot and the roles** played by the actors. Say whether you liked the film and would recommend it or not.
  Explain why.
- Check the Internet for online reviews and comments by people who have seen the film. Compare their evaluation with yours.

4 Camera operations

5 Important aspects of one or more film scenes

setting	contemporary / historical? • science fiction? • city / country? • exterior / interior?
characters	how many? • who? • appearance? • costumes? • body language?
story and storyline	dialogue? • interaction? • fight? • narrative structure?
camera	field size? • view? • zooming? • panning? • tracking?
light	colours? • brightness / darkness? • atmosphere?
cut	tempo? • rest? • correspondence with actions?
sound and music	voices? • atmosphere?
special effects	animation? • slow / fastmotion?

6 Presenting a film in class

- **Start by giving your audience more information** than just the title:
  - Who directed it?
  - Who acted in it?
  - Who produced it?
  - When was it made?
  - Who wrote the music?
  - Was it a success?
  - If the film is based on a literary text, say which one.
- Then briefly **introduce the setting and the characters and sum up the plot.**
- Say what is **good or bad** about the film and why you like it or not.
- **Present a scene** that has an important function in the film. The scene should enable you to say something about the characters, their relationship with each other, their role in the plot, their language and body language, the atmosphere of the film and what is typical of the way it tells its story. You should also be able to say at what point in the film it comes and what its function is.

Useful phrases

In the foreground / background there is … • The camera takes a long / medium / close-up / extreme close-up shot. • This brings us close to … / creates a distance between … • The camera position is … • The view of … is frontal / from above / below / behind. • The focus is on a … detail. • The camera zooms in / out of … • The camera pans from … to … • … is introduced in a panning shot. • The movement of … is followed in a tracking shot. • The shots follow each other quickly. / The … shot lasts for a while. This creates a / an … atmosphere. • … is shown in slow / fast motion.

Internet research

1 Subject searches and key word searches

- Browse a **subject guide or directory**, e.g. *Yahoo*, to choose a category, then a subcategory and so on, e.g. *travel* > *travel guides* > *United States* > *Las Vegas*.
- Use a **search engine**, e.g. *Google*, to look for certain key words, e.g. *history apartheid Mandela*.
- Most of the search engines use OR as a default. This means that you will get a list of sites that include any one of any of the key words you entered, e.g. you will get sites for South Wales (in Britain) as well as New South Wales (in Australia) if you enter *new south wales*.
  With most search engines you can **use + or – signs in front of certain key words** to make sure they are included or excluded from your search, e.g. *+martin +luther -king*. If you look for a certain phrase, like the title of a book, put it in **inverted commas**, e.g. *"lord of the rings"*.
- To get better results, it may help to put the **most unusual or relevant word first**.
- If you don't get many hits, check your spelling, try similar key words or use fewer words.
- If you get too many hits, be more specific and add some words.

2 Bookmarks *(Favoriten)*

- To make it easier to return to a site you like, you can add a **bookmark** either by clicking on the bookmarks *(Favoriten)* menu, by pressing Control-D *(Strg-D)* or by clicking on your right mouse button.
- If you forgot to add a bookmark, you can go back to sites you have visited during the last few sessions by using the forward or back buttons or by pressing Control-H *(Strg-H)*.

3 Evaluating your results

- Don't believe everything you read! Remember that anyone can publish anything on the Internet. **Judge the reliability** of a website before using information from it. Is it similar to *www.harvard.edu* or more like *www.aol/users/joedoe*?
- Is it a commercial website? Then it might be interested in selling something rather than giving objective information.
- Does it contain **facts or just opinions**?
- Is the **author** someone who is likely to know something about a subject, e.g. a university teacher or a journalist?
- Also check if the website has been **updated recently**, especially if you are looking for the latest news on a topic.

Projects and group work

1 Finding information

Set up an **'information centre'** in your classroom (or of your own) in which you keep a record of where to find information. Find and keep a record of:

- The name, address, email address, telephone and fax number of:
  - your local library
  - the nearest university or college library
  - your twin-town association (if your area has one)
  - the nearest newsagent or bookshop which stocks English newspapers and magazines. (Tip: Try your nearest main station.)
- The **website addresses** of search engines, schools and colleges, youth organisations, political parties, newspapers, magazines, government agencies in America and the UK.
- The names of classmates who have **contacts** (penfriends, relatives, friends, etc.) **in the English-speaking world**, and who might be willing to help you.
- The names of classmates or people in your neighbourhood who have an **English-speaking parent / parents** and who might help you. Collect **brochures** from travel agencies and tourist information bureaus. Collect material while you are on holiday (leaflets, magazines, postcards, advertisements, menus, timetables, etc.). Add information and addresses to your files when you find new material.

2 Doing a project

- Read the information you are given about the **project task** carefully.
- In your groups, **brainstorm** to find ideas about:
  - what you all already know about the topic.
  - which aspects you want to concentrate on.
  - where you can find information.
- If necessary, **decide which points are more important** (concentrate on these) and which are less important (and can possibly be left out).
- Decide **which tasks each member of the group are going to do**. Make sure the workload is divided equally.
- If not specified in the task, decide how you want to **present your material**.
  You can produce: a talk using visual aids • a video • a CD • a leaflet • a brochure • a file of written information • a written report • a poster or wall chart • a website.
- Remember to **keep a record of your sources**, i.e. where you found material, where quotes or extracts from original material were taken from, etc.

Questionnaires and surveys

1 Before doing a survey

- It is important to have a clear idea of **what kind of information** you hope to get from your survey.
- Write one or two **sentences describing your topic** and explaining why you are doing the survey. (Later you can include these sentences at the start of your questionnaire so that the people you ask (interviewees / participants) have a clear idea of what the survey is about.)
- Briefly **state what you expect the results of your survey to be** – or give alternatives.
- Decide **how many people** you want to interview and **which social groups** they should belong to. For example, is the age of participants important? Should they be male or female? Should they have a certain job or hobby?

2 The questionnaire

- The success of a survey depends largely on **how good your questions** are.
  If possible, ask an independent person to answer your questions before you carry out the survey to make sure your questions are clear.
- Decide what **type of questions** you want to ask. The most common types of questions are described in the box below.
- Your questions need not all be of the same type, but it is best not to include too many different types.
- Always keep the **aim of your survey** in mind when you are formulating questions.
- Word your questions **clearly and concisely**. Use formal language.
- **Don't ask too many questions** (between 10 and 15 is usually enough).
- Put your questions in **logical order**.
- Group questions relating to particular aspects together.
- Start off with simpler, more general questions and then go on to more detailed questions.
- Your last question can be an open-ended question.

3 Types of questions

Multiple choice questions

The interviewee chooses from given answers.

Which of the following do you own?

a) a TV ☐ *b) a DVD player* ☐
c) an MP3 player ☐ *d) a CD player* ☐

Yes / No questions

Questions that can be answered with 'Yes' or 'No'.

Do you exercise more than three times a week?

☐ *YES* ☐ *NO*

Graded questions

The interviewee has to choose to what extent they agree / disagree with, like / don't like / … something.

How often do you eat fruit or vegetables on average per day?

☐ *never*
☐ *less than three times*
☐ *more than three times*

Open-ended questions

Questions to which the interviewees must give their own answer.
The questions usually begin with a question word: who, what, when, where, why or how.

How, in your opinion, could the recycling system in your area be improved?

____

4 Presenting the results

- When you summarise and present your results, always **think of your aims**, for example:
  - proving a certain expectation right or wrong
  - comparing the answers of different groups
  - giving the majority opinion
  - presenting the most surprising results.
- Never forget to say **how many and what kind of people took part** in your survey! Most answers can be turned into statistics straight away, so you can present your statistics as percentages and use diagrams to support the presentation visually.

Example:

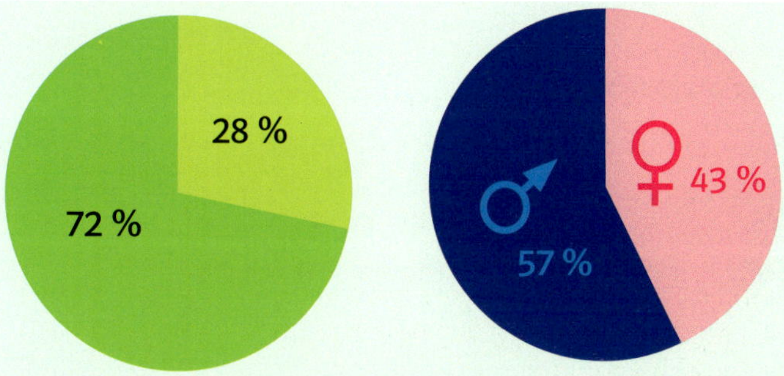

Of all the pupils in the tenth form at our school 72 % have got their own computer, 57% of them are boys.

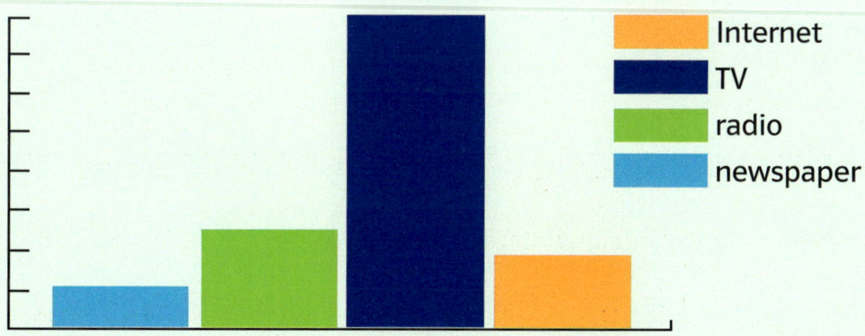

Popular sources of information for tenth graders

- Ratings may require a different **form of presentation**, e.g.:
  When asked about the importance of foreign languages, 26 out of 30 people answered that foreign languages were generally very important to them, 3 out of 30 thought foreign languages were only important in some situations, and only one person said they were not important at all.
- Presenting **answers to open-ended questions**, you may be able to make a top three, five or ten using similar answers or you may quote the most surprising ones, e.g.:
  The top three breakfast favourites in our class are: 1. rolls 2. cereals 3. jam.

Presentation

1 Preparation

Gather material on your topic:
- Brainstorm to find ideas on the topic and make a word web.
- Find information from relevant sources (library, school books, the Internet, newspapers, etc.)

Choose which main points you want to talk about.
Make a set of prompt cards in English, which you can look at during your talk to remind you of what you want to say (→ prompt cards p. 265).
- Write down the key words, phrases and vocabulary which you will need.
- Note down any examples or quotations.
- Note down any visual aids (OHPs, photographs, posters, flip charts, etc.) which you plan to use.

Arrange your prompt cards in logical order. You could present points:
- in terms of importance, from the most to the least important (or vice versa)
- chronologically
- with all those in favour first, followed by all those against.

Make a prompt card for your introduction (→ card 1 p. 265). Catch the listeners' attention with:
- an interesting question or fact
- a quote or joke
- a picture or cartoon on an OHP transparency.

Make a prompt card for your conclusion (→ card 7 p. 265):
- Note the point(s) you want to emphasise.
- Write down key words and phrases.
- Make a note of a final quotation or an example you wish to use.

2 Giving a talk or presentation

- **Practise your talk or presentation** out loud, preferably in front of a mirror, or ask a friend/relative to listen to you!
- **Speak slowly and clearly!**
- Use short, clear sentences.
- **Vary your voice** so that you don't sound boring. For example, emphasise particularly important points by speaking a little more loudly.
- **Look at your audience** as often as possible. Don't look at your prompt cards all the time.
- Try not to make distracting movements such as waving your hands, etc.
- **Smile!** (But don't laugh nervously!)
- **Start by introducing yourself** (if necessary) and your topic. **Finish by thanking** your audience for listening. Ask if anyone has any questions.

3 A market place

- **Form groups** and **prepare** your product.
- Choose a **speaker** for your group.
- **Present** your product in the classroom. Your classmates walk around and look at the different products. The **speaker** presents the product to the people who pass by and answers their questions.
- **Discuss** the products in class.

4 A gallery walk

- **Prepare** your product (on your own or in a group).
- Prepare an **evaluation sheet** in class.
- **Present** your product in the classroom and give the evaluation sheets to your classmates.
- Your **classmates** walk around, look at the different products and **fill in the evaluation sheet**.
- **Discuss** the results of the evaluation sheets in class.

5 Prompt cards

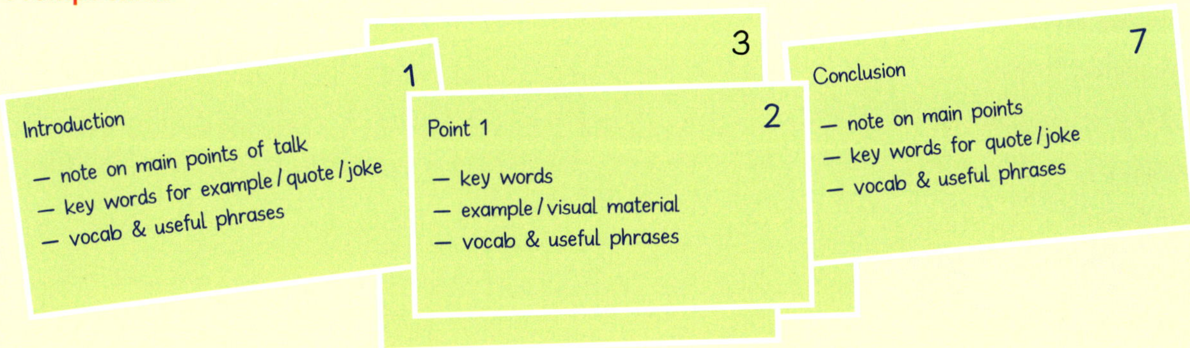

Useful phrases

Good morning / afternoon, my name is … • Today I'm going to talk about … • The subject of my talk today is … • Can everyone hear me alright? • Can everyone see the board / screen / etc.? • I'd like to begin by (+ *-ing form*) … • Let me start by saying a few words about … • Let me give you an example. • As you can see on the chart / graph / cartoon … • I'd like to finish / conclude by (+ *-ing form*) … • Let me finish by (+ *-ing form*) … • Finally … • Thank you very much for your attention. • I hope you all enjoyed my talk. • I'd be happy to answer any questions

Grammar files

Tenses

Simple present

Positive sentences	Negative sentences	Questions
I play football. You play football. He/she/it plays football. We play football. You play football. They play football.	I don't play football. You don't play football. He/she/it doesn't play football. We don't play football. You don't play football. They don't play football.	Do I play football? Do you play football? Does he/she/it play football? Do we play football? Do you play football? Do they play football? Questions with question word: Why do I play football? Why do you play football? Why does he/she/it play football? Why do we play football? Why do you play football? Why do they play football?
! Be careful with these verbs: be, have		

Examples of typical use:

1. Facts and general statements: Cats eat mice.
2. Everyday activities or habits: Our team plays football on Sundays.
   Tense markers: always, often, sometimes, never, usually, every day/week/month/year, on Mondays/…, at 7 o'clock/…
3. A set sequence of events or actions: The two knights fight, the Queen screams, and then the King saves her.
4. For scheduled future events with an adverbial phrase of time: The train leaves at 14:35.

Present progressive

Positive sentences	Negative sentences	Questions
I am singing.	I'm not singing.	Am I singing?
You are singing.	You aren't singing.	Are you singing?
He/she/it is singing.	He/she/it isn't singing.	Is he/she/it singing?
We are singing.	We aren't singing.	Are we singing?
You are singing.	You aren't singing.	Are you singing?
They are singing.	They aren't singing.	Are they singing?

Positive sentences	Negative sentences	Questions
		Questions with question word: What am I singing? What are you singing? What is he/she/it singing? What are we singing? What are you singing? What are they singing?

! Some verbs are never used in the progressive form, especially those which express feelings or belief: believe, love, hate, seem, have (in the sense of own), can, mean, want to, feel, notice, realise

Examples of typical use:

1. An activity that is going on right now and will continue for a certain limited or temporary period of time: Greg is cooking dinner (now).
   Tense markers: now, just now, at the moment
2. Planned future events with an adverbial phrase of time: They are visiting us in three weeks.

Simple past

Positive sentences	Negative sentences	Questions
I played football. You played football. He/she/it played football. We played football. You played football. They played football.	I didn't play football. You didn't play football. He/she/it didn't play football. We didn't play football. You didn't play football. They didn't play football.	Did I play football? Did you play football? Did he/she/it play football? Did we play football? Did you play football? Did they play football? Questions with question word: Why did I play football? Why did you play football? Why did he/she/it play football? Why did we play football? Why did you play football? Why did they play football?

! Be careful with irregular verbs

Examples of typical use:

1. For activities that began and ended at a specific time in the past: They returned from Canada a week ago.
   Tense markers: yesterday, ago, last week/month/year, in 2007/…, on Tuesday/…
2. For a series of events in the past as in a story, often called the 'narrative past':
   As the train left the station, Helen looked around the compartment. There was no one else in sight. She took out the letter and started to read it.

Past progressive

Positive sentences	Negative sentences	Questions
I was singing. You were singing. He/she/it was singing. We were singing. You were singing. They were singing.	I wasn't singing. You weren't singing. He/she/it wasn't singing. We weren't singing. You weren't singing. They weren't singing.	Was I singing? Were you singing? Was he/she/it singing? Were we singing? Were you singing? Were they singing? Questions with question word: What was I singing? What were you singing? What was he/she/it singing? What were we singing? What were you singing? What were they singing?

Examples of typical use:

1. An activity in the past that was already in progress when something else happened:
   They were cleaning the house when the guests arrived.
2. Several activities or events that were happening at the same time in the past:
   While Patty was mowing the lawn, Sid was cleaning the windows.

Present perfect simple

Positive sentences	Negative sentences	Questions
I have finished. You have finished. He/she/it has finished. We have finished. You have finished. They have finished.	I haven't finished. You haven't finished. He/she/it hasn't finished. We haven't finished. You haven't finished. They haven't finished.	Have I finished? Have you finished? Has he/she/it finished? Have we finished? Have you finished? Have they finished? Questions with question word: What have I finished? What have you finished? What has he/she/it finished? What have we finished? What have you finished? What have they finished?

! Be careful with irregular verbs
With the present perfect simple the result of the action is usually more important than the action itself.
Never use the present perfect with adverbs of past time, e.g. yesterday, last week, three years ago, in 2007.

Examples of typical use:

1. Activities that happened recently, and whose effects are still felt in the present:
   They have moved to Stratford and they are still living there.

2. With certain adverbs: just, so far, ever, never, recently, lately, today, this week, already, (not) yet
   The test results have just arrived. – I have had good marks so far this year. – Have you ever been to New York?

3. With for and since, for activities that started in the past and are continuing:
   I haven't eaten chocolate for three weeks! – I haven't seen Melanie since 2008.

Present perfect progressive

Positive sentences	Negative sentences	Questions
I have been waiting. You have been waiting. He/she/it has been waiting. We have been waiting. You have been waiting. They have been waiting.	I haven't been waiting. You haven't been waiting. He/she/it hasn't been waiting. We haven't been waiting. You haven't been waiting. They haven't been waiting.	Have I been waiting? Have you been waiting? Has he/she/it been waiting? Have we been waiting? Have you been waiting? Have they been waiting? Questions with question word: Why have I been waiting? Why have you been waiting? Why has he/she/it been waiting? Why have we been waiting? Why have you been waiting? Why have they been waiting?

Examples of typical use:

1. Activities that have either been going on either continuously or at intervals up to the present, often with adverbials of time such as all day, for a week, etc.: We have been looking for a camping site all day.

2. With no mention of time, the activity has taken place very recently and the result is clearly visible:
   It has been raining.

Past perfect simple

Positive sentences	Negative sentences	Questions
I had finished. You had finished. He/she/it had finished. We had finished. You had finished. They had finished.	I hadn't finished. You hadn't finished. He/she/it hadn't finished. We hadn't finished. You hadn't finished. They hadn't finished.	Had I finished? Had you finished? Had he/she/it finished? Had we finished? Had you finished? Had they finished?

Positive sentences	Negative sentences	Questions
		Questions with question word: What had I finished? What had you finished? What had he/she/it finished? What had we finished? What had you finished? What had they finished?
! Be careful with irregular verbs		

Examples of typical use:

1. An activity that happened before another activity in the past, showing the connection between the two activities:
   When we arrived at the station, the train had already left.
   After I had watched the news, I decided to go out.

2. In reported speech, when the original statement is in the past or present perfect:
   Jane said that she had forgotten to do her homework.

Past perfect progressive

Positive sentences	Negative sentences	Questions
I had been waiting. You had been waiting. He/she/it had been waiting. We had been waiting. You had been waiting. They had been waiting.	I hadn't been waiting. You hadn't been waiting. He/she/it hadn't been waiting. We hadn't been waiting. You hadn't been waiting. They hadn't been waiting.	Had I been waiting? Had you been waiting? Had he/she/it been waiting? Had we been waiting? Had you been waiting? Had they been waiting? Questions with question word: Why had I been waiting? Why had you been waiting? Why had he/she/it been waiting? Why had we been waiting? Why had you been waiting? Why had they been waiting?

Examples of typical use:

1. A past activity that occurred before another where there is a direct relation to the activity that followed:
   He was tired because he had been working so hard.

2. In reported speech, when the original statement is in the present perfect progressive:
   He said that he had been working hard.

Going to-future

Positive sentences	Negative sentences	Questions
I am going to leave early. You are going to leave early. He/she/it is going to leave early. We are going to leave early You are going to leave early. They are going to leave early.	I'm not going to leave early. You're not going to leave early. He/she/it's not going to leave early. We're not going to leave early. You're not going to leave early. They're not going to leave early.	Am I going to leave early? Are you going to leave early? Is he/she/it going to leave early? Are we going to leave early? Are you going to leave early? Are they going to leave early?

Examples of typical use:

1. For an action in the future that has already been planned or prepared:
   They're going to buy Tom a new computer for his birthday.
2. For a prediction about the future, when you can see that something is about to happen:
   Look at those clouds. It's going to rain soon.

Future simple (will-future)

Positive sentences	Negative sentences	Questions
I will play football. You will play football. He/she/it will play football. We will play football. You will play football. They will play football.	I won't play football. You won't play football. He/she/it won't play football. We won't play football. You won't play football. They won't play football.	Will I play football? Will you play football? Will he/she/it play football? Will we play football? Will you play football? Will they play football? Questions with question word: Why will I play football? Why will you play football? Why will he/she/it play football? Why will we play football? Why will you play football? Why will they play football?

! English will = German werden
English want = German wollen

Examples of typical use:

1. Things that are likely to happen at a defined or undefined time in the future:
   You'll be a great movie star some day.
2. For forecasts, such as the weather forecast: On Saturday, there will be rain for most of the day.
3. In 'if'-clauses Type 1 – future situations that are probable/possible:
   If the weather is fine, I'll play football.

Future progressive

Positive sentences	Negative sentences	Questions
I will be singing. You will be singing. He/she/it will be singing. We will be singing. You will be singing. They will be singing.	I won't be singing. You won't be singing. He/she/it won't be singing. We won't be singing. You won't be singing. They won't be singing.	Will I be singing? Will you be singing? Will he/she/it be singing? Will we be singing? Will you be singing? Will they be singing? Questions with question word: What will I be singing? What will you be singing? What will he/she/it be singing? What will we be singing? What will you be singing? What will they be singing?

Example of typical use:

Events – often planned – that will be going on at a certain time in the future when another event occurs:
You will be sleeping by the time I get home.

Future perfect simple

Positive sentences	Negative sentences	Questions
I will have finished. You will have finished. He/she/it will have finished. We will have finished. You will have finished. They will have finished.	I won't have finished. You won't have finished. He/she/it won't have finished. We won't have finished. You won't have finished. They won't have finished.	Will I have finished? Will you have finished? Will he/she/it have finished? Will we have finished? Will you have finished? Will they have finished? Questions with question word: When will I have finished? When will you have finished? When will he/she/it have finished? When will we have finished? When will you have finished? When will they have finished?
! Be careful with irregular verbs		

Example of typical use:

Future activities that take place before other future activities to show a relation between them. The simple present is used for the other activities:
Joanna will have finished the college course by the time she is 20.

Future perfect progressive

Positive sentences	Negative sentences	Questions
I will have been waiting. You will have been waiting. He/she/it will have been waiting. We will have been waiting. You will have been waiting. They will have been waiting.	I won't have been waiting. You won't have been waiting. He/she/it won't have been waiting. We won't have been waiting. You won't have been waiting. They won't have been waiting.	Will I have been waiting? Will you have been waiting? Will he/she/it have been waiting? Will we have been waiting? Will you have been waiting? Will they have been waiting?

Example of typical use:

Used in the same way as the future perfect simple but placing more emphasis on the activity:
They will have been studying English for eight years before they take the exam.

Conditional I

Positive sentences	Negative sentences	Questions
I would play football. You would play football. He/she/it would play football. We would play football. You would play football. They would play football.	I wouldn't play football. You wouldn't play football. He/she/it wouldn't play football. We wouldn't play football. You wouldn't play football. They wouldn't play football.	Would I play football? Would you play football? Would he/she/it play football? Would we play football? Would you play football? Would they play football? Questions with question word: Why would I play football? Why would you play football? Why would he/she/it play football? Why would we play football? Why would you play football? Why would they play football?

Examples of typical use:

1. For suggestions, polite questions and requests:
   Which ring would you take? – Well, I would take that ring.
   Would you like a drink?
   Would you help me, please?
2. In 'if'-clauses Type 2 – future situations that are improbable/unlikely:
   If you studied hard, you would pass the exam.

Conditional II

Positive sentences	Negative sentences	Questions
I would have helped. You would have helped. He/she/it would have helped. We would have helped. You would have helped. They would have helped.	I wouldn't have helped. You wouldn't have helped. He/she/it wouldn't have helped. We wouldn't have helped. You wouldn't have helped. They wouldn't have helped.	Would I have helped? Would you have helped? Would he/she/it have helped? Would we have helped? Would you have helped? Would they have helped? Questions with question word: Why would I have helped? Why would you have helped? Why would he/she/it have helped? Why would we have helped? Why would you have helped? Why would they have helped?
! Be careful with irregular verbs		

Example of typical use:

In 'if'-clauses Type 3 – past situations that are unreal/impossible/hypothetical:
If you had studied hard, you would have passed the exam.

If-clauses

There are three main types of 'if'-clauses (or conditional sentences) in English. They are basically used in the same way as conditional sentences in German. You can put the 'if'-clause at the beginning or at the end of the sentence.

1. Type 1 - Future situations (probable/possible):

a.	'if'-clause: simple present – main clause: 'will'-future If you study hard, you will pass the exam. Wenn du fleißig lernst, wirst du die Prüfung bestehen.
b.	'if'–clause: present perfect – main clause: 'will'- future If you have studied hard, you will pass the exam. Wenn du fleißig gelernt hast, wirst du die Prüfung bestehen.
c.	'if'-clause: simple present – main clause: can + infinitive If you study hard, you can pass the exam. Wenn du fleißig lernst, kannst du die Prüfung bestehen.
d.	'if'-clause: simple present – main clause: might + infinitive If you study hard, you might pass the exam. Wenn du fleißig lernst, wirst du eventuell die Prüfung bestehen.

2. Type 2 – Future situations (improbable/unlikely)

a.	'if'-clause: simple past – main clause: conditional I (would + infinitive) If you studied hard, you would pass the exam. Wenn du fleißig lernen würdest, würdest du die Prüfung bestehen.
b.	'if'-clause: simple past – main clause: could + infinitive If you studied hard, you could pass the exam. Wenn du fleißig lernen würdest, könntest du die Prüfung bestehen.

3. Type 3 – Past situations (unreal/impossible/hypothetical)

a.	'if'-clause: past perfect – main clause: conditional II (would + have + past participle) If you had studied hard, you would have passed the exam. Wenn du fleißig gelernt hättest, hättest du die Prüfung bestanden.
b.	'if'-clause: past perfect – main clause: could + have + past participle If you had studied hard, you could have passed the exam. Wenn du fleißig gelernt hättest, hättest du die Prüfung bestehen können.
c.	'if'-clause: past perfect – main clause: might + have + past participle If you had studied hard, you might have passed the exam. Wenn du fleißig gelernt hättest, hättest du eventuell die Prüfung bestanden.

! Exceptions to the rules:

1. The present tense is used in both clauses in general statements and for repeated activities or habits:
   If plants don't get enough water, they die. – If she has time, she goes to the fitness club.
2. For recommendations and advice use 'were' in the 'if'-clause and conditional I in the main clause:
   If I were you, I would study a bit harder.
3. 'If' can be left out when the order of the verb and subject are reversed:
   Had I studied harder, I would have passed the exam.

! Frequently made mistakes:

1. Be careful with commas. If you start with an 'if'-clause, use a comma. Don't use a comma if you start with the main clause:
   If you study hard, you will pass the exam.
   You will pass the exam if you study hard.
2. Don't use 'will' in the 'if'-clause, except to express willingness:
   They can come to Britain if they'll work.
3. Don't use 'would' in the 'if'-clause except when you are making a polite request:
   I would be grateful if you would hand in your homework on time in future.

The passive

The passive is often used when the action is more important than who or what performed it. The passive is frequently used in scientific and technical writing. The passive can be formed with or without an 'agent'. The 'agent' is the person or thing that causes an action to occur.

Form the passive using a form of 'to be' + past participle **(+ by + agent)**

Bank robbers often steal money.

Money is often stolen **by bank robbers**.

Simple present	Present progressive
I am invited to the party. You are invited to the party. He/she/it is invited to the party. We are invited to the party. You are invited to the party. They are invited to the party.	I am being terrorised by the neighbours. You are being terrorised by the neighbours. He/she/it is being terrorised by the neighbours. We are being terrorised by the neighbours. You are being terrorised by the neighbours. They are being terrorised by the neighbours.
Simple Past	**Past progressive**
I was invited to the party. You were invited to the party. He/she/it was invited to the party. We were invited to the party. You were invited to the party. They were invited to the party.	I was being terrorised by the neighbours. You were being terrorised by the neighbours. He/she/it was being terrorised by the neighbours. We were being terrorised by the neighbours. You were being terrorised by the neighbours. They were being terrorised by the neighbours.
Present perfect	**Modal verbs**
I have been invited to the party. You have been invited to the party. He/she/it has been invited to the party. We have been invited to the party. You have been invited to the party. They have been invited to the party.	I can be found in the office. You must be informed. He/she/it mustn't be informed. We needn't be informed. You ought to be informed. They should be informed.
Future	**Future perfect**
I will be invited to the party. You will be invited to the party. He/she/it will be invited to the party. We will be invited to the party. You will be invited to the party. They will be invited to the party.	I will have been invited to the party. You will have been invited to the party. He/she/it will have been invited to the party. We will have been invited to the party. You will have been invited to the party. They will have been invited to the party.
! Be careful with irregular verbs	

Relative clauses

Relative clauses are used to describe people or things. A relative clause usually begins with a relative pronoun.

Relative pronoun	refers to
who	people (subject or object)
whom	people (object), formal English
which	things
that	people or things (subject or object)
whose	possessions

1. Defining relative clauses:
A defining relative clause is important for the meaning of the sentence. Without the relative clause the sentence would not make sense. Defining relative clauses are not set off from the rest of the sentence by commas:
The house that/which we live in is very old.
This is the woman who(m) I saw yesterday.
This is the boy whose bike was stolen.

The pronoun 'that, which, who(m)' can be left out if the pronoun is the object of the relative clause. This type of relative clause is known as 'contact' clause:
The house we live in is very old.
This is the woman I saw yesterday.

2. Non-defining relative clauses:
In non-defining relative clauses the information is additional descriptive information. The sentence is clear even without a relative clause. These relative clauses are separated with commas:
My grandmother, who will be 85 in December, walks her dog every morning.

Adjectives

Adjectives describe people and things: the tall man – bright lights

1. The comparison of adjectives

Positive form	Comparative form	Superlative form
cold	colder	the coldest
hot	hotter	the hottest
funny	funnier	the funniest
modern	more modern	the most modern

! Remember the irregular forms:
good – better – the best
much – more– the most
bad – worse – the worst
far – further – the furthest

2. Making comparisons:
Use more/-er than, not as ... as and as ... as to make comparisons:
The black car is more modern than the red car.
The blue car is newer than the red car.
The red car is not as new as the blue one.
The white car is as new as the blue one.

3. Adjectives used as collective nouns:
Adjectives can be used as collective nouns. In such cases, the + adjective refers to a particular group of people as a whole:
We raised money for the blind.
The very young and the very old are particularly at risk.

4. Participles as adjectives:
The present participle (-ing form) and past participle of verbs can often be used as adjectives:
an interesting book
the finished report

5. Verbs followed by adjectives:
Verbs are usually followed by adverbs, however some verbs are followed by adjectives:

to be	Sally was tired.
to become	Anne became ill.
to feel	Thomas felt happy.
to get	The child got dirty.
to look	Mary looks sad.
to seem	Her new boyfriend seems very nice.

Adverbs

Adverbs are formed by adding -ly/-ily to an adjective.

Adjective	Adverb
safe happy real reasonable	safely happily really reasonably
! Remember the irregular forms:	good – well fast – fast hard – hard

1. Adverbs which describe actions (verbs): He walked quickly.
   She spoke slowly.
2. Adverbs before other adjectives: This is an extremely good essay.
3. Adverbs before other adverbs: He was driving incredibly fast.
4. Adverbs before past participles: Credit cards are frequently accepted.
5. The comparison of adverbs:

Positive form	Comparative form	Superlative form
fluently	more fluently	the most fluently
! Remember the irregular forms:	well – better – the best badly – worse – the worst fast – faster – the fastest	

6. Some useful adverbs: always, usually, often, frequently, sometimes, seldom, rarely, never, recently, soon, lately, in the past, in the future, largely, for the most part, partly, probably, possibly, hardly, definitely, obviously, clearly, basically, consequently, as a result

Question tags

A question tag is added to the end of a sentence turning it into a question. In German you use expressions like '…, nicht wahr?' and '…, oder?' in a similar way.

1. If the statement is positive, the questions tag is negative:
   He likes chocolate, doesn't he?
2. If the statement is negative, the question tag is positive:
   He doesn't like chocolate, does he?
3. The subject of the verb is the same in the statement and in the question tag:
   He likes chocolate, doesn't he?
4. If the statement is in the simple present or simple past tense, the question tag uses 'do/don't' or 'did/didn't':
   He likes chocolate, doesn't he?
   He went to England, didn't he?
5. If the statement uses an auxiliary verb (to be, to have, will, etc.) or a modal (can, must, etc.), use the modal or auxiliary in the same tense in the tag:
   Tom is here, isn't he?
   Roger has bought a new car, hasn't he?
   Jill will be at the party, won't she?
   You can speak English, can't you?

Modal auxiliaries

1. Will/would/can/could/may:

Asking someone to do something: Will/Would/Can/Could you do me a favour?
Asking for permission/giving permission: May I use your phone? – Yes, of course, you may.
Talking about abilities: She can speak English.

2. Must/mustn't/needn't:

Instructing someone to do something or not to do something: You must wear a safety helmet. You mustn't smoke in the office.
Talking about a necessity or duty: I must finish the project by Friday. You needn't pay in advance.

3. May/might/could/must/will:

Expressing a possibility or probability: It may/might/could/will rain. You must be Mr Jones.
Making a suggestion: We could go to that new Spanish restaurant.

4. Should/ought to/shouldn't/ought not to:

Giving advice: You should/ought to use a dictionary. You shouldn't arrive late for the interview.

5. Modal auxiliaries only have a present and/or past tense form. For other tenses substitutes are used:

Modal auxiliary	Substitutes	Examples
can/could	be able to	He won't be able to lift the piano.
may/mustn't	be allowed to not be allowed to	We were allowed to visit the church. We weren't allowed to see the pope.
must/needn't	have to not have to	The Millers will have to sell their house. We didn't have to wait long.

-ing forms

An -ing form can be either a present participle or a gerund.

The present participle

1. The present participle is used in the progressive tenses (present progressive, past progressive, etc.):
   Mary is playing the guitar. – The plane was flying at a height of 10,000 metres.
2. The present participle can be used as an adjective: the winning party – a growing child
3. The present participle can be used to shorten clauses, often after a conjunction, e.g: after, while, before, when
   I was riding my bike to work when I met her. → While riding/Riding my bike to work, I met her.
   I saw a woman who was wearing a silly hat. → I saw a woman wearing a silly hat.
   After we had eaten a burger, we went home. → After eating a burger, we went home.
   Read the text before you answer the questions. → Read the text before answering the questions.
   Although I felt tired, I couldn't sleep. → Although feeling tired, I couldn't sleep.

The gerund

1. The gerund is used after prepositions: You're very good at speaking English.
2. The gerund is often used after certain verbs: like, hate, enjoy, love, mind, prefer
   I don't mind watching TV but I prefer reading and I also enjoy playing computer games.
3. The gerund can be used as a noun: Laughing is good for you. – Studying is very important.
4. Some verbs have the construction verb + preposition + gerund:
   to be afraid of, to look forward to, to feel like, to talk about, to insist on, to decide against, to think about/of, to succeed in, to apologise for
   I'm afraid of flying.
5. When the following expressions are followed by a verb, use the gerund:
   There's no point in waiting any longer.
   It's not worth going to see the new James Bond film.
   A waste of money/time: It's a waste of time talking to you.
   To spend/waste/time/money: He spent all his money playing on the fruit machines.

Reported speech

Reported speech (or indirect speech) is used to report what someone has said without quoting them.

1. Start the reported speech with a reporting verb:

   a. Statements: say (that), tell sb. (that), answer, mention, explain, reply, etc.
   "I'm tired." → She says (that) she's tired.

   b. Questions: ask, want to know
   "Are you hungry?" → She asks me if I'm hungry.
   "Where do you go to school?" → She wants to know where I go to school.

   c. Commands: tell sb. to + infinitive
   "Leave me alone!" → She told me to leave her alone.

2. If the reporting verb is in the present, present perfect or future tense, the tense stays the same:
"Watching TV is bad for your eyes". → Mr Jones says watching TV is bad for our eyes.
→ Mr Jones has said watching TV is bad for our eyes.
→ Mr Jones will say watching TV is bad for our eyes.

3. If the reporting verb is in the past tense, the tense of the reported speech changes:

simple present "I walk the dog every day."	→	simple past She said she walked the dog every day.
present progressive "I'm walking the dog."	→	past progressive She said she was walking the dog.
simple past "I walked the dog last night."	→	past perfect She said she had walked the dog last night.
past progressive "I was walking the dog."	→	past perfect progressive She said she had been walking the dog.
present perfect "I have walked the dog."	→	past perfect She said she had walked the dog.
present perfect progressive "I have been walking the dog."	→	past perfect progressive She said she had been walking the dog.
past perfect "I had walked the dog."	→	past perfect She said she had walked the dog.
past perfect progressive "I had been walking the dog."	→	past perfect progressive She said she had been walking the dog.
will future "I will walk the dog every day."	→	conditional I She said she would walk the dog every day.

4. Questions follow the same tense changes as statements:
"Where did you park the car?" → The policeman asked the man where he had parked the car.

5. Some adverbs of time also change in reported speech, for example:

now	→	then
yesterday	→	the day before/the previous day
here	→	there
last year	→	the year before/the previous year
today	→	that day
tomorrow	→	the next day

6. Statements involving truths and facts do not have to change:
"Cats eat mice". → The teacher said that cats eat mice.

Videotraining: Englische Aussprache

Perfekte englische Aussprache leicht gemacht: Mit dem Lernprogramm zur englischen Lautschrift können Sie alle Laute einüben. Wählen Sie einfach in der Navigation rechts den entsprechenden Reiter (*Vowels* oder *Consonants*) aus und dann klicken Sie auf das gewünschte phonetische Symbol. Sprechen Sie die Wörter laut nach.
Unter www.klett.de geben Sie einfach den Online-Link 808201-1000 ein. Von dort aus können Sie die Webanwendung online starten.

Abkürzungen

etw. = etwas	sb. = somebody	BE = britisches Englisch
jmdm = jemandem	coll. = umgangssprachlich	AE = amerikanisches Englisch
jmdn = jemanden	sg = Singular	fml = formal
sth. = something	pl = Plural	infml = informal

Pronunciation

In this book the following phonetic symbols are used:

Consonants		Vowels		Diphthongs	Additional symbols
[ŋ] morning	[ʃ] she	[ɑː] father	[i] happy	[aɪ] I, my	[ˈ] Primary stress on the following syllable
[r] red	[tʃ] lunch	[ʌ] but	[iː] teacher, she	[aʊ] now, house	[ˌ] Secondary stress on the following syllable
[s] this	[ð] the	[e] pen	[ɒ] got	[eə] there, pair	[‿] Link between two words
[z] is	[θ] thanks	[ə] a sister	[ɔː] ball	[eɪ] name, they	[x] Pronounced like the German acht
[ʒ] television	[v] video	[ɜː] girl	[ʊ] book	[ɪə] here, idea	
[dʒ] page	[w] wow, one	[æ] flat	[u] January	[ɔɪ] boy	
		[ɪ] it	[uː] too, two	[əʊ] hello	
				[ʊə] sure	

All other letters are pronounced roughly the way they are written, e.g [b], [j], [l] etc.

The page numbers refer to the first occurrence of the word.

A

to abandon [əˈbændən] aufgeben 188

to abolish [əˈbɒlɪʃ] abschaffen 144

to accelerate [əkˈseləreɪt] beschleunigen 61

access [ˈækses] Zugang 177

accessible [əkˈsesəbl] zugänglich, befahrbar 18

accommodation [əˌkɒməˈdeɪʃn] Unterbringung 60

accomplishment [əˈkʌmplɪʃmənt] Leistung 66

to account for [əˈkaʊnt fɔː] ausmachen, (eine Anzahl) stellen 14

accusation [ˌækjʊˈzeɪʃn] Anschuldigung 54

to achieve sth. [əˈtʃiːv] etw. erreichen 25

to acknowledge [əkˈnɒlɪdʒ] anerkennen 55

to act on sth. [ˈækt‿ɒn ˌsʌmθɪŋ] auf etw. reagieren 64

addictive [əˈdɪktɪv] süchtig machend 65

to adjust [əˈdʒʌst] anpassen, sich anpassen 196

admiration [ˌædmɪˈreɪʃn] Bewundering 106

advance [ədˈvɑːns] Fortschritt, Vorstoß 74

to advance [ədˈvɑːns] fortführen, vorangehen 72

advantage [ədˈvɑːntɪdʒ] Vorteil, Vorzug 42

adviser [ədˈvaɪzə] Ratgeber(in) 12

advocate [ˈædvəkət] Befürworter(in) 158

aerospace [ˈeərəʊspeɪs] Luft- und Raumfahrt 82

to affect [əˈfekt] Einfluss nehmen auf 150

affection [əˈfekʃn] Zuneigung 48

affiliation [əˌfɪlɪˈeɪʃn] Verbindung, Zugehörigkeit 156

to afford sth. [əˈfɔːd] sich etw. leisten können 60

affordable [əˈfɔːdəbl] bezahlbar 55

agenda [əˈdʒendə] Tagesordnung 83

agility [ə'dʒɪlətɪ] Gewandtheit 181
agriculture ['ægrɪkʌltʃə] Landwirtschaft 177
aid [eɪd] Hilfe 54
to aid [eɪd] helfen, unterstützen 42
to aim at ['eɪm‿ət] zielen auf 14
air-freighted ['eəˌfreɪtɪd] per Luftfracht 160
allegedly [ə'ledʒədlɪ] angeblich 122
alongside [əˌlɒŋ'saɪd] neben 118
ambitious [æm'bɪʃəs] ehrgeizig 57
to announce [ə'naʊns] ankündigen, verkünden 31
to anticipate [æn'tɪsɪpeɪt] erwarten 14
anxiety [æŋˌzaɪətɪ] Angst 114
to apologise [ə'pɒlədʒaɪz] sich entschuldigen 40
appeal [ə'pi:l] Anziehung(skraft), Anreiz 10
appearance [ə'pɪərəns] Aussehen 57
applicant ['æplɪkənt] Bewerber(in) 31
application [ˌæplɪ'keɪʃn] Anwendung 177
to apply to sb. [ə'plaɪ tə ˌsʌmbədɪ] für jdn gelten 14
to appoint [ə'pɔɪnt] ernennen, verpflichten 46
to appreciate [ə'prɪ:ʃɪeɪt] schätzen, zu schätzen wissen 66
appreciation [əˌpri:ʃɪ'eɪʃn] Wertschätzung 59
apprenticeship [ə'prentɪʃɪp] Berufsausbildung, Lehre 62
approach [ə'prəʊtʃ] Haltung, Herangehensweise, Ansatz 80
approval [ə'pru:vl] Billigung, Zustimmung, Beifall 74
to approve [ə'pru:v] genehmigen, billigen 119
to arise [ə'raɪz] anfallen 183
to ascend [ə'send] aufsteigen 32
aspirational [ˌæspɪ'reɪʃənl] erstrebenswert 155
to aspire [ə'spaɪə] anstreben 43
to assault [ə'sɒlt] angreifen 122
to assemble [ə'sembl] zusammenstellen 58
assembly [ə'semblɪ] Versammlung, Rat 45
to assess [ə'ses] beurteilen 60
asset ['æset] Vermögen(swerte) 146
assumption [ə'sʌmpʃn] Annahme 106
astonishing [ə'stɒnɪʃɪŋ] erstaunlich 64
at one's disposal [ət wʌnz dɪ'spəʊzl] zur Verfügung 155
attainable [ə'teɪnəbl] erreichbar 25
attitude ['ætɪtju:d] Haltung 44
authoritarian [ˌɔ:θɒrɪ'teərɪən] autoritär 34
aware [ə'weə] bewusst 82
awareness [ə'weənəs] Bewusstsein 110
awkward ['ɔ:kwəd] seltsam 160

B

to back [bæk] unterstützen 176
backdrop ['bækdrɒp] Hintergrund 10
ball bearing [ˌbɔ:l'beərɪŋ] Kugellager 89
to banish ['bænɪʃ] verbannen 175
barrier ['bærɪə] Hindernis 10
to battle ['bætl] für/um etw. kämpfen 62
to bear in mind [ˌbeər‿ɪn 'maɪnd] beachten 91
to be exposed to sth. [bɪ‿ɪk'spəʊzd tə] etw. ausgesetzt sein 124
behaviour [bɪ'heɪvjə] Verhalten 154
to be held responsible for [bɪ ˌheld rɪ'spɒnsəbl fə] verantwortlich gemacht werden für 108
to be in charge of sth. [bɪ‿ɪn 'tʃɑ:dʒ əv] zuständig sein für etw. 46
to be more likely to do sth. [bɪ ˌmɔ: 'laɪklɪ tə 'du:] es ist wahrscheinlicher, dass man etw. tut 71
beneficial [ˌbenə'fɪʃl] förderlich, nützlich 55
benefit ['benəfɪt] Leistung, Nutzen 55
to be opposed to sth. [bɪ‿ə'pəʊzd tə ˌsʌmθɪŋ] gegen etw. sein 50
to be rewarded [bɪ rɪ'wɔ:dɪd] belohnt werden 57
to be set [bɪ 'set] erwartet werden 70
to be split over ['splɪt ˌəʊvə] geteilter Meinung sein über 160
to be sworn in [bɪ ˌswɔ:n ɪn] vereidigt werden 31
betrayal [bɪ'treɪəl] Verrat, Treuebruch 28
beyond [bɪ'ɒnd] jenseits, außerhalb 150
biased ['baɪəst] voreingenommen 122
bidder ['bɪdə] Bietende(r) 60
biotechnology [ˌbaɪəʊtek'nɒlədʒɪ] Biotechnologie 82
blank [blæŋk] unbeschrieben, leer 119
to blend [blend] mischen 107
to bless [bles] segnen 109
blessing ['blesɪŋ] Segen 149
blog [blɒg] Internet-Tagebuch 11
bold [bəʊld] mutig, entschlossen 18
bone marrow ['bəʊn ˌmærəʊ] Knochenmark 77
to boost [bu:st] in die Höhe treiben 51
to bother ['bɒðə] sich die Mühe machen 66
brand [brænd] Marke 154
brand value [ˌbrænd 'vælju:] Markenwert 143
breakthrough ['breɪkθru:] Durchbruch 114
breed [bri:d] (hier:) Generation 109
broad [brɔ:d] weitgehend 198
broadcasting ['brɔ:dkɑ:stɪŋ] Rundfunk und Fernsehen 8
byproduct ['baɪˌprɒdʌkt] Nebenprodukt 143

C

to call for ['kɔ:l fɔ:] verlangen 166
calling ['kɔ:lɪŋ] Berufung 67
canning ['kænɪŋ] Konserven- 89
canvas ['kænvəs] Segeltuch 119
capability [ˌkeɪpə'bɪlətɪ] Fähigkeit 67
capable ['keɪpəbl] fähig 49
to cast (a vote) [kɑ:st] (hier:) (Stimme) abgeben 31
casual ['kæʒjʊəl] Gelegenheits- 198
casualty ['kæʒjʊəltɪ] Opfer 11
cautious ['kɔ:ʃəs] vorsichtig 45
CCTV (closed circuit television) [ˌsi:si:ti:'vi:] Videoüberwachung 41
censorship ['sensəʃɪp] Zensur 10
census ['sensəs] Volkszählung 195

challenge ['tʃælɪndʒ] Herausforderung 141

to challenge ['tʃælɪndʒ] herausfordern 113

channels ['tʃænlz] Wege, Kanäle 11

charity ['tʃærɪtɪ] Wohltätigkeit, Wohltätigkeitsorganisation, -verein 60

to chart [tʃɑ:t] vermessen, skizzieren 96

chit-chat ['tʃɪttʃæt] Geplauder 180

citizen ['sɪtɪzn] Bürger(in), Staatsangehörige(r) 114

civic ['sɪvɪk] bürgerlich 119

civil service [ˌsɪvɪl 'sɜ:vɪs] öffentlicher Dienst 42

cloak [kləʊk] Umhang 99

clone [kləʊn] Klon 82

to clone [kləʊn] klonen 74

to coin [kɔɪn] prägen, erfinden 10

to coincide [ˌkəʊɪn'saɪd] übereinstimmen 155

to collaborate [kə'læbəreɪt] zusammenarbeiten 139

to combat ['kɒmbæt] bekämpfen 155

commander-in-chief [kəˌmɑ:ndər‿ɪn 'tʃi:f] Oberbefehlshaber 30

to commission [kə'mɪʃn] in Auftrag geben 70

commitment [kə'mɪtmənt] Bindung, Engagement 110

committed [kə'mɪtɪd] motiviert, entschlossen 93

commute [kə'mju:t] Pendelstrecke 38

compelling [kəm'pelɪŋ] faszinierend 19

to compete [kəm'pi:t] konkurrieren, mithalten, teilnehmen 139

competitive [kəm'petɪtɪv] konkurrenzfähig 141

to compliment sb. ['kɒmplɪmənt] jmdm Komplimente machen 28

to comply [kəm'plaɪ] übereinstimmen 58

to comprise [kəm'praɪz] umfassen 118

compulsory [kəm'pʌlsrɪ] obligatorisch, vorgeschrieben, **verpflichtend** 12

to compute [kəm'pju:t] rechnen 83

to conduct [kən'dʌkt] ausführen 74

to confer [kən'fɜ:] übertragen 87

confident ['kɒnfɪdənt] sicher, selbstbewusst 57

confidential [ˌkɒnfɪ'denʃl] vertraulich 58

congestion [kən'dʒestʃn] Verkehrsstau 174

to conquer ['kɒŋkə] besiegen, erobern 42

conscience ['kɒnʃəns] Gewissen 141

consistent with [kən'sɪstənt wɪð] übereinstimmend mit 158

to consolidate [kən'sɒlɪdeɪt] vereinigen 199

constituency [kən'stɪtjʊənsɪ] Wahlbezirk, Wahlkreis 46

constitution [ˌkɒnstɪ'tju:ʃn] Verfassung 46

construction [kən'strʌkʃn] Baugewerbe 82

contemporary [kən'temprərɪ] gegenwärtig 114

contentious [kən'tenʃəs] umstritten 60

contestant [kən'testənt] Teilnehmer(in) an einem Wettbewerb 98

contract ['kɒntrækt] Auftrag 143

to contribute [kən'trɪbju:t] beitragen 15

convenience [kən'vi:nɪəns] Annehmlichkeit, Bequemlichkeit 90

convention [kən'venʃn] (hier:) Parteitag 31

convergence [kən'vɜ:dʒəns] Zusammenlaufen, Annäherung 83

to convert [kən'vɜ:t] verwandeln, umwandeln 172

to convey [kən'veɪ] vermitteln 106

convulsive [kən'vʌlsɪv] erschütternd 109

core [kɔ:] Kern; Kern-, Haupt- 67

corporate ['kɔ:pərət] Unternehmens- 155

to counter ['kaʊntə] erwidern, dagegen sprechen 11

counterpart ['kaʊntəpɑ:t] Gegenüber, Pendant 181

to cover ['kʌvə] senden 167

to crawl [krɔ:l] krabbeln 32

to credit sb. with sth. ['kredɪt] jmdm etw. zuschreiben 22

criticism ['krɪtɪsɪzm] Kritik 34

crop [krɒp] Feldfrucht, Getreide 196

to crowd [kraʊd] überfüllen 58

crucial ['kru:ʃəl] entscheidend, äußerst wichtig 44

to crush [krʌʃ] unterdrücken 11

curative ['kjʊərətɪv] heilend 75

to cure [kjʊə] heilen 74

currency ['kʌrənsɪ] Währung 143

current ['kʌrənt] aktuell, gegenwärtig 114

current affairs [ˌkʌrənt‿ə'feəz] aktuelle Nachrichten, Zeitgeschehen 156

curriculum [kə'rɪkjələm] Lehrplan 12

curse [kɜ:s] Fluch 149

cut [kʌt] Senkung, Kürzung 62

cute [kju:t] süß 145

D

dawn [dɔ:n] Morgendämmerung, Beginn 176

debt [det] Schuld, Schulden 60

decade ['dekeɪd] Jahrzehnt 14

decline [dɪ'klaɪn] Rückgang 48

to decline [dɪ'klaɪn] abnehmen, zurückgehen 14

decreasingly [dɪ'kri:sɪŋlɪ] immer weniger 44

deep-seated [ˌdi:p'si:tɪd] tiefsitzend 34

deficit ['defɪsɪt] Defizit 50

defining [dɪ'faɪnɪŋ] entscheidend 32

degeneration [dɪˌdʒenə'reɪʃn] Abnahme, Degeneration 74

to delay [dɪ'leɪ] hinauszögern 177

delicate ['delɪkət] empfindlich 106

to demand [dɪ'mɑ:nd] verlangen, fordern 166

demographic [ˌdemə'græfɪk] demografisch 198

denial [dɪ'naɪəl] Ablehnung 184

to denounce [dɪ'naʊns] verurteilen 60

densely populated [ˌdenslɪ 'pɒpjəleɪtɪd] dicht bevölkert 31

to deny [dɪ'naɪ] abstreiten, verweigern, vorenthalten 13

dependency [dɪ'pendənsɪ] Abhängigkeit 92
to deploy [dɪ'plɔɪ] einsetzen 50
to deposit [dɪ'pɒzɪt] ablagern 172
to depreciate [dɪ'pri:ʃɪeɪt] abschreiben 39
deprived [dɪ'praɪvd] heruntergekommen 195
to derive sth. from [dɪ'raɪv frəm] etw. beziehen aus 81
to derive from [dɪ'raɪv frəm] sich ableiten von 114
derogatory [dɪ'rɒgətrɪ] abschätzig, abwertend 131
desirable [dɪ'zaɪərəbl] wünschenswert, erstrebenswert 127
desire [dɪ'zaɪə] Wunsch, Verlangen 154
desolate ['desələt] verlassen 38
to despise [dɪ'spaɪz] verschmähen 29
despite [dɪ'spaɪt] trotz 64
deterioration [dɪˌtɪərɪə'reɪʃn] Verschlechterung 33
to determine [dɪ'tɜ:mɪn] bestimmen, feststellen 66
devastating ['devəsteɪtɪŋ] verheerend 87
to diminish [dɪ'mɪnɪʃ] kleiner werden 97
disability [ˌdɪsə'bɪlətɪ] Behinderung 71
disadvantaged [ˌdɪsəd'vɑ:ntɪdʒd] benachteiligt 62
to discard [dɪ'skɑ:d] wegwerfen, abwerfen 99
to discriminate against sb. [dɪ'skrɪmɪneɪt‿əˌgenst ˌsʌmbədɪ] jdn diskriminieren 15
discrimination [dɪˌskrɪmɪ'neɪʃn] Diskriminierung 43
to disguise oneself [dɪs'gaɪz ˌwʌnself] sich verkleiden 126
to dishonor [dɪ'sɒnə] entehren 28
to dismiss sth. as … [dɪ'smɪs] etw. als … abtun 110
to disobey [ˌdɪsə'beɪ] nicht gehorchen 127
disparity [dɪ'spærətɪ] Ungleichheit 33
to disperse [dɪ'spɜ:s] verstreuen 194
to displace [dɪ'spleɪs] ersetzen 175
dissent [dɪ'sent] Widerspruch 109
to distinguish [dɪ'stɪŋgwɪʃ] unterscheiden 49
distinguished [dɪ'stɪŋgwɪʃt] angesehen, bedeutend 98
disunited [ˌdɪsju:'naɪtɪd] entsolidarisiert, uneinig 44
to ditch [dɪtʃ] aufgeben 70
domestic market [dəˌmestɪk 'mɑ:kɪt] Heimatmarkt 143
to dominate ['dɒmɪneɪt] beherrschen 114
dominion [də'mɪnjən] Herrschaft, Machtgebiet 43
to donate [dəʊ'neɪt] spenden 60
doomed [du:md] verdammt 49
double-edged sword [ˌdʌblˌedʒd 'sɔ:d] zweischneidiges Schwert 73
doubt [daʊt] Zweifel 65
downturn ['daʊntɜ:n] Abschwung 150
to draft [drɑ:ft] entwerfen 110
drill [drɪl] Übung 22
dull [dʌl] langweilig 65
dystopia [dɪs'təʊpɪə] Dystopie, Antiutopie 114

E

eager ['i:gə] eifrig 106
early riser [ˌɜ:lɪ 'raɪzə] Frühaufsteher 57
economic cycle [ˌi:kənɒmɪk 'saɪkl] Konjunktur 143
edible ['edɪbl] essbar 197
eerie ['ɪərɪ] gespenstisch 32
to elaborate [ɪ'læbəreɪt] näher ausführen 148
to eliminate [ɪ'lɪmɪneɪt] abschaffen, beseitigen 42
elusive [ɪ'lu:sɪv] *(hier:)* schwer zu erreichen 103
embarrassment [ɪm'bærəsmənt] Beschämung, Peinlichkeit 154
embedded [ɪm'bedɪd] eingelassen 174
embryonic [ˌembrɪ'ɒnɪk] Embryo- 74
to emerge [ɪ'mɜ:dʒ] heraus-kommen 38
emergence [ɪ'mɜ:dʒəns] Entstehung 114
to emit [ɪ'mɪt] emittieren, ausstoßen 172
emphasis ['empfəsɪs] Betonung 15
to emphasise ['emfəsaɪz] betonen 10
to empower [ɪm'paʊə] befähigen 112
to enable [ɪ'neɪbl] ermöglichen 112
to encompass sth. [ɪn'kʌmpəs] etw. umfassen 42
to encourage [ɪn'kʌrɪdʒ] ermutigen, animieren 62
encouragement [ɪn'kʌrɪdʒmənt] Ermutigung 156
to endorse [ɪn'dɔ:s] billigen, unterstützen 122
to engage [ɪn'geɪdʒ] involvieren 113
to engage in sth. [ɪn'geɪdʒ] sich an etw. beteiligen 95
engaged [ɪn'geɪdʒd] verlobt 127
engaging [ɪn'geɪdʒɪŋ] einnehmend, faszinierend 97
to enhance [ɪn'hɑ:ns] steigern, verbessern 95
enhancement [ɪn'hɑ:nsmənt] Verbesserung 82
to enlist [ɪn'lɪst] *(hier:)* in Anspruch nehmen 154
to enslave [ɪn'sleɪv] versklaven 114
to ensure (that) [ɪn'ʃɔ:] gewährleisten; dafür sorgen (, dass) 13
to entail [ɪn'teɪl] beinhalten 183
entire [ɪn'taɪə] ganz 15
entirely [ɪn'taɪəlɪ] ganz, vollständig 50
equal ['i:kwəl] gleich 13
essential [ɪ'senʃl] notwendig, wesentlich 96
ethics ['eθɪks] Werte 67
to evict [ɪ'vɪkt] jmdn hinauswerfen, (hier:) ausschließen 98
evidence ['evɪdəns] Beweis, Nachweis 92
evident ['evɪdənt] offensichtlich 97
evidently ['evɪdəntlɪ] offensichtlich 49
exaggeration [ɪgˌzædʒə'reɪʃn] Übertreibung 93
to exceed [ɪk'si:d] übersteigen, übertreffen 143
excluded [ɪk'sklu:dɪd] ausgegrenzt 109
executive [ɪg'zekjʊtɪv] leitend(e/r) 66
to exert [ɪg'zɜ:t] ausüben 199
exhibition [ˌeksɪ'bɪʃn] Ausstellung 163

to expand [ɪk'spænd] (sich) ausdehnen 147

expansion [ɪk'spænʃn] Expansion, Erweiterung 194

to expel [ɪk'spel] ausschließen 32

expenditure [ɪk'spendɪtʃə] Auslagen, Ausgaben 55

expense [ɪk'spens] Kosten 112

exploit [ˌeksplɔɪ'teɪʃn] Tat 162

to exploit [ɪk'splɔɪt] ausbeuten 60

exploitation [ˌeksplɔɪ'teɪʃn] Ausbeutung 55

to explore [ɪk'splɔ:] erkunden 113

to expose [ɪk'spəʊz] enthüllen 150

to extend [ɪk'stend] ausdehnen, verlängern 72

extent [ɪk'stent] Ausmaß 44

F

facility [fə'sɪlətɪ] Einrichtung 146

to factor in [ˌfæktər‿ɪn] berücksichtigen, einbeziehen 160

failure ['feɪljə] Versagen 150

feasible ['fi:zəbl] machbar 43

to feature ['fi:tʃə] zeigen 155

fee [fi:] Gebühr 60

fertiliser ['fɜ:tɪlaɪzə] Dünger 114

fertility [fə'tɪlətɪ] Fruchtbarkeit 74

to file for divorce [ˌfaɪl fə dɪ'vɔ:s] die Scheidung einreichen 76

fish fingers [ˌfɪʃ'fɪŋgəz] Fischstäbchen 90

flattering ['flætərɪŋ] schmeichelhaft 76

flawed [flɔ:d] fehlerhaft 135

fluency ['flu:ənsɪ] Flüssigkeit 14

to foreclose [fɔ:'kləʊz] zwangsvollstrecken 38

foremost ['fɔ:məʊst] führend 42

forerunner ['fɔ:ˌrʌnə] Vorreiter(in) 199

foreseeable [fɔ:'si:əbl] absehbar 82

to forge [fɔ:dʒ] schmieden 110

fortnight ['fɔ:tnaɪt] vierzehn Tage 109

fortunate ['fɔ:tʃənət] glücklich 129

to found [faʊnd] gründen 130

fraction ['frækʃn] Bruchteil 23

fragile ['frædʒaɪl] zerbrechlich, schwach 125

freedom ['fri:dəm] Freiheit 25

frequently ['fri:kwəntlɪ] häufig 159

fried [fraɪd] frittiert 90

fringe [frɪndʒ] Rand 120

from scratch [frəm 'skrætʃ] ganz von Anfang an 90

to frown [fraʊn] die Stirn runzeln 145

to fulfil [fʊl'fɪl] erfüllen 25

to fund [fʌnd] finanzieren 71

G

gain [geɪn] Gewinn, Vorteil 71

to gain [geɪn] gewinnen 112

to gain ground [ˌgeɪn 'graʊnd] an Boden gewinnen 10

to gain momentum [ˌgeɪn mə'mentəm] an Boden gewinnen 38

to gather ['gæðə] zusammenkommen, sammeln 58

to gauge [geɪdʒ] nachprüfen 74

GDP (Gross Domestic Product) [ˌdʒi.di:'pi: ˌgrəʊs dəˌmestɪk 'prɒdʌkt] Bruttoinlandsprodukt 51

gender ['dʒendə] Geschlecht 178

generous ['dʒenərəs] großzügig, freigebig 66

genetic [dʒə'netɪk] genetisch, Gen- 74

gentle ['dʒentl] sanft 103

to gentrify ['dʒentrɪfaɪ] verbürgerlichen 38

genuine ['dʒenjʊɪn] echt, aufrichtig 98

to get out of hand [ˌget‿aʊt‿əv 'hænd] außer Kontrolle geraten 114

the gist [ðə 'dʒɪst] Kernaussage, das Wesentliche 90

gloomy ['glu:mɪ] düster 38

gorgeous ['gɔ:dʒəs] sehr schön 66

to govern ['gʌvn] leiten, lenken 50

grant [grɑ:nt] Beihilfe, Unterstützung, Subvention 62

grape [greɪp] Traube 196

to grapple with sth. ['græpl wɪð] sich mit etw. auseinandersetzen 33

gravy ['greɪvɪ] (Braten-)Soße 90

to grieve [gri:v] trauern 98

groundbreaking ['graʊndˌbreɪkɪŋ] bahnbrechend 88

to grow [grəʊ] anbauen 140

growth [grəʊθ] Wachstum 50

guardian ['gɑ:dɪən] Erziehungsbeauftragte(r) 68

to guess [ges] glauben, schätzen 144

guidance ['gaɪdəns] Anleitung, Beratung, Ratschläge 92

H

habit ['hæbɪt] Gewohnheit 154

handicapped ['hændɪkæpt] Behinderte(r) 64

to harvest ['hɑ:vɪst] ernten 198

hazard ['hæzəd] Gefahr 73

hazardous ['hæzədəs] gefährlich 83

healthcare ['helθkeə] Gesundheitspflege 74

heathen ['hi:ðən] Ungläubige(r) 29

heir [eə] Erbe; Thronfolger 48

hence [hens] daher, deshalb 42

to hesitate ['hezɪteɪt] zögern 22

high-flying [ˌhaɪ'flaɪɪŋ] erfolgreich 70

to highlight ['haɪlaɪt] hervorheben 130

to hinge [hɪndʒ] abhängen 160

to hire [haɪə] einstellen 189

honesty ['ɒnəstɪ] Aufrichtigkeit, Ehrlichkeit 66

to hook up [hʊk 'ʌp] (hier:) zusammenfügen 76

horrendous [hə'rendəs] übermäßig, horrend 161

host [həʊst] Gastgeber(in) 25

humble ['hʌmbl] bescheiden 172

hybrid ['haɪbrɪd] Hybrid, Misch- 8

hyphen ['haɪfən] Bindestrich 64

hypocritical [ˌhɪpə'krɪtɪkl] scheinheilig, heuchlerisch 145

I

illiteracy [ɪ'lɪtrəsɪ] Analphabetismus 112

imaginary [ɪ'mædʒɪnərɪ] erfunden 114

immigrant ['ɪmɪgrənt] Einwanderer, Einwanderin 96

impact ['ɪmpækt] Auswirkung 15

to impair [ɪm'peə] beeinträchtigen 83

impediment [ɪm'pedɪmənt] Hindernis 33

to implement ['ɪmplɪment] einführen, umsetzen 50

to impose [ɪm'pəʊz] auferlegen 50

to impose sth. [ɪm'pəʊz] jmdm etw. aufzwingen 11

impressive [ɪm'presɪv] beeindruckend 145

inability [ˌɪnə'bɪlətɪ] Unfähigkeit, Unvermögen 92

inaccurate [ɪn'ækjərət] ungenau, falsch 199

inappropriate [ˌɪnə'prəʊprɪət] unpassend, unangemessen 167

inauguration [ɪˌnɔ:gjə'reɪʃn] Amtseinführung 31

inclined [ɪn'klaɪnd] geneigt 148

inconsiderate [ˌɪnkən'sɪdərət] rücksichtslos 174

inconvenience [ˌɪnkən'vi:nɪəns] Unannehmlichkeit(en) 40

inconvenient [ˌɪnkən'vi:nɪənt] ungünstig 172

increase ['ɪnkri:s] Zunahme, Anstieg 62

increasingly [ɪn'kri:sɪŋlɪ] zunehmend 66

in demand [ˌɪn dɪ'mɑ:nd] gesucht/gefragt 71

to indicate ['ɪndɪkeɪt] zeigen 194

indigenous people [ɪnˌdɪdʒɪnəs 'pi:plz] Einheimische 42

indignation [ˌɪndɪg'neɪʃn] Empörung 109

indistinguishable [ˌɪndɪ'stɪŋgwɪʃəbl] nicht unterscheidbar 72

to indulge in sth. [ɪn'dʌldʒ ɪn] sich etw. hingeben 96

inevitable [ɪ'nevɪtəbl] unvermeidlich 151

infant mortality [ˌɪnfənt mɔ:'tælətɪ] Säuglingssterblichkeit 33

inferior [ɪn'fɪərɪə] minderwertig 120

infrequently [ɪn'fri:kwəntlɪ] selten, unregelmäßig 64

ingredient [ɪn'gri:dɪənt] Zutat 91

injection [ɪn'dʒekʃn] Spritze, Injektion 75

injustice [ɪn'dʒʌstɪs] Ungerechtigkeit 55

inn [ɪn] Gasthaus 28

innovation [ˌɪnəʊ'veɪʃn] Neuerung 88

inspirational [ˌɪnspɪ'reɪʃənl] inspirierend 19

instant ['ɪnstənt] sofortig 97

instantly ['ɪnstəntlɪ] sofort, augenblicklich 162

insurance [ɪn'ʃɔ:rəns] Versicherung 113

to intensify [ɪn'tensɪfaɪ] verstärken 114

interface ['ɪntəfeɪs] Schnittstelle 97

to intervene [ˌɪntə'vi:n] einschreiten 34

to intimidate [ɪn'tɪmɪdeɪt] einschüchtern 131

intriguing [ɪn'tri:gɪŋ] faszinierend, fesselnd 173

intruder [ɪn'tru:də] Eindringling 83

invaluable [ɪn'væljʊəbl] außerordentlich wertvoll, unschätzbar 183

invention [ɪn'venʃn] Erfindung 42

to investigate [ɪn'vestɪgeɪt] erforschen, untersuchen, recherchieren 188

invincible [ɪn'vɪnsəbl] unbesiegbar 109

irreversible [ˌɪrɪ'vɜ:səbl] unumkehrbar 32

issue ['ɪʃu:] Frage, Problem 22

to issue ['ɪʃu:] ausgeben 182

J

to join forces [ˌdʒɔɪn 'fɔ:sɪz] zusammenarbeiten, sich zusammenschließen 140

judiciary [dʒu:'dɪʃərɪ] Gerichtsbarkeit 46

justice ['dʒʌstɪs] Gerechtigkeit 145

juvenile ['dʒu:vənaɪl] Jugend- 123

K

to keep track of sth. [ˌki:p 'træk‿əv] über etw. Aufzeichnungen machen 128

key [ki:] Haupt-, Schlüssel- 9

L

laboratory [lə'bɒrətrɪ] Labor 82

labour ['leɪbə] Arbeitskräfte 140

lack of ['læk‿əv] Mangel an 185

to lack sth. ['læk ˌsʌmθɪŋ] etw. vermissen lassen 64

large-scale [ˌlɑ:dʒ'skeɪl] großflächig, in großem Maßstab 140

the latter [ðə 'lætə] Letztere(r,s) 22

launch [lɔ:ntʃ] Markteinführung 178

to launch [lɔ:ntʃ] auf den Markt bringen 158

layer ['leɪə] Schicht 177

to leap [li:p] springen 19

to lessen ['lesn] verringern 43

letter of application [ˌletər‿əv æplɪ'keɪʃn] Bewerbungsschreiben 58

licensees [ˌlaɪsən'si:z] Lizenznehmer 161

license plate ['laɪsəns ˌpleɪt] Autokennzeichen, Nummernschild 28

likelihood ['laɪklɪhʊd] Wahrscheinlichkeit 50

limitless ['lɪmɪtləs] grenzenlos 107

lingua franca (Latin) [ˌlɪŋgwə 'fræŋkə] internationale Verkehrssprache 10

littered ['lɪtəd] übersät 199

livestock ['laɪvstɒk] Vieh 197

loan [ləʊn] Darlehen, Kredit 61

longing ['lɒŋɪŋ] Sehnsucht 42

to loom [lu:m] sich abzeichnen 97

to lose out on s.th. [ˌlu:z‿'aʊt ɒn ˌsʌmθɪŋ] ins Hintertreffen geraten 196

loss [lɒs] Verlust, Einbuße 43

M

to maintain [meɪn'teɪn] aufrechterhalten, beibehalten; behaupten 15

majority [mə'dʒɒrətɪ] Mehrheit 30

to make a living [ˌmeɪk‿ə 'lɪvɪŋ] seinen Lebensunterhalt verdienen 140

to make choices [meɪk 'tʃɔɪsɪz] Entscheidungen treffen 97

malnourished [ˌmæl'nʌrɪʃt] unterernährt 54

manipulation [məˌnɪpjə'leɪʃn] Manipulation, Beeinflussung 16

manufacturer [ˌmænjə'fæktʃərə] Hersteller 90

to marginalize ['mɑ:dʒɪnəlaɪz] an den Rand drängen 29

to mask [mɑ:sk] verbergen 120

mass transit [ˌmæs 'trænzɪt] Massenverkehr 38

to mature [mə'tʃʊə] reifen 155
measurable ['meʒərəbl] messbar 111
medium ['mi:dɪəm] Medium 8
merchant ['mɜ:tʃənt] Händler, Kaufmann, Handelsmann 91
mere [mɪə] bloß 118
merely ['mɪəlɪ] lediglich 111
millennium [mɪ'lenɪəm] Jahrtausend 82
mind-set ['maɪndset] Einstellung 67
minimally invasive surgery [ˌmɪnɪməlɪ ɪnˌveɪzɪv 'sɜ:dʒərɪ] minimalinvasive Operationstechnik 73
model ['mɒdl] Vorbild 94
to monitor ['mɒnɪtə] überwachen 86
monitoring ['mɒnɪtərɪŋ] Kontrolle, Überwachung 80
monopoly [mə'nɒpəlɪ] Monopol 42
mother tongue [ˌmʌðə 'tʌŋ] Muttersprache 127
motive ['məʊtɪv] Antrieb 42
mystery ['mɪstərɪ] Rätsel 76

N

nanotechnology [ˌnænəʊtek'nɒlədʒɪ] Nanotechnologie 82
native ['neɪtɪv] Ureinwohner(in) 96
native ['neɪtɪv] eingeboren, einheimisch 8
native speaker [ˌneɪtɪv 'spi:kə] Muttersprachler(in) 8
to negate [nɪ'geɪt] zunichtemachen 33
neglect [nɪ'glekt] Nichtbeachtung 150
to negotiate [nɪ'gəʊʃɪeɪt] verhandeln 186
negotiation [nɪˌgəʊʃɪ'eɪʃn] Verhandlung 8
notion ['nəʊʃn] Konzept, Idee 44
to nourish ['nʌrɪʃ] ernähren 199
nuclear ['nju:klɪə] nuklear, Atom- 73
to nurture sth. ['nɜ:tʃə ˌsʌmθɪŋ] etw. fördern 66
nutrition [nju:'trɪʃn] Ernährung 112

O

objective [əb'dʒektɪv] Ziel, Absicht 58
obligation [ˌɒblɪ'geɪʃn] Verpflichtung 183
obsession [əb'seʃn] Besessenheit 154
obvious ['ɒbvɪəs] offensichtlich 154
obviously ['ɒbvɪəslɪ] offensichtlich 145
offender [ə'fendə] Straftäter(in) 122
official language [əˌfɪʃl 'læŋgwɪdʒ] Amtssprache 8
to offset [ˌɒf'set] kompensieren, ausgleichen 161
offshore [ˌɒf'ʃɔ:] vor der Küste 162
open source [ˌəʊpn'sɔ:s] offener Quellcode (bei Software) 22
opponent [ə'pəʊnənt] Gegner(in) 51
oppressive [ə'presɪv] unterdrückend 34
ordinarily [ˌɔ:dən'erɪlɪ] für gewöhnlich, normalerweise 64
otherwise ['ʌðəwaɪz] ansonsten 113
outcome ['aʊtkʌm] Ergebnis 14
to outweigh sth. [ˌaʊt'weɪ] schwerer wiegen als etw. 91
overpaid [ˌəʊvə'peɪd] überbezahlt 64
overseas [ˌəʊvə'si:z] ausländisch; im Ausland 50
overwhelming [ˌəʊvə'welmɪŋ] überwältigend 45

P

pace [peɪs] Geschwindigkeit, Gangart 97
(cardiac) pacemaker [ˌkɑ:dɪæk 'peɪsˌmeɪkə] Herzschrittmacher 89
partially ['pɑ:ʃəlɪ] teilweise 70
to partition [pɑ:'tɪʃn] aufteilen 43
to partner with ['pɑ:tnə wɪð] sich mit jmdm zusammenschließen 198
patriotism ['pætrɪətɪzm] Vaterlandsliebe 91
pattern ['pætn] Muster 14
to pave the way [ˌpeɪv ðə 'weɪ] den Weg ebnen 90
peak [pi:k] Höhepunkt 108
to perceive [pə'si:v] wahrnehmen 155
perception [pə'sepʃn] Wahrnehmung 134
peril ['perəl] Risiko 103
periodical [ˌpɪərɪ'ɒdɪkl] Zeitschrift 8
perishable ['perɪʃəbl] (leicht) verderblich 91
to permit [pə'mɪt] erlauben 51
pertinent ['pɜ:tɪnənt] relevant 161
phenomenon [fə'nɒmɪnən] Phänomen, Erscheinung 47
pillow ['pɪləʊ] Kopfkissen 28
policy ['pɒləsɪ] Strategie, Richtlinie 14
poll [pəʊl] Umfrage 98
portfolio [pɔ:t'fəʊlɪəʊ] Mappe 58
to portray [pɔ:'treɪ] darstellen 114
to pose [pəʊz] darstellen 160
post [pəʊst] Ziel(markierung) 47
poultry ['pəʊltrɪ] Geflügel 161
power plant ['paʊə ˌplɑ:nt] Kraftwerk 73
praise [preɪz] Lob 66
to praise [preɪz] loben; anpreisen 66
precious ['preʃəs] wertvoll 76
predecessor ['pri:dɪˌsesə] Vorgänger(in) 109
to predict [prɪ'dɪkt] voraussagen 75
predictable [prɪ'dɪktəbl] vorhersehbar 172
prediction [prɪ'dɪkʃn] Vorhersage 82
predominance [prɪ'dɒmɪnəns] Vorherrschaft 11
prejudice ['predʒədɪs] Vorurteil 43
premonition [ˌpremə'nɪʃn] Vorahnung 32
pre-requisite [ˌpri:'rekwɪzɪt] Voraussetzung 61
to preside over sth. [prɪ'zaɪd ˌəʊvə] über etw. walten 33
presidency ['prezɪdənsɪ] Präsidentschaft 31
pressure ['preʃə] Druck 60
to pressure ['preʃə] Druck ausüben 90
to pressure sb. ['preʃə] jmdn unter Druck setzen 34
to prevent [prɪ'vent] verhindern, vermeiden 150
preventable [prɪ'ventəbl] vermeidbar 146
primarily [praɪ'merɪlɪ] hauptsächlich, vornehmlich 139
primary ['praɪməri] Vorwahl 31
privilege ['prɪvɪlɪdʒ] Privileg 60
to process ['prəʊses] verarbeiten 115
production costs [prə'dʌkʃn ˌkɒsts] Herstellungskosten 143

production facilities [prə'dʌkʃn fəˌsɪlɪtɪz] Produktionsanlagen 143

progress ['prəʊgres] Fortschritt 114

prohibition [ˌprəʊhɪ'bɪʃn] Untersagung, Verbot 183

projection [prə'dʒekʃn] Projektion, Hochrechnung, Fortschreibung 194

to promote [prə'məʊt] fördern, unterstützen 55

to prompt [prɒmpt] hervorrufen 176

property ['prɒpətɪ] Eigentum; Eigenschaft 126

proponent [prə'pəʊnənt] Befürworter(in) 51

proposal [prə'pəʊzl] Vorschlag 158

to propose to sb. [prə'pəʊz tə ˌsʌmbədɪ] jmdm einen Heiratsantrag machen 38

prospect ['prɒspekt] Aussicht 14

prosperity [prɒs'perətɪ] Wohlstand 110

prosperous ['prɒspərəs] wohlhabend, florierend 150

to provide (for) [prə'vaɪd] geben, bieten; sorgen für, versorgen 47

punishment ['pʌnɪʃmənt] Strafe, Bestrafung 130

to purchase ['pɜ:tʃəs] erwerben 50

purpose ['pɜ:pəs] Zweck 118

to pursue sb. [pə'sju:] jmdn bedrängen/jagen 126

to pursue sth. [pə'sju:] etw. verfolgen 61

pursuit [pə'sju:t] Streben 107

R

radical ['rædɪkl] radikal 27

ramification [ˌræmɪfɪ'keɪʃn] Auswirkung 48

random ['rændəm] per Zufall, willkürlich 13

range [reɪndʒ] Reichweite 174

to ratify a treaty [ˌrætɪfaɪ‿ə 'tri:tɪ] einen Vertrag ratifizieren, anerkennen 30

ready-made [ˌredɪ'meɪd] Fertig- 90

to reap [ri:p] ernten 198

to rear [rɪə] großziehen 75

to recede [rɪ'si:d] sich entfernen 29

recession [rɪ'seʃn] Konjunkturabschwung, Rezession 50

recipe ['resɪpɪ] Rezept 67

to reckon ['rekən] vermuten 70

recognition [ˌrekəg'nɪʃn] Erkenntnis; Anerkennung; Erkennung 59

to recommend [ˌrekə'mend] empfehlen 185

recommendation [ˌrekəmen'deɪʃn] Empfehlung 58

to recount [rɪ'kaʊnt] erzählen 131

to redefine [ˌri:dɪ'faɪn] neu definieren 108

redistribution [ri:dɪstrɪbju:ʃən] Umverteilung 102

reference ['refrəns] Referenz, Bezug 58

referendum [ˌrefə'rendəm] Bürgerentscheid 44

refuge ['refju:dʒ] Zufluchtsort 38

refugee [ref.jʊ'dʒi:] Flüchtling 107

to regard [rɪ'gɑ:d] betrachten 51

regardless of [rɪ'gɑ:dləs‿əv] ungeachtet, unabhängig von 44

regenerative [rɪ'dʒenərətɪv] regenerativ 75

regime change [reɪ'ʒi:m ˌtʃeɪndʒ] Regimewechsel 34

to reinforce [ˌri:ɪn'fɔ:s] verstärken 49

to reject [rɪ'dʒekt] ablehnen 58

relapse ['ri:læps] Rückfall 77

to relate to sth. [rɪ'leɪt tə] sich mit etw. identifizieren 124

reliability [rɪˌlaɪə'bɪlətɪ] Glaubwürdigkeit, Vertrauenswürdigkeit 156

reliable [rɪ'laɪəbl] zuverlässig 28

reliance [rɪ'laɪəns] Verlass 93

relief [rɪ'li:f] Erleichterung 145

reluctant [rɪ'lʌktənt] widerwillig, widerstrebend 123

to rely on [rɪ'laɪ‿ɒn] sich verlassen auf 51

to remain [rɪ'meɪn] bleiben 32

remark [rɪ'mɑ:k] Bemerkung, Äußerung 110

remarkably [rɪ'mɑ:kəblɪ] bemerkenswert 109

remote working [rɪˌməʊt 'wɜ:kɪŋ] Telearbeit 71

to remove [rɪ'mu:v] entfernen 167

renewable [rɪ'nju:əbl] erneuerbar 114

renewed [rɪ'nju:d] erneut 145

to replace [rɪ'pleɪs] ersetzen 12

reputation [ˌrepjə'teɪʃn] Ruf 90

requirement [rɪ'kwaɪəmənt] Anforderung 14

research [rɪ'sɜ:tʃ] Forschung 14

to resemble [rɪ'zembl] ähneln 172

reserve [rɪ'zɜ:v] Scheu, Förmlichkeit 180

to reshape [ˌri:'ʃeɪp] umformen, wieder verformen 55

to reside [rɪ'zaɪd] seinen Sitz haben 119

resident ['rezɪdənt] Einwohner(in) 128

residual [rɪ'zɪdjʊəl] restlich 48

resistance [rɪ'zɪstəns] Widerstand 114

respectively [rɪ'spektɪvlɪ] beziehungsweise 47

to respond [rɪ'spɒnd] reagieren 141

responsibility [rɪˌspɒnsə'bɪlətɪ] Verantwortung 34

to restore [rɪ'stɔ:] wiederherstellen 75

résumé [ˌrezjʊ'meɪ] Lebenslauf 58

to retain [rɪ'teɪn] behalten 119

retirement [rɪ'taɪəmənt] Ruhestand 102

to reveal [rɪ'vi:l] enthüllen, aufdecken, aufzeigen 55

to reverberate [rɪ'vɜ:bəreɪt] nachhallen 32

to reverse [rɪ'vɜ:s] umkehren 48

to revitalize [ˌri:'vaɪtəlaɪz] wiederbeleben 38

reward [rɪ'wɔ:d] Belohnung 66

rigorous ['rɪgərəs] peinlich genau, gründlich 75

to ring out [rɪŋ 'aʊt] schallen 32

riot [raɪət] Aufruhr 11

rise [raɪz] Anstieg, Zunahme 14

rival ['raɪvl] Konkurrent(in) 119

robotic [rəʊ'bɒtɪk] Roboter- 73

role models ['rəʊl ˌmɒdlz] Rollenvorbilder 62

root [ru:t] Wurzel 150

roughly ['rʌflɪ] ungefähr 14

row [raʊ] Auseinandersetzung 54

to rule [ru:l] herrschen, regieren 96

to rule out [ˌru:l‿'aʊt] ausschließen 182
rundown [ˌrʌn'daʊn] heruntergekommen 38
rural ['rʊərəl] ländlich 113

S

sample ['sæmpl] Beispiel 58
satisfaction [ˌsætɪs'fækʃn] Zufriedenheit 65
scale [skeɪl] Maß, Maßstab, Ausmaß 10
scarcely ['skeəslɪ] kaum 10
scope [skəʊp] Ausmaß, Umfang 95
to scramble for sth. ['skræmbl ˌfɔ:] um etw. kämpfen 42
scrutiny ['skru:tɪnɪ] Kontrolle, Prüfung 48
to secure [sɪ'kjʊə] absichern, unter Vetrag nehmen 19
sedentary ['sedəntrɪ] sitzend 94
segregation [ˌsegrɪ'geɪʃn] Rassentrennung 27
self-esteem [ˌselfɪ'sti:m] Selbstwertgefühl 112
self-evident [ˌself'evɪdənt] selbstverständlich 28
sensible ['sensɪbl] vernünftig, sinnvoll 103
sentiment ['sentɪmənt] Ansicht 131
separation [ˌsepər'eɪʃn] Trennung 156
to set out [set 'aut] (hier:) darlegen 161
settler ['setlə] Siedler(in) 26
to shape [ʃeɪp] formen 97
share [ʃeə] Anteil 99
shares [ʃeəz] Aktien 143
sharp [ʃɑ:p] steil, stark, scharf 194
to shatter ['ʃætə] zerschmettern 44
shift [ʃɪft] Veränderung 55
to shift [ʃɪft] wechseln 145
to showcase ['ʃəʊkeɪs] demonstrieren 58
side effect ['saɪd‿ɪˌfekt] Nebeneffekt 73
sincere [sɪn'sɪə] aufrichtig 66
to skip sth. [skɪp] ausfallen lassen 70
slave [sleɪv] Sklave/Sklavin 137
smooth [smu:ð] fließend 120
to soar [sɔ:] hochschnellen 110
solar energy [ˌsəʊlər‿'enədʒɪ] Solarenergie 115
solar panel [ˌsəʊlə 'pænl] Sonnenkollektor 73
sole [səʊl] einzig, ausschließlich 10
solicitor [sə'lɪsɪtə] Anwalt/Anwältin 71
sophisticated [sə'fɪstɪkeɪtɪd] hoch entwickelt 80
sore [sɔ:] Wunde 33
to spark [spɑ:k] entzünden 34
to speculate ['spekjəleɪt] spekulieren 39
spinal cord [ˌspaɪnl 'kɔ:d] Rückenmark 74
spirit ['spɪrɪt] Geist 109
to spoil [spɔɪl] verderben 91
to spot [spɒt] entdecken 122
to spread [spred] verbreiten, ausbreiten 11
staff [stɑ:f] Angestellte(r), Personal 163
stain [steɪn] Fleck 127
state [steɪt] Zustand 12
storage ['stɔ:rɪdʒ] Speicherung 89
straightforward [ˌstreɪt'fɔ:wəd] einfach, unkompliziert 178
strain [streɪn] Belastung 44
strategic [strə'ti:dʒɪk] strategisch 12
to strengthen ['streŋkθn] verstärken 35
striking ['straɪkɪŋ] verblüffend 118
to strive [straɪv] streben nach 151
stroke [strəʊk] Schlaganfall 92
to struggle ['strʌgl] kämpfen, sich abmühen 15
subliminal [sʌb'lɪmɪnəl] unterschwellig 122
to submit [səb'mɪt] vorlegen, abschicken 40
subsequent ['sʌbsəkwənt] anschließend, nachträglich 108
substantial [səb'stænʃl] beträchtlich 32
subtle ['sʌtl] dezent 155
to succeed [sək'si:d] erfolgreich sein 13
sufficient(ly) [sə'fɪʃənt, sə'fɪʃəntlɪ] ausreichend 15
suitability [ˌsu:tə'bɪlətɪ] Eignung 60
suitable ['su:təbl] geeignet, passend 87
superstition [ˌsu:pə'stɪʃn] Aberglaube 120
supervision [ˌsu:pə'vɪʒn] Beaufsichtigung 71
supervisor ['su:pəvaɪzə] Leiter(in), Kontrolleur(in) 66
supplies [sə'plaɪz] Vorräte 176
to supply [sə'plaɪ] liefern, zur Verfügung stellen 141
supposedly [sə'pəʊzɪdlɪ] angeblich 48
surface ['sɜ:fɪs] Oberfläche 80
surgery ['sɜ:dʒərɪ] Operation 73
to surpass [sə'pɑ:s] (hier:) überholen 199
surveillance [sə'veɪləns] Überwachung 83
survey ['sɜ:veɪ] Umfrage 58
to survive [sə'vaɪv] überleben 140
susceptible to [sə'septəbl tə] anfällig für 87
suspicion [sə'spɪʃn] Misstrauen, Verdacht 65
sustainability [səˌsteɪnə'bɪlətɪ] Nachhaltigkeit 155
sustainable [sə'steɪnəbl] nachhaltig 110
sweatshop ['swetʃɒp] Ausbeutungsbetrieb 137
to sweep [swi:p] rauschen, fegen 196
sympathetic [ˌsɪmpə'θetɪk] mitfühlend 66

T

to tackle ['tækl] angehen, in Angriff nehmen, bewältigen, bekämpfen 62
to take off [ˌteɪk‿'ɒf] abheben 54
to take the initiative [ˌteɪk ðɪ‿ɪ'nɪʃətɪv] die Initiative ergreifen 35
to target ['tɑ:gɪt] ins Visier nehmen, anpeilen 91
to target sb. ['tɑ:gɪt] jmdn als Zielgruppe haben, auf jmdn abzielen 14

temporary ['temprərɪ] vorübergehend, zeitweilig 62
tense [tens] angespannt 186
tension ['tenʃn] Spannung 49
tentative ['tentətɪv] vorsichtig 109
to terminate ['tɜ:mɪneɪt] beenden 55
terrifying ['terəfaɪɪŋ] furchterregend 114
testimony ['testɪmənɪ] Zeugnis, Beweis 74
therapeutic [ˌθerə'pju:tɪk] therapeutisch 83
therapy ['θerəpɪ] Behandlung 74
think tank ['θɪŋk ˌtæŋk] Expertenkommission, „Denkfabrik" 176
tie [taɪ] Bindung 15
tight [taɪt] knapp 111
tissue ['tɪʃu:] Stoff, Material 74
tongue-in-cheek [ˌtʌŋɪn'tʃi:k] ironisch 40
totalitarian [təˌtælɪ'teərɪən] totalitär 11
to track [træk] verfolgen 58
to trade in [ˌtreɪd‿'ɪn] eintauschen 196
trait [treɪt] Charakterzug, Eigenschaft 58
to transform [træns'fɔ:m] verwandeln 96
transition [træn'zɪʃn] Übergang 177
to treat [tri:t] behandeln 26
treatment ['tri:tmənt] Behandlung 27
trial [traɪəl] Versuch 74
to triple ['trɪpl] verdreifachen 63
tuition [tjʊ'ɪʃn] Unterricht, Unterweisung 63
turnover ['tɜ:nˌəʊvə] Umsatz 143
to turn over [ˌtɜ:n‿'əʊvə] umsetzen 143

U

unanimously [ju:'nænɪməslɪ] einhellig, einstimmig 11
unashamed [ˌʌnə'ʃeɪmd] schamlos 199
uncanny [ʌn'kænɪ] unheimlich 32
unchallenged [ʌn'tʃælɪndʒd] unbestritten 10
to undermine sth. [ˌʌndə'maɪn ˌsʌmθɪŋ] etw. untergraben 51
undoubtedly [ʌn'daʊtɪdlɪ] zweifellos 44
union ['ju:nɪən] Gewerkschaft 166
unique [ju:'ni:k] einzigartig 139
unjust [ʌn'dʒʌst] ungerecht 27
to unleash [ʌn'li:ʃ] freisetzen 54
unparalleled [ʌn'pærəleld] beispiellos 10
unprecedented [ʌn'presɪdəntɪd] beispiellos, nie dagewesen 146
unpredictable [ˌʌnprɪ'dɪktəbl] unvorhersehbar, unberechenbar 186
uprising ['ʌpˌraɪzɪŋ] Aufstand 108
urban ['ɜ:bən] städtisch, urban 118
urge [ɜ:dʒ] Drang, Trieb 42
to urge [ɜ:dʒ] drängen, ermahnen 67
urgent ['ɜ:dʒənt] dringend 150

V

vacancy ['veɪkənsɪ] Stellenangebot, Leere, Lücke 62
vacant ['veɪkənt] frei 38
valuable ['væljʊəbl] wertvoll 112
value ['vælju:] Wert 11
valued ['vælju:d] (wert)geschätzt 71
varying ['veərɪɪŋ] wechselnd 45
vehicular language [vɪˌhɪkjələ 'læŋgwɪdʒ] Verkehrssprache 10
venture ['ventʃə] Unternehmen, Unterfangen 19
venue ['venju:] Veranstaltungsort 113
to verify ['verɪfaɪ] belegen 58
to veto a law [ˌvi:təʊ‿ə 'lɔ:] ein Gesetz ablehnen 30
violation [ˌvaɪə'leɪʃn] Verletzung, Nichteinhaltung 55
virtue [vɜ:tju:] Tugend 107
vocational [vəʊ'keɪʃənl] beruflich, Berufs- 188
to voice [vɔɪs] äußern, zum Ausdruck bringen 11
volunteer [ˌvɒlən'tɪə] Freiwillige(r) 60
vulnerable ['vʌlnərəbl] angreifbar, verwundbar 62

W

weight [weɪt] Gewicht 112
whereas [weə'ræz] während, wohingegen 65
to withdraw [wɪð'drɔ:] sich zurückziehen 27
withdrawal [wɪð'drɔ:əl] Ausstieg 51
to witness ['wɪtnəs] beobachten 130
working knowledge [ˌwɜ:kɪŋ 'nɒlɪdʒ] praktische Kenntnisse 8

Y

to yield [ˌji:ld‿'ɪntrəst] hervorbringen 195

Z

zest [zest] Eifer, Ziel 93

Bildquellennachweis

4 iStockphoto (The Power of Forever Photography), Calgary, Alberta; **4** iStockphoto (LifesizeImages), Calgary, Alberta; **4** Getty Images (Dan Kitwood), München; **4** shutterstock (mihaicalin), New York, NY; **5** iStockphoto (Vladislav Ociacia), Calgary, Alberta; **5** iStockphoto (David Jones), Calgary, Alberta; **5** Picture-Alliance (abacausa), Frankfurt; **5** Perez, Armando, McLean; **6** Corbis (Pawel Kopczynski/ Reuters), Düsseldorf; **6** shutterstock (RF/Losevsky Pavel), New York, NY; **7** BBC Information and archives, London; **7** Thinkstock (iStockphoto), München; **7** iStockphoto (Lisa F. Young), Calgary, Alberta; **10** Agency: Ogilvy & Mather Budapest. Creative: Dalbir Singh.; **12** iStockphoto (The Power of Forever Photography), Calgary, Alberta; **14** Mauritius Images (Alamy), Mittenwald; **15** John C Fewings, Peterborough, On; **16** www.CartoonStock.com (Goddard, Clive), Bath; **17** shutterstock (c.), New York, NY; **19** Classical Comics Ltd, Litchborough,Towcester; **21** Mit freundlicher Genehmigung der Berliner Stadtreinigung und der Heymann Brandt de Gelmini Werbeagentur AG; **24** Getty Images (AFP/Paul J. Richards), München; **24** Getty Images (Digital Vision), München; **24** iStockphoto (LifesizeImages), Calgary, Alberta; **25** Alamy Images (Jeff Greenberg), Abingdon, Oxon; **25** Ullstein Bild GmbH (AP), Berlin; **25** iStockphoto (Juanmonino), Calgary, Alberta; **26** Corbis (Brian A. Vikander), Düsseldorf; **26** Alamy Images (PhotoStock-Israel), Abingdon, Oxon; **27** Corbis (Leif Skoogfors), Düsseldorf; **27** Getty Images (Craig Allen), München; **28** Wikimedia Deutschland (PD), Berlin; **30** JupiterImages photos.com (photos.com), Tucson, AZ; **30** Wikimedia Deutschland (PD), Berlin; **30** Corbis (Wally McNamee), Düsseldorf; **31** Corbis (SABA/Freeland), Düsseldorf; **32** Picture-Alliance (dpa), Frankfurt; **32** Süddeutsche Zeitung Photo, München; **34** Süddeutsche Zeitung Photo (AP), München; **34** Das Fotoarchiv (Markus Matzel), Essen; **35** Corbis (Sygma/Stone), Düsseldorf; **35** Fotosearch Stock Photography (Design Pics), Waukesha, WI; **35** Corbis (Anthony Dobson/US Navy/Hanout/CNP), Düsseldorf; **38** Picture-Alliance (dpa/EPA/JUSTIN LANE), Frankfurt; **40** Ullstein Bild GmbH (Liverani), Berlin; **40** Corbis (Ashley Cooper), Düsseldorf; **40** iStockphoto (Duncan Walker), Calgary, Alberta; **41** Topham Picturepoint, Edenbridge Kent; **41** shutterstock (Pres Panayotov), New York, NY; **43** Schrank, Peter, Aldeburgh; **44** Getty Images (Dan Kitwood), München; **46** Ullstein Bild GmbH (Reuters), Berlin; **46** Corbis (Bettmann), Düsseldorf; **46** Getty Images (Tim Graham), München; **47** Klett-Archiv (nach: The Huddersfield Daily Examiner), Stuttgart; **48** Getty Images (Chris Jackson), München; **48** Getty Images (BEN STANSALL/AFP), München; **50** iStockphoto (pagadesign), Calgary, Alberta; **53** www.CartoonStock.com (Clive Goddard), Bath; **54** iStockphoto (Gawrav Sinha), Calgary, Alberta; **56** iStockphoto (dra_schwartz), Calgary, Alberta; **56** iStockphoto (Gene Chutka), Calgary, Alberta; **56** iStockphoto (Lisa F. Young), Calgary, Alberta; **56** iStockphoto (Catherine Yeulet), Calgary, Alberta; **57** iStockphoto (pavlen), Calgary, Alberta; **57** iStockphoto (Dan Tero), Calgary, Alberta; **57** iStockphoto (Panagiota Vorgia), Calgary, Alberta; **57** iStockphoto (fredy sujono), Calgary, Alberta; **57** iStockphoto (Mark Stay), Calgary, Alberta; **57** iStockphoto (Er Ten Hong), Calgary, Alberta; **58** iStockphoto (Nikada), Calgary, Alberta; **60** iStockphoto (YinYang), Calgary, Alberta; **63** www.CartoonStock.com (Morgan, Ron), Bath; **64** Getty Images (Ulf Andersen), München; **64** iStockphoto (Dmitry Vasilyev), Calgary, Alberta; **66** iStockphoto (Karl Dolenc), Calgary, Alberta; **70** shutterstock (mihaicalin), New York, NY; **72** shutterstock (koya979), New York, NY; **72** shutterstock (dervish11), New York, NY; **73** iStockphoto (Blend_Images), Calgary, Alberta; **73** iStockphoto (LeicaFoto), Calgary, Alberta; **73** shutterstock (higyou), New York, NY; **74** Telegraph Media Group Limited, London; **74** Fotolia.com (Alexandr Mitiuc), New York; **76** Getty Images (David Levenson), München; **78** Picture-Alliance (dpa), Frankfurt; **80** iStockphoto (alengo), Calgary, Alberta; **81** Goff, Ted, Kansas City; **82** iStockphoto (Vladislav Ociacia), Calgary, Alberta; **86** Reuters, Frankfurt; **87** www.CartoonStock.com (Flanagan, Mike), Bath; **88** iStockphoto (David Jones), Calgary, Alberta; **88** Thinkstock (istockphoto), München; **88** iStockphoto (Alex Slobodkin), Calgary, Alberta; **88** Fotolia.com (ricardoazoury), New York; **89** www.CartoonStock.com (Goddard, Clive), Bath; **90** iStockphoto (Kelly Cline), Calgary, Alberta; **92** Copyright Guardian News & Media Ltd 2011, London; **92** iStockphoto (AlbanyPictures), Calgary, Alberta; **94** iStockphoto (Catherine Yeulet), Calgary, Alberta; **96** iStockphoto (Scott Betts), Calgary, Alberta; **96** The Sunday Times, London; **98** Getty Images (Ben Pruchnie), München; **102** iStockphoto (tumpikuja), Calgary, Alberta; **103** nach: OECD http://www.oecd.org/dataoecd/28/10/47571423.pdf; **104** iStockphoto (JasonRWarren), Calgary, Alberta; **104** iStockphoto (Vallarie Enriquez), Calgary, Alberta; **104** iStockphoto (eva serrabassa), Calgary, Alberta; **104** iStockphoto (Silvia Jansen), Calgary, Alberta; **104** iStockphoto (Angela Sorrentino), Calgary, Alberta; **105** Avenue Images GmbH (Brand X Pictures/Colin Anderson), Hamburg; **106** iStockphoto (De Meyer), Calgary, Alberta; **107** www.CartoonStock.com (Schwadron, Harley), Bath; **108** Picture-Alliance (abacausa), Frankfurt; **110** PantherMedia GmbH (speedfighter), München; **110** iStockphoto (GYI NSEA), Calgary, Alberta; **110** shutterstock (Alexander Zavadsky), New York, NY; **112** iStockphoto (Robert Churchill), Calgary, Alberta; **115** Frank R. Paul Estate (used with the acknowledgement of the Frank R. Paul Estate), Questa, NM 87556; **115** Foster and Partners, London; **118** Picture-Alliance (Photoshot), Frankfurt; **118** shutterstock (Stephen Finn), New York, NY; **120** Corbis (Colin McPherson), Düsseldorf; **120** Cheron Bayna, USA; **121** Picture-Alliance (Photoshot), Frankfurt; **122** www.CartoonStock.com (Glenn Foden), Bath; **124** Penguin Group (UK), London WC2R ORL; **126** Picture-Alliance (EFE/Toni Garriga), Frankfurt; **128** Perez, Armando, McLean; **128** laif (Yiannis Liakos/IML), Köln; **130** Getty Images (Paul Kane), München; **133** PantherMedia GmbH (Christian Winter), München; **134** iStockphoto (jan kranendonk), Calgary, Alberta; **134** Getty Images (Marco Secchi), München; **135** Cagle Cartoons (by Vince O'Farrell www.politicalcartoons.com), Santa Barbara, CA; **136** Corbis (Strauss/Curtis), Düsseldorf; **136** Getty Images (RR/Iconica), München; **136** DHL Worldwide Express, Langen; **136** Corbis (Pawel Kopczynski/Reuters), Düsseldorf; **136** WILDLIFE Bildagentur GmbH (S.E. Arndt), Hamburg; **136** laif (Redux), Köln; **138** iStockphoto (HultonArchive/Getty Images), Calgary, Alberta; **138** iStockphoto (Grafissimo), Calgary, Alberta; **138** shutterstock (Stephen Coburn), New York, NY; **139** www.CartoonStock.com (Karsten Schley), Bath; **139** Getty Images (David Levenson), München; **140** Fairtrade International (FLO), Bonn; **141** Fairtrade International (FLO), Bonn; **142** Daimler AG Medienarchiv, Stuttgart; **142** The Body Shop Deutschland & Österreich (The Body Shop), Neuss; **142** iStockphoto (Michael Krinke), Calgary, Alberta; **143** Interbrand Zintzmeyer & Lux GmbH, Köln; **143** BMW AG, München; **143** Toyota Deutschland GmbH (Probst), Köln; **143** Daimler AG Medienarchiv, Stuttgart; **144** Getty Images (Michael Buckner), München; **146** iStockphoto (ranplett), Calgary, Alberta; **147** www.CartoonStock.com (Flanagan, Mike), Bath; **151** Imago (bonn-sequenz), Berlin; **152** iStockphoto (rabbit75_ist), Calgary, Alberta; **152** Thinkstock (Hemera/Keith Bell), München; **153** Corbis (Walter McBride/Retna Ltd.), Düsseldorf; **153** Imago (Moritz Müller), Berlin; **154** iStockphoto (Lisa-Blue), Calgary, Alberta; **156** iStockphoto (Yunus Arakon), Calgary, Alberta; **157** www.CartoonStock.com (Bacall, Aaron), Bath; **158** iStockphoto (Günay Mutlu),

Calgary, Alberta; **159** Cagle Cartoons (Brian Adcock), Santa Barbara, CA; **160** Corbis (Caste/PhotoCuisine), Düsseldorf; **162** shutterstock (Featureflash), New York, NY; **165** nach: http://images.ientrymail.com/webpronews/article_pics/media-preference-when.jpg; **166** shutterstock (RF/Losevsky Pavel), New York, NY; **167** Cagle Cartoons (Jimmy Margulies), Santa Barbara, CA; **168** BBC Information and archives, London; **169** BBC Information and archives, London; **170** BBC Information and archives, London; **171** BBC Information and archives, London; **172** iStockphoto (Marcello Bortolino), Calgary, Alberta; **173** Source: European Commission 2009; **174** Getty Images RF (Flickr), München; **175** Source: PRTM Worldwide; **176** shutterstock (Kirsty Pargeter), New York, NY; **178** The Observer, Guardian News & Media Ltd (David Levene), London; **179** Source: Flurry Analytics; **180** iStockphoto (Yuri_Arcurs), Calgary, Alberta; **181** iStockphoto (skynesher), Calgary, Alberta; **183** www.CartoonStock.com, Bath; **184** Getty Images (William Thomas Cain), München; **185** COX & FORKUM Editorial Cartoons, Nashville, TN; **186** Corbis (Kelly Redinger/Design Pics), Düsseldorf; **188** iStockphoto (Lisa F. Young), Calgary, Alberta; **198** Imago (Rüdiger Wölk), Berlin; **223** The Guardian, London; **223** The Mirror, London; **284** Klett-Archiv, Stuttgart; **COVER** Alamy Images (James Whitaker), Abingdon, Oxon

Textquellennachweis

9 From: English Next. Why global English may need the end of, English as a Foreign Language' by David Graddol © copyright British Council; **9** Source: „European Union, Eurobarometer" http://ec.europa.eu/public_opinion/archives/ebs/ebs_243_sum_en.pdf. The European Union does not endorse changes, if any, made to the original data and, in general terms to the original survey, and such changes are the sole responsibility of the author and not the EU; **9** Quelle: Job Trends Deutschland 2011 © 2011 by Staufenbiel Institut GmbH; **10/11** Source: Lingua Franca: Chimera or Reality? Studies on translation and multilingualism 1/2011 © European Commission, 2011; **12/13** © Independent News and Media Ltd. 2007; **14/15** Joe Friesen, „Canada to raise language bar", 19 June 2012 © Guardian News & Media Ltd 2012; **18/19** Alison Flood „Schools test ‚interactive graphic novel' version of Macbeth" 1 March 2010 © Guardian News & Media Ltd. 2010; **22/23** By Ruth Walker. Reprinted with permission from the June 30, 2010 issue of The Christian Science Monitor. © 2010 The Christian Science Monitor (www.CSMonitor.com); **28/29** Copyright © 2006 by Greil Marcus. Delivered as a commencement address at the University of California at Berkeley, May 19, 2006. Published by Salon.com on 4 July 2006. Veröffentlicht mit Genehmigung der Paul & Peter Fritz AG in Zürich; **32/33** 40 years after King's death …, Ed Pilkington, 03 April 2008 © Guardian News & Media Ltd.2008; **38/39** Lara Farrar, Is America's suburban dream collapsing... From CNN.com, 6/16/ © 2008, Cable News Network, Inc.. All rights reserved. Used by permission and protected by the Copyright Laws of the United States. The printing, copying, redistribution, or retransmission of this Content without express written permission is prohibited; **44/45** © Guardian News & Media Ltd 2011; **48/49** Stuart Jeffries, „How the royals became cool", 11 April 2012 © Guardian News & Media Ltd. 2012; **50/51** © Independent News and Media Ltd. 2012; **54/55** Praful Bidwai, „Why India needs aid", 7 Febr 2012 © Guardian News & Media Ltd.; **58/59** By Mary Nestor-Harper. From: eHow.com © 2011, Demand Media, Inc.; **60/61** Career-boosting internships for sale', Rachel Williams, 24 May 2011 © Guardian News & Media Ltd. 2011; **62/63** © BBC News at bbc.co.uk/news; **64/65** From: THEN WE CAME TO THE END by Joshua Ferris. Copyright © 2007 by Joshua Ferris. By permission of Little, Brown and Company. All rights reserved; **66/67** By Marily Gardner. Adapted with permission from the January 28, 2008 issue of The Christian Science Monitor. © 2008 The Christian Science Monitor (www.CSMonitor.com)"; **70/71** © Independent News and Media Ltd. 2005; **74/75** © Telegraph Media Group Ltd. 2011; **76/77** From „My Sister's Keeper" by Jodi Picoult © Hodder & Stoughton, London 2004, pp. 7–8/9–10; **78/79** © SPIEGEL ONLINE 2008; **80/81** © BBC News at bbc.co.uk/news; **82/83** From: Richard Watson ‚Future files: A brief history of the next 50 years', p. 40 © Nicholas Brealey Publishing, 2009; **86/87** Alok Jha, „Glow cat: fluorescent green felines could help study of HIV", 11 Sept 2011 © Guardian News & Media Ltd. 2011; **90/91** The rise and rise of convenience food', Tim Dowling, 19 May 2006 © The Guardian News & Media Ltd., 2006; **92/93** Jerome Monahan and Joe Clancy, Lifelong learning is the secret to happiness in old age, 17 May 2011 © Guardian News & Media, 2011. 93 © SPIEGEL ONLINE 2010; **94/95** From: www.life123.com © Text: LuAnn Schindler; **96/97** From: Sunday Times © Times Newspapers Ltd.; **98/99** From: Dead Famous by Ben Elton © Bantam Press (a division of Random House) 2001; **102/103** Anna Coote, „A shorter working week would benefit society", 30 July 2010 © Guardian News & Media Ltd. 2010; **106/107** Michael White, Why national dream is a foreign concept, 5 February 2011 © Guardian News & Media Ltd. 2011; **108/109** John Harris, Global protests: is 2011 a year that will change the world? 15 November 2011 © Guardian News & Media Ltd. 2011; **110/111** From: Remarks to Non-Governmental Organizations. Source: UN News Center Website, 19.10.2012; **112/113** From: Society Guardian.co.uk © Guardian News and Media Limited 2011; **115** Quelle: Rainer Hermann, Hightech für die Umwelt: Die Stadt der Zukunft. Deutschland Online, 2007.; **118/119** © BBC 120 Jacky Kay, In my country. From: Other Lovers © Bloodaxe Books Ltd., 1993; **120** „Legal Alien" is reprinted with permission from the publisher of „Chants" by Pat Mora (© 1994 Arte Público Press-University of Houston); **121** Windrush Child by John Agard. From: Half-Caste and other Poems by John Agard © Hodder Children's Books, 2005; **122/123** Marguerite Rigoglioso, Racial Stereotypes Can Be Unconscious but Reversible © Stanford Graduate School of Business Board of Trustees, Leland Stanford Junior University Stanford, Calif.; **124/125** Transcript from American Public Media's Speaking of Faith (now on Being) © 2008 American Public Media. Used with permission. All rights reserved.; **126/127** From: Chris Cleave, Little Bee, pp. 1-3 © Simon & Schuster UK, 2010; **128/129** © Armando Perez, Virginia, USA; **130/131** Stephen Brook, „It's Australia Day. Don't let the ‚we grew here, you flew here' crew spoil it", 26 Jan 2011 © Guardian News & Media Ltd. 2011; **134/135** From: Welcome to Everytown by Julian Baggini © granta Books, 2007.; **137** Globalization Blues © words and music: Ray Korona; **138/139** From: Thomas L. Friedman, A World is flat: A brief history of the twenty-first century © 2005 Farrar, Straus and Giroux, Penguin, 2006; **140/141** © Fairtrade International; **142/143** Quelle: www.boerse-online.de © 1996 - 2012 BÖRSE ONLINE; **144/145** From Jennifer Government by Max Barry, copyright © 2003 by Max Barry. Used by permission of Doubleday, a division of Random House, Inc.; **146/147** From Jennifer Government by Max Barry, copyright © 2003 by Max Barry. Used by permission of Doubleday, a division of Random House, Inc. 150/151 © Kofi Annan Foundation; **154/155** Sylvia Rowley,

Can brands make consumers see sustainable behaviour as desirable?, 5 October 2011 © Guardian News & Media Ltd. 2011; **156** New media fail to click on the reliability scale by Ari Sharp. From: The Sydney Morning Herald, March 16, 2010 © Text: Ari Sharp; **157** Quelle: WinFuture.de, Berlin; **158/159** Used with permission of Network World Copyright © 2012. All rights reserved.; **160/161** Organic movement split over air-freighted food, Martin Hickman, 29 May 2007 © Independent News & Media Ltd. 2007; **162/163** From: Steve Martin, An object of beauty, pp. 5–8 © Orion Publishing Group, 2010; **166/167** © Independent News & Media Ltd. 2007; **172/173** © BBC 174/175 © BBC; **176/177** Dawn of the age of robots, Dominic Rushe, 30 December 2010 © Guardian News & Media Ltd. 2010; **178/179** Mark King, „A working life: The app developer", 5 March 2011 © Guardian News & Media Ltd. 2011; **180/181** Copyright © The Economist Newspaper Limited 2009. All rights reserved; **182/183** Olivia Perrott and Nick Atkins, „Top tips for web startups", 21 Aug 2012 © Guardian News & Media Ltd.; **184/185** Gozde Zorlu, „New holistic approach to treat child obesity", 1 Aug 2012 © Guardian News & Media Ltd. 2012; **186/187** Guardian Professional „Just another day in court as a social worker", 13 Jan 2012 © Guardian News & Media Ltd. 2012; **188/189** Jessica Shepherd, „Has England finally found the formula for vocational education?" 31 May 2012 © Guardian News & Media Ltd. 2012; **194/195** Mark Tran, Ethnic minorities to make up 20% of UK population by 2051, 13 July 2010 © Guardian News & Media Ltd. 2010; **196/197** © The Times, 2007; **198/199** From: Naomi Alderman, Get down on the FarmVille, 13 May 2011 © Guardian News & Media Ltd. 2011

Sollte es in einem Einzelfall nicht gelungen sein, den korrekten Rechteinhaber ausfindig zu machen, so werden berechtigte Ansprüche selbstverständlich im Rahmen der üblichen Regelungen abgegolten.